ART OF THE ANDES

ART OF THE ANDES

Pre-Columbian Sculptured and Painted Ceramics from the Arthur M. Sackler Collections

Introduction and catalogue by
PAUL A. CLIFFORD
Essays by
ELIZABETH P. BENSON
MAUREEN E. MAITLAND
MICHAEL E. MOSELEY
DONALD A. PROULX
ALAN R. SAWYER

Edited by LOIS KATZ
Curator, The Arthur M. Sackler Collections

THE ARTHUR M. SACKLER FOUNDATION
AND
THE AMS FOUNDATION FOR THE ARTS, SCIENCES AND HUMANITIES
WASHINGTON, D.C.

EXHIBITIONS:

The City Art Centre, Edinburgh, Scotland
August 15, 1983–October 2, 1983
Bayley Art Museum, University of Virginia
November 15, 1983–January 15, 1984

COVER: No. 151, *Spouted Jar in the form of a Dignitary*(?), Coastal Huari

END PAPERS: No. 38, *Vessel in the form of an Antlered Deer*, Moche III

FRONTISPIECE: No. 20, *Stirrup Spout Effigy Bottle in the form of a Supernatural Figure*, Moche I

Designed by Victor Trasoff
Assistant to the Editor: Judith Groppa
Photographs by Otto E. Nelson
Additional photographs by Murray Shear

LIBRARY OF CONGRESS CATALOGUING IN PUBLICATION DATA

Art of the Andes:
Pre-Columbian Sculptured and Painted Ceramics from the Arthur M. Sackler Collections
Exhibition held at the City Art Centre, Edinburgh, Scotland; Bayley Art Museum, University of Virginia
Bibliography: p. 338
1. Ceramics, Andean—Exhibitions.
2. Sackler, Arthur M.—Art Collections—Exhibitions.
I. Paul A. Clifford. II. Elizabeth P. Benson, Maureen E. Maitland, Michael E. Moseley, Donald A. Proulx, Alan R. Sawyer.
III. Title.
IV. Arthur M. Sackler Collections.
No. 83-77267
ISBN 0-913291-00-5

Published in 1983 by The Arthur M. Sackler Foundation, Washington, D.C., and The AMS Foundation for the Arts, Sciences and Humanities, Washington, D.C.

TABLE OF CONTENTS

Plate I. *Seated Couple with Child*
Bahía Culture, Ecuador, 500 BC–AD 300 (*App. no. 1*)

Preface

BY ARTHUR M. SACKLER, M.D.

CULTURE IN THE AMERICAS derived from those ancients who entered the New World in the Pleistocene period 50,000-25,000 years ago. During the last great ice age it is believed massive glaciation lowered the sea level and the Bering Straits Land Bridge surfaced, allowing waves of migration from the Asian continent. Without in any way negating that probability, I believe there is evidence to suggest that the Western Hemisphere was populated over time by several later migrations using different routes.

On a visit to China, seated in Guilin facing an official of the People's Republic of China, I was so absorbed by the visual impact he made on me that my almost hypnotic stare made him extremely uncomfortable. Had we been transported to Mexico or seated together in Peru, I would have been convinced I was facing an Indian of Mexico or Peru. This feeling was reinforced as I encountered different individuals in those sections of China closest to Indochina. I recalled that in my collection of Pre-Columbian textiles, the cotton was a genetic cross between a native cotton and one of southeast Asia. Similarly, I noted some Mexican or Mesoamerican and South American Indians have a closer resemblance to individuals living today in south China than to their New York Long Island Indian brethren. And, some Long Island Indians look more like members of the Mongol tribes of north China than they look like other American Indians.

Chinese Art and the Pacific Basin

These observations were linked in my mind with others expressed at the seminar we sponsored at Columbia University in August 1967, "Early Chinese Art and Its Possible Influence in the Pacific Basin," chaired by L. Carrington Goodrich. The publication of those proceedings was dedicated to Robert von Heine-Geldern, a key participant in the symposium. The collegium was triggered by a unique document—an artifact and art object—our Ch'u Silk Manuscript, and the the distribution in the Pacific basin of its iconography. Clearly, those iconographic elements, such as the antlered demons, horned man and long tongue, were not restricted to the Ch'u State or to a primary or contiguous diffusion to Taiwan, but, as the accompanying exhibition at the University demonstrated, to the Americas as well.

Routes of Diffusion

The diffusion of that iconography, regardless of the debate on the "Jomon-Valdivia theory," forces us to examine the possibility of a series of trans-Pacific migrations taking place over time from different regions of Asia. If trans-Pacific migrations had taken place by sea, they could only have been possible under near-ideal conditions, in a craft adequate to make the voyage (weather notwithstanding) and, of course, with sufficient food and fresh water. As Heyerdahl has demonstrated, transoceanic crossings could have been possible on simple ships or even primitive rafts.

Provisioning an Expedition

As to the provision of food and water for such journeys, I have long been intrigued with the thought of investigating the possibilities either experimentally or in some other way, but could not free the time necessary. Theoretically, adequate food supplies could have been assured because, in the earliest periods in China, rural peasants clearly understood the principles of the "balanced aquarium," or the current concept of a balanced biosphere or ecosystem; for instance: man eats pig, pig eats offal, man eats pig. Interestingly, the Chinese ideograph for home is a pig under a roof (家). Furthermore, millennia earlier than even the most primitive Neolithic societies, the Chinese had developed and effectively deployed fishhooks and fishnets. Between fishing and the utilization of a family of pigs raised on human offal, adequate caloric and protein stores were theoretically available on simple ships and large rafts.

The transportation of fresh water, however, had to have been a problem, for it would have been hazardous in the extreme to venture forth depending solely on the collection of rainwater for drinking purposes. I have wanted to investigate, but could not engage the problem of desalinization of seawater with the simplest possible technology. What I had hoped to investigate, among other possibilities, was the use of porous ceramics of different types as well as that all-purpose giant Chinese weed, the bamboo plant. Hopefully, someone with more time and more imagination may come up with some answers for possible desalinization of seawater during long journeys in ancient times.

As I sought to convert psychiatry from a "soft," subjective science into the "harder," more objective science of metabolism and biochemistry, I realized that to call mathematics an absolute, objective science is to disregard its virtually totally subjective origins. Furthermore, as to theoretical abstractions, Linus Pauling maintains that medicine can gain as much from theoretical medicine as physics has from theoretical physics.

The Arts and Sciences

Clearly, the solution of the problems of human migrations and cultural diffusion will call upon the skills of modern technology and science. Culture encompasses the arts, sciences and humanities, and rightly so. The arts and sciences increasingly utilize techniques commonly considered as part of one or the other domain.

Science as we know it in the modern sense is a very recent development and much of it based not only on hard data, but also on fundamental theoretical postulates such as those of Copernicus, Galileo and Newton. It also has other not so scientific antecedents. The alchemist, in his search for gold, may be seen as the unwanted forefather of the great chemists of today. Metallurgy was manifested in the highest form in the technology of the Shang bronzecaster and in the skills of the Achaemenian silver- and goldsmiths. Paradoxically, ceramic technology, which actually reached a higher stage of perfection as an art form than is generally available to us today, has spawned industries in glass, engineering and the communication systems of the future.

Among the critical elements characterizing science is our ability to predict, and, ultimately, to control, phenomena. Recently, on the occasion of a symposium at Harvard in conjunction with the exhibition "Art from Ritual: Ancient Chinese Bronze Vessels,"chaired by the great art historian, Max Loehr, I was moved to that point. When our British colleague, Dr. Jessica Rawson, commented that in Britain some archaeologists tend to look askance at art historians, I remarked that Max Loehr, on the basis of art historical studies, anticipated the findings of field archaeology in China and therefore could be characterized as a theoretical archaeologist. Thus, today, even as in an earlier day, technology and the arts are closely linked and the sciences and humanities reciprocally serve each other.

The Humanities and Humanity

Language and literature, history and philosophy, have long been closely linked to the arts and sciences as a cultural manifestation. Unhappily, they have not always served humankind. Whereas the original migration from the Orient opened to a sector of humanity a fertile hemisphere rich in resources and potentials, the earliest entry of western man from the Occident manifested neither a beneficent nor humane aspect. We must note the baneful influence of some who throughout history have loudly proclaimed the virtues of their "civilization." Spain, at one of the peaks of its history, not only engaged in the Inquisition of people on its own soil but also deployed its power in sending forth explorers to other continents. Then, in one of the worst examples of imperial exploitative savagery, an "advanced" European nation brought down the indigenous ancient civilizations of Peru and Mexico. There is a lesson to be learned from both the submissiveness of the victims and the brutality of their conquerors. Fortunately, democratic social structures afford the opportunity for a governmental flexibility that did not exist under the Inca who, despite their political and social organizational skills, became the victims of just 168 soldiers, several score horses and four cannons. The incredible military achievement of the conquerors was matched only by their gross cupidity—the thoughtless greed with which they melted down objects of the greatest beauty, a heritage of all mankind, into gold bullion—and the brutality with which, in the name of faith, they destroyed the culture of other peoples seven to eight thousand miles from their own country.

For the Preservation of Homo sapiens

At a time when the accumulated nuclear arsenals deriving from the most brilliant minds of science and technology can destroy the world, when the responsibility for the ultimate decision of a nuclear Armageddon devolves upon the decision not of 168 men but on far fewer, we need more than ever to build links of understanding and mutual respect between peoples of different civilizations. All, in our mutual interest, must seek to reach a goal which can best be fulfilled through the building of the most important bridges between civilized men and women of culture, of all cultures—the arts, the sciences and the humanities.

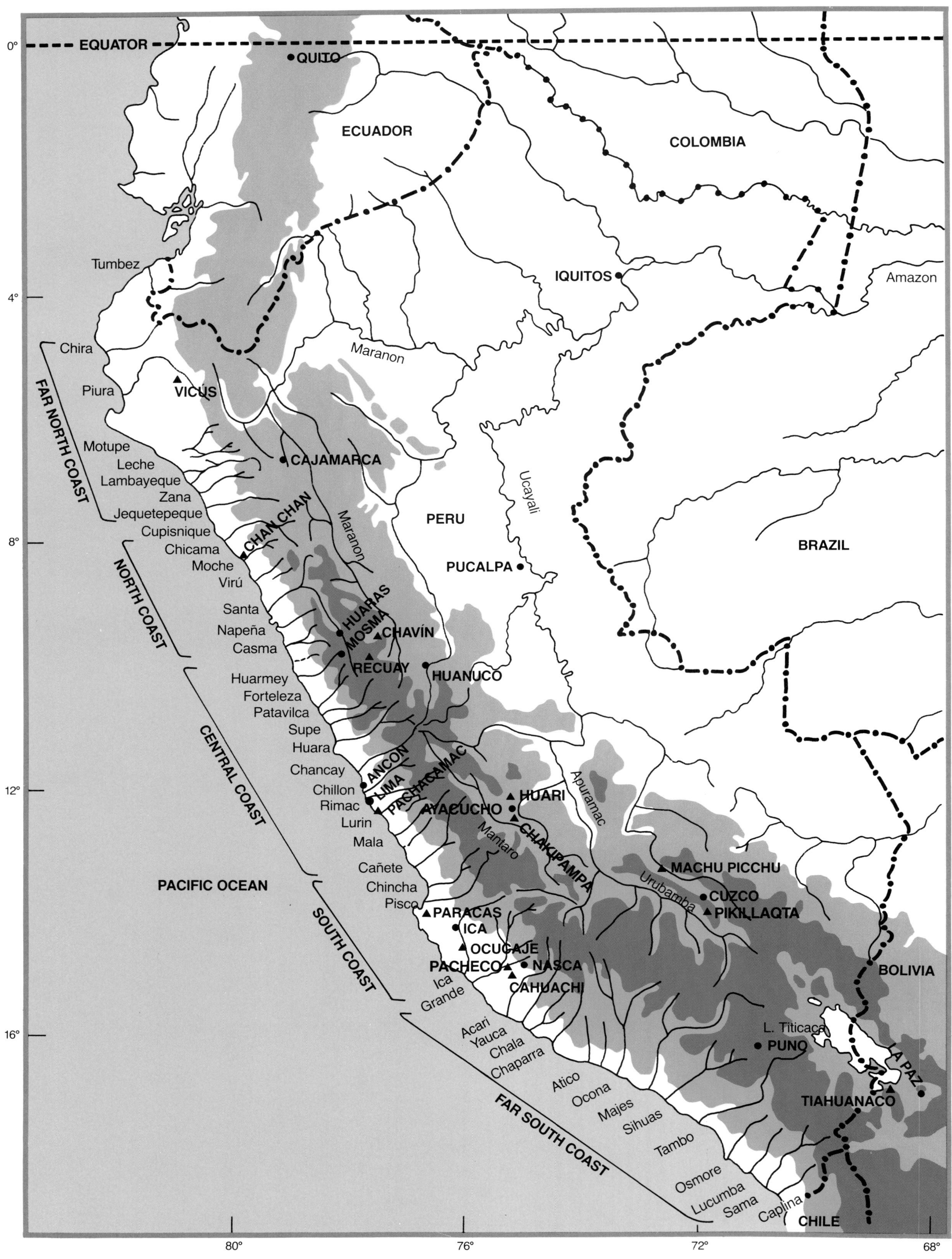

0°
EQUATOR
QUITO
ECUADOR
COLOMBIA
Tumbez
IQUITOS
Amazon
4°
Chira
Maranon
Piura
VICUS
FAR NORTH COAST
Motupe
Leche
Lambayeque
Zana
Jequetepeque
Cupisnique
CAJAMARCA
Ucayali
CHAN CHAN
Maranon
PERU
8°
Chicama
Moche
Virú
PUCALPA
BRAZIL
NORTH COAST
Santa
Napeña
Casma
HUARAS
MOSMA
CHAVÍN
RECUAY
HUANUCO
Huarmey
Forteleza
Patavilca
Supe
Huara
CENTRAL COAST
Chancay
Chillon
Rimac
Lurin
Mala
ANCON
LIMA
PACHACAMAC
12°
AYACUCHO
HUARI
Apurimac
Mantaro
CHAKIPAMPA
PACIFIC OCEAN
Cañete
Chincha
Pisco
MACHU PICCHU
Urubamba
CUZCO
PIKILLAQTA
PARACAS
ICA
OCUCAJE
PACHECO
NASCA
CAHUACHI
SOUTH COAST
Ica
Grande
BOLIVIA
16°
Acari
Yauca
Chala
Chaparra
L. Titicaca
PUNO
LA PAZ
Atico
Ocona
Majes
Sihuas
FAR SOUTH COAST
TIAHUANACO
Tambo
Osmore
Lucumba
Sama
Caplina
CHILE
80°
76°
72°
68°

Introduction

PAUL CLIFFORD

IT IS NOW GENERALLY ACCEPTED that ancient man did not evolve in the New World, but entered it from the Asian continent during the Pleistocene period some time between 50,000 and 25,000 years ago. This period coincides with the last great ice age when waters of the oceans were frozen in glaciers. The consequent lowering of the sea level caused a natural land bridge, known as the Bering Straits Land Bridge, to appear at intervals, connecting what is now Siberia and the tip of Alaska. Ancient man, as a hunter-gatherer, followed the migration of animals, unknowingly crossed over the Bering Straits Land Bridge and entered the New World. The best evidence indicates that his entry took place during the Wisconsin Glacial stage and possibly as early as the Iownian substage, 20,000 to 40,000 years ago. His passage must be deduced from very meager and scattered traces.

The latest evidence indicates no concerted migration, but many small family groups entering over a long period of time.[1] Possibly hundreds of years elapsed between migrations, resulting in a heterogeneous population apparently on a "low" cultural plane, equal to Middle or Late Paleolithic man in Europe. The immigrants must have brought a minimum of Old World Paleolithic-level culture to the New World: fire, a tradition of flint-working, the use of particular tools and weapons, clothing made from animal skins, and ideas about social groupings and the supernatural.

Probably following natural ice-free corridors from the Bering Straits Land Bridge south into continental North America, early man fanned out both to the east and south. Richard S. MacNeish suggests there were at least two distinct entries during the early period.[2] The evidence for the first migratory wave is found in crude stone tools and Carbon-14 dates associated with them from such sites as Lewisville and Friesenbaken in Texas and Tlapacoya in Mexico. The second great influx may have occurred between 18,000 and 15,000 BC. From this period the Clovis people, whose fluted points are associated with Pleistocene megafauna, have left traces of their camps in the western United States. Since populations of the greatest antiquity are found in North America, undoubtedly each new wave of migrating people pushed beyond earlier peoples.

Crossing into Middle America and settling around the lakes in the Valley of Mexico, early man left only traces of his passage. Fossil evidence and lithic weapons have been found here in association with the bones of such prehistoric animals as the mastodon. An engraving on a mammoth bone of 20,000 years ago from the Valley of Mexico reveals a clue to the relationship between man and his environment at that time.[3]

Land hunters and gatherers may have migrated to the South American continent by way of Panama, entering the Andean highlands by way of the Cauca and Magdalena River valleys in Colombia. Here, game and other wild foods were reasonably plentiful, and there were no barriers to a continued southward migration. Evidence as far south as Tierra del Fuego points to man's having been there as early as 12,000 BC.[4] Cave habitations found in the northern highlands of Peru at Lauricocha, located at an elevation of 15,000 feet, indicate that early man in South America made the high altitudes his home rather than the lowland coast. Lithic workshops also have been found at many sites 10,000 feet above sea level. At Punin, Ecuador, a human skull was discovered with mastodon, sloth, deer, and camel bones as well as an extinct form of horse.

Geography, Climate and Environment

Topographically the South American continent is divided into three major zones: the Andean chain of mountains along the Pacific coast, the tropical and temperate plains, and the highlands of east Brazil and the Guianas. These major zones, topographical features of which undoubtedly influenced migration and cultural diffusion, extend from north to south and within them are many contrasting environments. The rugged Andes rise in marked contrast to the flat plains of the Argentine Pampas and present formidable mountain barriers with numerous peaks over 20,000 feet high and few passes under 12,000 feet. The three parallel ranges in Colombia are reduced to two in Ecuador and break up into short diagonal chains in Peru, expand

Plate II. *Spouted Bottle punctate-marked and burnished*, Late Chavín Period, Peru, North Coast, 400–200 BC (*App. no. 3*).

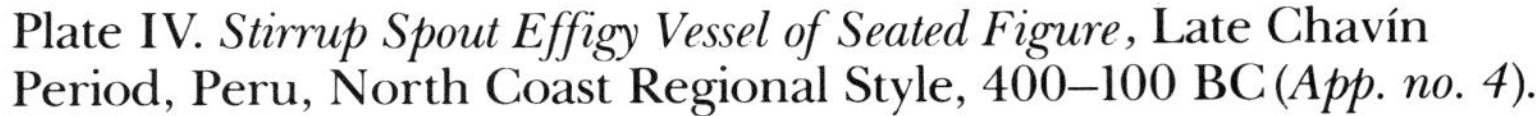

Plate IV. *Stirrup Spout Effigy Vessel of Seated Figure*, Late Chavín Period, Peru, North Coast Regional Style, 400–100 BC (*App. no. 4*).

Plate III. *Spouted Bottle with Monkey Head*, Late Chavín Period, Peru, North Coast, 400–200 BC (*App. no. 2*).

Plate V. *Hollow Male Figurine*, Late Chavín Period, Peru, North Coast, 400–200 BC (*App. no. 5*).

again to a pair in Bolivia, and finally narrow to a single range in Chile.

Northern Chile and sections of the coast of Peru contain one of the world's most arid deserts, while the Amazon river which rises in the Andes in the west and flows east, together with its tributaries, passes through one of the world's largest known stretches of rain forest. Obviously early man could not use large sections of the South American continent for agricultural purposes. Dense rain forests, pampas with deep sods where the richest soils were located but where there were no draft animals or plows to work them, waterless deserts, or high, wind-swept altiplano, were of no use to the agriculturalists. Furthermore, a hemisphere with little in the way of animals suitable for domestication precluded a herdsman society. The llama and alpaca of the Andean highlands were the only large animals of the Americas suited for herding and as beasts of burden.

The habitable sections of South America are the intermontane basins, the plateaus, and the valley flatlands of rivers which drain into the Amazon. These basins and flatlands have well-watered, fertile soils, though without a deep sod cover. They also have many resources such as stone and clay suitable for building and pottery making, as well as easily mined copper, silver, gold, and tin. All these were incentives to cultural development. Archaeological evidence indicates that these intermontane valleys were the first areas to be chosen by early man for seasonal camps. A number of such areas are extensive enough to have supported a reasonably large population.

The coastal shelf along the Pacific presents a considerable contrast in environment. It is widest in Ecuador and Colombia where it lies within the tropics. High temperatures and excessive rainfall result in a jungle forest cover. The narrower coastal plains of southern Ecuador, Peru, and northern Chile form the west coast desert. Along Peru's west coast the desert shelf is at most thirty miles wide with the Andes to the east abruptly soaring to 22,000 feet. Close to the coast the Humboldt current moves from south to north. Extremely cold waters cool the air of the off-shore winds sufficiently so that little or no precipitation falls over the hot coastal land. Habitable areas of this coastal area, except for small fishing sites where early subsurface agriculture was carried on, are limited to the valleys of some fifty rivers that have their source in the mountains and flow rapidly to the Pacific.

Contrast between coastal deserts and the high Andean valleys is enormous, but in terms of the subsistence patterns of early man, the differences proved no barrier to transition from one to the other. Both the high valleys and the coastal river systems share such favorable features as rich, easily cultivated soils, an absence of deep-rooted grasses and jungle cover, a relatively moderate climate, and a sufficient water supply to encourage controlled agriculture. Early man, traveling only a few hundred miles from west to east, passed through the driest desert, well-watered upland valleys, intensely cold high peaks and plateaus, and then down the eastern slopes of the Andes to the stifling rain forests. Evidence from all these areas proves that he traveled, traded, and built high cultures in all regions.

Temperatures in the Andes are more or less constant, reflecting altitude rather than latitude, with the result that most sections are cool to cold during the entire year. Although trees grow in some areas, much of the region is unforested and may be classed as either grassland, brushland, or desert. The northern Andes, which include Colombia, Ecuador, and a small part of Peru, are characterized by a double rainy season, which supports wet rain forests in areas of high altitude between 10,000 feet and the snowline. Because the northern highlands are not favorable for grazing llamas and alpacas, these, the two most important domesticated animals of pre-Spanish America, were not of great importance to the earlier peoples of that area. The central Andes, on the other hand, have alternate rainy and dry seasons and their highlands support abundant grass ideal for grazing animals.

Early Man in Peru

The history of ancient Peruvian civilization is the history of man's successful efforts to adapt himself to a varied and difficult environment. When early man settled into camps in the Andean mountain valleys, he traveled from the highlands to the coast as the seasons changed. The Pacific Ocean was important, both as a controller of the climate and as the source of a rich food supply. Fogs, created by the cold Humboldt current flowing along the west coast, lasted up to eight months during the winter season and caused the formation of fog meadows or *lomas*. These *lomas*, with their lush foliage and consequent plentiful supply of seeds, snails, wild potatoes, as well as lizards, birds, and sometimes deer, attracted early man to move down from the valleys.

From about 7000 to 2500 BC cultural patterns based on seasonal migration from highland to coastal *lomas* continued to develop. Towards the end of this period, however, a change in climate conditions caused the *lomas* to shrink and some groups of people, discovering the rich bounties of the sea, moved their camps to the seashore. About 2500 BC the first true village sites can be identified near the present coastal town of Ancón. Evidence has been found of a farming community as well as a fishing community. This then was

Plate VI. *Stirrup Spout Effigy Vessel of Seated Man*, Moche II, Peru, North Vicús, Piura Valley, 300 BC–AD 600 (*App. no. 8*).

Plate VII. *Stirrup Spout Effigy Vessel of Squatting Man*, Moche II, Peru, North Coast, Vicús, Piura Valley, 300 BC–AD 600 (*App. no. 9*).

Plate VIII. *Effigy Vessel of Kneeling Prisoner*, Negative Vicús, Peru, North Coast, Vicús, Piura Valley, 300 BC–AD 600 (*App. no. 10*).

Plate IX. *Effigy Vessel of Squatting Prisoner*, Negative Vicús, Peru, North Coast, Vicús, Piura Valley, 300 BC–AD 600 (*App. no. 11*).

the beginning of a stable and settled civilization in the Peruvian area. As time progressed, the small village sites along the coast prospered and grew. Here, early man practiced specific rituals for the burial of the dead. The distinctive mortuary goods, including mats and garments used in burials, indicate advances in textile technology, while remains of twined fibers point toward the beginnings of a true textile industry.

Cultural Development and the Question of Outside Influences

Anthropologists generally agree that civilization, in the usual sense of the term, cannot appear until a truly productive agricultural system has been developed. Field work over the last decade has focused on the origins of agriculture as complex systems. The most complete record of early planting in the New World comes from the coast of Peru where the arid climate preserved the evidence of cultivated plants. It is also now apparent that the important cultivated plants did not originate there but were brought from elsewhere. George W. Beadle has recently suggested that the earliest known cultivated corn (maize), the staple food of the New World which appeared in the Tehuacan Valley of Mexico about 6000–5000 BC, shows a level of genetic modification which can only be understood in terms of at least one thousand to two thousand years of prior development under primitive cultivation.[5]

Much prior development was needed to support a formative level of culture. Both the standardization of elaborate agricultural practices and the genetic modification of key plants were gradual processes. But once man became tied to the land and a way of life beyond mere subsistence from day to day, he was free to explore ways of improving his living standards. The ability to control plant genetics so that more food could be raised than was needed for sustenance also allowed man to spend more time on political and social systems as well as the development of arts and crafts.

Origins of New World culture, so far as Old World contact and stimuli are concerned, are still a matter of debate. Although it is generally felt that New World cultural development is indigenous, occasional trans-Pacific contacts are not ruled out. Nevertheless, the influence of such contacts appears to have been minimal. Certain puzzles, however, remain to be solved. In general, agricultural products of the New World are unique to its hemisphere and include a long list of fruits, among them the avocado, and vegetables, such as white and yellow potatoes. Yet sweet potatoes and gourds are found in both the New World and the Old World. Cotton, which was grown in both parts of the world, poses special problems: Old World cotton has thirteen large chromosomes; New World cotton has thirteen small chromosomes. Yet cotton domesticated in early Pre-Columbian times in coastal Peru contains both thirteen large and thirteen small chromosomes.

Other similarities between Old World and New World cultures which remain unexplained include the appearance in the Andean area, during the first millenium BC, of an advanced technological knowledge of metalworking such as lost wax casting and gilding which, in the present state of our knowledge, had no antecedents; pottery shapes in Ecuador are akin to those of the Joman Culture in Japan; bark cloth, found in Peru around 2000 BC, is otherwise known only in the Old World; techniques, such as the tie-dye method of producing designs on cloth, or the use of weapons and instruments such as star-shaped mace heads, blow guns, and pan pipes, are found in many areas of the world; and pottery house models and headrests occur in both the New World and the Orient. There is also similarity between New and Old World art motifs, for instance, the tiger of the Zhou dynasty in China and the feline motif of Chavín Culture in the northern highlands of Peru, both of which appeared during the first millenium BC.[6] If parallels resulted from Old and New World contact one would also expect to have seen the introduction in the New World of one of man's most important inventions, the wheel, but its true use in transportation and pottery making was not known in the New World until the Spanish conquest.

The Making of Pre-Columbian Pottery

Since the potter's wheel, which had been used throughout the Old World from earliest times, was unknown in the New, the Peruvian potter employed other methods which, though slower, produced ceramics that rivaled those made elsewhere on the wheel. With the coiling process, coils of clay were built up in spirals to form a vessel, the outside and inside of which were then scraped and smoothed to make the joints invisible. Using this technique, an amazing symmetry could be achieved even on very large vessels. Pastillage, appliqué, and strapwork techniques were similar to coiling in that strips of clay were pressed onto the surface to adorn a figure or decorate a vessel, for instance, on the large Chancay urn in Number 170. Coiling is still used in remote areas of the Americas.

In block modeling and slab building, the potter began either with a block of clay to which he gave the desired shape by hollowing out and thinning the block, or he flattened a slab of clay into rectangular shape and then bent it into a circle and joined it. To this he added a bottom, and the result was a flat-bottomed, straight-sided vessel. The earliest utility vessels were probably

Plate X. *Effigy Vessel of Feather-Crowned Squatting Prisoner*, Negative Vicús, Peru, North Coast, Vicús, Piura Valley, 300 BC–AD 600 (*App. no. 12*).

Plate XI. *Effigy Vessel of Crowned, Kneeling Man*, Negative Vicús, Peru, North Coast, Vicús, Piura Valley, 300 BC–AD 600 (*App. no. 13*).

Plate XII. *Effigy Vessel of Kneeling Prisoner*, Negative Vicús, Peru, North Coast, Vicús, Piura Valley, 300 BC–AD 600 (*App. no. 14*).

Plate XIII. *Stirrup Spout Effigy Vessel of Two Warriors*, Negative Vicús, Peru, North Coast, Piura Valley, 300 BC–AD 600 (*App. no. 15*).

made in this way but slab-sided vessels were popular primarily in Meso-America and are not found in Peru.

Direct modeling was done by manipulating the clay by hand into expressive forms such as figurines or effigy vessels. This method allowed for more detail and three-dimensional effects than could be achieved by using molds but it was slow and time-consuming

The most popular method for the mass production of pottery in ancient Peru involved the use of molds. This technique evolved quite early. A two-piece press mold was used either by itself or in combination with others to build up the object. The finished vessel was then cleaned up, details enhanced, and such features as handles, lugs, and spouts added. It is not always easy to tell if a vessel of one of the early cultural periods is mold-made, but later on less care was taken and mold lines are more clearly visible. Among grave goods from central and north coast burials there are groups of molds used to create various pottery shapes and we find multiple vessels were made from the same mold (see Fig. 1). Molds made possible pottery which was at once complicated, light in weight, and relatively resistant to breakage during firing.

Glazes were unknown in the New World before the Spanish conquest; consequently decoration and surface finish had to be obtained by other means. Some vessels, especially early ones, depended on the surface treatment of the clay for their decoration. Different areas of a vessel might be contrasted: one part highly burnished while another was left matte or given a textured surface. Incising and cutting out sections of the surface to form relief decor could be done after the vessel was sun-dried and before it was fired. Designs could also be pressed or rolled into the clay from a negative form. In addition, methods of appliqué were used (see No. 2).

Designs were also painted on a vessel using clay slip, a watered-down version of the potting clay. By adding minerals or other material to the clay slip, the potter could obtain up to nine different colors as well as shades in between. Postfired painting using resinous paints was another method of decoration. Although the areas to be painted were roughened to retain the paint, often much of the original postfired paint has been lost, especially on ceramics from northern sites where the climate is moister.

Resist decoration was another popular method of pottery design throughout the Americas. An organic material such as honey or resin was applied to the surface of the unfired vessel. Such material "resisted" the heat of the fire, keeping the covered area from oxidizing and thus changing color. After firing, the resist substance was cleaned off and the once-covered area

Fig. 1. Two-piece pottery press mold for a figurine. Author's collection.

stands out because it lacks the color of the clay exposed to the heat of the fire. A somewhat similar method consisted of painting designs on the surface of the vessel with an organic substance after firing and then charring the substance in a fire.

The natural color of the clay bodies could also be controlled by the method of firing. While kaolin, a clay formed where it is worn down by water, produces a white body, most clays contain iron and, if heated in an oxidizing fire, will turn a light red or red-brown. If, however, the oxygen is removed from the kiln during the firing, as is done in making charcoal, a soot-blackened gray or black pottery will result. During certain periods of early Peruvian history such blackware was much admired and produced in large quantities.

As far as we know, Pre-Columbian pottery was fired by placing vessels, separated by potsherds, in bonfires. Such pottery, obviously made under other than controlled conditions, was a low-fired ware and all the more amazing for the heights of refinement of shape and design that much of it achieved.

Classification and Chronology

In the course of modern Peruvian archaeology, certain identified cultures have at various times been known by different names and the chronology proposed for them has undergone repeated revision. All Pre-Columbian cultures have a relative chronology within a limited geographical area, a chronology essentially based on the knowledge that one particular culture preceded or followed another. Absolute dating in a culture which is without writing is obviously problematic, just as it is

Plate XIV, a & b. *Effigy Vessels with Man and Woman*, Negative Vicús, Peru, North Coast, Vicús, Piura Valley, 300 BC–AD 600 (*App. nos. 17, 18*).

Plate XV. *Effigy Vessel with Feline(?)*, Negative Vicús, Peru, North Coast, Vicús, Piura Valley, 300 BC–AD 600 (*App. no. 20*).

Plate XVI. *Effigy Vessel with Seated Female(?)*, Negative Vicús, Peru, North Coast, Vicús, Piura Valley, 300 BC–AD 600 (*App. no. 19*).

problematic to relate the dates for a culture in one area to remains or sites in other locations. What scholars thought was a simple, straightforward development has often turned out to be a complicated series of interrelationships. In the present catalogue we have called the various cultures by the names most commonly used by modern scholars. As for chronology, we have tried to incorporate the conclusions of the latest research, some of it, in fact, first presented in essays in this catalogue. Needless to say, any chronology may simply represent a temporary stage in the state of knowledge, and it is valid only until new facts are discovered or new relationships understood.

The Arthur M. Sackler Collection of Pre-Columbian Peruvian ceramics includes examples from every major Peruvian culture and time period up to the Spanish conquest. Since all the objects in the exhibition were made to accompany the dead, each piece is part of the intriguing history of the ceremonial ceramics of ancient Peru. Some vessels are so realistic they leave no doubt about what inspired their creator, but others, painted or modeled to represent deities or mythical monsters and beings, defy quick interpretation. Ancient Peruvians left no written records, but their material remains imply intimate involvement with natural forces and unseen spirits. Nothing seems to have been done without purpose and everything appears to have been fraught with meaning.

The history and art of certain cultures and time periods have been amply treated in separate essays, following this Introduction. Remarks here, therefore, shall be primarily confined to discussing certain characteristics of pottery illustrated by examples in the present exhibition and catalogue. Some of the examples are from The Arthur M. Sackler Collections in the Museum of the American Indian, Heye Foundation, New York City. These are included in the Plates and in the Appendix to the catalogue but are not in the exhibition. References to Plate numbers in this text are to some of these vessels.

Plate XVII. *Effigy Vessel with Animal*, Negative Vicús, Peru, North Coast, Vicús, Piura Valley, 300 BC–AD 600 (*App. no. 16*).

Plate XVIII. *Effigy Jar in form of Llama Head,* Negative Vicús, Peru, North Coast, Vicús, Piura Valley, 300 BC–AD 600 (*App. no. 24*).

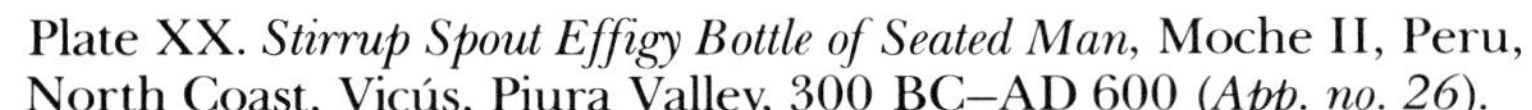

Plate XX. *Stirrup Spout Effigy Bottle of Seated Man,* Moche II, Peru, North Coast, Vicús, Piura Valley, 300 BC–AD 600 (*App. no. 26*).

Plate XIX. *Effigy Bottle of Squatting Man Holding Bowl,* Moche II, Peru, North Coast, Vicús, Piura Valley, 300 BC–AD 600 (*App. no. 25*).

Plate XXI. *Effigy Vessel of Seated Warrior with Striped Headdress,* Moche II, Peru, North Coast, Vicús, Piura Valley, 300 BC–AD 600 (*App. no. 27*).

ARCHAEOLOGICAL AND ART HISTORY

NORTH COAST AND HIGHLANDS

The Chavín Culture

Apparently the production of competent pottery began at least 1000 years earlier in Ecuador than in Peru and Mexico. Investigations by Donald Lathrap and Donald Collier in Ecuador, particularly in Guayas province, have established that there were sizable pottery-producing communities on the coast of Ecuador before 3000 BC.[7] This early ceramic horizon in Ecuador has been given the name Valdivia and lasted from circa 3000 to 1500 BC.

Two periods, the Machililla and the Chorrera, followed the Valdivia. The Chorrera Culture flourished along the coast of Ecuador during a time when the early communities of the Peruvian north highlands and coast were laying the foundation for all later cultural development in the central Andes, and when the Olmec Culture in Mexico was establishing the basic Meso-American artistic and iconographic traditions. Influences moving from Ecuador to Peru and Mexico can be traced over a thousand-year period beginning about 1500 BC. After circa 1000 BC both Peru and Meso-America surpassed Ecuador in social complexity and gradually evolved towards the complex states encountered by the Spaniards.[8] It is interesting to note that both Mexican Olmec and Peruvian Chavín art seem to be based on the same religious systems, cosmology, and origin myths.

In ceramics, the Machililla and the Chorrera periods in Ecuador saw the development of the stirrup spout vessel, which was to be so important to north coast and highland Peruvian civilization.[9] Other innovations which developed during this time included realistically modeled zoomorphic and anthropomorphic vessels, the use of resist decoration, the double spout and bridge bottle, often with a whistle, and the use of an iridescent slip which has been identified as far away as the Pacific coast of Guatemala.[10] Ceramics from this period and area of Ecuador seem to have influenced, perhaps even to have been exported to, the very earliest formative culture complexes of Meso-America and Peru. An example of Ecuadorian ceramic sculpture is a seated family group in Plate I. The figures come from Los Esteros, Bahía de Manta, Manabi, where several hollow, large-scale figures were found. The size of the group, the vividness of their color and their exaggerated features make it a remarkable and distinctive example of Bahía art.

The first great civilization to produce fine pottery in Peru is called Chavín after the spectacular ceremonial center at Chavín de Huantar in the northern highlands. The influence of its religious beliefs and art styles spread from this highland center to the coast and as far south as the Paracas peninsula. Chavín de Huantar itself is primarily known for its fine stonework in the form of carved reliefs and other sculptural monuments. Subjects of design on these Chavín stone carvings include powerful representations of deities combining the features of man, jaguar, eagle, cayman, and serpent. These motifs, reproduced on pottery from various sites, enable us to trace the influence of this first center of Pan-Peruvian Culture as it spread across Peru.

Formerly, scholars tended to classify all the pottery of this early period as Chavín and to regard the variations found in different sites on the coast as simply the result of local influences. We now know that the true picture is far more complicated. Even before Chavín styles began to spread, there already existed a pre-Chavín group of interrelated cultures in the north coast valleys, evident from the iconographic and other similarities of their pottery. Centers of these pre-Chavín north coast valley cultures, such as Cerro Sechin in the Chicama Valley and its counterpart Chongoyape in the Lambayeque Valley, continued to develop during the Chavín Period.

Pre-Chavín Culture centers are also found in the highlands. Perhaps the best known is Kotosh where diggers found a large quantity of early ceramics, the so-called Tutishcainyo ware, consisting of trade pieces possibly brought in from further east. In all, three pre-Chavín phases have been recognized, and many of their characteristics continued to appear on local pottery even after the rise of Chavín Culture as a religious power. Open vessels predominate, but the stirrup spout bottle is also found for the first time in the central Andes. Various decorative techniques were employed, including incising with anthropomorphic representations and geometric motifs and the use of punctates filled with red, white, or yellow pigments.

The Chavín Period is traditionally believed to have lasted from about 900 to 100 BC, and its pottery can be divided into three phases.[11] Phase I Chavín pottery is closely related to Chavín lithic art and had strapwork relief on it that imitates stone carving. Its influence is not found outside the immediate Chavín de Huantar area. Phase II Chavín pottery shows the influence of the later Chavín sculpture. Bottles have angular and circular stirrups with unflanged lips. The design motifs are geometric and uncrowded. During this phase Chavín influence begins to spread to the coast and to

Plate XXII. *Effigy Vessel of Kneeling Prisoner,* Moche II, Peru, North Coast, Vicús, Piura Valley, 300 BC–AD 600 (*App. no. 28*).

Plate XXIII. *Effigy Vessel of Frog*, Moche II, Peru, North Coast, Vicús, Piura Valley, 300 BC–AD 600 (*App. no. 29*).

Plate XXIV. *Effigy Vessel of Seated Man with Cakes(?)*, Moche IV, Peru, North Coast, Chicama Valley, AD 200–500 (*App. no. 31*).

Plate XXV. *Stirrup Spout Effigy Vessel of Warrior Head Portrait* Moche IV, Peru, North Coast, AD 200–500 (*App. no. 34*).

Fig. 2. Rubbing from neck design of Number 1 with winged rapacious bird.

Fig. 3. Drawing of incised design on Number 2 of mythical creatures.

blend with local styles. Phase III Chavín pottery uses Chavín-related imagery in a more distinctly regional manner. Much more emphasis is placed on naturalistic representation of vegetable and animal subjects. Vessels of this phase from Tembladera in the Jequetepeque area display well-preserved postfired paint. The most common Chavín vessel forms are straight-sided bowls with flat or slightly rounded bottoms and bottles with straight spouts (No. 1). The stirrup spout bottle makes its appearance somewhat later in the period (see No. 2).

Plastic decorative techniques, distinguished by extraordinary workmanship, are the most important. The very heaviness of the potting and the use of deep incising, polishing, and thick pastillage are reminiscent of the stone carving at Chavín de Huantar. The motifs, such as saurians, birds, and felines, are also much the same as those on stone, and their forms seem to reflect the efforts of the stone carver rather than the potter. The Chavín and Chavinoid pottery in this exhibition are typical of that produced in both the highlands and coastal areas. The large Chavín spouted bottle (No. 1) combines two distinct shapes into a single vessel: above is a massive bottle with a straight spout and below is a dish with flared sides. This vessel demonstrates two typical characteristics of Chavín ceramics already mentioned: heavy potting and thick pastillage reminiscent of highland Chavín de Huantar stone carving. The decorative motif on the sides, a winged rapacious bird, and the smaller version of it on the neck are both done in heavy strap pastillage (Fig. 2).

Outside of Chavín de Huantar, Chavín-style or Chavín-influenced pottery has been known as Cupisnique or Coastal Chavín. Its centers of distribution were Cupisnique in the Chicama Valley, Tembladera in the Jequetepeque Valley and Chongoyape in the Lambayeque Valley on the north coast. A common vessel in these valleys was the globular flat-bottomed bottle with stirrup spout. Number 2 is a doughnut-shaped vessel whose stirrup is slightly bowed and has a graceful spool-shaped spout. Appliquéd to the side of the vessel and extending over the top and under the spout is a serpent with a feline head and incised interlocked teeth and body markings. Combining different animal characteristics is common in Pre-Columbian ceramics in general and certainly in Chavín pottery. Incised on the sides of the vessel here are mythical creatures which combine bird, serpent and feline elements (Fig. 3).

Coastal potters influenced by Late Chavín styles also produced various modeled vessels. In particular, aquatic and terrestrial animals are often modeled on stirrup spout bottles. Number 3, probably from Chongoyape, represents a rat-like animal seated on its haunches with its paws to its mouth. Surface contrast was obtained on this gray clay vessel by heavily stippling the rodent body to represent fur and smoothly burnishing the heavy stirrup, which typically has a turned spout. An example of another bottle form from the Late Chavín Period on the north coast is Number 4, an ovoid orangeware bottle with a long, delicate neck spout which is turned at the mouth rim. An animal face with button eyes and tab ears is incised and modeled on one side, conforming to, yet appearing to push out from, the matrix of the ovoid body. Another example of a similarly shaped bottle, with a monkey face modeled out of the upper section of one side of the body can be seen in Plate III. The latter was produced in a reducing environment, resulting in a brown-black body that has been further decorated with postfired red and green pigment. There is another Chavín bottle of brownware with a globular body and tall, tapering spout (Pl. II). Its textured globular base with punctate markings contrasts with its neck which was polished by burnishing.

As the Chavín Period came to an end, pottery tended to become lighter, thus pointing the way towards more delicate vessels and the use of modeling and slip painting for decoration rather than incising and appliqué. At the very end of Phase III, pottery was fired in an oxidizing environment so that slip painting was possible. This could be combined with incising, the lines of which often define the color areas, as in Number 5. Another example is seen in Plate IV which also retains the Chavinoid spout. In addition, small, hollow figurines were also created during the Late Chavín Period (Pl. V).

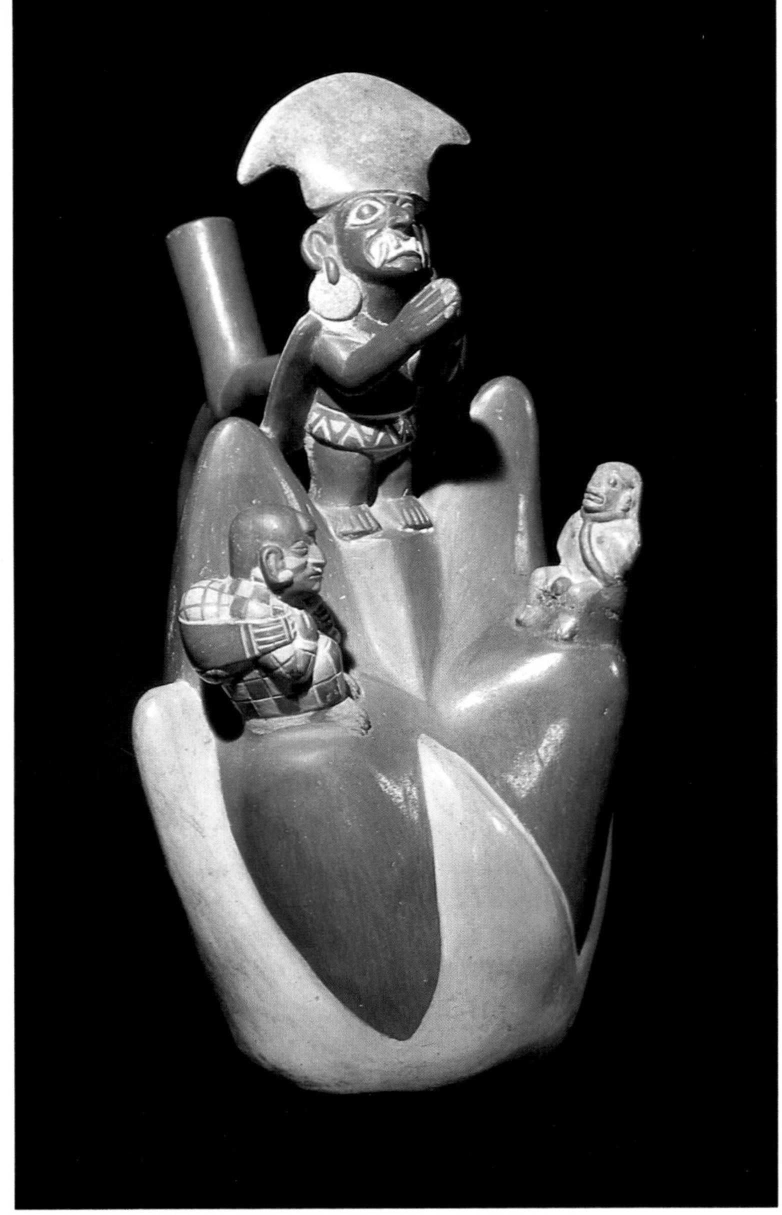

Plate XXVI. *Stirrup Spout Effigy Vessel of Mountain Scene*, Moche IV, Peru, North Coast, AD 200–500 (*App. no. 35*).

Plate XXVII. *Stirrup Spout Effigy Vessel with Foxes in Relief on Side*, Moche IV, Peru, North Coast, AD 200–500 (*App. no. 36*).

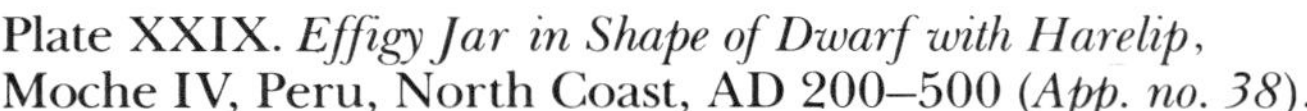

Plate XXIX. *Effigy Jar in Shape of Dwarf with Harelip*, Moche IV, Peru, North Coast, AD 200–500 (*App. no. 38*).

Plate XXX. *Effigy Jar in Shape of Warrior Holding Shield and Club*, Moche IV, Peru, North Coast, AD 200–500 (*App. no. 39*).

During the Late Chavín Period, perhaps by the final century before the Christian era, strong regional orientation started to develop in all areas of Peru. Earlier forms and iconography were not totally abandoned: the cult of the jaguar, for instance, continued to exert its influence. But in certain valleys local cultural autonomy developed, with independent patterns of settlement and individual styles.

The Salinar Culture

One early culture, known as Salinar, spread through the north coast, taking over parts of the Chicama and other river valleys. The Salinar introduced two new bottle types: the spouted bottle with a strap handle from the spout to the shoulder and the two-spouted bottle with a strap handle between the two spouts, one of which is "blind," that is, not a pouring spout. The Salinar also used the stirrup spout bottle.

The technological competence of the Salinar potters is evident in the quality of execution of their ceramics and the improved control of firing, which produced a pale-colored pottery. Molds were sometimes used. Decoration was by incising and painting, with white and red the most frequent colors. Designs tended to be based on triangles, stepped lines, and other geometric shapes. The principal modeled and mold-made forms include representations of humans and felines. In addition, Salinar vessels depict burrowing owls, monkeys, rats, and other animals, as well as sexual scenes. Number 6 shows a feline in a pouncing position with large pop eyes and fangs. The curve of its body flows into its spread legs. A tapered spout rises obliquely from the rear and is attached by an arched tubular handle to the back of the head. The surface is burnished red.[12]

Virú Culture

In the Virú Valley the Gallinazo Culture, dated circa 300 BC to AD 300, followed that of the Salinar and seems to be related to it. At first Gallinazo elements are mixed with Salinar traits. The best known pottery of this period is decorated with negative painting but there are other associated styles that lack it. Vessels are usually a reddish-orange color with burnishing. Whistle spout double bottles are common. Vessel necks often appear as modeled faces with appliquéd button eyes and with ears in low relief.

Eventually, a style evolved in the Virú Valley, possibly under outside influence, called Virú. Elements of this style include tapered spouts and arched tubular handles on double vessels containing whistles. Typical Virú vessels are Numbers 7 and 8, one a double bottle with macaw head, the other a bird-house vessel with its

Plate XXVIII. *Bowl with Interior Relief of Nude Female Giving Birth*, Moche IV, Peru, North Coast, AD 200–500 (*App. no. 37*).

Plate XXXI. *Jar with Design of Copulating Figures*, Imperial Chimú, Peru, North Coast, Lambayeque Valley, AD 1000–1470 (*App. no. 43*).

Fig. 4. Warrior with llama, Recuay Culture, AD 100–700. Height 6¾". Private collection.

Fig. 5. "Temple" vessel with ritual scene, Recuay Culture, AD 100–700. Height 8". Private collection.

Fig. 6. Vessel with resist design showing stylized feline motif, Recuay Culture, AD 100–700. Height 6". Museum of the American Indian, New York (14/3880).

blind spout modeled in house form. Both of these show the Moche influence of cream slip painting on red. During Moche Phase III the Virú Valley was overrun by the Moche. Double whistle vessels continued to be produced for a short time, but were never of major significance later.

The Recuay Culture

The people of the Recuay Culture lived on the southern outskirts of the Moche area, and the period of their cultural florescence is dated circa AD 100 to 700. One of their main ceremonial centers was located close to Chavín de Huantar. In fact, their stonework has been confused with that of the Chavín, who lived earlier, as well as with the Huari, who came later.

Recuay ceramics, found in the upper reaches of the Santa River, are made of a fine-textured white kaolin and are thin-walled and skillfully modeled. While their pottery styles are in many ways peculiar to the area, they sometimes show the influence of the Moche and Salinar cultures. The numerous examples of Recuay pottery depicting the warrior and his llama suggest that warfare occupied an important place in daily life (Fig. 4).[13] There also seems to have been a cult in which the feline, the condor, and the serpent played important roles.

The typical Recuay vessel, as seen in Number 10 in this exhibition, is a globular bottle, sketchily modeled as a figure, with a double spout for filling and pouring. In this example the pouring spout is in the form of a musical instrument held to the mouth, but more often it is part of the figure's ornate headdress. Other Recuay forms include doughnut-shaped vessels with trifid spouts and large vessels topped by "temples" with small tab-like figures engaged in what seems to be various rituals (Fig. 5).[14]

Recuay vessels are also noted for their painted decoration which often depicts anatomical detail or the textile patterns of clothing. Painting techniques included the use of negative resist in black and white. Red on white, and black, white, and red positive painting was also employed. One technique applied red slip to areas previously treated by smoking, thus creating a contrast between light and dark red. Number 11 also shows the use of a brown slip. A common resist design motif is a highly stylized feline (Fig. 6), a theme shared with Moche pottery, as illustrated in Number 43. A Recuay ceremonial dipper *(pacha),* sometimes erroneously called a "corn popper" is especially noteworthy for its fine painting (No. 12). The vessel itself is painted in orange and black resist on white. Half of it is left plain, but the other half is ornamented with solid color zones and a belt patterning which includes the so-called Greek key, step-fret and sun symbol designs in an unusually brilliant black on the white body.

Huari incursions into the north coast and highlands put an end to the pure Recuay tradition. While the Huari held sway, outside influences produced a hybrid culture which is reflected in the pottery, for instance the Recuay technique of surface decoration is combined with the modeling and tapered spout of the Huari.[15] Yet another outside influence came in with the Inca conquest, and this too is reflected in the pottery, as in Number 190, a Recuay-Inca piece with its straight spout and flat flanged mouth rim extending out beyond the spout in typical Inca fashion.

The Vicús Culture

In 1961 a new culture came to light along the north coast of Peru near the Ecuadorian border. Experts were alerted to this new area by the appearance in the marketplace of a new style of pottery decorated with negative painting. At first the new culture was called Ayabaca after the name of the town near the alleged original area of discovery. In fact, the finds were not at Ayabaca but at a burial ground in the Morropón district. Later the name was changed to Vicús when it was understood that the cemeteries were discovered near the site of that name in the Piura River Valley.

There is still much to be learned and clarified about this area and culture. The large burial grounds included graves containing negative painted vessels of less refined style, but there were also others which contained very fine ceramics resembling the best of early Moche pottery. This second type is produced from the finest clay and is powerfully modeled. It rivals all but the best pottery from the very heartland of the Moche Culture to the south, namely the Chicama, Moche, and Virú valleys. The presumption is that its production was between 400 BC and AD 100.

In 1968, Alan Sawyer proposed that this Moche-related pottery be called "Classic Vicús."[16] He considered this northern variant both technically and artistically superior to that of the Moche homeland and called attention to its preference for sculptural as opposed to painted decoration. By 1976, Alan Lapiner, in his revision of the Moche timetable, felt safe in including this pottery from Vicús as the product of the most ancient Moche Culture[17] (see Plates VI and VII).

The other pottery style found in the cemeteries at Vicús is known simply as "Negative Style Vicús." Carbon-14 tests of related organic material, found along with the ceramics in the burials, have yielded dates of circa AD 300, and the range for Negative Style Vicús ware is given as AD 100 to 700. This pottery shows none of the characteristics of Moche iconography; neither do the gilded copper objects such as cutout plaques, mace heads, and *"tumis"* or ceremonial knives which were discovered with the pottery. In fact, this Vicús pottery may be compared with the pottery which was being produced to the north in Ecuador and Colombia.

Technically the pottery is of poor quality and in appearance it is rather primitive.[18] The clay body, when fired, produced a brown ware. Decoration was mainly by a resist technique which resulted in a negative black configuration on the brown clay body. Occasionally positive slip colors were also used, namely red and white. Vessels are generally globular or sausage-shaped bottles with effigy figures superimposed on the surface or modeled as blind spouts. In addition, there are vessels with short, blunt spouts attached to the top of an effigy head and others with heavy, crude stirrups.

Typical of the type with the effigy figure superimposed on the surface are Numbers 13 and 15, the first depicting a seated warrior with a conical helmet, the other a warrior with a shield. The design of Number 14 shows the influence of the earlier Moche potters who typically modeled bottles in the form of kneeling prisoners with arms tied in front. Here there is a pouring spout on the back attached by an arched strap handle to the back of the head which forms the air-return spout for the vessel. Such a blind spout often contains a whistle, which sounds as air enters it when liquid is being poured out. Five other bottles that were modeled in the form of prisoners appear in Plates VIII, IX, X, XI and XII.

All of these were said to have been excavated near Ayabaca but were apparently from the cemeteries at Cerro Vicús, and they all exhibit typical Vicús features: large, hooked noses, coffee-bean eyes and slit mouths. The figures in Plate XIII also have the typically Vicús, large, flanged ears, seen here as pierced for the insertion of ear ornaments. A very common form in Vicús pottery is the double bottle connected by tube and handle, one bottle being modeled and the other containing a whistle. Five examples of the type are seen in Plates XIV, XV, XVI and XVII. These five were also apparently excavated from the Vicús cemeteries.

Number 16 in the exhibition is a modeled bottle in the form of a predator's head. The short spout has a Vicús arched handle attached to the top of the head. The lower half is a black color, which was the result of reduction firing. A band of positive cream paint from below the ear to the nose and around the teeth is all that remains of the color decor on the upper half, which was probably more extensive at the time of manufacture. The head jar with top spout and arched strap handle in Number 17 exhibits the more vivid tones of black with cream and red slip, which were probably evident on the predator's head before the original color wore off or the surface became pitted. Its face with its broad, toothy grin and B-shaped tab ears with incised dotted centers is duplicated in color and form, but in larger size, by a vessel in the Museum of the American Indian.[23] A spouted effigy vessel with comparable features and ears of similar shape and decoration was pub-

Plate XXXII. *Bowl with Incised and Postfired Painted Décor,* Paracas, Peru, South Coast, Ocucaje, Ica Valley, 500–300 BC (*App. no. 61*).

Plate XXXIII. *Double Spout Whistling Vessel,* Paracas, Peru, South Coast, Ocucaje, Ica Valley, 500–300 BC (*App. no. 62*).

Plate XXXIV. *Large Ovoid Vase, Incised Décor,* Paracas, Peru, South Coast 500–250 BC (*App. no. 63*).

lished by Alan Lapiner as coming from Vicús in the Piura Valley. Lapiner associated the vessel with "Middle Moche (?)" and identified the head, whose toothy grin includes feline fangs, as *Ai-Apec*, the fanged god of the Chavín, Moche and Chimú.[19] Number 18 is a footed cup which is modeled in the form of a human head and slip painted with a cream color. It is further embellished with black to represent hair. Around the back of the neck is a very elegant band of "S" decorations containing reed-circle motifs. This may represent a woven scarf or headdress ornamentation. The Recuay characteristics of this cup, which allegedly comes from Vicús, puts the Vicús attribution in question. Another type of Vicús cup, in the form of a modeled redware llama head with a knobbed handle on each side of the head is also in the Sackler Collection at the Museum of the American Indian (Pl. XVIII). Number 19 is unusual in that it seems to be a brazier or incense burner. The very amusing face, with appliqué nose and ears, has its mouth and eyes in the form of crosses cut through the walls like a jack-o'-lantern. The vessel does not have a bottom and inside the saucer-like cap the top of the head is pierced. There are traces of original resist painting, but the face is streaked with a positive cream slip.

The Moche Culture

The greatest flourishing of ancient Peruvian art occurred in what has sometimes been called the "Mastercraftsman Period." On the north coast this is identified with the celebrated Moche empire, which lasted for over a thousand years, from 400 BC to AD 700.

The great Moche ceremonial centers are in the Chicama and Moche River valleys. The most spectacular site is the massive terraced and truncated pyramid known as the Huaca del Sol in the Moche Valley. The whole pyramid is built up of solidly packed adobe brick (Fig. 7). Michael Moseley, who worked in this complex for many years, has shown that it is a true ceremonial center that was visited by pilgrims from outlying villages. Each village was assigned a building area, and whenever pilgrims from the village came to the ceremonial center, they brought adobe bricks to add to their section. Thus different parts of the building are made of different adobe clays which have been traced to specific distant points of origin.[20]

It is not possible to assign exact dates to the various Moche phases because dates in Peru before the Spanish conquest are not based on written evidence. The problems of the relative chronology of the various Moche styles are also quite complex.

The major archaeological work has been done in the Moche heartland, the valleys of the Moche and Chicama rivers on the north coast; but a thorough inves-

Fig. 7. Moche ceremonial center, the pyramid of Huaca del Sol, Moche River Valley.

tigation of the Virú Valley, an area into which the Moche expanded, has helped to clarify our understanding of Moche chronology. Yet as we saw earlier, discoveries in the Piura Valley of graves containing Vicús cultural remains, together with graves containing Moche cultural remains, complicated the problems of dating and led to a number of theories concerning the origin of regional developments and the interaction among regional cultures and Moche Culture after the demise of the earlier Chavín highland and regional cultures in the north. In 1969, large quantities of gold and gilded metalwork were discovered in Loma Negra in the Piura Valley, and the definite Moche characteristics which they display reinforced the impression that the producers of this metalwork were related to the Moche.

If the dates and chronology proposed by Alan Lapiner are correct, the basic scheme of Moche Culture is as follows:[27]

Early Moche	400 BC — AD 100
Middle Moche	AD 100 — 500
Late Moche	AD 500 — 700

Lapiner's Early Moche incorporates the material from the Piura Valley which Alan Sawyer designates "Classical Vicús." If one follows Lapiner's scheme, dates obtained through Carbon-14 tests on associated burial materials in the Moche and Chicama valleys would place Moche development in those two valleys in the Middle Moche Period though this is the heartland of Moche Culture. The relationship among Early Moche, Classical Vicús, Salinar and Virú still awaits a satisfactory solution.

Plate XXXV. *Whistling Vessel with Human Head Blind Spout,* Paracas, Peru, South Coast, Ocucaje, Ica Valley 500–300 BC (*App. no. 64*).

Plate XXXVI. *Kero with Modeled Lizard Head,* Painted, Tiahuanaco, Bolivia, La Paz, AD 400–700 (*App. no. 67*).

Plate XXXVII. *Vessel in form of Puma Head and Body,* Polychromed, Tiahuanaco, Bolivia, La Paz, AD 400–700 (*App. no. 68*).

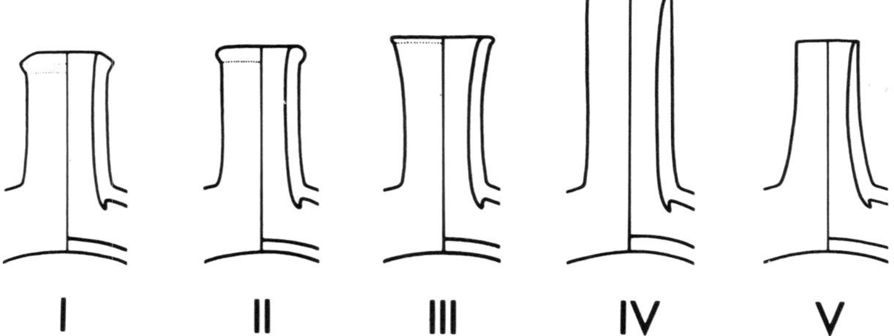

Fig. 8. Moche vessel spouts, Phases I–V, after Donnan.

The famous Peruvian archaeologist Rafael Larco Hoyle was the first to work out a satisfactory chronology for Moche pottery styles.[22] He based it largely on changes in the development of the stirrup spout and distinguished five basic phases. His sequence has been generally accepted and confirmed through more recent work, especially that of Dorothy Menzel and Christopher Donnan.[23] As Donnan has pointed out, the most telling characteristic is usually the upper part of the spout (Fig. 8).[24]

Phase I spouts are short and rather thick, with a pronounced lip at the rim. For instance, Numbers 24 and 26 in the exhibition, both of which are extremely well formed and show the exceptional realism of early Moche pottery, are from this phase. Additional examples are in Plates XIX, XX, XXI, and XXII.

In Phase II the short, thick spout form is maintained, but the lip is considerably reduced, in some cases even to a slight thickening. Typical of this is the spout on Number 34 which depicts a squatting man with one leg under him. Yet another Phase II vessel, Number 37, shows the turn of the lip nearly gone. The stirrup spout on the feline frog effigy vessel in Plate XXIII is another example of a Phase II vessel.

Phase III spouts have a flaring contour and tend to have concave sides. The stirrup itself is somewhat narrower and lighter in appearance. Such a spout may be seen on Number 40, an effigy vessel in the form of a crouching dog. For many vessels it is difficult to determine classification as Phase III or IV since their stirrups exhibit characteristics of both phases. These have been placed in an intermediate category called Phase III-IV. Plate XXIV, showing a man seated on a bottle with a bowl of food in front of him, belongs to this intermediate category. The stirrup itself is thinner and has a larger loop but the spout is still slightly concave, and this is a characteristic of Phase III. Other examples are Number 45, a feline head, Number 47, a vessel with modeled monkeys and Number 46, a marine scene.

In Phase IV the spout is taller and its sides are straight. The stirrup is still lighter and with a larger loop. Plates XXV, XXVI, and XXVIII, a vessel in the form of a portrait head of a chieftain, a five-peaked mountain jar and a bottle with the relief of a fox impressed on either side, belong to this phase. The inside of the upper portion of the lip also has been thinned, as in Numbers 51 and 52, which depict a seated blind man and a seated dignitary. Phase V spouts taper towards the top, but are about the same height as the Phases I to III spouts. However, there are no vessels with Phase V spouts in the collection.

Most Moche vessels were partly or wholly slip painted and burnished before firing. The slips were usually a shade of red or white. Most firing was done in an oxidizing atmosphere which resulted in a light-colored reddish body. In the early Moche phases, however, some vessels were fired in a reducing atmosphere which produced a gray-black or black body (No. 28). A secondary method of decoration was to paint the fired vessel with a black organic pigment that was then scorched onto the surface to provide additional detail to the costume and face. Since this black pigment is fugitive, only traces of it usually survive, and it was doubtless used on many more vessels than are apparent now. Number 37 is a Phase II vessel on which fugitive black was used to outline the cream bands and volutes on the surface.

The phase of a given piece can also be determined by an analysis of the painting and fine-line drawing on it.[25] Vessels were painted during all five Moche ceramic phases. Use of red and white slip began in Phase I and is the principal means of decoration through Phase V. As a rule, the figures or designs were drawn in a red slip on a cream ground. In Phase II the decoration was painted in broad lines in geometric designs or in patterns borrowed from textiles. True fine-line drawing was not fully developed until early in Phase III and continued to be important through Phase IV. Phases III and IV saw geometric decoration replaced by fine-line painting of scenes that are often symbolic or mythological, such as the sea-serpent warriors on Number 58, which is an example of a Phase IV painted vessel. The controlled use of fine-line drawing and open space in Phase IV painting stands in marked contrast to the use of broad lines and solid areas of color in Phase III. The shape of the stirrup and spout here correspond to the phase identified by the painting style.

Warfare, and motifs derived from it, are quite common in painted scenes. A favorite theme was that of the warrior or procession of warriors running through the desert carrying pouches of beans and coca leaves. No attempt was made to use perspective: figures usually appear in profile, though eyes and chests are sometimes shown from the front (Fig. 9).

During the close of Phase IV and throughout Phase V, there is a proliferation of the fine-line painted motifs on vessels. Phase V painting shows still further improvement in controlling the fine-line drawing. Fea-

Plate XXXVIII. *Kero with Polychrome Figural and Geometric Designs*, Coastal Huari, Peru, Central Coast, ca. 700–800 (*App. no. 69*).

Plate XXXIX. *Kero with Polychromed Figural Designs*, Coastal Huari, Peru, Central Coast, ca. 700–800 (*App. no. 70*).

Plate XL. *Kero with Polychromed Figural Design*, Coastal Huari, Peru, Central Coast, ca. 700–800 (*App. no. 71*).

tures are more clearly delineated and elaborate details of clothing and ornamentation are depicted. On Phase V vessels all the space, including that on the stirrup spout, is filled with detailed figures and various filler elements. As a result of the artist's desire to cover every particle of space, they are often drawn so crowded together that they lose their individual identity. The characteristics of fine-line drawing are consistent with each phase and enable us to assign to their proper phase vessels which do not have a stirrup, such as some bottles and bowls.

Certain vessel shapes can also be assigned to particular phases.[26] Single spout and handle bottles are almost all from Phase IV and have chamber forms similar to the stirrup spout bottles of this phase (see No. 57 and App. no. 40). Dippers shaped as the Recuay example in this exhibition (No. 12) are fairly common in Moche Phases III and IV (see App. no.33). A Phase III dipper usually has its design painted on the upper part of the bowl, while in Phase IV the design is painted on the lower part. Flaring bowls can be attributed to Phases III, IV or V, though the majority come from III and IV (see Plate XXVIII). There are many effigy jars, such as Number 41 in the form of a human figure with the face modeled into the neck of the jar and the body as the vessel's body. Phase III jars are distinguishable from those of Phase IV by the way the upper part of the jar's neck is treated. In Phase III it forms part of the headdress, while in Phase IV the spout rises above it: for example, in Plates XXIX and XXX, one a standing dwarf and the other a standing warrior, and Number 42 in the exhibition.

Moche pottery has long been popular because of the realism achieved by its potters, who were truly sculptors in clay. Every aspect of daily life has been depicted in minute detail including explicit sexual scenes. Details of clothing on sculpted or painted figures show how they were embellished and worn (see No. 25). In Number 54 a well-dressed man holds a pouch containing coca leaves in one hand and a container of powdered lime in the other. The two had to be chewed simultaneously to release the cocaine.

While it has long been believed that the goal of the Moche artist was merely to model and paint grave goods to accompany the deceased to the next world, recent studies of large collections of Moche pottery by Christopher Donnan, Elizabeth Benson, and others have resulted in some interesting refinements of the earlier conclusions. Donnan has pointed out that "...although Moche art gives the impression of having an almost infinite variety of subject matter, analysis of a large sample of it indicates that it is limited to the representation of a very small number of basic themes." He further believes that "...the iconography expresses only the nonsecular aspects of Moche Culture [and]...certain depictions, which appear to illustrate secular or daily occurrences, may in fact be pieces of a symbolic system which expresses only the supernatural and ceremonial aspects of this ancient culture."[27] Whatever their ultimate purpose, it is the immediacy of the figures and the scenes depicted on Moche pottery that makes it so appealing.

Fig. 9. Scene with running warriors, fine-line drawing on Moche IV vessel, after Donnan.

The Moche potter was a master at using most of the techniques known in his time to produce finely sculptured and painted pieces. These techniques include coiling, direct modeling, stamping, and the use of molds. Molds had been used since the very earliest times. The best mold-made pottery was cleaned up after all its parts were assembled. The joints were smoothed over, blurred lines sharpened, and often additional details were appliquéd on the clay body before the final slip painting. Despite these individualized touches, duplicate vessels are found which were made from the same mold and apparently by the same artist.[28] Three examples of this duplication exist in a private collection in southern Florida (Fig. 10). In the present exhibition Number 48, a pair of cup vessels is from the same mold.

At some point during Phase V, outside influences apparently exerted sufficient pressure to cause radical changes in Moche pottery. It no longer appears in the cemeteries, and new and strange pottery shapes and styles take the place of the earlier Moche shapes and styles. Usually such abrupt changes of style in an area which had hitherto remained quite stable was thought to reflect some catastrophic event such as internal collapse or foreign invasion. Actually, the new pottery

Fig. 10. Three mold-made vessels with figures playing drums. Moche III, AD 100–200. Height 6″. Private collection, Florida.

styles are strikingly similar to those found in the Huari heartland north of Lake Titicaca in the southern Andean highlands, and it is therefore presumed that this change resulted from Huari domination.

The Pan-Peruvian Huari empire and its pottery are discussed elsewhere in this introduction. Here we are concerned only with the effect of its formation and development on the north coast. By about AD 700 the Huari, by means of either an outright military conquest or a religious crusade, had reached the northern coast and put an end to the great Moche empire. This incursion from the south coast brought Huari pottery styles to the north where they are found in both their pure Huari form and in combination with local pottery styles. This blend of styles is known as "North Coast Huari." Diagnostic features of the so-called "North Coast Huari" Style are head-neck bottles, oblique tapered spouts, kero forms, and Huari Style polychrome painting. North Coast Huari pottery was decorated with geometric designs in black and red on white. Stiff, multicolored designs depicting Huari divinities were substituted for three-dimensional modeling and scenic painting. The color of plain pottery changed from red to reduced black, and the use of molds almost entirely replaced modeling.[29] To the far north, where Huari influence was diluted, some Moche traits continued. The predominant shapes, however, are clearly Huari.

The Lambayeque-Chimú Culture

The great city-state of Huari in the southern highlands seems to have collapsed about AD 900, perhaps exhausted by several centuries devoted to extensive military expansion. Yet the Huari had devised a sophisticated system of military support based on an elaborate network of army roads and supply posts, and much of the credit given to the later Inca for their organizational abilities and road building should be accorded to the Huari. When this central control was gone, regional states again blossomed from north to south, and with them came a resurgence of local pottery styles.[30]

One strong local tradition that emerged was in the Lambayeque River Valley area on the north coast. Legend had it that a hero named Naymlap, who came "over the seas," founded a dynasty which ruled the area. Early Lambayeque pottery shows a number of older Moche traits such as a light oxidized surface decorated with a charred-on fugitive black. Vessel shapes, however, were a blending of Huari and local styles. Footed bottles with tapered spouts and a handle and double spout and bridge handle bottles were popular, the spouts themselves showing the typical Huari taper and angle. A favorite style was a bottle with the head of Naymlap modeled on the tapered spout and adoration figures on the walls of the vessel and on the strap handle (Nos. 72 and 73). Similar scenes occur on spout and bridge bottles (No. 70). The artisans of this period were also outstanding metalworkers and exact replicas of pottery vessels are found in gold or silver (Fig. 11).[31]

After a period of local rule, the Lambayeque area was absorbed into the emerging Chimú kingdom. Vessel shapes remained the same but the most popular decorative technique became the black reduction firing of the Chimú.

The Chimú Kingdom

The Chimú kingdom is said to have been founded by a legendary figure named Tacaynamo who came from the north into what had been the old Moche heartland. The date of his arrival is uncertain but it was sometime after the Huari empire collapsed. The Chimú kingdom grew and expanded, eventually conquering the Lambayeque to the north and gaining control of the coastal valleys to the south as far as the Patavilca. It came to dominate the entire north coast and remained in control until the Inca conquest just sixty years before the arrival of the Spanish.

The great urban centers in the Chimú area indicate that the urban center had become important to the political, economic, and social life of the people of that time. The Chimú capital city was Chan Chan which was well planned and well laid out. It covered some thirteen square miles and was divided into ten walled sectors. Each sector contained houses, terraces, reservoirs, parks, roads, and public buildings. The walls of palaces and temples were beautifully decorated with relief friezes carved in clay and originally painted.

The period of Chimú dominion was one of mass production. The growing demand of an enlarging urban population for goods in quantity was reflected in the emergence of household industries and specialization in pottery-making, gold-working, and textile weaving. Chimú pottery is primarily recognized by its black color and metallic sheen and its predominantly angular form. Both ceremonial and domestic vessels were mold-made. Firing was done in a reduction atmosphere, where the lack of oxygen and the resultant smoke and soot turned the unfired, but burnished, pottery into a burnished blackware. Some polychrome pottery painted in red, black, and white with geometric ornamentation continued to be produced, but this was eventually replaced by vessels which were decorated in relief, had three-dimensional figures on their upper portion, or were completely modeled. Although stirrup spouts came back into favor, Huari shapes remained popular, among them vessels with two conical, slanted spouts and a bridge handle in between, and jars with faces on the neck. Subject matter included fruits, vegetables, animals, birds, and inanimate objects. The vessel with a llama giving birth, Number 63, is an example of an Early Chimú vessel of the eighth or ninth century from the Moche or Chicama Valley. North coast blackware vessels sometimes have long, tapering spouts and broad, arched handles as seen here. They are generally taken to indicate Tiahuanaco-Huari influence. Since such features are found throughout the coast from that period, this llama vessel may be contemporary with coastal Tiahuanaco Culture. Its blind spout containing a whistle is in the form of the llama's head.

A distinctive Chimú decorative touch was the adding of a small nub or figure, such as a monkey, at the join of the stirrup and the spout (see No. 81, profile view). The Chimú apparently also felt the need of some textural decoration on their otherwise plain black pottery. This was achieved on pressed-ware pieces by stippling and by contrasting areas of matte finish with those that were burnished (see Nos. 75, 83, 84, 86, 87 and App. no. 49). Some vessels were decorated by stamping and/or modeling. An example from Chiclayo in the Lambayeque Valley is in the Sackler Collections in the Museum of the American Indian (Pl. XXXI). The erotic scenes on the bottle are both stamped and modeled.

About 1470 the Chimú kingdom finally fell before the repeated onslaught of the Inca armies. Its power was broken and, in accordance with Inca custom, many of its people were transported to other areas. Chimú blackware pottery continued to be produced; there are even a few examples of Early Chimú Style oxidized and slip-painted pottery, such as Number 88, a pressed-ware bottle in the form of a celestial house. On the whole, however, later pottery shows a blend of Chimú and Inca stylistic elements. The Inca introduced shapes and features that were hitherto unknown: the aryballos form, as in Number 186, the shallow dish with a bird or animal head handle, and the flared rim on spouts, as on the pressed-ware bottle in the form of a human head in Number 87.

Inca (Tallan) Culture

To the far north in the coastal valleys of the Chira and Piura rivers there emerged a little-known regional style called "Tallan" which seems to be a composite of various elements. Tallan pottery is relatively scarce, but Number 90 is an interesting variant of a stirrup spout bottle in which part of the stirrup takes the form of an anthropomorphic figure rising out of the bottle top. The light-orange color of the pottery is produced in an oxidizing rather than reducing environment and is painted with geometric designs in cream slip.

SOUTH COAST AND HIGHLANDS

Paracas

The Paracas peninsula in southern Peru juts out into the Pacific. Nearby is a sheltered bay where the Pisco River Valley meets the sea. Remains of an ancient town parallel the bay high above the sea. In 1925 the famed Peruvian archaeologist Julio C. Tello conducted extensive excavations in the grave fields near Cerro Colorado which lay nearby. The excavators discovered deep shaft tombs with chambers of multiple burials placed at the base. It was from these excavations that the Paracas Culture derived the name "Paracas Cavernas." From these finds came decorated textile fragments and incised pottery painted with a resinous paint after firing.

Further excavations among the ruins on the northern slope of Cerro Colorado uncovered a cache of several hundred large funerary bundles. The find was spectacular. Each bundle contained a seated body wrapped in alternate layers of elaborately embroidered clothing and plain cotton shrouds. Various artifacts in gold, stone, and gourd, and rather plain pottery, were also included with the funerary bundles. Dr. Tello named

Fig. 11. Vessel with double spout and bridge handle, gold, Chimú, AD 1000–1470. Height 11¾". Private collection, Lima.

this find "Paracas Necropolis," believing the tombs of the necropolis, or city of the dead, on the northern slopes of Cerro Colorado were a repository for the funerary bundles of exceptionally important personages from the entire Paracas area. His opinion is still being debated.

After many years of investigation, the time span for Paracas Culture is now considered to be much longer and its area much larger than was earlier believed. Interrelationships of valleys also appear to be more complex. Work has been done in every south coast valley from Cañete to the Rio Grande de Nasca. Alan Sawyer dates the Paracas Culture to a period between about 900 BC and AD 100. He divides its earlier development into the Formative Paracas Period, when Chavín influence was dominant, and the Early Paracas Period, which is characterized by the florescence of regional styles growing out of the Formative Paracas Period with perhaps the continuation, though diminished, of Chavín influence.[32] Then the Paracas Cavernas Culture appeared throughout the south coast affecting these Early Paracas regional styles unequally. Sawyer therefore calls the period of its ascendancy "Middle Paracas." He further divides the time span covered by Tello's term "Necropolis" into Late Paracas and Proto-Nasca.

The divisions of Paracas Culture are handled somewhat differently by Menzel, Rowe, and Dawson, who place the beginning of the Early Horizon between 1000 BC and 600-700 BC.[33] On the basis of vessel shapes and changes in motifs they then divide its later history into ten phases which they blend into Early Nasca.

Early Paracas pottery exhibits an important vessel shape foreign to other Chavinoid complexes: the double spout. There are, however, a number of Chavinoid elements, among them globular stirrup-spouted vessels,

Fig. 12. Bowl with incised and painted owl design, Late Chavín Period, 700–400 BC, Jequetepeque Valley (?). Height 2¾″. Private collection.

the use of incision to delineate decorated zones, and many designs copied directly from Chavín art. Over a period of time changes and alterations resulted in a different style.

Menzel, Rowe, and Dawson have divided the evolution of Paracas ceramics in the Ica River Valley into ten phases of which the first eight fall into the middle of the Early Horizon.[34] Phases I and II are closely related to pottery complexes of the central and north coasts, including Cupisnique, and are represented at the earliest levels of the Ica Valley Cerrillos site: Number 91 is similar to a bowl excavated from a grave lot comprising two bowls with well-preserved resinous paint showing typical traits of the Cerrillos time range. It is a straight-sided, heavily potted bowl decorated with an incised and painted human face with a modified Chavinoid eye. The representation is evidently of a human being rather than an anthropomorphic feline deity, for the mouth lacks the god's feline fangs. Circles without incisions have been painted on the remainder of the sides except for the pouring lip. The thick resinous paint is in bright yellow, red, white, and black. The unincised painted circles are red.

A bowl in the Sackler Collections in the Museum of the American Indian displays a motif that played a major role in the design of Formative Paracas and Early Paracas Period ceramics (Pl. XXXII). This blackware bowl with red and yellow pigment has on it an incised design of a frontal feline mask characteristic of late Chavinoid conventionalized eyes and mouth which exhibits overlapping fangs and an upturned button nose in relief. The bowl exhibits two different sizes of feline mask, one with two pairs of opposing or overlapping fangs, but the other smaller mask with only one pair. The body of the feline creature extends on the panels to the side of each mask. The site from which this bowl derives is not known, but the design suggested Chiquerillo or Ocucaje in the Ica River Valley.

Other ceramics in the exhibition are associated with several different Paracas phases and styles. Number 92 is possibly an Early Paracas Style vessel from Carhua, a site on the south coast below the Paracas peninsula. This small object with curved sides has a carbon-blackened body set off by incised lines defining an owl's eyes and its modeled beak and is painted in resinous red and yellow. Its similarity to a bowl with the incised face of an owl, associated with the Late Chavín Culture from the Jequetepeque Valley on Peru's north coast, demonstrates the strong influence of Chavín art on that of Paracas (Fig. 12).[35]

The exhibition also contains several objects which can be related to the Early Paracas Period style of the upper Ica Valley site of Juan Pablo.[36] Juan Pablo ceme-

Fig. 13. Mummy mask with postfired paint, Late Paracas, 300–100 BC, Chongos (?), Pisco River drainage. Height 11¼". The Brooklyn Museum, New York (64.94).

teries are found north of Ocucaje and above the city of Ica at the foot of Cerro Teojate. The style of Juan Pablo ceramics was essentially conservative, being the most Chavinoid of Early Paracas wares. At the same time, it gave special emphasis to important local non-Chavinoid motifs, such as the fox and the *vencejo,* a local whippoorwill. Juan Pablo continued to develop its Early Paracas Period iconography throughout the Middle Paracas and well into the Late Paracas Periods.

A ceramic type that is characteristic of the Juan Pablo Early Paracas Period and represents a distinctive South Coast tradition is the large melon-shaped bottle, Number 93. It is ornamented across the top and down the shoulders. The motif, incised and painted with pastel-colored pigments which tend to powder, is a highly abstract feline.

The double-spouted bottle ornamented with a frontal feline mask in Plate XXXIII is an example of a ceramic type which continued throughout the Paracas sequence at Juan Pablo even when the feline design disappeared in the vocabulary of the Paracas sites of Ocucaje and Callango. The vessel here is from the Middle Paracas Period, contemporary with the Paracas Cavernas Style, when Juan Pablo bottle forms became more compressed and ovoid in shape. The bird-head blind spout, like the feline mask motif, remains as a characteristic of Juan Pablo style although it disappears at Ocucaje and Callango. The feline mask design as seen here has an elaboration of the three brow whiskers in multiple pelt markings but all the paw elements of the feline mask of the Early Paracas are absent. A band of the *vencejo* motif, like the feline mask motif, continuing at Juan Pablo throughout the Paracas sequence, passes under the handle between the spouts. It has a large, double-circle eye and whisker elements curling to meet the beak. The wings, body, and tail are reduced to horizontal geometric components like examples of the last phase of the Formative Paracas Period. The colored pigments, originally much like those on vessels from Ocucaje, have deteriorated for the most part, due to the ground water to which the burials at Juan Pablo were subject for over 2000 years.

A good example of the Juan Pablo *vencejo* motif is Number 94. The *vencejo* was a motif of special importance in the south coast region. This example, incised and resin-painted, belongs to the last phase of the Formative Paracas Period. The large double-circle eye is typical, as are the whisker-like elements circling to meet the beak. The wings, body, and tail are reduced to horizontal geometric components. The secondary motif consists of a panel containing a row of three reed circles connected by short lines.

Also attributed to the Juan Pablo site is the large, incised globular bowl or jar with the Oculate Being in the Sackler Collections in the Museum of the American Indian (Pl. XXXIV). The figure has two serpents on its face and carries weapons and two trophy heads. The original postfired resinous pigment has deteriorated. The face on the jar has characteristics similar to Paracas mummy masks with concave eyes and snakes drawn above and below the eyes and nose, also of the Late Paracas Period, circa 300 to 100 BC, from Chongos, in the Pisco River drainage (Fig. 13).[37]

An example of a Juan Pablo feline figure is Number 95, a Phase 6 bowl with incised and resin-painted designs. Alan Sawyer has classified four versions of this abstract feline motif. The feline figure here combines what Sawyer describes as the second and third of four versions. The nose on the feline mask has been eliminated and the canine teeth reduced to parallel lines. Body markings are the same as in version two. There are Chavinoid eye patterns below the body markings.

There are two examples of Phase 6 bottles from the Upper Ica Valley, probably the Teojate Cemetery site: Number 96 is a bottle with a spherical body and a hyperboloid or "spool-shaped" neck. The resin-painted pastel designs are probably elaborated god's eye motifs and geometric designs which may be stylized facial features. These include the continuous mouth band and elaborated eye which is used in decorating both bottles and bowls. The bottle in Number 97 is similar. Its collar band is incised and resin-painted in step-fret designs with dot decoration.

Phase 9 falls within the Middle Paracas Period. The bowls in Nos. 98 and 99 belong to the Ocucaje style and have incised and resin-painted geometric designs. The most common geometric motifs in Phase 9 are diagonal step and twined-fret designs. Diagonal step designs are used exclusively in rim bands on the

Fig. 14. Bottle with spout and strap handle and figural blind spout, Late Paracas, 300–100 BC. Height 5⅝/16″. Morton D. May Collection, St. Louis Art Museum (368:1978).

outside of bowls. The second design used on the bowls noted above is the step-block design, drawn at very acute angles, a distinctive Phase 9 innovation.

The Ocucaje basin in the central part of the Ica Valley became a major center for the trophy head cult in the Middle Paracas Period. During the Late Paracas Period changes took place in iconography and style that show the gradual transformation of the imported trophy head cult into a true south coast cult. At the end of the period, south coast religious concern was focused on the assurance of agricultural fertility.

Another postfired, resin-painted vessel from Ocucaje is one with a single spout with strap handle attached to a blind spout in the form of a human head in relief (Pl. XXXV). The head sports an elaborate headdress with a whistle hidden at its base. The vessel was said to have been found in a grave together with another of similar type now in the Morton D. May Collection in St. Louis (Fig. 14). The Sackler vessel is of a different shape, however, with sharply delineated shoulder, and is more elaborately decorated with figures of the trophy head cult incised and painted on each side of the shoulder. The vessel is dated to the Late Paracas Period at Ocucaje.

An undecorated, reduction-fired, double-spouted vessel, Number 100 is also from the Late Paracas Period. Others of similar shape but with postfired resinous paint decorations are said to have been found at Chucho, south of the Pisco River drainage (Fig. 15).[38] The site is probably the same as that indicated by Julio Tello, spelled "Chuchio" and shown as being on the Bahía de Independencia, south of the Paracas peninsula.[39] Alan Sawyer has attributed this vessel to Callango, located in the southern end of the Ica Valley.[40] A bowl (No. 101), also attributed to Callango, is similarly severe in its black, burnished and mostly undecorated surface; only a small undulating band of postfired, cream-colored resinous paint encircles the mouth rim.

A set of panpipes with four joined pipes (No. 102), made in a reduced and burnished blackware, has also been attributed by Sawyer to the Late Paracas Period at Ocucaje. Its bulging shape and its more primitive form distinguish it from the elegant panpipes (No. 142), of ten-pipe size, attributed to a later Nasca Period.

The example in the exhibition of the last Late Paracas Period phase, Phase 10, is the bowl in Number 103. Bowls like this, according to Menzel, Rowe, and Dawson, are referred to as shape 56, and have simple, standardized line patterns on the outside.[41] On rarer vessels of the type two diagonal blocks, composed of from four to six lines, cross each other to form an "X" and, as seen here, create a lozenge pattern in between.[55] The inside rim is decorated with short line designs in the form of line triangles analogous to the line designs on the exterior side. The remaining interior decoration of the bowl consists of small, tightly curved S-shaped figures, worm- or snake-like.

The transition from the Late Paracas Period to the Proto-Nasca Period was gradual. William Duncan Strong, who excavated in the Nasca area in 1952-53, recognized a Proto-Nasca Period which seems to bridge Paracas and Nasca.[43] It is possible, as Alan Sawyer has suggested, that the Nasca polychrome slip tradition resulted from outside influence, possibly from the Topará Culture, referred to in the two valleys immediately to the north of the Nasca Valley, as the Chincha and Cañete cultures. Their ceramics, thin-walled and highly controlled in firing, were simple, natural forms whose surfaces were covered with a white or cream-colored slip applied before firing. The invention of this slip-painted pottery may have occurred in the Chincha-Alta in the northern Paracas area.

Fig. 15. Double spouted bottle with postfired painting, Late Paracas, 300–100 BC, Chongos (?), South of Pisca River drainage. Height 12½″. Private collection.

Nasca Culture: 370 BC–AD 540

Nasca Culture, located in much the same area as the earlier Paracas Culture, appears to have superseded it. The long period of Nasca development on the south coast has been named the "Mastercraftsman" period, just as Moche development has been on the north coast. All the arts flourished, including pottery of a highly developed technical level.

One major area of Nasca Culture consists of a series of rivers culminating in the Rio Grande de Nasca. Located on it is Cahuachi, the largest known Nasca site. It is a ceremonial center consisting of a series of platforms on artificially leveled hills which were once surrounded by numerous dwelling sites and extensive cemeteries. A second important Nasca area was the Ica River Valley where the major cemetery sites are located on the Hacienda Ocucaje, also well known for its remains of the Paracas Culture. Further upstream on the Ica are the Nasca sites of Cerro Soldado and Cerro Blanco. Nasca pottery has also been found in the Acari Valley further south, and Nasca influence reached as far north as the Pisco and Cañete valleys and as far inland as Ayacucho in the Andean Highlands.

Ceramics in this exhibition provide a cross-section of most of the phases of Nasca pottery chronology. Early Nasca pottery forms tend to be simple and show stylistic continuity with the earlier Paracas Culture. Vessel shapes remained largely the same as those of the Paracas but a thin-walled, well-fired polychrome pottery gradually supplanted the thick-walled, incised, and resin-painted vessels of the earlier culture. From the so-called Proto-Nasca Period incised, resin-painted sherds have been excavated on the same levels as those that are either incised and slip painted or only slip painted. A precise chronology, therefore, for the Proto-Nasca Period is difficult to formulate, just as it is difficult to formulate a proper nomenclature for the people of the culture of that time and place.

Nasca polychrome pottery has a long history and its development was gradual. In contrast to the north coast, modeling was only an adjunct to slip painting. Effigy vessels tend to be stiff and the shape of the vessel itself dictated the representation to the effigy (No. 106). Often modeling merely consists of pushing out the walls of the vessel to form a head spout or to indicate the roundness of a head on a vessel wall. Noses may be appliquéd. It is in the realm of slip painting that the glorious artistic expression of Nasca pottery is realized.

The Nasca artist used up to nine different colors, ranging from almost pure white to cream, buff, tan, orange and red-browns, Indian red, mauve, gray and black. During the Early Nasca Period decoration was often naturalistic, usually painted against a white or dark background. Motifs include fruits and vegetables as well as animals, birds, reptiles and fish. Fertility or agricultural deities also began to appear, nearly always depicted with face whiskers, what appear to be gold mouth masks, and winged forehead ornaments. Whiskers may be divided into two types: one has tufts extended to the sides as in Number 115, which denotes the monkey deity of the trophy head cult; the other has whiskers sweeping up to the ears, as in Number 114, characteristic of the cat-like otter, *Lustra felina,* found in the Nasca area.

The earliest example of Nasca ceramics in the exhibition, Number 104, comes from the style complex referred to as Nasca, Phase 2. Its shape, that of an effigy bottle in monkey form, is typically early. The flattened face has an appliquéd nose, and the eyes and mouth are incised as well as slip painted. This combination of decorative techniques is also characteristic of the Proto-Nasca Phase of Paracas.

The small bowl in the form of the cat-like otter head, Number 105, represents the early Nasca realism of Phase 3. The eyes are a holdover from early Chavinoid/Paracas stylistic expressions. The protruding tongue now becomes an important motif in Nasca art. Two early naturalistic examples of human effigy bottles are Numbers 106 and 107. The former represents an important figure, possibly a shaman, with cap projection and hawk silhouette painting around each eye. In his mouth he holds an early representation of a musical instrument, a panpipe similar to Number 102. The seated figure in Number 107 has a similar cap projection. In each vessel it is apparent that the container shape is more important than the realistic modeling.

Examples in the exhibition of realistic painting of the Early Nasca Phase 3 type are bowls painted with natural figures, such as the bands of recognizable birds in polychrome on a white ground in Numbers 109, 110 and 111, and one with a floral motif, Number 113. The importance of agriculture is emphasized by the bowl in Number 120, which is decorated with a horizontal row of half-beans. The Nasca painter sometimes did not plan ahead, as in Number 113, where it became necessary to add a vertical blossom to fill up the remaining space. Another example of not planning ahead is the large bowl of Phase 6, Number 136, where three of the heads in the encircling band of heads have only one eye rather than two. Bowls of Nasca Phase 3 were also painted with simple geometric patterns, as in Numbers 112 and 118.

During the Early Nasca Period some vessels were decorated with complex fertility deities. Number 115, as an example, is painted with a representation of the Serpentine Creature featuring the typical straight whiskers, winged forehead ornament, and strings of discs hanging beside the head. Its front feet end in feather-like toes. A double spout and bridge-handle bottle, Number 114, is also painted with the Serpentine Creature. This one, however, has cat-like otter whiskers and a very feline-looking head, but lacks the winged forehead ornament. The ability of the Nasca painter to fit his subject to a curved surface is noteworthy.

The last example from Phase 3 is Number 117; it is unusual in that, in contrast to the north coast, scenes representing everyday life, like the figures on it, are scarce. Here is a row of Nasca warriors, each with a different face paint, and each holding darts in one hand and a bundle of darts in the other. While the images are recognizable, the draftsmanship does leave much to be desired.

Early Nasca Phase 4 is characterized by a distinct break with many of the traditions of Phase 3 and by the sudden appearance of many new mannerisms of drawing. Several new vessel shapes appear as well, such as collared and straight-sided jars and very deep-bottomed bowls. There is an increase of mythological motifs, such as the Horrible Bird (No. 123), and geometric designs become more frequent, as in Number 119.

Only one example in the exhibition, Number 122, is an Early Nasca Period Phase 4 collared jar. Painted on its horizontal white band is a circle of foxes: the first fox in line has captured a stylized worm. The bowl in Number 124 is painted with an exterior rim band in an interlocking pattern of stylized fish motifs. Such painting may have taken its inspiration from the designs of the Nasca textile-weaving industry. Stylized interlocked patterns are dictated by the nature of the weaving produced in ancient Peru on the back-strap loom, which further imposes angularity on woven designs.

Middle Nasca Period Style corresponds with Nasca Phase 5. In this brief period motifs depart even further from naturalism, becoming increasingly abstract. The transformation from naturalism to abstraction probably results from foreign influence, possibly from the highland Ayacucho area.[44] The same deity figures continue to be painted, but now their anthropomorphic forms are very stylized. Typical of the painting style of this phase are the anthropomorphic mythical beings painted on the walls of Number 131, a double spout and bridge-handle bottle. The human face is rounded and has the usual marsh cat whiskered mouth and forehead ornaments. Although bent at right angles and with the legs dangling below, the body is that of a human. One hand holds a trophy head, the other a cluster of darts. Trophy heads, which must have had considerable significance to the theocratic military society of this period, decorate the feathered train.

Head vessels of this style phase may represent either prisoners of importance or those who have died. Numbers 127 and 129 are partially modeled and painted representations of living persons. The former seems to represent an important personage with a large, sling-bound turban and hawk wing painting under the eyes. A very simple miniature head vessel is in the author's collection (Fig. 16). Number 125 illustrates the painting of such heads on the walls of a vessel and shows a free-hand linear treatment of detail. Numbers 128 and 130 are trophy heads with closed eyes. The former has lips pinned shut, a feature also found on actual trophy heads in burial sites.

The vessel in Number 126, whose rim band decoration consists of multiple representations of the *vencejo*, demonstrates the use of abstraction in this phase.[45] Here the *vencejo* is reduced to a "haired" head, an eye, and a tuft of feathers. Such figures should be compared with the birds on Phase 2 vessels to appreciate the transformation from naturalism to abstraction.

In Phase 6, the heads and bodies of figures were replaced by proliferated motifs consisting of faces with octopus-like arms adorned with hairy, "cactus-like" projections representing trophy hair. These presentations imply that such trophy heads have fertility connotations.[46] The vessel in Number 135 has such a band of heads encircling the top of a human head.

During the final Nasca periods pressures from the highland Tiahuanaco people become evident. The quality of pottery declined and new forms appeared. Among them were tall beakers as in Numbers 137 and 138 in this exhibition, both of which display double tiers of female heads. The former emphasizes the heads by pushing out the vessel walls to give plasticity to the head shape; its wide rim band contains replicas of darts and clubs or throwing sticks. The latter, with its clumsily painted faces and sloppy geometric designs, illustrates the general decline in artistic quality.

A large bottle, Number 139, whose neck is painted with a female head and whose upper body has arms holding vegetable forms, is an interesting example of the marriage between Nasca painting and Huari pottery form. The painting of the head on the spout is typically southern highland style which can be traced as it moves up the coast. Both this vessel with its loop handles and a similar one, Number 140, illustrate the changes which took place during the transition between the long Paracas/Nasca Period and that of the intrusive Huari Period.

Among the innovative pottery styles of the south coast, ceramic panpipes are especially intriguing. The set of ten joined pipes, Number 142, illustrates the problems faced by the potter in producing uniform narrow tubes which will produce notes of the desired pitch. It has been suggested that the individual pipes were made by slip-casting in molds. Slip-casting is done by repeatedly shaking a wash of clay in a closed mold until the desired thickness of the walls is attained. If the technique was used on the pipes shown here, it would be the earliest known use of such casting anywhere in the world.

In the Ayacucho zone of the southern Huarpa highlands of the Andes a culture developed which is now referred to as Huarpa. Its development coincided with that of the Moche on the north coast and the Nasca on the south coast, and was a manifestation of the regional development of the time. Terracing—the use of shelves in mountainside farming in order to retain soil—was begun quite early in this period. Irrigation was practiced, and canals and reservoirs were used to catch and hold rainwater.

Pottery was produced in a variety of forms and was thin-walled. The principal decorative technique was the use of a red and black slip on a white-slipped surface. Some motifs resemble surrealistic and unidentified plants and animals. One of the most common figures is that of an octopus with two bodies and six or eight volute appendages. Toward the end of the period this motif made its way from the highlands into the Nasca area.

SOUTH HIGHLANDS

Tiahuanaco

The most famous ruins in the south highlands are those of Tiahuanaco. The history of this area and that of the Huari empire are thoroughly covered by Donald Proulx elsewhere in this catalogue. Among the examples in the exhibition of Tiahuanaco ceramics from this period is Number 147, an effigy vessel in the form of a llama with a large flaring spout at the rear. It is well-modeled and realistic, and recalls the large modeled llamas found on the coast.[47] This depiction is all the more striking as most of the art of this area deals with the supernatural.

A new pottery shape was introduced from the highlands, namely the kero, or slant-sided goblet or cup. An example can be seen in Plate XXXVI, a slant-sided polychrome goblet with a partially modeled lizard on one side. A variant of this form, often with an undulating rim and the head of a feline or bird against a raised square, is called a "fumigator," a term used by the Spanish although the meaning is not clear. Such vessels show some modeling in the rather stiffly rendered head and, occasionally, the tail.[48] The vessel in Number 146, with bird head against the square, is fully painted in black with repeated stylized bird heads but sometimes the painting is of a highly abstract rendering of the body parts of the modeled form. Number 145 is similar in style but has feline attributes. The wonderfully modeled bowl in the feline-headed llama form in Plate XXXVII, is a variant of the kero with feline attributes in Number 145. Tiahuanaco and Huari textiles are treated iconographically and stylistically in much the same way. The late John Wise, a connoisseur of Pre-Columbian Peruvian art, referred to these people as the "Picassos of South America."

This second Pan-Peruvian wave came from the south, and it is possible to trace the movement of its style and motifs from a distant spot in the south highlands, namely that of the great city-state of Huari in the Ayacucho area just north of Lake Titicaca. The first impact of it on the south coast occurred between AD 600 and 700. Nasca Phase 10 ceramics gave evidence of increasing pressures and influence from the highlands. An important new sub-style now appeared on the south coast and has been called the Atarco. Atarco ceramics are finely potted and blend highland motifs, imported pottery shapes, and the best of the Nasca polychrome painting style. A popular vessel in this style phase was the double whistling bottle, a shape imported from the north coast. One such double bottle vessel, Number 150 has one bottle shape modeled in human effigy form with the head forming the blind spout which contains the whistle. The second bottle of the vessel has a typically tapered Huari spout and is connected to the effigy bottle by a tube and an arched strap handle. The effigy figure is painted quite realistically, including the patches of paint on the cheeks. The spouted bottle is decorated with a painted row of fruit or vegetables.

A fine single-spouted bottle, Number 149, has a row of bodyless profile heads painted on the shoulder in Indian red, yellow, tan, gray-white and black. Like Number 150 the surface is highly burnished. The headdress has trailing plumes that include a stylized feather, a typical motif of Huari iconography. Each head is separated by a vertical dart motif, and a chevron design circles around the slender tapered spout. Number 148 is a head-spout bottle with modeled ears, nose and mouth. The body of the bottle is painted with right-angled stripes to represent a tunic, and the top of the spout is painted to form a cap. It is instructive to compare this bottle with Number 139, which is also a head-spout bottle from Phase 6 of the Nasca Period, since they clearly illustrate the change in bottle styles from the Late Nasca to coastal Huari.

Toward the end of the Huari expansion, certain regional administrative and ceremonial centers gained sufficient importance to pull away from the control of the central highlands. The great ancient ceremonial center of Pachacamac on the coast below Lima was one such regional center. As the control of the highland Huari began to weaken, Pachacamac continued to thrive independently and separately. Many of the same vessel shapes continued to be produced, but new motifs became important. The most distinctive mythical figure was a griffin with a winged feline body and an eagle head. Geometric fillers consisting of S-shaped elements, painted circles with dots, and sausage-shaped, cream-colored bands with black dots, are all quite common. The large bottle, Number, 152 is an example of coastal Huara Valley Style, derived from Pachacamac. Painted around its shoulder is the motif of a highly stylized, open beak parrot, with diagnostic feather crest. Areas around the spout are filled with black S-shaped elements.

Ica-Chincha

After the collapse of the Huari empire, and probably as early as AD 1000, several more or less homogeneous cultures extended over several valleys along the south coast.[49] Although they share cultural elements, there are also local variations. The regional area they occupied is usually known by the name Ica-Chincha. In general, ceramics of the area and period follow a uniform pattern with polychrome painting style of white and black on a red surface. Their decorative motifs are geometric, with most of the designs adapted from textile patterns. An example in the exhibition is the large pottery vessel, Number 144. This kidney-shaped bottle closes to a short neck with a flaring rim. Painted around the shoulder of the vessel and enclosed in parallel black and white lines are fox-like motifs taken from textile designs and multiple tiny motifs appearing to be a flock of birds in flight or a school of small fish. Toward the close of the period in this regional area, vessel shapes from the Inca empire are found mixed with the traditional Ica shapes.

THE CENTRAL COAST

The decline of the Huari empire disrupted the unity that had been imposed on the central Andes. This permitted a resurgence of local or regional influences. Huari influences in pottery style and motifs lingered on the central and north coasts, although they often blended with local styles and decoration. Coastal pottery is generally painted in black and red on white. The dominant style is known as Pachacamac. As this style moved up the central coast, the traits implanted during the Huari Period were gradually transformed. This transformation style is referred to as three-color (red, white and black) geometric. In the area of the Chancay and Huara valleys it is known as the Huara Style. Early Huara Style seems directly influenced by the earlier Huari Style at Pachacamac but later ceramics show an independent movement toward greater abstraction and freer expression. Typical Huari kero shapes from the central coast are seen in Plates XXXVIII, XXXIX and XL. They are painted with designs of sky deity figures and lunate faces, and have stylized arms and legs which terminate in Huari feather motifs. Each figure wears a slightly different cap and is framed by horizontal and vertical bands containing god's eyes. Number 155, a Huari kero shape, has a highly simplified geometric motif painted in black, white and red on orangeware walls; perhaps the design represents a single bird's eye joined with wing markings. Number 154 from the same area, is a head vessel which has a lunate face similar to those painted on textiles and keros as well as on mummy masks.[50] Here, however, the face is partly modeled as well as painted red, white and black. The rim of the tall kero-like spout is painted with a narrow geometric border. Number 153 is a deep, rounded bowl with curving, outwardly splaying sides. A standing figure modeled in the round and with upturned broad face and squat body, like those of the small tomb figurines produced by this culture (see Nos. 158 and 159), is placed in the bottom of the bowl. The interior walls of the bowl are painted in swirl-like designs. An almost identical bowl can be found in the collection of the Krannert Art Museum.[51]

From the same area comes a charming collection of small hollow figurines in orangeware with markings and decorations painted in black, white and red. Numbers 156 and 157 are zoomorphic figures with feline attributes. Numbers 158 and 159 are more human in appearance and are the forerunners of the numerous black and white Chancay Culture figurines. The former is especially interesting since it is still dressed in a small textile shawl. Numerous small textile garments indicate that many of these figures were dressed when they were laid in the grave as offerings.

From the Huacho area on the central coast comes Number 163, a large frog effigy with agricultural motifs impressed on its sides. The style and size place it within the coastal Huari Period; however, the red and cream coloration indicates a lingering of Moche influence.

The Chancay Culture

Intervalley activity on the central coast took place in the valleys of the Rimac and Lurin rivers, as well as the valleys of Chancay and Chillon. The most typical urban center of the period was that of Pisquillo Chico in the Chancay Valley where a ceremonial sector and various temple mounds are connected by ramps with a rectangular plaza. Constructed nearby are former habitation quarters and an administration center. Similar centers are found in other valleys. Most of their buildings were of clay and adobe, and are poorly preserved.

Development of the Chancay Style began with the emergence of a series of regional offshoots after the coastal Huari Period. This development is sometimes referred to as the Epigonal or Huara Period. Huara designs in black and white on red continued some of the Tiahuanacoid designs. The so-called three-color geometric style that followed was characterized by abstract black and red on white decoration. This style then gave rise to the distinctive Chancay black on white.

Much of the information concerning the Chancay Culture originally came from collections of pottery vessels from extensive cemeteries near Ancón and in the Chancay Valley. These vessels are somewhat crude and the workmanship often careless. Molds were used extensively, either for complete figures or for vessel details. A gritty body clay was used and its finished surface is seldom smooth. Painted decoration consists of designs, often textile patterns, painted on the surface in blackish or brown slip on a white ground. Vessel shapes vary. Bowls such as Number 172 and App. no. 77 are semicircular or annular based. Jars with narrow necks, like Number 177, often have small modeled appliqué figures or lugs attached. Canteen-shaped vessels such as Number 176 have bulbous necks resembling small bowls and strap handles. Tall, pedestal-based vases such as Number 173 resemble *floreros* (flower vases). Large, globular vessels like Number 178, with flaring neck rim and strap handles, sometimes have an animal modeled around the neck with its head and forelegs on one side and the tail and hind legs on the other. Probably the most characteristic Chancay vessel is a large, egg-shaped urn with the neck modeled in the form of a human head, as in App. no. 80. The upper rim forms the hat. These urn figures are probably votive since rudimentary arms and hands hold a small cup against the breast.

Chancay figurines were abundantly produced; many of them, like App. no. 88, were mold-made. The large hollow female figures, as in Numbers 168, 169 and 170, are impressive in size. They always have their arms outstretched to either side. The majority were embellished on their faces with a diagonal line extending from the outer edge of the eyes toward the temples, giving them the appearance of wearing eyeglasses. There are many varieties of these figures, although the same general type is maintained (see App. no. 85). Zoomorphic vessels were also produced and are quite charming, particularly the birds and llamas, like Numbers 179 and 180.

At the end of the Chancay Period, double spout vessels with whistles made their appearance. Characterized by a long spout on one bottle and a human or animal form surmounted on the top of the other, these vessels incorporated a small whistle built into the effigy (see Nos. 181 and 182). The act of pouring liquid from the spout causes the whistle to sound as air is returned.

The Inca Culture

The last civilization to emerge in Pre-Columbian Peru was that of the Inca who rose to power in the mid-15th century in the southern highlands. The Inca themselves were a small, Quechua-speaking tribe of nomadic people. They pushed into the Cuzco area and, thanks to the ferocity of their army, gained control of it between 1430 and 1440. The Empire of Tawantinsuyu, as it was called, became the dominant political power not only in Peru but also in Chile to the south and Ecuador to the north. With the ninth ruler, Pachacuti Inca Yupanqui (AD 1438-1471), there began a period of imperial expansion. From their own beginnings as a small tribal nation, the Inca grew, in a span of about three hundred years, to become the largest political entity in the Americas in both territory and population. Inca power extended north and south, up and down the Andes for more than 2000 miles.

After the Inca's rise to power in AD 1438, Pachacuti and his son Topa Inca moved through the central Andean region from Ecuador to southern Chile and brought most of that area under control. Where their rule was accepted by the local inhabitants, the subjugated kingdoms were allowed to maintain their own ways of life under Inca supervision. Conquering Incan armies appear to have had little effect on the ongoing life of the people.

No one in the New World could rival the Inca in their ability to organize politically and socially, yet their cultural achievements were at best only equal to that of their neighbors. Inca architectural features may be found at such religious centers as Pachacamac and in fortified administration centers such as Puruchuco in the Lima suburbs.

Certain characteristic shapes and styles of Inca pottery were, as one would expect, adopted or imported from the conquerers. The Incas did introduce some new pottery forms with their most characteristic shape being the aryballos, so-called because of its resemblance to the ancient Greek vessel of that name. It is a large jar with broad, rounded lower body and a conical and pointed base, and with a long neck terminating in a flared lip or mouth rim, which often had small ornamental pendant lugs suspended from its undersides. Two vertical loop or strap handles on the sides, and a small modeled figure or lug on the shoulder, at the base of the neck halfway between the loop handles, were used for holding it by a carrying strap or to suspend the vessel by a tump line on the bearer's back. Number 186 is a fine example of the classical Inca aryballos and is decorated with austere and simplified Inca geometric designs. Many variations of this vessel type appear in the conquered areas on the coast. In the area of Imperial Chimú the shape is retained but the vessels are produced in the preferred blackware. The flaring spout rim appears on other vessels as a typical trait of the Inca Period. A flaring spout rim can be seen on the central coast, Provincial Inca, stirrup spout effigy vessel in Number 189, with the unusual figure of a man poised on one end of a rectangular bottle and holding panpipes to his mouth. The attention to detail in the hair, the expressive face, dynamic coloring and extraordinary condition make this a unique example.

Double bottle whistling vessels were modified to exhibit certain Inca styles. Number 187, from the central coast, is painted with bands of Inca geometric motifs. Other adopted stylistic traits on it are the flattened, outward-flaring lip or mouth rim on the spouts and the vertical bridge handle. The faces on this vessel are unusual since the Inca rarely used the human face or figure on pottery. The whistle is built into the blind spout under the crouching feline. A second double bottle whistling vessel, Number 188, is somewhat simpler in form. The flared mouth rims are missing, but the vertical bridge handle and the painting on the shoulders indicate Inca Period manufacture.

The last example of the Provincial Inca Style is Number 190, a fine effigy bottle in the form of a seated male with a small llama tied across his shoulders. It comes from the Santa River area on Peru's north coast. The manner of modeling the llama and the facial treatment and expression of the seated man place the workmanship in the Recuay area. Treatment of the hat, however, which becomes the spout with flattened mouth rim, is typically Inca, suggesting that this piece may have been produced after the Inca conquest.

In September 1532 the Spanish, led by Pizarro, landed on the Peruvian coast near the modern city of Tumbes. Pizarro succeeded in leading 110 foot-soldiers, 67 horsemen and 4 cannons across the Andes and into the intermontane valley where the provincial capital of Cajamarca was located. Once there, he met the Inca ruler Atahuallpa whom he seized and strangled. In only a few decades the Spanish conquerors brought to an end the cultural flourishing of 2000 years.

1. MacNeish 1971, pp. 36-46, and Canby 1979, pp. 330-363.
2. *Ibid.*
3. *Ibid.*
4. Bennett/Bird 1960, p. 26.
5. Beadle 1972, pp. 2-11, and Lathrap 1975, p. 21, citing Beadle.
6. von Heine-Geldern 1967, pp. 787-791, esp. p. 788, fig. 3, the drawing of a Zhou Dynasty tiger after a bronze in the Freer Gallery, Washington, D.C.
7. Lathrap 1975, p. 27.
8. *Ibid.*, pp. 56 and 61.
9. *Ibid.*, p. 33.
10. *Ibid.*, pp. 33-37.
11. See the essay on Chavín by Sawyer and Maitland in this catalogue for chronological determinants.
12. See the vessel in Lapiner 1976, fig. 231, from the Charlotte Thomson Collection, Boston. It is possible that the vessel in this exhibition was once similarly resist painted.
13. Published also in Lapiner 1976, fig. 438; see also figs. 434, 436 and 437, and additional notes to these figures on p. 445.
14. Published also in Lapiner 1976, fig. 424; see also figs. 417-433, and additional notes on this piece on p. 444.
15. Lumbreras 1974, fig. 124 and fig. 183.
16. Sawyer 1968, p. 25.
17. Lapiner 1976, p. 112.
18. The shapes and styles of Negative Style Vicús pottery are thoroughly documented and classified in Larco Hoyle n.d.(a).
19. Lapiner 1976, p. 116.
20. Moseley/Watanbe 1974.
21. Lapiner 1976, p. 112.
22. Larco Hoyle 1963.
23. Menzel 1977, p. 59; Donnan 1976: in the following paragraphs I am primarily relying on this excellent summary of the development and date determinants of Moche pottery.
24. Donnan 1976, and revised edition 1978, fig. 71, p. 52.
25. *Ibid.* 1978, pp. 52-55.
26. *Ibid.* 1976, Chapter 4: discussion on chronology begins on p. 54.
27. Donnan 1978, pp. 158 and 174.
28. *Ibid.* fig. 61 shows a pair of vessels which are clearly from the same mold and painted by the same hand.
29. Lumbreras 1974, p. 173.
30. See the essay by Michael Moseley in this catalogue, p. 77.
31. See also another gold, double spout vessel from the collection of Dr. Peter Ludwig, Aachen, Germany, illustrated in Lapiner 1976, fig. 621, and additional notes on this vessel, p. 447.
32. Sawyer 1966, p. 73.
33. Menzel et al. 1964, p. 4.
34. *Ibid.*
35. In the last twenty years, clandestine activity at Carhua, a site on the coast south of the Paracas peninsula, produced ceramics close to Chavín in style. See discussion in Number 92.
36. See Sawyer 1966 for a discussion of Juan Pablo style.
37. See also Lapiner 1976, fig. 146, from the Jay C. Leff Collection, Uniontown, Pa., with the additional notes on this piece on p. 440; and fig. 150, from a private collection.
38. Lapiner 1976, fig. 212.
39. *Ibid.*, with additional notes to fig. 209, p. 441.
40. See Sawyer 1966, pp. 115-121, for a discussion of Callango ware.
41. Menzel et al. 1964, p. 231.
42. *Ibid.* fig. 64C.
43. Strong 1957, p. 21.
44. Sawyer 1966, p. 125.
45. Sawyer 1975a, fig. 137.
46. Sawyer 1966, p. 131.
47. As illustrated in Lothrop 1964, p. 212, and elsewhere.
48. Lumbreras 1974, pp. 143-144, especially fig. 156.
49. *Ibid.*, p. 195.
50. Waisbard 1965, p. 30.
51. Sawyer 1975a, fig. 184.

No. 189

No. 190

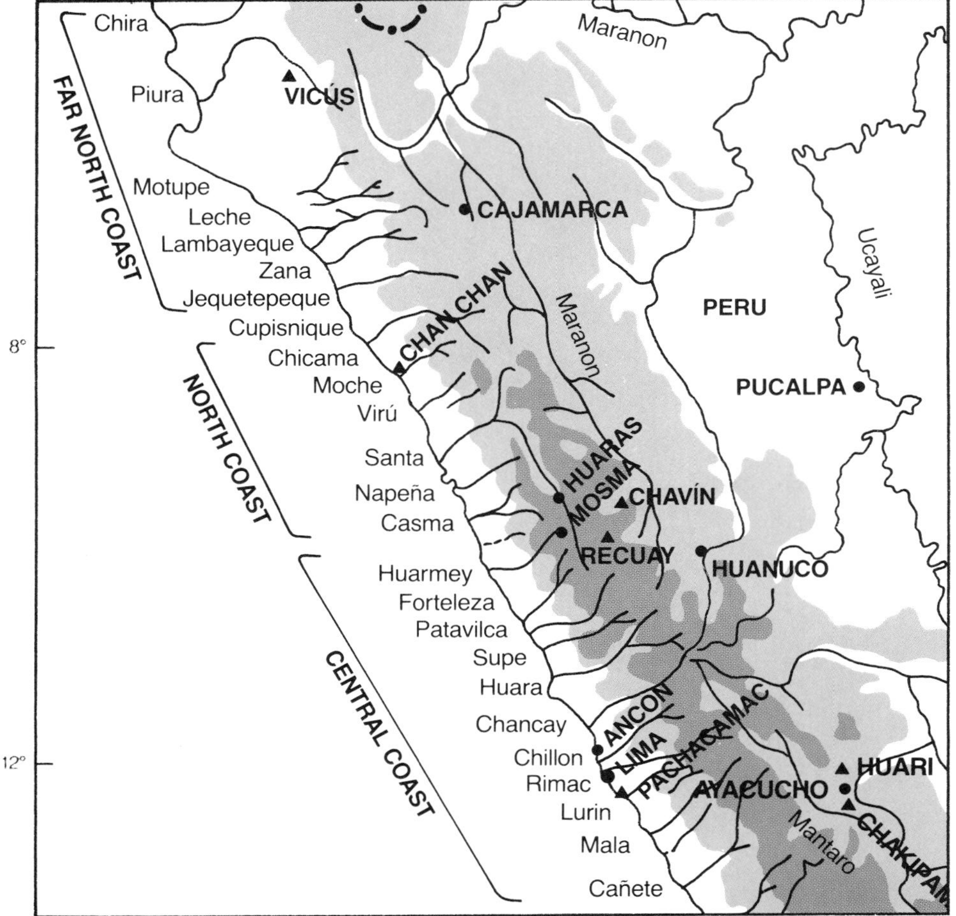

Fig. 1. Drawing of the Raimondi Stele (after Willey).

A Reappraisal of Chavín

Alan R. Sawyer
Maureen E. Maitland

The impressive stone ruins of Chavín de Huantar, located in the north central highlands of Peru, were visited as early as the 16th century by post-Conquest travelers such as A. Vásquez de Espinosa (1616), who described the site as an ancient oracle and pilgrimage center to which people journeyed from all parts of Peru.[1] The site became renowned for its four-and-a-half-meter stone anthropomorphic feline image that was set in a gallery deep within the temple. The Spaniards called it the "Lanzón" because its overall form resembled the shape of a dagger. It is the oldest central cult object still in its original place in the Americas and has always been held in awe by the Andean natives, as evidenced by offerings left at the site by pilgrims as late as Inca times.[2]

The famous geographer Antonio Raimondi visited the site in 1873 and had a carved stone monument transported to Lima where it was the subject of much debate concerning its antiquity and cultural affiliations.[3] It is now known as the Raimondi Stele (Fig. 1).

In 1886, E. W. Middendorf, who had visited the ruins, recognized that Chavín was associated with a pre-Inca culture, but he was unable to determine its antiquity.[4]

The recognition of the cultural significance of Chavín was left to Julio C. Tello who conducted archaeological investigations at the site in 1919, 1934 and 1940. Tello's findings enabled him to contribute fundamental information regarding the temporal position and importance of the Chavín Culture in Andean civilization.[5] During his first visit, Tello was able to survey the ruins, and upon his return in 1934, he found that part of a temple platform had been washed away by a change in the course of the Mosna River. From this fortuitous excavation, Tello recovered ceramic fragments that enabled him to determine the characteristics of "classic" Chavín pottery.[6] He was the first to define Chavín as an art style, and this enabled him to recognize Chavín-related motifs on artifacts in private and public collections throughout Peru. Tello also conducted an intensive examination of early sites on the coast and in the highlands, which he identified as belonging to the Chavín sphere of influence. This led him to conclude that Chavín was the center of a culture that had extended over diverse geographical areas.[7]

At the time of Tello's final expedition to Chavín in 1940, carved stones consisting of a single cornice block and several tenoned heads still ornamented the southern external walls of the temple. Other fragments of similar type, and various wall reliefs, were scattered about the site or encountered in his excavations. Tello set up a field museum in a colonial chapel on the top of the temple to house these materials. Unfortunately, in 1945, a massive landslide covered the temple complex (Fig. 2), and the contents of the chapel and tenoned heads were swept away and buried under tons of debris. Tello died shortly thereafter, believing that the most important discovery of his lifetime had been lost.

Although some of the missing stones have since been found, a great many have not, and it is fortunate that Tello had recorded almost everything in his site museum in the form of plaster casts, drawings, or rub-

Fig. 2. Ruins of Chavín de Huantar.

bings. These appear in the Chavín reports, prepared by Tello between 1940 and 1945, and published posthumously.[8]

In addition to this information recorded by Tello, Wendell C. Bennett had surveyed the site in 1938, providing further statistical information as well as drawings and rubbings of many stone carvings. He also provided observations on the style and iconography of the carvings and technical information on ceramic remains. Bennett's descriptions of archaeological sites excavated by Tello on the coast are also important in that they summarized what were thought to be Chavín-related finds up to that time.[9]

Tello's identification of Chavín-related artifacts over widespread areas of Peru led scholars to designate Chavín as an "Horizon Culture."[10] In the early years of Chavín studies, incised ceramics and carved stones were often seen to be Chavín-related even though they displayed little iconographic similarity to the Chavín Style (Fig. 3). Since Tello's death, scientific excavations and

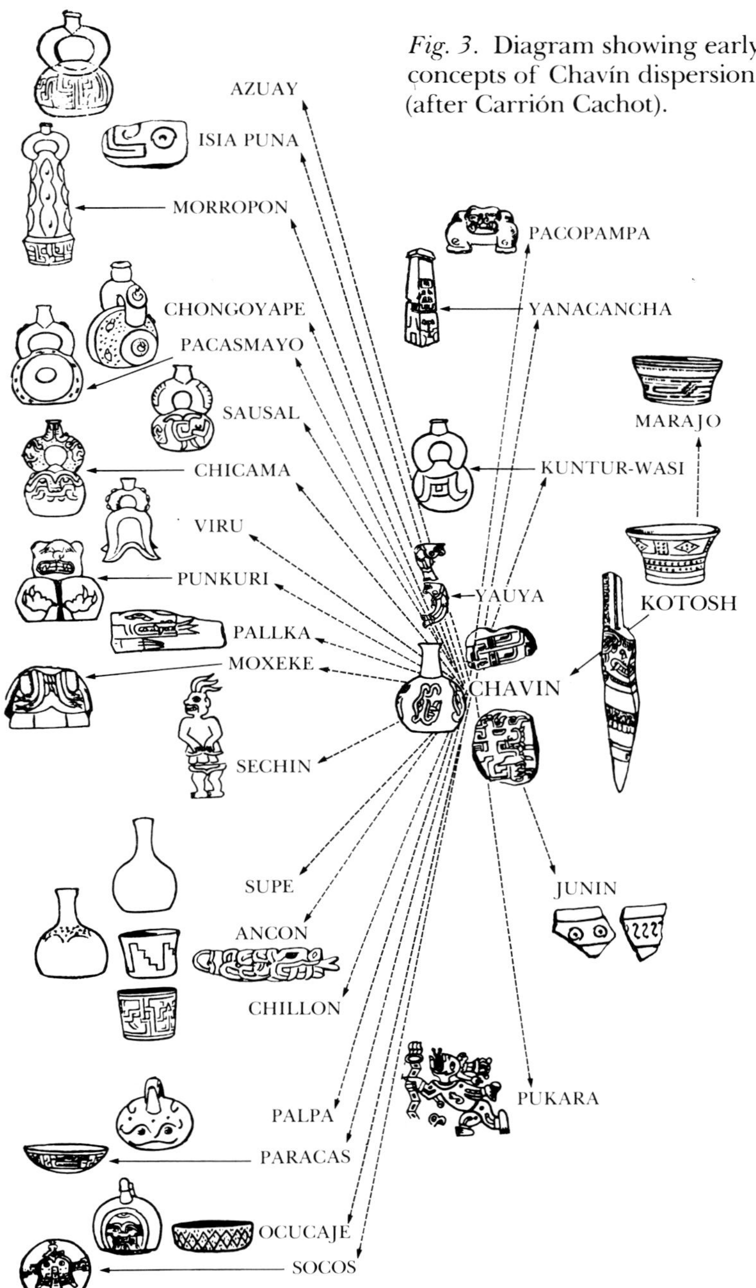

Fig. 3. Diagram showing early concepts of Chavín dispersion (after Carrión Cachot).

the activities of professional treasure hunters have frequently brought to light new evidence that has caused Peruvianists to continually reevaluate and refine Tello's original concepts of Chavín and its sphere of influence. As a result of this process, a much clearer understanding of early cultural styles has emerged.

The Discovery of the Black and White Portal

The first important new discovery following Tello's death was made by Marino Gonzáles Moreno, an inhabitant of the local town of Chavín, who had worked with Tello and was appointed by him as the Archaeological Commissioner of the site.

Following the landslide, Gonzáles collected carved stones from the wreckage of the town and recovered a number of the materials that had been stored in Tello's site museum from the Mosna riverbed. He then began to clear away the debris covering Tello's excavations on the southeast corner of the main temple. In 1956, a few meters beyond the point that Tello had stopped digging, he discovered two elaborately carved, round stone columns and fragments of stylistically related cornice reliefs (Fig. 4). This new discovery revolutionized the interpretation of the site since it indicated that a principal entrance to the temple had been located on the east face of its south wing. A stairway beginning halfway up the wall to the south of the portal was now seen as one of two entrances into the upper part of the temple, formerly reached by flights of stairs rising to the north and south along the east wall from the newly discovered portal.

The columned entrance was named the Black and White Portal because the south half of its steps was constructed of light gray rhyolite porphyry and the north half, of black limestone.

The Contributions of John H. Rowe

In 1961, John H. Rowe and Gonzáles surveyed the ruins and Rowe published their results along with his proposed chronology of Chavín lithic art in 1962. He returned to Chavín the following year and an amplified version of his original paper appeared in 1967. From their survey of interior galleries, Rowe concluded that two symmetrical wings had been added to the original structure containing the Lanzón, which he called the "Old Temple." During a subsequent building phase, the south wing of the temple was extended by a further addition and another unfinished section was begun, which, if completed, would have placed the newly discovered portal at the center of the east face of the south wing (Fig. 5).

Rowe noted that the construction in front of the portal, which he called a "Patio," and an impressive

Fig. 4. East Portal with columns and cornice fragments.

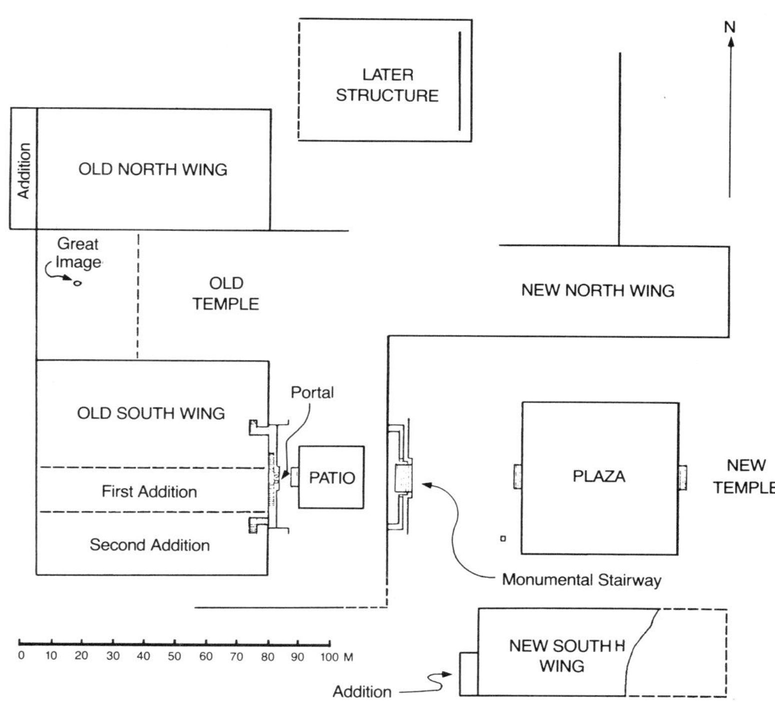

Fig. 5. Rowe's site plan from his 1961 survey of the temple complex.

stairway leading down to a large plaza, which he called the "Monumental Stairway," were both centered on the Black and White Portal. He observed that the lithic construction of the Monumental Stairway was divided into black and white sections in the same manner as that of the Black and White Portal.

While searching for evidence of the sequence of temple construction, Rowe noted that certain carvings had been associated with specific phases of its development, either as cult objects or as structural embellishments. Some cornice blocks and tenoned heads had been reused and were unsuitable as chronological indicators; but others, such as the Lanzón and the Black and White Portal sculptures, clearly related to building phases.[11] By correlating architecturally associated stone carvings with unassociated reliefs of similar style, Rowe proposed a relative stone chronology comprising four phases: AB, C, D and EF. Phase AB is represented by the Lanzón and some stylistically related cornice fragments, including those motifs illustrated in Figure 11, a and c.

The Tello Obelisk (Fig. 6), a major cult object found by Tello at the doorway of the church in the town of Chavín, was placed in Phase C on the basis of Rowe's stylistic analysis. Because the Obelisk was stylistically different from any other Chavín monuments then known, its place in the evolution of Chavín art remained problematical.[12]

Tello believed that the image on the Tello Obelisk was feline, but Rowe has argued for a crocodilian or, more precisely, for a cayman interpretation.[13] In 1971,

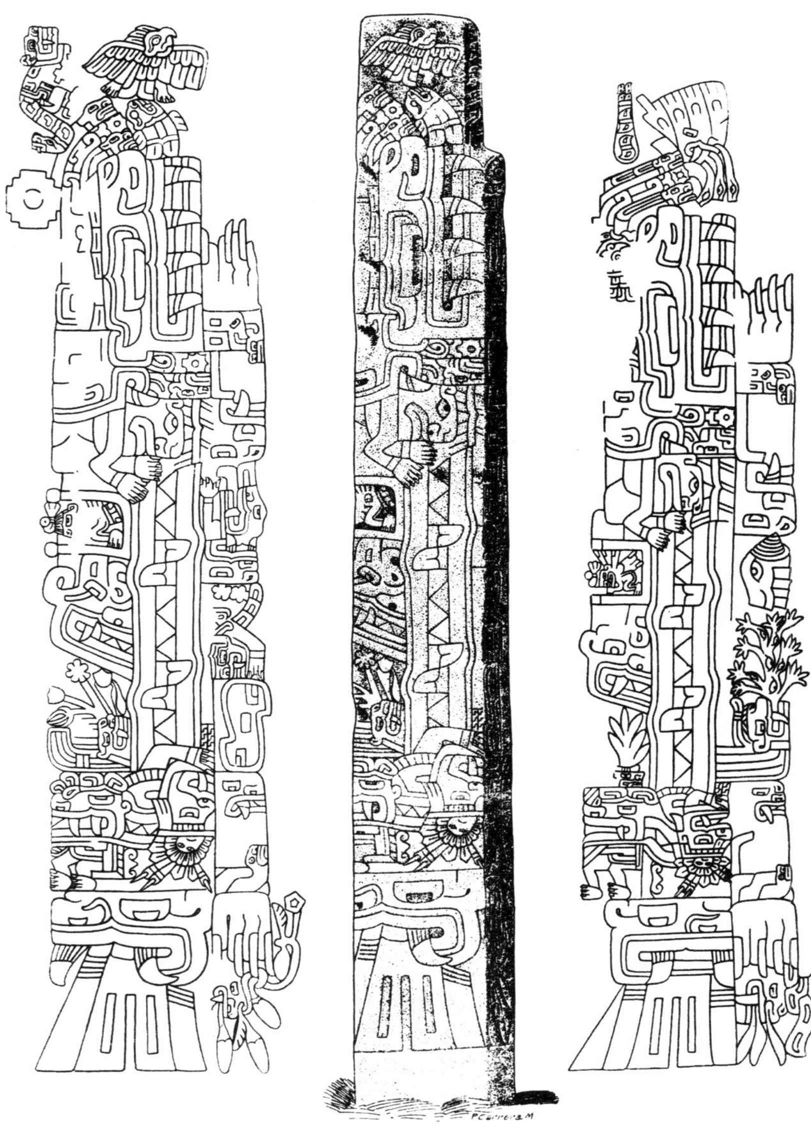

Fig. 6. Drawing of the Tello Obelisk (after Tello).

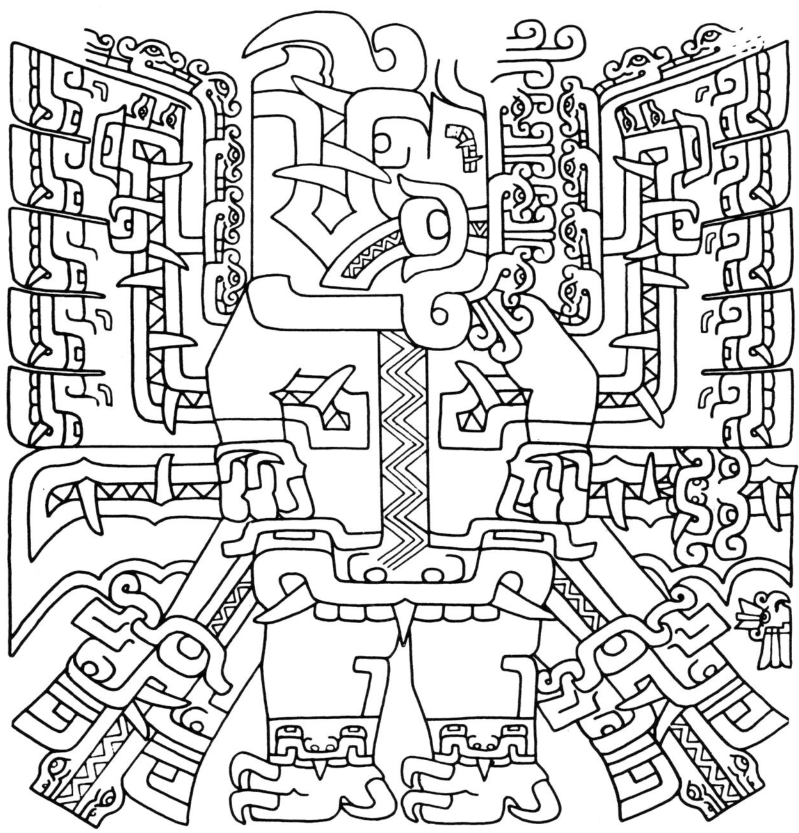

Fig. 7. Rollout drawing of north column relief, Black and White Portal (after Lumbreras) 1970.

Fig. 8. Painted Carhua textile showing splayed cayman imagery, *Carhua (?)*.

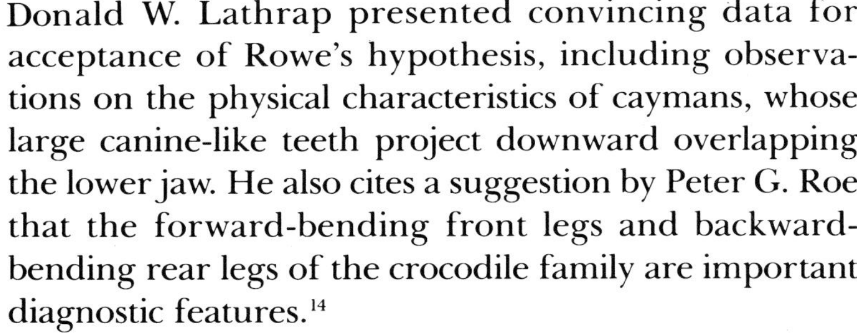

Donald W. Lathrap presented convincing data for acceptance of Rowe's hypothesis, including observations on the physical characteristics of caymans, whose large canine-like teeth project downward overlapping the lower jaw. He also cites a suggestion by Peter G. Roe that the forward-bending front legs and backward-bending rear legs of the crocodile family are important diagnostic features.[14]

The Black and White Portal sculpture corresponded to the establishment of a new ceremonial axis and served to represent Rowe's Phase D style (Fig. 7). The principal monument assigned to his Phase EF was the Raimondi Stele (Fig. 1). He also cites unspecific fragments of similar style and the Gotosh Monument[15] (see Fig. 10). The latter is a section of a carved stele found at a site five kilometers from Chavín on the other side of the Mosna River.

Rowe's relative sequence of construction and stone carvings was a major breakthrough in establishing the chronological evolution of Chavín culture. Of equal importance were his perceptive definitions of Chavín artistic conventions.

Excavations by Lumbreras and Amat

In 1966, Luís Guillermo Lumbreras and Hernán Amat Olazábal joined Gonzáles in a program of excavations at Chavín. In a series of galleries located in the masonry construction within the northern portion of the U-shaped bay of the Old Temple, large deposits of broken ceramics were recovered (see Fig. 9). The galleries were called "Ofrendas" since the elaborate ceramics they contained represent a wide diversity of styles and appear to be offerings brought to the site from areas within the Chavín sphere of influence. A second group of ceramics called "Rocas" was found by Amat in 1969 in subterranean storm drains in front of the south wing of the Old Temple.[16]

Lumbreras has published three chronologies attempting to clarify the temporal placement of the ceramics.[17] His most recent one corresponds closely to Rowe's stone sequence, with Ofrendas ceramics assigned to the Tello Obelisk Phase C, and Rocas ceramics dated to the Black and White Portal Phase D.[18]

Excavations conducted in the center of the U-shaped bay near the Ofrendas gallery revealed a sunken Circular Plaza. The walls of the northeast and southeast quadrants of the Plaza were ornamented by two relief friezes. The lower, near the floor, consists of horizontal rectangular blocks displaying profile feline images; the other, above, separated from the first by two plain stone courses, consisted of square blocks bearing elaborately costumed anthropomorphic figures. Single reliefs of each type also flank the western exit of the Plaza.[19] Lumbreras later informed Alan Sawyer that he found evidence of an earlier plaza located underneath the one excavated.[20]

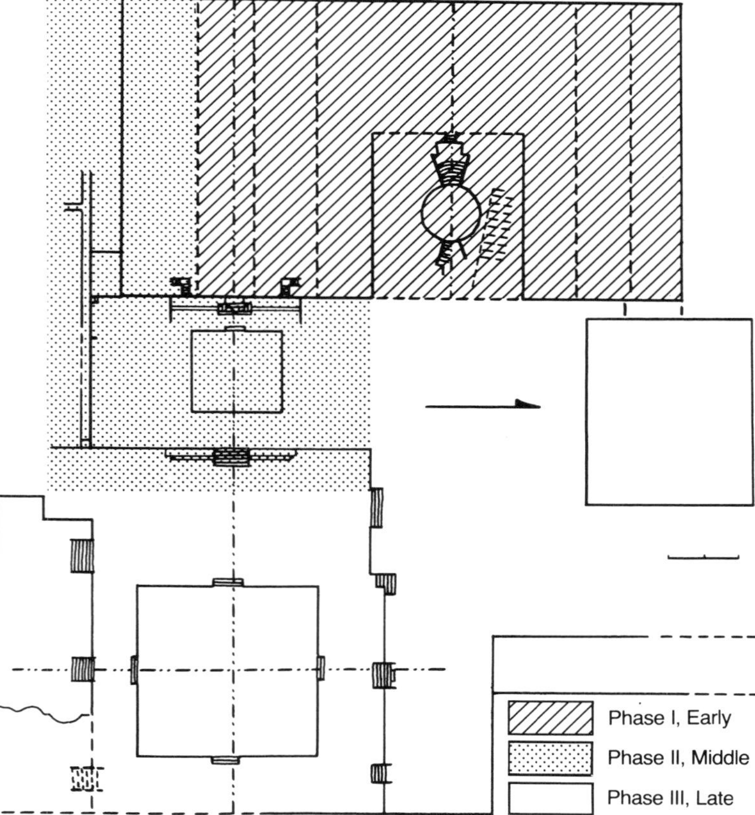

Fig. 9. University of British Columbia site plan.

Carhua Textiles

In 1960, two distinctly Chavinoid painted textiles, now in the Dumbarton Oaks collection, which were said to come from the south coast Paracas area, appeared on the art market (Fig. 8). Nine years later, well over one hundred examples of varying completeness were obtained by New York dealers. They were said to come from the site Carhua on the south coast just below the Paracas Peninsula. The major portion of this lot was lent to the Textile Museum in 1970 for study by Alan Sawyer and were made available for viewing by participants of the Dumbarton Oaks Conference on the Feline later that year. Sawyer presented a paper at that conference, citing the feline iconography of the Carhua textiles, and suggested a revision of our interpretation of the impact of the Chavín on the south coast Paracas culture. At that time Sawyer did not challenge the Chavín chronology published by Rowe and dated most of the textiles to his C-D phases in recognition of both Tello Obelisk and Black and White Portal traits.[21]

The Carhua textiles are amazingly close in their iconography to the stone carvings at Chavín de Huantar. Indeed, they appear to have been painted by individuals familiar with the stone reliefs at that site. One motif which occurred disporportionate to its known occurrence in Chavín lithic art was the staff god, of which only one complete example, the Raimondi Stele, is presently known from Chavín. In 1974, Dwight T. Wallace cited technical evidence which indicated that the painted textiles were of northern manufacture, and that they were brought to the south coast by individuals proselytizing Chavín religion.[22]

The same group of textiles studied by Sawyer were later forwarded to the University of California at Los Angeles where they formed the subject of a Doctoral Dissertation by Alana Cordy-Collins in 1976. Her analysis dated the majority of textiles to Phase D of Rowe's chronology and noted concepts of agricultural fertility associated with the staff god motif.[23]

The University of British Columbia Chronology

During the two academic years 1974-76, members of a University of British Columbia seminar directed by Sawyer undertook a reexamination of Rowe's Chavín chronology in the light of new evidence not available to him at the time it was proposed. This evidence included Carhua textiles, Ofrendas ceramics, the Circular Plaza sculptures and other recently discovered architectural features at Chavín de Huantar.[24]

Following Rowe's lead, three phases of architectural development were identified: I, Early (AB and C), II, Middle (D and part of EF) and III, Late (EF) (Fig. 9). These were keyed to the stylistic evolution of their stone carvings. The result paralleled Rowe's chronology with the exception of the placement of the Tello Obelisk which was redated to a final late phase (EF) of the sequence, with the Circular Plaza taking its place in the earlier phase (C).

First we shall describe the characteristics of style found in Phases I–III, the principal monuments and our summary of the period. We shall then present the

Fig. 10. Drawing of the Gotosh Monument.

Fig. 11. Circular Plaza reliefs (right) compared to Rowe's AB and D style reliefs.

University of British Columbia seminar's placement of the Circular Plaza sculptures, substituting them for the Tello Obelisk in Rowe's chronology that is now placed in the Late Phase.

The first stylistic phase was characterized by round-cornered, discontinuous curved lines that often end in elaborate serpent or feline "kennings."[25] Multiple imagery, guilloches, S-curves and repetitive designs that are tightly controlled within the outline of individual figures are typical artistic conventions. This early style is represented by the Lanzón, some cornice figures and almost all of the tenoned heads. It is associated with the Old Temple construction and includes Rowe's Phase AB. The Circular Plaza was found to follow this phase, making a logical transition to Rowe's D. The labyrinth-like placement of the Lanzón and constricted space within the Circular Plaza appear to indicate an intense religious cult, affording limited access to individuals within its sacred precincts.

The Middle Phase (II) is characterized by rectilinear lines with rounded corners and tightly curved volutes. Emphasis is placed on variety and occult balance rather than on repetition or exact symmetry. This style is dynamic and animated. It is associated with the New Temple and Black and White Portal and related fragments judged to predate the Raimondi Stele. There is discernible, in the fragments falling stylistically between these two monuments, a trend toward greater elaboration and more rigid arrangement of design components. The art of this period would seem to express a vital and expanding religious cult with a growing elaboration of ceremonial spaces to accommodate an increasing sphere of influence. Phase II comprises Rowe's D and part of his EF Phase.

Phase III is difficult to characterize because of the diversity of style in its major monuments: the Raimondi Stele, the Tello Obelisk and the Gotosh Monument. They each appear to be experimental innovations attempting to meet the agricultural concerns of the people of diverse environments then falling within the Chavín cult's expanded sphere of influence.

The Raimondi Stele is seen as a logical end result of the stylistic evolution of Phases I and II and appears to be an attempt to evoke a new concept of supernatural power in control of agricultural fertility. The staffs may represent growing plants, perhaps maize, and the rising volutes and their related central symbols, abstract expressions of growth force (see Fig. 1).

The Tello Obelisk is seen as the culmination of a cayman cult represented in two earlier monuments featured in Rowe that fall late in our Phase II.[26] The first, which we refer to as the Monumental Gateway Lintel, will be discussed later and is partially reconstructed in Figure 17. The second, the Yauya Stele, is probably more or less contemporary with the Raimondi Stele and, like the lintel, features two opposed cayman figures.[27] The Tello Obelisk departs from the previous two monuments' accommodation with earlier stylistic conventions to establish a looser and compartmentalized design structure incorporating naturalistic plants, human and other elements, including the traditional feline and raptorial bird motifs reduced to secondary roles (see Fig. 6).

The Gotosh Monument is an incomplete fragment showing only the top of what was evidently a massive monument bearing a frontal staff god on its principal face and a cayman-like motif on its sides (Fig. 10). Only the head and shoulders of the staff god are preserved and it appears to be a somewhat simplified version of the Raimondi deity, but with deeply incised bowl-shaped eyes that were probably inlaid.

The head of one staff is preserved and is stylistically distinct from any other Chavín monument so far discussed. Its eye is also a deeply incised but inverted bowl shape. Its most distinguishing feature is an upper lipband which curls around the nostril, with a row of fangs and teeth which completely border the profile of the face. U-shaped bands in front of the face are reminiscent of those associated with the cayman imagery of the Monumental Gateway Lintel and the Yauya Stele. The association with caymans is further reinforced by the image on the side of the monument with its forearm extended forward beneath the jaw, its long hooked claws, and L-shaped band on the arm. These traits correspond closely to both previously cited cayman images, and the figure might very well be a variation on the cayman theme. Another distinctive feature, not found in previous monuments, is the feather-like projections from the front of the being's lips. The importance of the Gotosh Monument lies in the frequent occurrence of its distinctive features, such as the surrounding toothband and the feather-like appendages to the mouth in late coastal Chavín-related styles. It may have been a final Chavín attempt to combine the concepts of the Raimondi staff god image and the Tello cayman image.

The survival of at least three major cult objects belonging to the Late Phase of Chavín indicates the existence of a pantheon of deities that grew in response to a variety of concerns among the followers of the Chavín religion.

The architectural history of the site is one of continuous expansion of ceremonial facilities most likely to accommodate ever-increasing numbers of worshippers. In Phase III, the large Eastern Plaza was built and flanked by north and south temple platforms, each ascended by three stairways indicating the location of at least six new temples. A seventh stairway in the northwest corner of the plaza allowed visitors access to the Old Temple area and the Monumental Stairway ascended to the Black and White Portal area. Spaces were therefore available for a large number of cult objects, each within its own shrine.

The Dating of the Circular Plaza

The carved surface of many of the Circular Plaza reliefs is badly spalled, making their iconography difficult to decipher, but a sufficient number are well preserved to indicate that, as a group, they form a smooth stylistic transition between Rowe's AB and D phases.[28] Comparative examples are arranged in Figure 11 with typical motifs of AB and D to the left and the Circular Plaza reliefs to the right. The AB feline cornice (a) is larger and more elaborate than the smaller Circular Plaza feline (b) but they share the same ear, eye and mouth conventions. Another plaza feline (d) has a lipband that curls up behind its fangs as does an AB eagle cornice (c). This feline also has fangs that overlap the lip, a trait found in other AB feline cornice fragments mentioned by Rowe.[29] The Circular Plaza figure relief (f) has a lipband that curls around the nose and chin and long curved fangs overlapping the lip, both features characteristic of Black and White Portal reliefs (e). The only "D" trait it lacks is a frontal fang.

The Dating of the Tello Obelisk

The Tello Obelisk does not display significant stylistic similarities to Rowe's AB or D lithic phases or to the Circular Plaza reliefs. It does, however, share many traits appearing on ceramics found in the Ofrendas

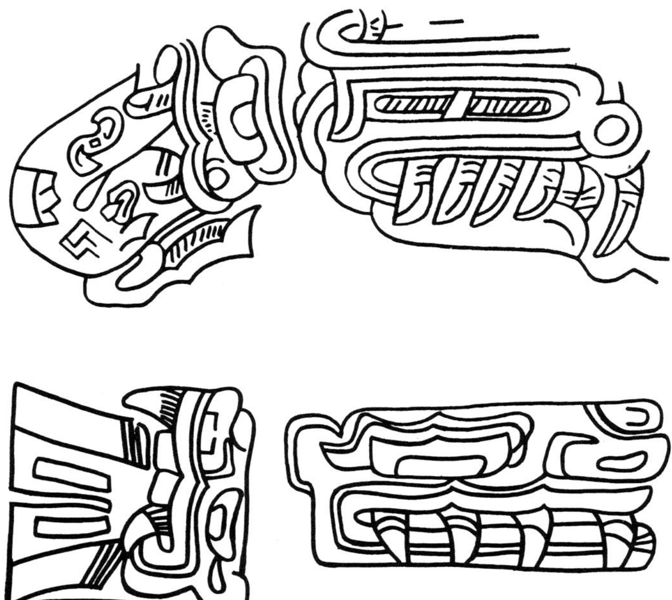

Fig. 12. Motif from Ofrendas ceramic (above) compared with head and tail of cayman on Tello Obelisk.

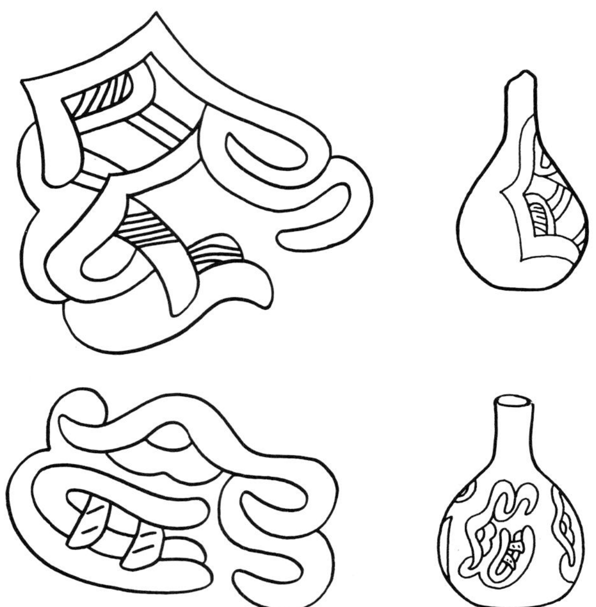

Fig. 13. Comparison of Ofrendas motif (top) and motif on sherds found by Tello in south platform.

Fig. 14. Late Cayman Stele. Upper portion from rubbing, Bennett 1942; with newly discovered fragment added from Sawyer photo.

Galleries located in close proximity to the Circular Plaza (Fig. 12). These facts, together with Rowe's proposed chronology, posed a dilemma for Lumbreras in dating the ceramics and accounts for his vacillating interpretations. Two factors indicate a late date for Ofrendas ceramics. Pottery which we believe to be post-Chavín styles (called "Wacheqsa" and "Mosna" by Lumbreras) occur in the same deposit, suggesting a period of accumulation beginning in Late Chavín times and extending into the post-Chavín era. Secondly, Tello found sherds in association with the late southern temple platform that are Ofrendas in style (Fig. 13).

Another piece of evidence indicating that the Tello Obelisk belongs to the final phase of Chavín is a smaller and less elaborate cayman obelisk. Part of it was found by Tello in 1919 and it is extended by a recently found fragment (Fig. 14). The body and mouthband correspond very closely to the Tello Obelisk, and it also displays traits related to the Gotosh Monument such as the extensions beyond the lip.

Further support for the dating of the Tello Obelisk to a later phase was derived from a detailed stylistic analysis of painted Carhua textiles. Staff gods and feline figures, which had been dated "D" by Sawyer and Cordy-Collins because of the three-point corner lipbands similar to those on the Black and White Portal reliefs, were found to exhibit late traits as well, such as scroll feet as in the Raimondi Stele and feather-like protrusions from lips like those of the Gotosh Monument figure.[30] It was observed that, on the basis of their most advanced traits, none of the textiles could be dated earlier than Late Phase II and that most belonged to Phase III. This means that they would all date to Rowe's Phase EF as he defined it.

Several Carhua painted textiles feature cayman figures that follow the conventions of Chavín lithic art very closely. One large hanging is of special interest in that it features one splayed and two profile cayman figures in configurations that occur, respectively, on the Yauya Stele and the Tello Obelisk (Fig. 15). Its rectilinear style more closely resembles that of the cayman image in Figure 14 than it does the Tello Obelisk.

Hypothetical Reconstruction of Phase II Architectural Features:

THE BLACK AND WHITE PORTAL

The Black and White Portal foundations show that the Portal and its stairways protruded from the east face of the temple and were enclosed on three sides by a screening wall, the lower portion of which consisted of large square blocks, some of which were found *in situ*.

In his 1962 and 1967 publications, Rowe proposed a reconstruction of the Black and White Portal in which he placed the cornice directly above a lintel resting on the columns and showed the screening wall rising to a height of little over 5 meters, to the point where the upper stairways entered the temple structure.[31]

The reconstruction above this point is problematical. It is proposed that many fragments of large rectangular feline-raptorial bird reliefs, closely related to the columns in style, may have constituted an ornamental frieze across the face of the screening wall above the level of the portal (Fig. 16).

The feline-eagle and -hawk cornice fragments found near the Portal and now erroneously placed across the top of the carved columns may have been located at the top of the screening wall at the same level as the other temple cornices. This proposed reconstruction is highly speculative, but in view of the awkward nature of a low screening wall which would have precluded privacy and allowed other visitors to see people entering the stairways cut into the upper temple wall, the possibility must be considered. It is unlikely that the tenoned heads on that portion of the wall would have been concealed. (If this reconstruction is correct, they may have been moved to the screening wall to continue the band of tenoned heads surrounding the temple.) For stability, a high screening wall, as suggested here, would have been tied into the upper wall of the temple. Unfortunately, the upper wall of this section was destroyed by colonial treasure hunters, eradicating any evidence that might have existed of tie beams (see Fig. 19).

THE MONUMENTAL GATEWAY LINTEL AND FORECOURT AREA

In 1919, Tello discovered a fragment of a massive carved lintel in a house near the Chavín ruins. It was lost in a landslide but Tello had had a drawing and photo made.[32] The light-gray stone from which this and other Chavín reliefs were made is volcanic stone called rhyolite porphyry although Tello and others have erroneously called it granite. While clearing the site in 1955-56, Gonzáles discovered two adjoining fragments of the same lintel at the foot of the Monumental Stairway. The three fragments reunited would measure 2.33 × .56 × .35 meters and display two elaborate cayman images

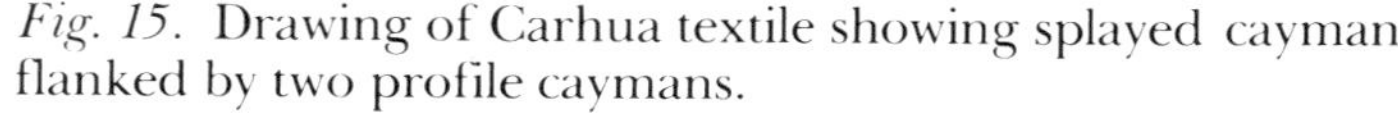
Fig. 15. Drawing of Carhua textile showing splayed cayman flanked by two profile caymans.

Fig. 16. Wall relief fragment of Feline-Hawk figure.

Fig. 17. The Monumental Gateway Lintel. Reconstructed from three known fragments (solid line) with further reconstruction (in dotted line).

nose to nose (Fig. 17). Each cayman has two profile faces sharing a single mouth with pairs of long sharp fangs. The body consists of a similar mouth band with agnathic frontal masks above and below with U-shaped motifs. Two forelegs side by side were evidently matched by two backward-facing hind legs. Assuming a short fan-like tail such as on the Tello Obelisk, the lintel probably was originally at least 4.3 meters long.

Above the Monumental Stairway, fragments of four round columns were found. Two of dark-grey limestone are badly shattered but were richly carved in relief similar in style to that of the Black and White Portal columns. The other two are better preserved but have spalled surfaces; they are of rhyolite porphyry and were decorated with abstract symbols, still faintly visible, that are almost identical to those appearing in a Carhua textile (Fig. 18). This correspondence tends to confirm the impression stated earlier that the painters of the Carhua textiles were thoroughly familiar with the lithic art at the Temple of Chavín de Huantar. The authors suggest that the massive cayman lintel (Fig. 17) may have been supported by the columns—the two to the right white and the two to the left black—repeating the black and white division of the portal and stairway. It would have formed part of an impressive portico at the top of the Monumental Stairway which entered into an atrium or forecourt in front of the Black and White Portal (Fig. 19). The walls of this enclosure are presently preserved to a depth of about 1.5 meters below ground level in front of the temple with steps rising to the portal level.[33] The walls may originally have been higher considering the number of similar stones uncovered in this area, some of which bear carved reliefs. The walls are constructed of double courses of rec-

Fig. 18. Carhua textile with motifs similar to those found on column from the area of the forecourt, seen in photograph at right.

tangular blocks alternating with single courses of square stones, the same structural system found in the Circular Plaza and the Sunken Plaza between the late period north and south temple platforms.

The masonry construction adjoining the Circular Plaza rises over 2 meters above floor level, and it is conceivable that the portico structure, and possibly the plaza, were roofed over. It is likely that such roofs would have been made of wooden beams and thatch. The spalled plaza reliefs and fractured portico columns suggest that the structures were destroyed by fire and hint that the splendid Chavín culture may have come to a violent end.

The Chavín Sphere of Influence

In the northern sierra, Chavín-related temples have been discovered throughout the Mosna-Marañón drainage, at Kotosh to the east of Chavín in the Huanuco area near the headwaters of the Huallaga, at La Copa (Kuntur Wasi) near Cajamarca, and Pacopampa to the north. On the coast, Chavín influence extended from the Piura Valley in the far north, to the Nasca Valley in the south. Included in this area is Chongoyape, a ceremonial center in the upper Lambayeque Valley and the well-known temple complexes of Huaca de los Reyes in the upper Moche Valley, Cerro Blanco in the Nepeña Valley, and Garagay, seven kilometers north of Lima on the central coast. Although Chavín-related temple complexes have not been excavated on the south coast, there is ample evidence of Chavín influence in the area.

The Chongoyape Style

Chongoyape is a regional culture of the far north coast named after an early ceremonial center in the upper Lambayeque Valley. Its ceramics are distinct, being uniformly of somewhat heavy grey ware with thickened spout lips and surfaces that are textured by punctation, roulette, or applied and incised pads of clay. Traces of postfire paints survive on a few examples indicating that the ceramics were very colorful. It seems likely that the texturing in most cases may have been employed to help bond the paints to the surface since no traces of paint have been found on polished areas. Like the ceramics of Cupisnique in the Chicama Valley, their paints have been removed by groundwater in the cemeteries where they were buried.

The decoration of Chongoyape ceramics usually consists of geometric motifs either outlined by incision or applied in bosses or strapwork. All are left highly polished in contrast to their textured backgrounds. Bird, animal and human figure vessels are simply modeled and selected portions are left untextured (No. 3). Chavín-derived motifs are extremely rare, but when they occur, manifest Late Period III influence. Two examples are shown in Figures 20*a* and *b*. The agnathic faces on the body and stirrup of *a* are executed in strapwork

Fig. 19. Marino Gonzales stands behind column fragment next to forecourt. Note court walls and steps to area of Black and White Portal.

Figs. 20a, b. Chongoyape stirrup spout bottles showing Chavín-derived motifs. Private collection, Buenos Aires.

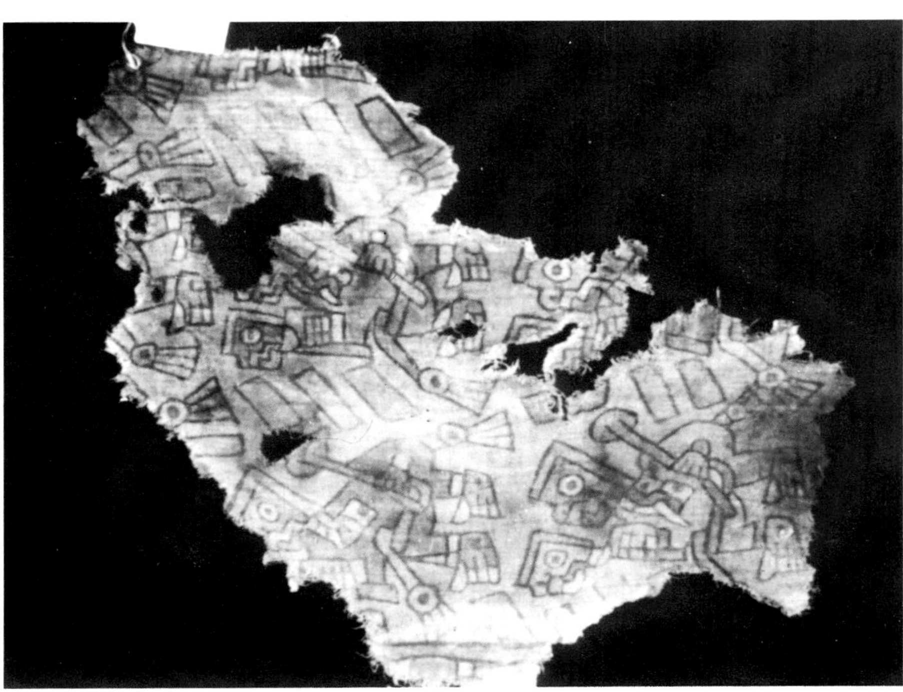

Fig. 21. A Carhua textile fragment showing figures holding masks on sticks.

Fig. 22. A Chongoyape Style ceramic figure holding a mask on a stick. Private collection, Buenos Aires.

and have L-shaped fangs similar to those found on the Raimondi Stele. The similarly placed incised profile faces on b are regional variants of late Chavín themes showing some relation to the heads on the Gotosh Monument (Fig. 10) and are closely comparable to regional variants found in Cupisnique ceramics discussed later in this paper.

The rarity of Chavín-derived motifs on Chongoyape ceramics may be misleading since not all ancient Andean cultures used ceramics as a primary vehicle for religious iconography. Several bits of evidence indicate that Chongoyape may have played a significant role in late Chavín culture. Some of the ceramics classified as "Rocas" at Chavín are in pure Chongoyape style and may well be offerings brought to the shrine by far north coast pilgrims .[34]

Stirrup spout bottles with thickened spout lips similar to those of Chongoyape are found among south coast Chavinoid ceramics. The stirrup spout was alien to the south coast and may have been inspired by northern bottles brought to Carhua by Chavín priests along with their painted textile icons. Wallace's textile structure evidence is consistent with this possibility.[35] One tantalizing piece of evidence supporting the speculation that proponents of Chavín culture came to Chongoyape is a Carhua textile that features human figures holding masks on sticks in front of their faces (Fig. 21). The same subject occurs on a Chongoyape ceramic (Fig. 22) but has not been encountered in any other area of Peru.

It is obvious that the Chongoyape culture had a long history before the arrival of Chavín influence and that its regional traditions strongly persisted throughout the Chavín-related period. This characteristic regionalism was typical of all cultures influenced by the cult of Chavín.

The Cupisnique Style

Chavín-influenced ceramics without provenience but said to have come from the north coast in the vicinity of the Moche and Chicama valleys are often referred to as "Cupisnique" in style. This designation was coined by Rafael Larco Hoyle in 1934 after a visit to the barren Cupisnique Quebrada located immediately to the north of the Chicama Valley. From the surface of the quebrada, Larco collected incised sherds that he felt were related to those which Tello called "Coastal Chavín." At this time, complete vessels were being sold by local pot hunters, and because he saw in them technical and stylistic similarities to the sherds he had found, he called them Cupisnique.[36] In 1938, Larco received information concerning cemeteries being looted on the Hacienda Sausal in the upper Chicama Valley. By 1939, he had located the activity and engaged the cooperation of the looters to record grave association at the sites.[37] Ceramics found in those burials, and some unassociated ceramics with alleged north coast provenience, were published by Larco in 1941. Some of these had been obtained by his uncle Victor Larco Herrera and are now in the Museo Nacional de Antropología y Arqueología in Lima.

Between 1964 and 1968, Alan Sawyer made several

Fig. 23a. Ceramic related in Style to sherds found by Sawyer in Cupisnique Quebrada. Private collection, Quito.

Fig. 23b. Monkey effigy bottle bearing little relationship to Cupisnique Style and probably post-Chavín in date. Private collection, Buenos Aires.

reconnaissance trips to the Cupisnique Quebrada in the company of the late Fritz Smischek, a local antiquarian who had visited the area numerous times and acted as his guide. Neither was able to identify any Chavín-related "motifs" on sherds they found, and Smischek stated that he knew of none from the area. Sherds collected by Sawyer from a way station on the trail leading across the Cupisnique Quebrada from the Jequetepeque Valley, had no Chavín influence, but were incised with geometric designs similar to those found on a clearly identified early ceramic style found at Kotosh called "Wairajirca," and other early sites. This led Sawyer to conclude that Larco's term "Cupisnique" may be a misnomer.

Chavín-related ceramics appeared on the art market in the late 1960's that were said to come from the Tembladera area in the upper Jequetepeque Valley. A number of individuals who had visited the area informed Sawyer that the ceramics had come from cemeteries in the upper parts of the valley closer to Kuntur Wasi. Richard W. Keatinge, who conducted an archaeological survey of the area, notes architectural similarities of Las Huacas, a temple complex at Tembladera, to Huaca de los Reyes in the upper Moche Valley. His sherd collections, however, did not show classic Chavín iconography.[38] To date, there is no solid evidence to suggest that Chavín-related ceramics said to come from the Tembladera area were actually found there. The sharp rise in ceramic prices on the antiquities market stimulated illegal digging throughout the north coast in the 1960's and ceramics said to come from Tembladera represent a wide range of styles; some are identical to the Chicama Valley Cupisnique style, while others are clearly of different regional and temporal styles (Fig. 23a and b).

In 1978, Maureen Maitland undertook a study of Chavín-related ceramics from the valleys of the Chicama and the Jequetepeque rivers, and ceramics alleged to have come from the north coast including the Tembladera area. The study clarifies much of the confusion surrounding identification of ceramics referred to as Cupisnique or Tembladera in style.[39] The University of British Columbia Chronology was utilized as a basis for stylistic comparisons between north coast ceramics and Chavín stone carvings.

The sample was divided into two groups: those exhibiting Chavín-derived iconography and those manifesting no Chavín influence. The interesting result of the separation was that it showed approximately 60% of the ceramics previously described as Chavín-related to be more closely associated with non-Chavinoid north coast regional styles.

The final Chavín-related sample consisted of 77 ceramics said to come from the north coast. *Los Cupisniques* was the principal reference because of its considerable number of illustrations and information on provenience of Chicama Valley ceramics.[40] Approximately 50% of the ceramics in Larco's sample were associated with the Chavín style. A study of many ceramics illustrated in *Los Cupisniques* as well as similar north coast examples was undertaken at the Museo Arqueologico "Rafael Larco Herrera" in 1978. It was possible to match many

Fig. 24. Chavín-related ceramics (Group I): *(a)* feline-raptorial bird motif in strapwork relief. Private collection, Buenos Aires; *(b)* feline-raptorial bird motif in broad line incision. Private collection, Buenos Aires.

Fig. 25. Chavín-related ceramic with fine line incised feline motif (Group II). Private collection, Buenos Aires.

of Larco's unidentified illustrations with the vessels from which they had been taken and thus obtain important data on correspondences between vessel shapes and iconography. The sample was augmented with ceramics from public and private collections, most of which had been photographed by Sawyer.

Seven thematic categories were identified and are listed in order of frequency of occurrence: felines, feline-raptorial birds, human beings, vegetal forms, snakes, feline serpents and anthropomorphic felines. An examination of regional traits suggested contemporaneity within the sample, while iconography, technology and ceramic shapes indicated three distinct but related groups.

Group I ceramics exhibit numerous Chavín traits that correspond to late stone reliefs such as the Tello Obelisk and the Raimondi Stele, as well as Ofrendas ceramics and sherds found at Chavín. Images are characterized by the use of kennings, multiple motifs and horror vacuii, a late design principle at Chavín. Reduction, a function of abstraction which eliminates individual traits or entire anatomical parts, was a particularly important artistic convention. The images on Group I ceramics were formed in strapwork relief with fine line incised details (Fig. 24a) or in broad line incision (Fig. 24b). Their spouts have thick, flaring lips, and the shape of the stirrup and spout is round with thick proportions, thus allowing for the increased design space necessary for strapwork relief imagery. This type of strapwork relief vessel is similar in style to sherds found by Tello at Chavín and illustrated in his 1960 publication.[41] The broad line incised example (Fig. 24b) is stylistically and iconographically related to a bottle form vase and a bowl found by Lumbreras in the Ofrendas Galleries at Chavín.[42]

The majority of Group II ceramics are found in Larco's Chicama Valley sample.Trait analysis shows they were influenced by Late Period III Chavín sculptures, in particular the Gotosh Monument (Fig. 10). This is demonstrated by a Group II vessel on which a fine line incised feline image shows bowl-shaped eyes, long, curved fangs and an upper lipband that curls around the nostril with a row of fangs and teeth bordering the profile of the face (Fig. 25). Vessels with triangular and circular stirrup configurations accompanied by flaring spouts with unflanged lips share the same iconography, indicating that they are contemporary (Figs. 26a and b). Their design motifs are less crowded than in Group I ceramics and tend towards geometric forms. The regional nature of the Chavín-related designs is char-

Fig. 26. Two Chavín-related ceramics of the Chicama Valley type (Group II). Victor Larco Collection, Museo Nacional de Antropología y Arqueología, Lima.

Fig. 27. Chavín-related ceramics with modeled and incised motifs (Group III). *(a)* modeled feline in a cactus landscape. Private collection, Buenos Aires. *(b)* human trophy head motif (?). Collection F. Landmann.

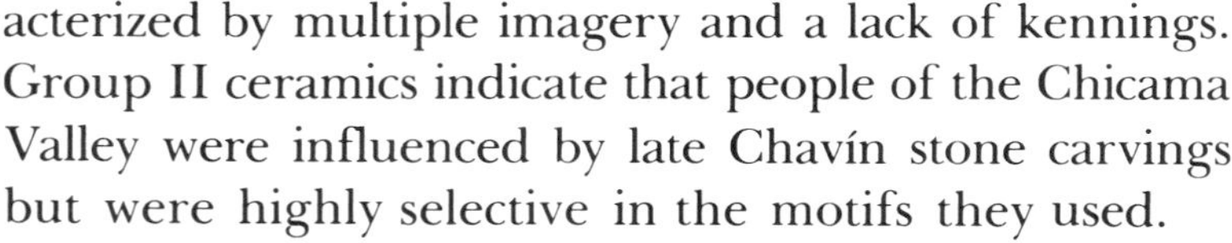

acterized by multiple imagery and a lack of kennings. Group II ceramics indicate that people of the Chicama Valley were influenced by late Chavín stone carvings but were highly selective in the motifs they used.

A vessel found in the Ofrendas Galleries and classified by Lumbreras [43] as "Raku," a substyle of "Mosna," is identical in iconography and ceramic shape to Figure 26b. Since Mosna pottery is thought to be post-Chavín, this indicates that the style continued on the coast after the collapse of centralized Chavín power. The form of this vessel is considered by Sawyer to be transitional to Formative Moche.

Group III ceramics display Chavín-related imagery depicted in an even more distinctive regional manner. The few Chavín traits observed in this group also derive from our Late Chavín Phase. Emphasis is on naturalism with imagery taken from human, vegetal or animal subject matter (Fig. 27a). Representations of the human figure bear some resemblance to the style of figures found on stone carvings at Cerro Sechín in the Casma Valley and may be part of a regional trophy head cult (Fig. 27b). The derivation of this motif is probably coastal since relatively few trophy heads occur in highland Chavín iconography.

Cupisnique type ceramics from Tembladera often

display well preserved postfire paint decoration. This indicates the likelihood that those from the Chicama Valley were similarly painted. Based on his experience with Paracas pottery, Alan Sawyer has long suspected this since Paracas ceramics are left roughened in areas to be painted, while the remaining surface is polished. A close examination of Cupisnique ceramics reveals the same characteristics.

Chavín-related motifs found on Cupisnique ceramics and other artifacts consistently exhibit stylistic traits found only in late Chavín stone reliefs such as the Raimondi Stele, Tello Obelisk and Gotosh Monument. This is true even though many of the subjects depicted are best known from earlier phases of Chavín art. They are, like the painted textile icons found at Carhua on the south coast, a composite of traits datable by their most advanced characteristics.

The late Chavín stylistic traits displayed by the three designated groups of Cupisnique ceramics overlap and suggest a relatively brief period of Chavín influence. Group I motifs are the most closely related to Chavín lithic art and exhibit traits characteristic of the Tello Obelisk. The strapwork vessels appear to imitate stone reliefs and may be an elite type of ceremonial ware. The broad line incised type features reduced shorthand versions of similar motifs. Group II ceramics show strong influence of the Gotosh Monument style and may, therefore, be slightly later in date. They manifest distinct north coast regional traits, indicating a weakening of Chavín influence. Group III motifs contain very few Chavín traits and are, by far, the most regional in character. They may be partially contemporaneous with Group II, but it seems more likely that they belong to the period immediately following the collapse of the highland Chavín culture.

The recognition of the late date and limited effect of Chavín influence on north coast religious iconography reveals the simplistic nature of the long-held concept of an Early Horizon dominated by the Chavín cult. It is now apparent that, during this period, north coast peoples developed a vigorous tradition of their own which was highly resistant to outside influence. This independent tradition is clearly expressed in the early ceremonial centers of Cerro Sechín and Mojeque in the Casma Valley and Punkuri in the Nepeña which Tello thought to be Chavín-related when he excavated them in the 1930's. The blending of their motifs and style traits with those of Chavín in some north coast artifacts has been interpreted by some Andeanists as evidence that Tello was correct.[44] An example is a well-known engraved conch shell trumpet from Chiclayo in the Lambayeque Valley.[45]

The best statement on the confusion that exists concerning early coastal styles and the problem of separating their local traditions from the Chavín style is given by Lumbreras in his description of what he calls the "Lower Formative":

> "The Lower Formative, as here defined is not a stylistic or chronological horizon. It represents the recognition that much of the Andean area was occupied by groups possessing varying kinds of Formative culture before the spread of Chavín influence. Where Chavín influence did not penetrate, existing chronological data are often insufficient to differentiate pre-Chavín from non-Chavín complexes, and some of the groups in this category may turn out to be later in time. They are more comparable to pre-Chavín manifestations than to Chavinoid ones, however, and for this reason have been included in the Lower Formative."[46]

North Coast Ceremonial Centers

In 1941, Larco argued for the existence of a feline cult originating in the Nepeña Valley, which he described as "similar" but different from that which had produced the stone carvings at Chavín. The territorial limits to the spread of Larco's "Nepeña" culture included Chavín and other sites in the central and northern highlands as well as the south coast.[47] Current studies of north coast sites suggest that a modified version of Larco's hypothesis may be correct. Richard L. Burger, who conducted stratigraphic excavations at Chavín, has recently suggested that architectural features found in coastal sites may have served as possible antecedents for similar traits found at Chavín.[48] His synthesis of radiocarbon dates from excavations on the coast shows that some phases of construction at Garagay in the Rimac Valley and Caballo Muerto (Huaca de los Reyes) in the Moche Valley date earlier than, or contemporary with, the earliest phases of Chavín development.[49] Larco had proposed a similar sequence of events which placed coastal Chavín influences at a later period, after the development of the sites of Punkuri, Cerro Sechín and Mojeque and the Cupisnique culture in the Chicama.[50]

The limited impact of Chavín cult iconography on highland cultures has been clearly demonstrated by excavations conducted at Kotosh, east of Chavín, near Huanuco.[51] A few Chavín traits, heavily overlaid with regional characteristics, were found in one level late in the stratigraphic sequence (600-800 BC). A similar picture is emerging from studies conducted on other highland sites but, because of the more complete data available on early coastal sites, our point can best be made by their brief review.

During two archaelogical surveys of the north

Fig. 28. A Chavín-related bone spatula. Collection, Museo Nacional de Antropología y Arqueología, Lima.

coast conducted by Tello in 1933 and 1937, the temples of Punkuri and Cerro Blanco in the Nepeña, and Pallka, Mojeque and Cerro Sechín in the Casma Valley were investigated. Punkuri is noted for a three-dimensional mud and stone feline executed in a naturalistic manner with a winged eye which is a north coast trait also found on Maitland's Group III Cupisnique ceramics. The Punkuri feline resembles a feline mural on the inner walls of the temple at Cerro Sechín. Tello mentions the discovery of Chavín-related ceramics at Punkuri but none of the sherds he illustrated relate to the iconography of Chavín lithic art.[52]

At Pallka, a site in the upper Casma Valley, a bone fragment incised in the coastal Chavín-related manner was recovered by Tello along with sherds that show some Chavín influence. However, they represent a small percentage of the total finds.[53] The bone figure is similar to one that is on display at the Museo Nacional de Antropología y Arqueología in Lima and both specimens exhibit the long snout, posture, vegetal motifs and semi-naturalistic style reflected in the Tello Obelisk (Fig. 28). Both cayman figures have winged eyes, which have been shown to correspond to the north coast regional style.

Adobe friezes uncovered at Mojeque show the remains of severed figures and human heads which bear little Chavín resemblance but are stylistically related to stone figures at Cerro Sechín.[54] Both sites portray an iconography of disembodied heads with eye markings and may be associated with a coastal warrior or trophy head cult. Similarities between Cerro Sechín and Mojeque and evidence of warrior/trophy head imagery in regional north coast cultures was also noted by Roe as a late preoccupation of coastal peoples.[55]

At the present time, Cerro Blanco and Huaca de los Reyes appear to be the only two north coast sites which exhibit adobe reliefs related to Chavín stone carvings. Adobe friezes found by Tello in 1933 at Cerro Blanco include L-shaped fangs, fangs overlapping lips and lipbands with bracket points, all traits that occur in the late phase at Chavín.[56]

Excavations conducted under the auspices of the Chan Chan–Moche Valley Project led to the discovery of the Caballo Muerto complex in 1969. Preliminary

Fig. 29. Chavín-related materials from the Central Coast.
(a) a ceramic bowl with a fish motif. Collection, Museo Nacional de Antropología y Arqueología, Lima.
(b) composite of Garagay adobe reliefs.

excavations undertaken by Luis Watanabe in 1972 uncovered a number of adobe reliefs in the mound called Huaca de los Reyes.[57] A subsequent excavation of the site was carried out in 1973-74 by Thomas Pozorsky.[58] The excavations showed that the facades of buildings facing open plazas had been ornamented with large-scale adobe reliefs, of which only the lower portions survive. They consisted of giant feline heads set in deep niches, feline figures of which only the feet and part of the tail remain, and a variety of large standing frontal figures of which the legs, flowing serpent belts and bases decorated with anthropomorphic faces are preserved to varying degrees.[59] The use of colossal adobe figures and reliefs can be divided into two phases

Fig. 30. Paracas-chavinoid bottles with feline and anthropomorphic feline motifs from Ocucaje. Collection Paul Truel, Lima.

Fig. 31. Stirrup spout bottle with frontal feline face in relief, incised and postfire painted, Callango (?) Ica Valley. Private collection, Quito.

closely paralleling ceramic Groups I and II in their use of traits derived from the Tello Obelisk and Gotosh Monument.

William J. Conklin has recently conducted an architectural study of the structures at Huaca de los Reyes in which he isolated ten phases of construction. The adobe reliefs of Chavín-related style were shown to belong to phase nine of the temple development.[60]

Chavín Influence on the Central Coast

In his search for evidence of the spread of Chavín influence, Tello noted Chavinoid style characteristics among the materials excavated by Max Uhle at Ancón-Supe in 1904.[61] In 1941, Gordon R. Willey and John M. Corbett excavated in the same area and recovered Chavinoid ceramics and two tapestry woven textile fragments featuring a Chavín feline-eagle motif.[62] These and other Chavín-related artifacts recovered from central coast sites all manifest late Chavín influence (Figs. 29 a and b). Lumbreras has noted their similarity to Ofrendas ceramics and, indeed, the Tello Obelisk cayman image appears to have been their primary inspiration.[63]

The Ancón interior decorated bowl (a) displays a fish with a cayman lip band and fang in a style similar to Ofrendas ceramics. The profile head (b) is a composite of four similar faces in adobe relief flanking a stairway in the Garagay temple in the Rimac Valley excavated by Rogger Ravines and William H. Isbell in 1974.[64] Again the influence of the Tello Obelisk and Ofrendas ceramics is evident in the eye form and downward sweeping fangs.

Chavín Influence on the South Coast

Between 1925 and 1930, Tello conducted excavations on the Paracas Peninsula on the south side of the Pisco Valley. He identified two cultural levels: "Paracas Cavernas" and "Paracas Necropolis." Cavernas ceramics were incised and postfire painted and, in an effort to expand his sample, he began to examine all similar materials he could find. In a private collection at Ocucaje in the Ica Valley, he found examples (Fig. 30) that led him to postulate that the Cavernas Culture began with an era of strong Chavín influence.[65]

Some Peruvianists supported Tello's interpretation, while others attempted to refute it.[66] His gathering together of stylistically diverse though technically related ceramics under the term "Cavernas" caused much confusion, but his observation regarding Chavín influence has been amply vindicated.

In 1955, Alan Sawyer and Lawrence E. Dawson made separate visits to Ocucaje, were intrigued by the research potential of the collections of Paracas ceramics they examined there, and independently began attempts to decipher their complex chronological development. Dawson placed Paracas ceramics in four temporary chronological phases which he named T1 through T4. All Chavinoid examples were placed in

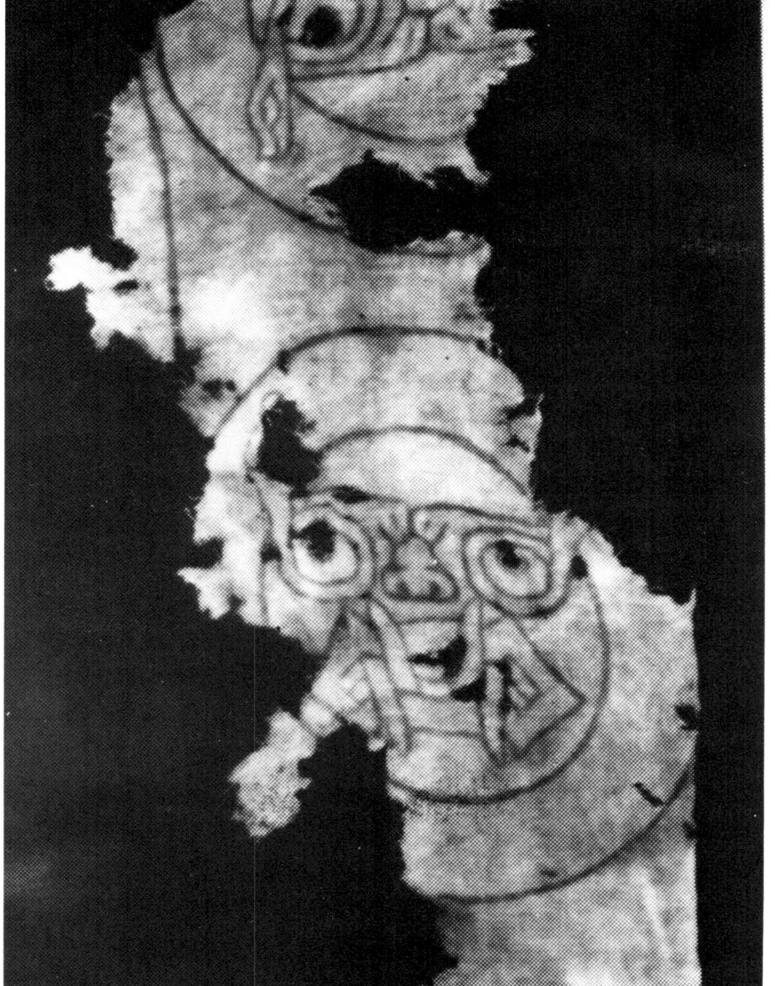

Fig. 32. Detail of Carhua textile fragment. Present location unknown.

Fig. 33. Paracas-chavinoid bottle. Raymond Wielgus Collection.

T3. His findings were published by Rowe in the 1958 *Revista del Museo Regional de Ica.* That same year Dwight T. Wallace conducted stratigraphic excavations at Cerrillos in the Upper Ica Valley, in which he found Chavín-related materials in the lowest Paracas levels.[67]

In 1960, Sawyer prepared his findings for publication in which he proposed a Formative Paracas Period manifesting strong Chavín influence followed by an Early Paracas Period characterized by regional styles based on the Chavinoid tradition. Two additional short periods covered the remainder of his Paracas sequence.[68]

Meanwhile, Dawson was preparing a detailed revision of his temporary classification with the assistance of Rowe and Dorothy Menzel. They proposed ten chronological phases called Ocucaje 1 through Ocucaje 10.[69] Basically their chronology paralleled that of Sawyer, though the two did not agree in their correlation of regional styles. The sparse Chavinoid sample covered by Sawyer's Formative Phase was divided into five phases paralleling the entire sequence at Chavín.

The appearance in 1969 of a large number of Chavín textiles from Carhua revealed the startling fact that Chavín religious functionaries had established at least one proselytizing mission on the south coast and brought with them painted icons revealing a complete inventory of classic Chavín iconography. This had not been suspected because of the distinctly regional adaptation of Chavín motifs on Paracas-chavinoid ceramics.

Fig. 34. Paracas-chavinoid bowl with toothband and "eye of god" motifs. Textile Museum, Washington.

A few ceramics, the one in Figure 31 for example, can now be seen to bear almost verbatim transcriptions of Carhua textile motifs (Fig. 32). Others, such as Figure 33, were obviously abstracted from more complete textile motifs such as the cayman image on the Dumbarton Oaks textile in Figure 8. The cayman motif per se evidently did not appear, but some ceramic motifs may have been drawn from its representations (Fig. 34). The toothband on the bowl may have been derived

Fig. 35. Paracas-chavinoid bottle with fox motif. Louis Slavitz Collection.

Fig. 36. Paracas-chavinoid bowl with *vencejo* motif. Private collection.

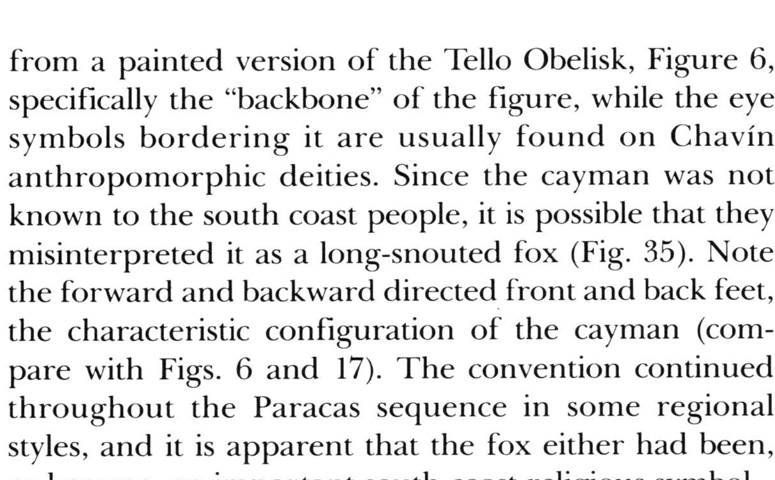

from a painted version of the Tello Obelisk, Figure 6, specifically the "backbone" of the figure, while the eye symbols bordering it are usually found on Chavín anthropomorphic deities. Since the cayman was not known to the south coast people, it is possible that they misinterpreted it as a long-snouted fox (Fig. 35). Note the forward and backward directed front and back feet, the characteristic configuration of the cayman (compare with Figs. 6 and 17). The convention continued throughout the Paracas sequence in some regional styles, and it is apparent that the fox either had been, or became, an important south coast religious symbol.

Another motif frequently encountered on Paracas-chavinoid, and lately south coast ceramics, and which has no obvious Chavín precedent, is a highly abstracted flying bird usually identified as the *vencejo* (Figure 36). It, like the fox, may have been a motif of regional importance before Chavín influence arrived. It may, however, have derived from a misinterpretation of the Chavín representations of the Harpy Eagle (Fig. 37) also known on the south coast. The motif to the right in Figure 36 is a stylized "hand of god," probably a shorthand symbol of the staff-god like the "eye of the god" symbol seen in Figure 34. Though the full-figure staff-god is the most common of Carhua textile motifs, it is rarely encountered in Paracas-chavinoid art, though a greatly simplified version of the god's head with serpent tresses is more common.

The two Ocucaje bottles in Figure 30 that were among those originally identified by Tello as being Chavinoid, are typical south coast adaptations to Chavín themes. The left-hand example represents a feline and the one to the right an anthropomorphic god. Both are reductions of figures to a frontal face rendered in distinctly south coast conventions in which the feline eye is standardized as lenticular and that of the god, rectangular. It is obvious that the south coast people did not readily adopt alien concepts but accepted and modified only those they could understand on their own terms.

Conclusions

The authors have sought to demonstrate the importance of establishing the chronology of Chavín Style and a thorough analysis of traits before attempting to evaluate the spread of Chavín influence.

Fig. 37. Carhua textile with harpy eagle motifs, Brooklyn Museum.

In applying our understanding of Chavín chronology to coastal cultures, we have concluded that the period of influence was late in Chavín times and of relatively short duration. A distinct difference in the impact of this contact can be seen between the north and south coast areas, probably due to the fact that the former were close enough to send emissaries to the site of Chavín, while the latter were not. No Paracas-chavinoid ceramics were found in the Ofrendas Galleries.

It also becomes obvious that the Chavín religion, which flourished in the high sierra, had roots in the jungle from which it derived most of its symbols. The birds and animals of the jungle were unfamiliar to the coastal peoples who could not understand them, except in terms of familiar species of their area. Thus, on the south coast, the powerful jaguar was translated into the small and benign Pampas Cat.

Without question, there was a florescence of cultures where contact with Chavín was made. That florescence, however, may have been caused more by the benefits of trade and the acquisition of new technologies than it was from the degree to which other cultures adopted Chavín religion.

1. Vasquez n.d.: 491
2. Lumbreras 1970: 42
3. Tello 1960: 188
4. Middendorf 1895: 88-104
5. Tello 1943
6. Tello 1943: 151-52
7. Tello 1929: 100; 1943: 157-59
8. Tello 1960
9. Bennett 1939
10. Bennett 1943; Kroeber 1944
11. Rowe 1967: 74
12. See also Rowe 1967: figs. 6 and 7
13. Tello 1923: 583-606; 1929: 83; Rowe 1962: 18; 1967: 83
14. Lathrap 1971: 3
15. Rowe 1967
16. Lumbreras/Amat 1969
17. Lumbreras 1971, 1974, 1977
18. Lumbreras 1977
19. Lumbreras 1977
20. Private correspondence; Lumbreras 1978
21. Sawyer 1972: 91-92
22. Wallace 1979: 48
23. Cordy-Collins 1976
24. Maitland, Mowatt, Phillips and Watson 1976
25. Kennings, visual comparisons or metaphors suggested by substitution, were first defined in Chavín art by Rowe, 1967: 78
26. Rowe 1967, figures 18 and 19
27. Rowe 1962: fig. 31
28. See Lumbreras 1977
29. See Tello 1960: fig. 67
30. Sawyer 1972:94-99; Cordy-Collins 1976:268-69.
31. Rowe 1967: figs. 3 and 4
32. Tello 1960, fig. 68, pl. XXXI c
33. See Lumbreras 1969: 9
34. Lumbreras 1971: 27
35. Wallace 1979
36. Larco 1941: 8
37. Larco 1946: 149
38. Keatinge 1980: 470-74
39. Maitland 1980
40. Larco 1941
41. Tello 1960: figs. 163—bottom right, and 164
42. See Lumbreras 1970: 150 and 1971: fig. 12
43. Lumbreras 1971: fig. 25b
44. Roe 1974
45. Larco 1941: fig. 174
46. Lumbreras 1974: 50
47. Larco 1941: 8
48. Burger 1978
49. Burger 1981: 559-600
50. Larco 1941: 9
51. Izumi 1971
52. Tello 1943
53. Tello 1956, Lammina IIId, Pl. XIV
54. See Tello 1943: pl. XIIIb and fig. 18
55. Roe 1974: 34-38
56. Tello 1943: pl. XIIIa
57. Moseley/Watanabe 1974
58. Pozorsky 1975
59. See Pozorski 1975: figs. 1-38
60. Conklin n.d.
61. Tello 1943: 136-39
62. Willey 1954: pl. 23-24
63. Lumbreras 1974: 72
64. Ravines/Isbell 1975: 253-76
65. Tello 1943: 157
66. Kroeber 1944 and 1953 supported and Willey 1951 refuted
67. Wallace 1962
68. Sawyer 1961
69. Menzel *et al* 1964

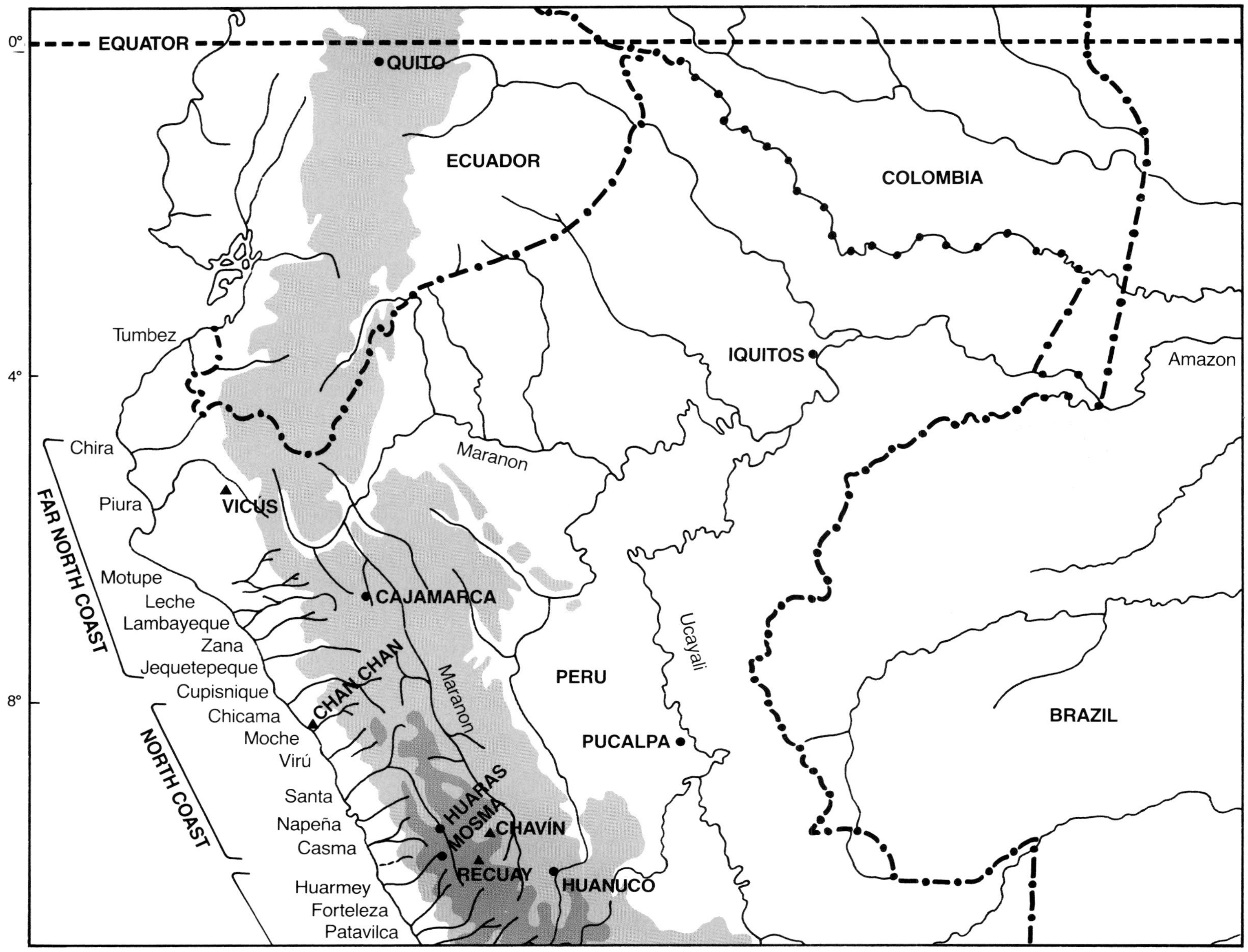

0°
EQUATOR
QUITO
ECUADOR
COLOMBIA
Tumbez
4°
IQUITOS
Amazon
Chira
Maranon
Piura
VICUS
FAR NORTH COAST
Motupe
Leche
CAJAMARCA
Lambayeque
Zana
Jequetepeque
CHAN CHAN
Cupisnique
8°
Maranon
PERU
Ucayali
Chicama
Moche
Virú
NORTH COAST
PUCALPA
BRAZIL
Santa
HUARAS
Napeña
MOSMA
CHAVÍN
Casma
RECUAY
HUANUCO
Huarmey
Forteleza
Patavilca

Drawing of "Dance of Death" figures on Number 61, Moche V.

Moche and Vicús

ELIZABETH P. BENSON

IN THE ARID DESERTS of the north coast of Peru, on the edges of fertile valleys irrigated by rivers from the high Andes, lie the remnants of a series of civilizations, dating from about 2400 BC until the arrival of the Spaniards in the early sixteenth century. Prominent in this sequence, in what is generally known to archaeologists as the Early Intermediate Horizon, is the Moche, or Mochica, Culture, which dates from before the birth of Christ, possibly as early as 400 BC, to the seventh or eighth century AD.[1] The culture is named for the site of Moche, in the Moche River Valley, which boasts a ceremonial center called the Huaca del Sol, with an enormous structure of sun-dried bricks, forty meters high and at least 350 meters long. From the remains of this site it is clear that Moche was the administrative center of this society, although the valley is smaller than the Chicama River Valley to the north, another major area of Moche society that must have grown in power at about the same time. Although the pattern of the early Moche momentum is not well understood, it is clear that the Moche and Chicama valleys were central to the development of Moche power and expansion.

The Moche Valley was occupied from very early times[2] but there are relatively few remains of early Moche Culture.[3] The Middle Moche Period, termed Moche III and IV, saw both the growth of population in the Moche and Chicama valleys and the expansion of Moche power along the coast to the Virú, Chao, Santa, and Nepeña valleys to the south, and the Jequetepeque, Lambayeque, and Motupe-Leche valleys to the north. In the peripheral valleys material from later Moche phases is normally seen above levels of earlier occupation by other peoples.

The end of Moche dominion was undoubtedly caused, at least in part, by the Huari-Tiahuanaco expansion from the southern highlands which marked the end of the Early Intermediate Horizon. Remains of the late Moche phase are rare at the Moche site itself and at some other sites of Moche Culture, but new sites appeared at this time with the ceramics of Moche V, the last phase of Moche ceramics. Moche V was a time of transition to another level of cultural development referred to as the Middle Horizon, and the pottery sometimes shows the direct effects on it of the Huari-Tiahuanaco Style. Moche V ceramics certainly show a change in painting which had developed gradually from the tight, strong, early style to a fussy *horror vacui*. There were also some differences in vessel forms as well as the introduction of new themes and the suppression of old ones.

A vast cemetery area, referred to generally as Vicús, although various parts of it are known by other names, lies in the Piura River Valley in the far north. Excavated mostly in uncontrolled conditions since the discovery of the site in 1961, the shaft tombs in this area have yielded quantities of ceramics, including some types similar to those found in the Virú, Moche, and Chicama valleys beneath Moche levels; these usually have negative, or resist, decoration. Some of the Vicús types may be related to the pottery of Ecuador or Colombia, to the north.[4]

Vicús vessels take a variety of forms. They are often effigy vessels with a stirrup spout or a tapered spout with a tubular or a flat handle (No. 14 or 16), or the negative Vicús types may be double vessels with an effigy vessel connected by a tube and a handle to a plain bottle. Double vessels are usually "whistling vessels," with holes in the effigy side; sound is produced when liquid pressure pushes air through the holes. In general, these Vicús vessels are more crudely made than Moche ceramics.

The Vicús area, however, has also yielded ceramics of extraordinarily fine craftsmanship, which are often very close in style and subject matter to the earliest Moche Style but are referred to as Vicús Moche. According to Alan Sawyer, "...from both a technological and artistic point of view, these Vicús Moche ceramics are superior to those of the Moche area."[5] Hans Horkeimer has also claimed that Vicús Moche pieces are among some of the most beautiful examples of prehispanic ceramics.[6] Some decorative themes are unique to Vicús Moche: a seated man with a bipartite-cap headdress (No. 28), for example, who often holds a vessel on one shoulder (Pl. XIX), or a monkey with a fanged mouth (No. 26). Llamas (No. 22), owls, bats, parrots and felines are common to both, as are warriors (No. 15), prisoners and figures engaged in a coca-chewing ritual (No. 25). Often, if the source is not known, it is difficult to tell whether a vessel is from the northern area or the central Moche area. The same theme may be depicted with equal quality in both Vicús and Vicús Moche shapes, that is, with lipped stirrup spout and with tubular spout and handle.[7]

The problems of source, relationship, and relative chronology of Vicús and Vicús Moche styles are many and complex; they are as yet unresolved.[8] There can be no doubt, however, that the period of Vicús Moche Style overlapped that of certain of the Vicús styles since vessels from each are reported to have been found in the same graves, although not from controlled excavation. That Vicús Moche vessels are prototypes of central-area Moche ceramics may even be possible. Problems of relationship and relative chronology of these styles are compounded by the fact that quantities of fine metalwork have also been found which appear to be somewhat later than the Vicús Moche ceramics.[9] The iconography and style of much of the metalwork resemble that of the central Moche region, especially in themes of human sacrifice, although there are distinct shades of difference in iconography.

It is extraordinary that this quantity of Moche-style artifacts was found in such a distant region, in shaft tombs, which are not a Moche trait, and without massive adobe architecture, which is a Moche trait.[10] The small amount of controlled archaeological excavation and testing that has been done has not answered the many questions raised by the finds. It is unlikely, however, that the early Moche of the Moche River Valley were powerful enough to have established a colony in the Piura River Valley where the Vicús Moche finds were made. Whether the people who built the great ceremonial center at Moche came from the north or whether the Vicús Moche and the central Moche both came from elsewhere is still unknown.

The Moche were farmers who needed to control the water sources far up in the valleys and to guard and fight for the land they irrigated, factors that were surely important in their expansion. They were also fishermen in one of the world's richest fishing grounds, the offshore Humboldt Current. They built reed rafts for use along the coast and such rafts are still made today. Undoubtedly they used the guano from nearby islands as fertilizer in their farming. The fertility of the land and the richness and dangers of the sea were of basic importance to their livelihood and to their religion. Their cosmology and art are rooted in these themes.

Moche architecture was embellished with mural paintings, fragments of which have been found in several sites.[11] Monumental sculpture is absent, but small sculpture exists: wooden figures and lapidary work, usually in turquoise, chrysocolla, shell, or bone. Burials in or near structures contained varying numbers of artifacts of many kinds. Textiles are rare because of salts in the north coast desert sands which have prevented preservation, but the few known examples show complex designs woven with considerable skill. Moche metalworkers were among the finest in the world. What has been unearthed includes masks, ear and nose ornaments, headdress decorations, plaques, and pins made of gold, silver, and copper, often in combination, and sometimes garnished with shell and stone inlay. Copper tools and weapons are also extant.

Pottery, of course, is the artifact unearthed in the greatest quantity. Simple ceramics were used for functional purposes. Decorated vessels were placed in graves. Many, if not all, of the decorated vessels may have been made expressly for burial: the vessels which have been found in a good state of preservation show little wear and their subject matter, often elaborate, was apparently appropriate to be taken to the other world.

Fine Moche vessels were surely made by craft specialists.[12] Since the potter's wheel was not used in the Pre-Columbian world, Moche vessels were made by working coils of clay, by modeling, or by use of a mold; surface decoration was produced by slip-painting in limited colors (No. 30), stamping (Nos. 61, 62), and incising (No. 54).[13] Some early vessels have stone inlay or metal attachments (No. 31). The most important form of Moche decorated pottery was the stirrup-spout vessel, the body of which may take a number of shapes. Globular forms are common (No. 37 and App. no. 32); an almost-globular shape, or more rarely, a box, may have modeled figures on the top (App. no. 40 and No. 52). The lower part may be plain-slipped (No. 56), or may have painted or relief, often stamped, motifs. Many stirrup-spout vessels are fashioned as effigies of gods (No. 20); men (Nos. 42, 50, 51 and 52); animals (Nos. 22 and 40); vegetables, houses, or even complex scenes (No. 46). Globular vessels sometimes have a spout and tubular handle, like a cruet (No. 57 and App. no. 40). Effigy or globular shapes may have a wide spout (App. no. 41, App. no. 32, and App. no. 40). Sometimes a conventional vessel is anthropomorphized by the addition of a human head, which is often the spout, and painted or incised hands and costume details (No. 42, App. no. 41 and No. 53). The broad-spouted form is related to the jug, a common shape, which usually has a modest amount of decoration, often a tie painted around the neck (App. no. 32). The jug may have been a very specific burial object; it is often represented on vessels with scenes that appear to show burial offerings.[14] Another frequent form is a "dipper" (App. no. 33), a vessel with a handle and a round opening in one of its curving sides. Many ceramic objects are sound-making like the double "whistling" vessels; cups, goblets, bowls, and *floreros*, a bowl with a flaring rim, are vessels that frequently have rattles in their bases.[15] Figurines, which are often whistles (No. 49), were also made from clay, as were recurved trumpets.

For the Moche people, as for most Pre-Columbian people, pottery had a symbolic significance that is difficult for modern, plastic-oriented people to imagine. The people of the high-cultures of the Americas were agriculturalists who worshipped the earth that produced vegetation, and the earth or underworld to which they committed their dead. The clay of their pottery was part of the earth; it came from the ground that they adored. Clay was mixed with water and fired to make pottery; the most basic and sacred elements of civilization went into its manufacture. It was very durable; it could break, but it did not disintegrate. It could hold or contain life-sustaining nourishment for human beings and perhaps for ancestors or gods. It could be made into shapes that represented gods and men. Moche pottery was the most important medium for myth-telling. Conventional vessels with a head added suggest a symbolic equivalence between ceramic vessels and human beings. In Moche art, a jug with a tie around the neck and a human head becomes a depiction of a captive (No. 42). The stirrup-spout form, an ancient form in the Andes, was probably sacred because it was thought to be a form used by the ancestors, whether actual ancestors or people with whose heritage the Moche wished to be associated. When it is depicted in scenes, the stirrup-spout vessel is shown with the most important person in the scene.[16] Pottery, therefore, was a significant item for the grave because it endured, because it was associated with ancestors, the earth, and regeneration, because it held nourishment for the deceased, and because it took the forms of gods and creatures who protected the deceased, telling of the requisite myths and ceremonies. Moreover, because its material came from the ground, it was appropriate to return it there for burial.

Moche pottery has been noted for its naturalism, and, indeed, the species of many of the flora and fauna it depicts are identifiable. Information about garments, weapons, hunting, house structures, fishing techniques, and diseases can also be obtained from their naturalistic representation on Moche ceramics. In addition, there are portraits of recognizable individuals with distinctive features and scars, headdresses, and ear ornaments (No. 44 and Pl. XXV).

This naturalism creates a false scent, however. By looking at other vessels, it becomes clear that naturalistic depictions were not intended as genre art, as glimpses of everyday life. Instead, they are at one end of a continuum that leads inexorably toward what we would call fantasy. Creatures composed of combinations of human and animal traits often repeat the poses and actions of human beings. Scenes with warriors in battle or runners carrying bags may show human beings; parallel scenes, however, may present creatures with human bodies but animal heads and tails. Some creatures, such as fish, are anthropomorphized by the addition of a human arm and leg. One frog may be shown with almost absolute realism; another frog, fairly realistic, will be draped with vegetation; and yet another will have a snakehead tail or a fanged mouth (see the Huari frog in No. 163). One vessel may depict a potato quite simply; another will show a human head emerging from a potato; and still another will show a face wherever there is an "eye." Maize is usually depicted with a fanged-mouth head emerging from it. A squash may sport the head of a bat (No. 55) or an owl. A deity head may rise from a guano island with sea lions and sea birds (No. 46), or a deity body may merge with mountain peaks (No. 60). Portrait vessels may portray a god with round, staring eyes and feline canines, or perhaps the head of a feline (No. 45), fox, or owl. All of these depictions belonged to a world of intricate symbolic language based on combining the attributes of creatures and things which probably symbolized the forces of nature. The "spiritual" world was as real as the "naturalistic" one.

The subject matter of Moche pottery has a wide range, yet it also has specific limitations and conventions. Despite the profusion of creatures and activities, there are only certain major themes. What was portrayed and what was not portrayed are interesting matters in themselves. But the interpreter wants primarily to understand the motivation for, and the significance of, the subjects depicted. It may be easy to identify a frog or a reed raft but the questions remain: Why was it important to picture these things? What symbolism were they charged with? Why were they appropriate subjects to be put into burials to be taken to the other world? The questions multiply with increasing exploration and knowledge.

No detail of Moche iconography is whimsical. Each element is saying something specific: an ear ornament or the lack of ear ornament, the kind of stripes on a shirt, the details of a headdress, the fact that two sets of panpipes are tied together, the manner in which a spear is held, how a figure is seated. Clothing and accoutrements indicate role and status in a specific ritual or occasion defined by associated objects, environment, and activity. The motifs are put together like words, and Moche iconography can be grouped by the clustering of such details. A cluster deals with a broad group of recurring traits that define the parameter of a related object. Clusters might be thought of as circles enclosing certain subject matter. Some circles overlap and some motifs seem to have been pivotal between them. All of the clusters can be thought of as parts of the intricately structured whole of a belief system.

Many depictions show warriors. Vessels may be effigies of individual human or anthropomorphic warriors in certain poses (No. 52) or of figures that are presumably the prisoners of these warriors (No. 42). Painted or relief scenes show warriors in procession, wearing helmets and carrying clubs and shields. Other scenes show human warriors fighting, two by two. Often one figure is clubbing another or holding him by a forelock, or the second figure is falling backwards from a blow; helmet and weapons fly off into the air. Differences in warrior regalia suggest that more than one battle or more than one battle ritual is depicted. Some show processions of warriors carrying captured gear or leading prisoners by a rope around the neck.

One group of warriors with distinctive garments is associated with the ritual chewing of coca leaves and this subject matter forms a cluster.[17] In the Andes, coca leaves are still chewed with a little lime to overcome the effects of altitude. Coca has long been a sacred and magical substance and it is clear that it was a ritual substance for the Moche.[18] Effigy figures are shown with coca bags held by a striped cord around the neck (No. 25) and, in their hands, the gourd that held the lime and a stick with which to pick up the lime (No. 50). Other figures illustrate other moments in the coca ritual, for example, figures holding up shirts or wearing shirts of characteristic patterns without putting the arms through the sleeves (No. 25). Some of these figures may hold small jaguars or spotted felines. Monkeys are also related to this rite and may be shown with coca bags. Human figures wearing coca-associated garments and holding coca bags and lime gourds are depicted in scenes with weapons, and certain figures in battle may have coca bags as part of their paraphernalia. Captive figures may be shown in the large scenes and as individual effigy figures (No. 42). Certain vessels depicting figures holding smaller figures or offering children may also belong to this cluster.[19]

Another cluster centers around one warrior, often supernatural, who wears a shirt of small metal plates and has owl associations, that is, he often is an anthropomorphic owl, shown together with another warrior with two rosettes on his headdress.[20] Captive figures, with hands tied behind them, who may be either sacrificial victims or rulers undergoing rites of humiliation, wear the garments of these two warriors. This cluster, which often shows musicians, dancing warriors and various kinds of vegetation, includes the Presentation Theme in which supernatural figures in warrior dress meet in connection with human sacrifice.[21] It overlaps another cluster of figures who appear to have priestly duties; some figures in these scenes wear a combination of warrior and priestly dress.[22] Scenes that show a figure on a rack or lying on the ground being pecked at by birds are on the periphery of this last cluster.[23]

The clusters described above account for a sizable percentage of the Moche oeuvre, and include some of the most elaborate painted scenes. Other battle scenes and figures with helmets, ear protectors and weapons, apparently belong to additional clusters (No. 53).

One cluster shows modeled mountain scenes in which there are usually five peaks in a shape like a hand; sometimes vessels are actually in the shape of a hand or an amputated forearm.[24] Five peaks may also appear on a warrior's helmet (No. 52). The mountain scenes are sometimes inhabited by a god, who is often shown with two snakes or a two-headed snake (No. 60). A modeled-and-relief type shows a many-figured scene (Pl. XXVI). In the example in the Sackler Collection in the Museum of the American Indian, New York City, the fanged god *Ai-Apec* is praying over a costumed person seated with a burden. On the other peak is a nude slave with hands bound behind his back, probably indicating a sacrifice.[25] In another prominent mountain jar of similar type in the Museo Nacional de Antropología y Arqueología, Lima, a god with a fanged mouth sits passively at one side, like a sculpture. Over the top of the central peak, a prone figure lies, with hair flowing downward, an apparent sacrifice. Another victim lies supine in the valley below. Usually, one of the attendant figures holds a small animal. Perhaps related to these scenes are vessels in the form of a stepped wave, or step-and-swirl motif, an ancient and widespread Andean motif. On the crest of the "wave" lies a prone figure with streaming hair; another figure sprawls on the lowest step. An active deity with fanged mouth, short garment and bent knees stands on one side; on the other side there is an anthropomorphic iguana.[26]

The deity and the iguana are seen together in a number of scenes, especially sea scenes, which present another complex major cluster.[27] A deity with a fanged mouth is depicted fighting sea monsters, or anthropomorphic fish, and a crab that has a deity face on the shell. A god may have a fish on a line or hold a sea bird by the neck, or may be shown in a reed raft, the ends of which usually turn into snakeheads; he is sometimes aided by anthropomorphic cormorants. Pots depicting guano islands may show a deity (No. 46) or may record sea-lion hunts in which human beings in specific dress club the animals; these scenes have a ritual aspect. The irregular faces and odd proportions of "fantasy" or "collage vessels" that show land and sea creatures, "real" beings and gods, may derive from the distortions of looking underwater.

Yet another cluster includes scenes of deer hunting and of a ritual that superficially resembles a badminton game in which figures hold long poles with a flower or cluster of feathers tied on the end.[28] The participants in the two scenes wear the same garments, so the scenes are related, and the deer hunt is apparently also a ritual.[29] Deer were hunted by being driven into a netted area where they were speared. Foxes were also hunted but with clubs; fox scenes appear to belong to another context (App. no. 32).

A large number of vessels have human figures or anthropomorphs running and holding a bag in one hand.[30] Commonly known as "bean runners", since some scholars think that the bags contain beans, the figures, bare-chested and wearing a headdress with a plaque on the front, usually run through a landscape strewn with various kinds of vegetation, although some scenes depict sea creatures. Two vessels show the goal of the trip. On one, the runners approach an uninhabited temple on an elaborate platform; the other shows the platform, or throne, inhabited by a large figure with a fanged mouth guarded by an anthropomorphic owl.[31]

Yet another cluster features "death priests."[32] These figures appear to be engaged in the preparation or ritual use of burial offerings. They are seen in specific dress, usually a light-colored garment with a fringed border, a tied cape or thick, scarflike overgarment, and a tied soft headdress with a diagonal fold. They often hold pottery, usually have a physical deformity (No. 33), blindness, or signs of disease and are closely related to the partially skeletal figures who also appear in scenes with pottery, dancing (No. 61 and No. 62), playing drums, flutes or panpipes, or engaging in sexual activity. Because the partially skeletal figures appear frequently in erotic scenes, sometimes wearing death-priest garments, they seem to belong to this cluster. It has been suggested that the skeletal figures are not dead but are living figures with flayed faces and emaciated bodies who imitate the dead.[33] This interpretation is quite possible but, since the vessels were put in burials, it is not unlikely that scenes with such skeletal figures describe the dead and the afterlife. An early Spanish source tells that Indians of the colonial period were "...persuaded that the dead feel, eat and drink."[34]

Human portrait vessels usually depict chieftains, ancestors or possibly priests, who may also be seen as full figures and who occasionally are shown in scenes.[35] Insofar as they can be placed in context, human, deity and animal heads may belong to various clusters.

From the major clusters briefly described above it may be noted that certain figures or elements seem to be pivotal between clusters. Death-priests, for example, appear in several clusters, such as scenes in which they themselves are featured together with plate-shirt/rosette-headdress figures, and in deerhunt, "badminton," and sea-lion-hunting scenes. Cormorants and seals may be dressed as death-priests. Owls appear in various guises in various contexts: they may be shown as warriors, death-priests or even women.[36] The grouping of clusters is complicated not only by overlapping but also by the fact that the Moche seem to have been culturally incapable of doing anything exactly the same way twice.

If the grouping is sometimes difficult, the interpretation of the themes is even more so. For example, is a battle scene the depiction of an actual historical battle, a reenactment of a battle far back in history or mythology, a mock battle performed as a ceremony to "capture" sacrificial victims, or an initiation rite?[37] There are undoubted ritual aspects to the scenes depicted and, in some instances; mythic aspects. Yet one must also remember that the Moche were aggressors who conquered territory, thus the depiction of an actual historical battle cannot be ruled out. Several clusters are apparently connected with human sacrifice; specific captive or victim figures are associated with them. It has been suggested that the theme of sacrificial decapitation may refer to a past custom, not one contemporary with the manufacture of the vessel on which this theme appears.[38] Such an interpretation is possible, although from what we know of human sacrifice in Mesoamerica and from the quantity of decapitated heads shown in Andean art, it seems likely that the sacrifice was real and that it was associated with the appeasement of forces of nature or of the nourishing of ancestors connected with these forces.

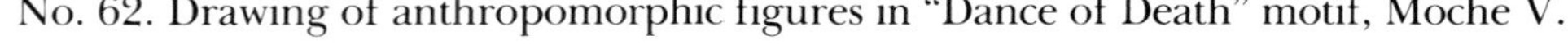

No. 62. Drawing of anthropomorphic figures in "Dance of Death" motif, Moche V.

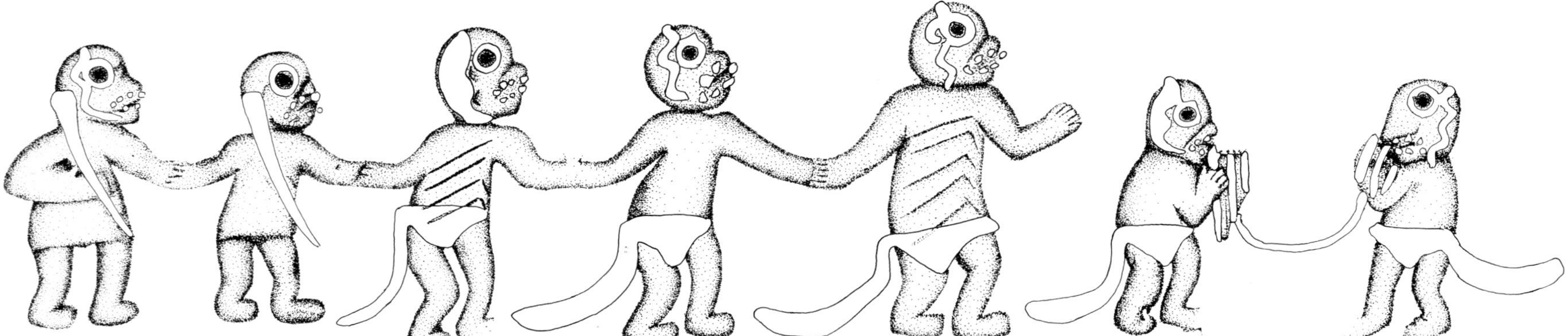

Drawing of "moon monster" from No. 43, Moche III.

There are no written sources that deal directly with the Moche since they, like all other Andean cultures, did not have writing and their civilization was followed by several others before the arrival of the Spaniards. The only primary sources, therefore, for the understanding of the Moche are their remains. But how are these remains to be approached? How are the questions of meaning best answered? One of the most basic needs of the iconographer is a large body of material to examine.

The basis of Moche studies is dirt archaeology, which began at the turn of the century with Max Uhle's University of California excavations at the Huaca del Sol and the Huaca de la Luna in the Moche Valley.[39] A.L. Kroeber followed up Uhle's work at Moche for the Field Museum, Chicago.[40] Slightly later, Rafael Larco Hoyle did independent excavation in the Chicama Valley.[41] It was Larco in 1948 who established the seriation of Moche pottery Phases I through V that is still generally used.[42] Wendell C. Bennett worked in the Lambayeque and Virú valleys for the American Museum of Natural History, New York City, and later became involved in the Virú Valley Project, which, conceived in 1945, was undertaken with scholars from a number of institutions.[43] Although the Virú Valley is relatively small, it has a long archaeological sequence and the Virú Valley Project was one of the most thorough undertaken in the Andes; from it resulted a number of important publications.[44] More recent archaeological work has been done by Heinrich Ubbelohde-Doering in the Chicama and Jequetepeque valleys, by Christopher B. Donnan in the Santa Valley and by Donald Proulx in the Nepeña Valley.[45] The Chan Chan-Moche Valley Project, with scholars from various institutions, included later occupancy of the Moche Valley by other cultures but produced work relating to the Moche as well.[46] Other recent work has been carried on by the Royal Ontario Museum Lambayeque Valley Project and the Princeton University Batan Grande-La Leche Archaeological Project.

Archaeology can also help to explain the meaning of pottery even though pottery itself is a basic source of archaeological information. Archaeological excavations provide knowledge about the sequence of pottery, the contexts in which it was placed, the things with which it was associated, and the physical and political world to which it belonged.

The publication of Moche objects, which began seriously in the early years of this century with the general Andean publications of Arthur Baessler, has also served as a major research tool for the iconographer by adding to the corpus of material that may be examined.[47] One of the first interpreters of Moche material was Larco Hoyle and one of the most important was Gerdt Kutscher.[48] A number of other authors have written general descriptions of the culture or about certain of its aspects. Some of the publications are essentially picture books; they may include material other than Moche, but nevertheless provide additional material with which to work.[49] Illustrated catalogues from exhibitions have also added to the published material and have been useful sources of data. Another important resource is the Archive of Moche Art established by Christopher B. Donnan at the University of California, Los Angeles, a photographic collection from which a number of valuable rollout drawings of complex vessel scenes have been made. The best resource, of course, is the actual object found in excavation or seen in museum and private collections.

Since there are many contexts in which Moche vessels and their iconography can be understood, various methods of approach to such understanding are being, and have been, used. Beginning with the information that is on the object itself, one basic method is to take a single motif and search for its associations. Jorge Muelle was a pioneer in this method in his study of the *chalchalcha*, the knife-shaped rattle worn at the back by many Moche warrior figures.[50] A more complex method is to take a figure characterized by certain motifs and to determine in what contexts it frequently appears.[51]

The single-motif approach often leads to the definition or clarification of themes or clusters. It is difficult to draw a firm line of distinction between what are referred to as themes and clusters. Generally, themes refer to a more limited amount of material, identifying the same group of figures appearing in a similar context. The cluster, on the other hand, deals with a broad group of recurring traits that define the parameter of related material, making it vital to know what motifs belong together. Both methods have the same limitations: although Moche artists provided a great deal of information in what they depicted, specific meaning of the themes or motifs is still elusive. Information must be obtained from other kinds of investigation if the problem of interpretation is to be solved. In addition to examining the objects themselves and learning whatever is possible from archaeological investigation, the interpreter looks for clues to meaning that may be found in the customs of contemporary people, in historical documents, and in comparisons made with what is known of other cultures that might be related; for example, that an implement like that shown in the "badminton" scenes was found in a burial at Moche.[52]

To add to the general knowledge about ancient culture and possibly to shed light on specific problems with regard to the reconstruction of the past, it is important to study modern ways of coping with the same environment in the present context, particularly the north coast environment inhabited by the Moche.[53] John Gillin's description of life in the village of Moche, published in 1947, is an important document since many everyday customs of the people had changed little, even by that time.[54] Of the ancient plant material seen on ceramics and other media, remains of many types have been found in graves or are still growing in the coastal valleys.[55] There is also lore connected with the growing of modern crops that undoubtedly relates to the past.[56]

Ethnographic information may also be significant in remnants of ancient beliefs and customs among the present-day Andean Indians. Most of this kind of data comes from cultures of other regions but, because they may deal with widespread themes, they may be useful as a basis for interpreting ancient Moche motifs.[57] The ethnographic data include studies of shamanism. There are still curers and performers of magic ritual on the north coast of Peru using practices that must have ancient roots, and this material has been used by iconographers.[58] Data on modern shamanism may be very instructive in indicating which elements have or had power and how ancient peoples may have thought about them. It must be remembered, however, that the contemporary religious-social-political structure is entirely different from that of the past. The accoutrements of gods and kings may still be reflected in the shaman's *mesa*, but they cannot have the identical meaning or power.

The writings of nineteenth and early twentieth-century travelers have been examined,[59] but of particular importance to the iconographer are the documents of early Spanish observers in the sixteenth and seventeenth centuries.[60] The sources of information were usually written by Europeans who were observing Indians as a strange species. In addition to information provided by the well-known early chroniclers there are various obscure documents and records that provide information on pre-Spanish concepts and procedures.[61] Yet even the earliest of these observations was made nearly a millenium after Moche glory had faded and largely concerned an Indian group from the southern highlands, the Inca, whose viewpoint was necessarily different from that of the Moche and who came from a very different agricultural environment; they certainly produced a very different art style. Few of the early sources concern the north coast; however, one might still hope to find clues in them. Anne Marie Hocquenghem, for example, has compared ritual scenes on Moche vessels to early descriptions of Inca calendrical festivals.[62] Certainly, ritual agricultural calendars and astronomical events were celebrated throughout the Pre-Columbian world, and Hocquenghem's comparative approach is based on a widespread substratum of similar ritual as well as on specific detail. Donnan and McClelland used a north coast legend about a curer, as in the seventeenth century, as part of the basis for their interpretation of the Burial Theme.[63]

To examine motifs as carefully as possible, to find whatever archaeological associations might exist, and then to apply whatever ethnographic and/or ethnohistorical material which seems relevant is the most fertile method for attempting the interpretation of the significance of Moche ceramics. Yet dangers even lurk here for the iconographer since there are pan-Andean beliefs that appear to have long continuity and motifs that carry over a wide area through a long period of time. For example, the motif of a man with a feline standing behind him cuts through various clusters and symbol systems.[64] Although the motif has staying power, its meaning may change. Iconography of a specific time and place may be as distinctive as a specific art style. It is clear that iconography shifts even within the Moche period. There are iconographic differences between the art of Vicús Moche and of the central Moche area, beginning with very early Moche pieces. Some important Late Phase Moche themes do not appear in the Early Phase. In Moche IV a radiant god is introduced, competing with earlier deities. Portraits are highly individualized only in Moche IV. The Burial Theme does not appear before Moche V, yet it uses many elements from earlier Moche iconography, such as a fanged god and an iguana, a figure on a rack, a conch-shell monster, pottery jugs and a laden llama that dates back to Moche I (No. 22). Although the theme itself does not occur before Moche V, when it does new elements appear in it as well.[65] Battle scenes, on the other hand, disappear in Moche V, probably because the Moche were no longer powerful warriors.[66] It is necessary, therefore, to use any comparative material tentatively.

There has been some exploration of relationships between Moche and the earlier Chavín civilization, while the results of recent archaeology of later periods in the valleys occupied by the Moche have provided additional patterns for comparison.[67] In terms of motif and theme comparisons with other cultures, however, more work is necessary. The Moche clearly had contact with the Recuay people, their nearby highland contemporaries. Many motifs that appear in the coca-ceremony scenes of Moche art are found in Recuay art. Fruitful comparisons might also be made with the contemporary Nasca Culture of the south coast, for many of the same motifs appear in the art styles of both cultures. Of the Pre-Columbian cultures, however, the Inca are the best known and have probably provided the richest source of comparative information.

A comparison that has not been attempted is with the contemporary Maya in Mesoamerica, i.e., southern Mexico, Guatemala, Belize and Honduras. Much more is known about the Maya than about any other Pre-Columbian people of that period for they were the only people who had a true form of writing which has now, to a large extent, been deciphered. A great deal of excavation has been done in the Maya area and there has probably been more scholarly study on the Maya than on any other Pre-Columbian people. Although the environments were almost entirely different, both the Moche and Maya people were farmers who occupied fairly large regions and were at a fairly comparable stage of development. Many similar iconographic elements appear in the material remains of both cultures.

Lists of the names of rulers and their dates of rule are known for most Classic Maya sites. The monumental inscriptions deal largely with the historical, ritual and supernatural biographies of kings, along with astronomical-astrological information. Political reality was interwoven with the supernatural. Rulers had immediate, known ancestors through whom they inherited power, as well as mythical ancestors in the dim past who reinforced that power and gave it another dimension. Maya rulers had power in this world and in the supernatural world as well as the underworld, the afterlife. They were, to some extent, god-kings. They were commanders-in-chief and leaders in war; on monuments they hold spears and shields as symbols of office. They stand on prisoner figures or prisoners kneel at their feet; one of their titles may be written as "captor." They were responsible for agricultural fertility and, in an accession ritual that conferred on them the inherited right, power and obligation of insuring the earth's fertility, they let their own blood. Rulers, as gods or demigods, are sometimes shown with supernatural attributes. They did not die but went to underworld palaces where they are shown on burial pottery surrounded by other figures and by the pottery, cloth and other objects that symbolize their rites of accession and their claims to power. The Maya elite were buried with fine vessels as grave goods; these vessels show mythical, ritual and afterlife scenes.

One cannot expect exact equivalences between the Moche and the Maya, but knowledge of the Maya may be a guide to a level of approach to the Moche, to the sorts of things to look for in Moche iconography. The dilemma of the Moche iconographer is that all available resources lie at some distance from the heart of the problem. It is hazardous to push the clues too far; and yet, they are all we have.

Many major problems of interpretation of Moche iconography have not been approached seriously. For example, virtually nothing is known about Moche deities. Is there one important deity with different manifestations, accompanied by various supernatural spirits or demigods, or are there many deities? What may be a major god has a mouth with canine teeth of feline type, a belt with extensions that end in snakeheads and, usually, snakehead ear ornaments. Sometimes this god sits in the mountains, like an ancient ancestral creator god, a *deus otiosus* (No. 60). A god with the same attributes is shown in active poses, with knees bent, often battling anthropomorphized sea creatures. Is this second god the active aspect of the mountain god, who, like the sun, comes down from the mountains to the sea each day? Is it a son of that god? Or is it an entirely different deity? Is it the same god whose head rises from a guano island (No. 46) or a pile of maize ears? The subject is further complicated by the fact that other deities may occasionally wear the snake earrings and belt extensions. A fanged mouth is widely used and may indicate a deity, a supernatural being, or possibly even a human being in a moment of great ritual sacredness. Some fanged-mouth figures may be rulers. It is necessary to look more closely to see what rulers do, what rites they are engaged in, what supernaturalness they mix with their political power, or how supernaturalness serves political power.

Attempts must also be made to identify the astronomical content of the art. Astronomical-astrological lore plays an important role in the belief system of the Pre-Columbian peoples—the Aztec, the Maya and the Inca—about whom we have more knowledge and there is visual evidence that it played such a role with the Moche: double-snake-headed "sky bands" and figures with radiances are among the motifs that suggest this.

Most known Pre-Columbian deities have some stellar or planetary association; such identities must have existed with the Moche. Hocquenghem has done some work with this subject in positing calendrical rituals and she has touched on another important question, i.e., that of the time sequence that relates the scenes. Scenes depict different moments in time but it is not simple to construct the time relationship between events or the time sequence within a ritual or myth. For example, one might ask at what moment in the coca ritual do figures wear shirts with empty sleeves? A similar kind of problem is that we do not understand the conventions for depicting the dead. A dualism exists if it is true that figures depicted as dead are actually living imitators of the dead and it may be equally true that those depicted as living, or the person in whose grave the depictions are placed, such as ancestors, perhaps, are actually dead. Moche art appears to be full of such inversions; for example, a captive figure dressed as a god.

Another aspect of dualism is the parallelism between human figures and anthropomorphs engaged in the same activities. Some scholars have suggested that the anthropomorphs are masked human beings in ritual activity, but only certain anthropomorphic owl figures are clearly masked and the fact that warriors' garments and weapons may also be anthropomorphized argues that all these beings were real in the minds of the ancient Moche.

The purest expression of the world and the beliefs of the Moche is found in the ceramics they placed in the grave. From them it is clear that we are dealing with a stratified society whose chieftains commanded a vast amount of labor to build ceremonial centers and had fine craftsmen to make funerary pottery and other offerings. Some figures sit enthroned while others sit on the ground; some figures are much more richly dressed than others. The Moche were farmers and hunters of deer and foxes; they were also sea-lion hunters, guano-gatherers and fishermen who went out in reed rafts to face the perils of the sea. The dichotomies of land and sea, mountains and coast, water and dryness were basic to their work, and undoubtedly to their cosmology. There must have been rituals related to astronomy and agricultural cycles. It appears that human sacrifice kept the agricultural world going. As with most ancient American peoples, death and fertility were strongly associated. Burial customs were important and sometimes elaborate.

1. Rowe 1962b
2. Donnan/Mackey 1978, pp. 13-54
3. Topic 1982b
4. Sawyer 1975a, p. 25; Lumbreras 1979, p. 24
5. Sawyer 1975a, p. 25
6. Horkheimer 1965, p. 15
7. Horkheimer 1965, p. 22; Disselhoff 1971, Taf. 40, 41; Lapiner 1976, p. 126; Lumbreras 1979, p. 40, 41
8. Horkheimer 1965; Larco Hoyle 1965a and 1967; Matos Mendieta 1965; Disselhoff 1971; Sawyer 1968 and 1975a, p. 25; Lapiner 1976, pp. 112-131; Lumbreras 1979
9. Lapiner 1976, pp. 148-161; Jones 1979; Lechtman et al. 1982; Lapiner 1976, p. 114
10. Horkheimer 1965, p. 23
11. Kroeber 1926-30, pl. XV; Schaedel 1951; Bonavía 1961; Donnan 1972
12. Topic 1982b
13. Donnan 1965
14. Benson 1975
15. Hocquenghem 1980a
16. Benson 1975
17. Kutscher 1950a, p. 22 and pp. 24-25; Disselhoff 1956; Benson 1976, 1979 and n.d.a; Berezkin 1978; von Schuler-Schömig 1979 and 1981
18. Mortimer 1901
19. Hocquenghem 1980c
20. Jímenez 1955; Benson n.d.c
21. Donnan 1976 and 1978
22. Benson 1975
23. Donnan/McClelland 1979; Hocquenghem 1980b
24. Donnan 1978, pp. 146-154
25. Dockstader 1967, pl. 118
26. Benson 1972, figs. 2-11, pp. 2-12; Hocquenghem 1980a, fig. 19
27. Kubler 1948
28. Kutscher 1958
29. Benson 1975 and 1979
30. Larco Hoyle 1938, pp. 85-125; Kutscher 1951; Kutscher 1954, pl. 26-29, pp. 67-73; Benson 1978
31. Kutscher 1954, pl. 72 and 73
32. Benson 1975
33. Sawyer n.d.
34. Arriaga 1968, p. 64; see also Hocquenghem 1977c
35. Hocquenghem 1977c; Benson n.d.c; see also this Cat. no. 44, and the Museum of the American Indian App. no. 34, pub. in Dockstader 1967, pl. 112
36. Benson n.d.b
37. Hocquenghem 1978; von Schuler-Schömig 1979 and 1981; Benson n.d.c
38. von Schuler-Schömig 1979 and 1981
39. Uhle 1913a; Kroeber 1925a; Menzel 1977
40. Kroeber 1926-30
41. Larco Hoyle 1938, 1945 and 1946
42. Larco Hoyle 1948; Donnan 1976, pp. 43-62
43. Bennett 1939
44. Ford/Willey 1949; Bennett 1950; Strong/Evans 1952; Willey 1953; Collier 1955
45. Ubbelohde-Doering 1959, 1960 and 1967; Donnan 1973; Proulx 1968 and 1973
46. Donnan/Mackey 1978
47. Baessler 1902-3
48. Larco Hoyle 1938, 1945, 1965b and 1966; Kutscher 1948, 1950a and 1954
49. Fuhrmann 1922a and 1922b; Lehmann/Doering 1924; d'Harcourt 1924; Montell 1929; Schmidt 1929; Valcárcel 1935; Jímenez 1937, 1950-51 and 1955; Tello 1938; Ubbelohde-Doering 1954; Sawyer 1966, 1968 and 1975a; Disselhoff 1967; Klein 1967; Lavallée 1970; Anton 1972; Benson 1972; Donnan 1976 and 1978; Lapiner 1976; Hocquenghem 1977a; Bankes 1980; Purin n.d.; della Santa n.d.
50. Muelle 1936
51. Benson 1982
52. Donnan/Mackey 1978, pp. 154-155; Donnan 1978, pp. 71-72
53. Kosok 1965; Nachtigall 1966; Buse 1981
54. Gillin 1947
55. Yacovleff/Herrera 1935 and 1939; Towle 1961
56. Weiss 1961
57. Hissink 1950; Hocquenghem 1979c
58. Sharon 1978; Sharon/Donnan 1974; Hocquenghem 1977d
59. Squier 1877; Middendorf 1893; Bandelier 1910
60. see also Rowe 1946 and 1948
61. Murra 1975; Duviols 1977; Rostworowski 1961, 1977 and 1981
62. Hocquenghem 1978, 1979a, 1979b, 1979c, 1980b and 1980c
63. Donnan/McClelland 1979; Calancha 1638
64. Benson 1974
65. Donnan/McClelland 1979
66. Berezkin 1978
67. Rowe 1971

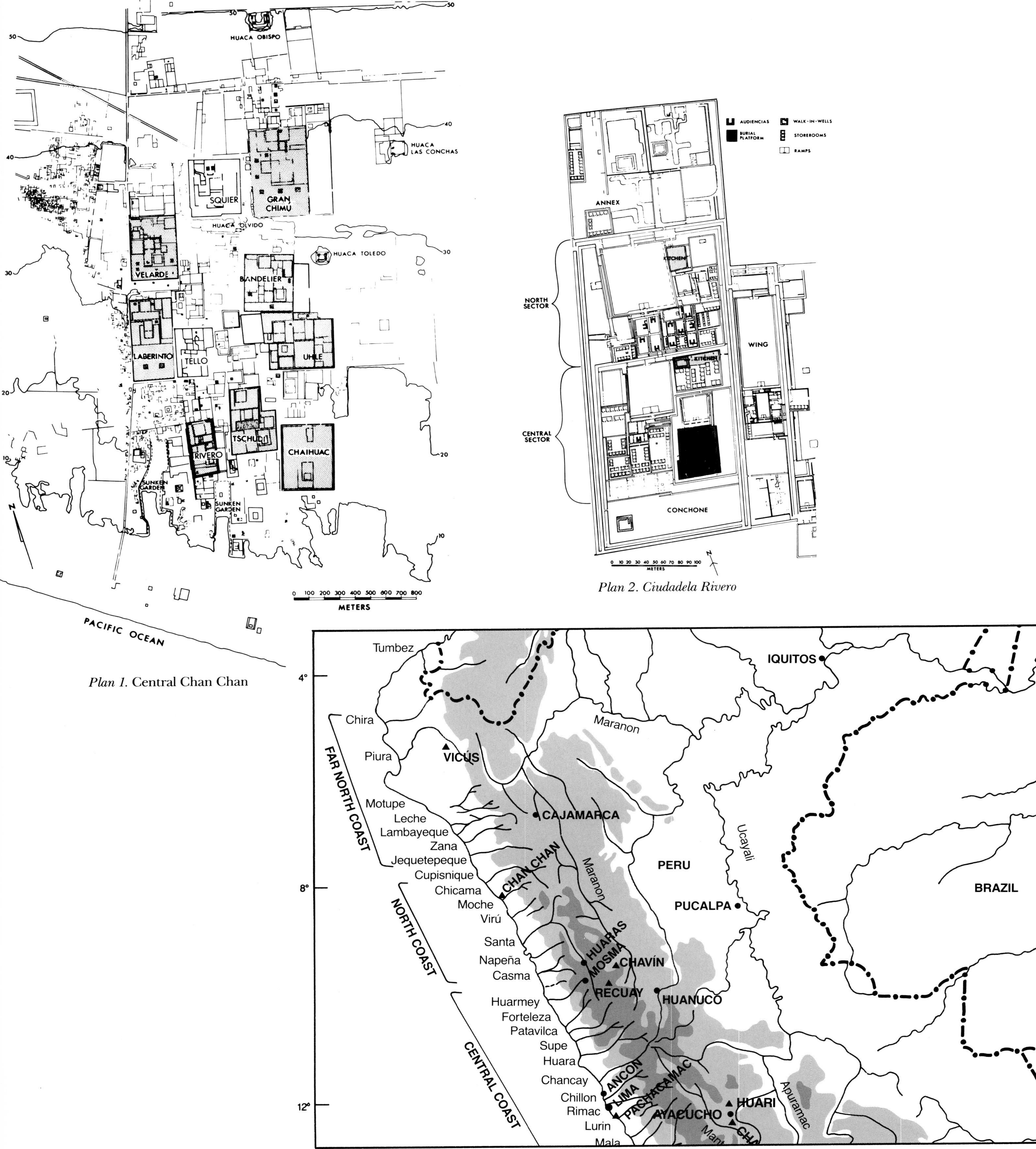

Plan 1. Central Chan Chan

Plan 2. Ciudadela Rivero

DESERT EMPIRE AND ART:
Chimor, Chimú and Chancay

MICHAEL E. MOSELEY

STRETCHING ALONG 1,000 kilometers of Pacific coastline, the desert empire of Chimor was the largest native state and the most developed center of South American civilization to battle the Inca for ultimate political domination of the sprawling Andean Cordillera. Of greater size than Mexico's Aztec domain, Chimor represents the second largest New World polity that can be documented on the basis of native accounts recorded by Spanish conquistadors and corroborated by archaeological exploration (see map).[1]

At the height of its territorial expansion about a century before Columbus' Caribbean landfall, the imperial frontiers reached from near southern Ecuador to about Lima, Peru's present capital, on the central coast (see map). By dint of armed conquest and by treaty, the empire incorporated not only diverse ethnic groups but also unusual ecological variety. The political frontiers encompassed societies and states using Lambayeque Chimú, Imperial Chimú, Chancay and other regional art styles. The frontiers of Chimor also embraced three global extremes in environmental conditions. The empire stretched down the world's driest desert, where showers of consequence fall but once or twice per century.[2] The eastern boundary ran along the tortuous flanks of the highest, most rugged mountain range in the Western Hemisphere, second only to the Himalayas in elevation and relief. The western boundary ran along the Pacific shoreline, which is swept by coastal currents supporting a prodigious marine food chain with fishery yields amounting to one-fifth of all seafood consumed the world over.[3]

The extreme conditions in mountain topography and marine and meteorological currents effectively juxtaposed the bleakest, most barren, yet broken and rocky, landscape on earth with the richest, most beautiful sea life in all the oceans. This juxtaposition had a profound influence on both the organization of the empire and the graphic content of its regional art styles.

Perspective

The conquistadors and chroniclers wrote down relatively little about Chimor because it had been largely dissolved under Inca subjugation and foreign rule. However, the Spanish discovered vast quantities of gold and silver objects in the tombs of the lords and nobles of Chimor. The wealth was so great that colonial corporations were chartered to systematically mine the ancient mausoleums. The looting of desert cemeteries for their art works has continued for centuries, resulting in large collections of objects and artifacts.

Appreciation of these collections and understanding of Chimor in general are undergoing a revolution. This change was triggered by systematic mapping and exploration of the ruins of Chan Chan, the sprawling imperial capital,[4] and by an ensuing, ongoing series of major archaeological programs addressing the empire's ancient cities, architectural monuments and engineering accomplishments. Within the last decade everything from artisans' workshops to royal palaces and shrines have come under scientific scrutiny, with new discoveries being made faster than they can be published by scholarly journals or disseminated to the public. It is the purpose of this essay to bring forth aspects of these new materials as they bear on issues surrounding the arts and organization of the desert empire and as they reflect the themes and concerns of Chimú and Chancay objects in the Arthur M. Sackler Andean Collection.

The Imperial Realm

Imperial capital of Chimor was Chan Chan, a sprawling metropolis of royal palaces, residences of the nobility and artisan quarters situated at the mouth of the Moche Valley (Plan 1). It was more or less at the midpoint of the political realm, in what may be termed the imperial heartland, the zone that stretched between the Rios Chicama and Chao. The lords of this region and the emperors of Chimor traced their origins to a legendary hero called Tacaynamo. Tacaynamo reputedly sailed from across the sea to land at the mouth of the Moche, where after various adventures he settled and founded a dynasty of ten successive potentates. These heirs expanded and governed the desert realm up to its subjugation by the Incas, about AD 1470.[5] Significantly, the towering monumental architecture at Chan Chan includes ten vast, high-walled compounds, called *ciudadelas* or "little cities," each of which served as a palace for one of the dynastic rulers and his royal lineage.[6]

The imperial metropolis with its imposing *ciudadelas* occupied a pivotal economic, as well as political, setting. To the north of Chan Chan the rugged foothills of the Andean Cordillera pull back from the shoreline, exposing wide plains crossed by several of the very largest desert rivers. These flatlands were the prime setting for large-scale irrigation agriculture that culminated in the Lambayeque canal complex linking several rivers into an integrated agricultural system. Until its conquest relatively late in the history of Chimor, this northern canal complex was governed by a federation of regional lords tracing their dynastic origins to the legendary hero Naymlap, who reputedly reached the land by sailing down the coast and founded his royal estate and shrine at Chot or Chotuna before ascending into the sky, leaving his heirs to rule.[7] It was in this northern setting that the Lambayeque Chimú Style arose.

South of Chan Chan the Andean Cordillera pushes out into the sea. The rough topography inhibits construction of large irrigation systems, whereas the rocky coast and rich shoreline currents support bountiful marine life and high yields from fishing. It was in this pivotal heartland that the Imperial Chimú Style arose. Farther south, the Rio Chancay, the largest river valley near the southern frontiers of Chimor, combined a rich coastal fishery with relatively abundant arable land. Heavily populated with ancient cities and towns, this region supported its own distinct art style, called Chancay. It was a relatively late political incorporation of Chimor. Unfortunately, early Spanish accounts provide little information about the governing nobility or beliefs and organization of the population.

The Hydraulic Order

Farming the world's driest desert is technologically complex because it depends upon water from distant rainfall high within the hemisphere's most rugged mountain range. Large-scale canal systems are required to carry river runoff out of the rocky foothills and across broken topography to reach and irrigate croplands. These conditions made Chimor not simply a conquest state but a very sophisticated "hydraulic" state. "Hydraulic" societies and states include the civilizations of antiquity and nations of today that have mastered arid environments by means of irrigation agriculture. Within the frontiers of Chimor lay both the largest canal systems ever built on the continent and fully two-thirds of all irrigated land ever reclaimed along the entire Andean desert coast. Roughly 30 to 40 percent more land was farmed in the past than at present in the same region, and recent engineering analyses of large abandoned Chimú canals indicate that native engineers a thousand years ago were employing concepts in fluid dynamics and channel flow design that Western technology did not begin to implement until about a century ago.[8] These canals are an impressive measure of technological development, even by modern standards.

A considerable body of theory surrounds the great irrigation civilizations of antiquity. Chimor has been compared with the hydraulic states of ancient China, and cited as reflecting the organizational principles of "Oriental Despotism."[9] These comparisons reason that, in a sense, large canal systems are large machines. Building, operating and maintaining large machines is a complicated business, which requires highly coordinated activity by a hierarchy of specialists ranging from laborers, mechanics, engineers and operators to financiers. The mechanical necessity for specialists and coordination in irrigation-dependent states underlie the principles of Oriental Despotism. In this authoritarian order, the upper echelon of the hydraulic hierarchy consists of a ranked hereditary nobility that acts as the managerial bureaucracy overseeing water, agricultural production and the general well-being of the nation.

There is considerable scholarly debate over how such despotic hydraulic states first arose.[10] However, Chimor, like Shang China, was a mature hydraulic society. The desert empire had been preceded by earlier irrigation states, notably the Moche polity, which dominated the north Andean desert at the beginning of the Christian era. Thus, Chimor constitutes the end point of millennia of prior coastal experience with canal building and irrigation management by the nobility.[11] This long evolution had seen the nobility evolve from a class into a closed hierarchical caste. The kings of Chimor were held as divine, and, along with their noble kindred, they reputedly descended from one set of stars within the Pleiades, while commoners and the rest of humanity descended from a different set of stars.[12] A vast gulf separated the agricultural peasantry from the managerial ranks of the nobility, who viewed ownership of wealth, chattel and property as their exclusive prerogative by divine right.[13] While Chimor was uniquely Andean in its authoritarian organization and attendant pomp and ceremony, it certainly shared many parallels with the despotic irrigation states of the ancient Orient, so the arts of the desert empire must be understood in this context.

In mature hydraulic states, development and expression in fine arts and monumental architecture, beyond the level of folk craft, are exclusively patronized by the bureaucratic nobility and therefore validate their values and encapsulate the cosmology rationalizing their rule. Andean societies—both past and present—attach great ritual value to ceremonial libations, toasting and drinking of *chicha* (maize beer). Thus, libation vessels are well represented in the Sackler Collection. Because of the ritual roles they fulfilled, the ornamentation of such vessels is often cosmologically charged. Indeed, since most of the collection derives from funerary offerings, the iconography of the ceramic pieces is, no doubt, value laden. Fortunately, several of the key motifs and themes can now be cross-tied to recently recorded monumental adobe friezes and architectural decoration at Chan Chan and Chot, thus placing much of the collection in its broader ideological context.

The Celestial Serpent

Chimor incorporated societies whose structure and content of beliefs shared general similarities with other peoples of the Northern Andes and greater Amazon Basin.[14] Underlying these similarities was a primordial cosmos in which air, earth and water comprised separate internested spheres, one within the other. Thus, the universe was stratified: earth, the solid realm, floated between an aqueous and a gaseous or celestial sphere. In this cosmos, fluids such as smoke, vapor, or rainwater flowed and threaded among the celestial, solid and aquatic orbits. Man's physical and spiritual well-being was predicated upon his manipulation of fluid threads so that the forces of nature would be benevolent. In a practical sense, this balance was the essence of irrigation agriculture, while in a ceremonial sense it involved the ritual creation and manipulation of fluid threads, such as burnt offerings of aromatic coca leaf to create ropes of smoke, or *chicha* libations by which man wove a common fate with maize and water.[15]

Much like a Western society may map its world view on a globe, the basic outline of the stratified Andean cosmos was encapsulated by certain spherical vessels used for ceremonial libations. Within the Arthur M. Sackler Collection, Number 71 is such a cosmological globe executed in Lambayeque Chimú Style. This object, like Number 70, is a so-called double-spout-and-bridge vessel. The symbolic sphere of water and liquid is contained within the chamber formed by earth and clay. Surrounded by air, the solid sphere is, in turn, overarched by a double-headed serpent, a celestial symbol. The spouts, through which liquid circulates in complementary flow, arise above and behind each head of the sky serpent and are bridged by the intertwined body of the serpent. Wearing noble attire, two figures with upraised arms have been press-molded onto the globe. The figures stand between the spouts of fluid circulation and beneath the overarching double-headed serpent. Here, the celestial serpent embodies a rainbow, the metaphor of water vapor and sunlight, capturing those key elements of the inner and outer cosmic spheres that made the desert agriculturally verdant.

The double-headed serpent is an ancient Andean motif, whose antiquity has been traced back to the preceramic, preagricultural origins of coastal civilization.[16] It served as a celestial symbol in the graphic arts of the Moche state, Chimor's predecessor.[17] Although it was not present in the design repertory of Imperial Chimú arts, the celestial serpent was a heraldic emblem of Naymlap, his heirs and the Lambayeque Chimú Style. This association of the double-headed serpent and Lambayeque royalty has its foundations in recent excavations of adobe friezes with celestial serpents at Naymlap's shrine of Chotuna.[18]

The imperial lore surrounding the heroic deeds of Naymlap includes the contention that as a revered old man he evaded mortal death by having the ability to fly; and, leaving his realm in prosperous order, he flew off into the heavens at the end of his reign. This theme is encapsulated in Number 70, where a central figure, flanked by two smaller attendants, rides atop the crest of the rayed, double-headed rainbow symbolizing ritual flight. It is interesting that like the celestial motif, the theme of a central "heroic" figure flanked by two attendants of smaller stature is a carryover from the earlier Moche Style. In Lambayeque Style renderings, the central hero is distinguished by unusual headgear, particularly the laterally projecting ear ornamentation.

The same cast of cosmic characters appears on a libation vessel of different form, Number 73. Here, the head of the central hero is flanked by the heads of the celestial serpent, while attendant figures ride on the handle of the vessel. In Number 72 and App. no. 45 and 48, the serpent heads are dropped, while attendant figures are retained and elaborated upon.

Although the celestial serpent and its associated hero and attendants are a dominant theme in the Sackler Lambayeque Collections, the style was rich and varied in its representational themes. As Numbers 63, 64 and 74 attest, artisans rendered rich portrayals of animal and plant life.

The Guardian of Rivero

As the nexus of the New World's greatest hydraulic state, the metropolis of Chan Chan flourished as the imperial focus of royalty and artistry. Although the royalty of the city was all-powerful, the artisans were more numerous, and the largest proportion of the urban populace consisted of gold-, silver-, and metalsmiths, lapidaries and jewelers, wood-carvers and sculptors, weavers and tailors of fine cloth and feathered mantles, and other craft specialists.[19] Neither farmers nor fishermen were allowed to reside in the sacred city. Instead, they were settled in planned, outlying satellite communities which could supply the city's wants without cluttering or crowding the imperial metropolis.

Artisans were residentially distinct from the general populace and enjoyed the privilege of residing within the capital. They were also socially distinct, and at Chan Chan enjoyed the privilege of wearing earspools, albeit small ones, fashioned from wood. The general respect for the fine arts is further reflected in the fact that certain high-ranking nobles held titles such as "Painter of Textiles" and "Master of Feathered Cloth." The physical and social proximity of the artisan and noble classes at Chan Chan relates to the fact that systematic production of exquisite works of fine art was integral to the political system. The economy did not employ currency or a standard medium of exchange; rather, commodities such as fine textiles and the fine arts in general served in certain ways as media of exchange and rewards for labor and loyalty among the hereditary nobility. Just as *chicha* libations were integral to all ceremonial occasions, the nobility cemented many ritual alliances with exchanges of works of art.

The concentration and numbers of artisans at Chan Chan made the metropolis not simply the political focus of the empire but its economic focus, involving large-scale production of fine arts, particularly works in gold and silver. If art acted as the coin of the realm, then Chan Chan was the national mint. Just as mints today generate an iconography of national symbols and concerns ranging from presidents and heroic figures to the national bird or beast, much of Imperial Chimú art has such symbolic qualities.

Following the subjugation of Chimor, the Inca divested Chan Chan of its economic base by resettling the artisan class adjacent to Cuzco, where they produced for a different imperial economy. Removal of the artisan class largely depopulated the coastal capital. Without even bothering to establish a local garrison, the Inca allowed Tacayanamo's defeated descendants to carry on an impoverished court as heirs to the lower Moche Valley. Interestingly, much the same pattern of subjugation and artisan "capture" is implicated earlier at Chan Chan, when a significant numerical increase in resident craftsmen occurred more or less coincident with the conquest of Lambayeque.[20] Presumably, the gold workers, metalsmiths and other skilled craftsmen who served Naymlap's noble descendants were relocated to serve Chan Chan. Then, in turn, the Chan Chan artisan class was resettled to serve at Cuzco. This pattern of artisan capture is intelligible in terms of the broader economic role of fine arts in Andean imperial organization.

Although Chan Chan's artisans were entitled to wear wooden earspools, they were not entitled to reside in elite architecture built of adobe. Instead, craftsmen's quarters—their houses and workshops—consisted of cane-walled rooms crowded around open patios to form compounds cramped into alley-lined neighborhoods. They were not, however, an undifferentiated population. Certain tracts of quarters and shops were built atop wide, low platforms immediately adjacent to or alongside one or another of the *ciudadelas*.[21] No doubt, these quarters served for production of works of fine arts patronized by the particular potentate or royal lineage holding court in the adjacent *ciudadela*.

This intimate physical association of royalty and artisans is in keeping with the truly vast wealth and finery contained within the *ciudadelas*. Each of the ten great *ciudadelas* contained banks of storerooms filled with artisan goods and other finery. In a sense, these stores comprised the national treasury, and they had been emptied, presumably by the Inca, by the time the conquistadors first encountered Chan Chan. The Spanish did, nonetheless, encounter vast treasure. Each *ciudadela* had served not only as royal quarters and coffers, but also as a mausoleum for a potentate and his heirs. Systematic looting of the tombs returned such great quantities of gold and silver objects that plundering became legally synonymous with mining, and the Spanish Crown established a government smelter nearby so that the treasures could be melted into bullion from which a royal tax of one-fifth was extracted. Large-scale commercial mining of Chan Chan's mausoleums continued up to about a century ago, making it the most intensively looted ancient city in the Western Hemisphere. What is particularly impressive is that the vast treasures that sustained hundreds of years of Spanish mining were but the residue of wealth left by the Inca after their conquest of Chimor.

The original names of the city's *ciudadelas* are not known, so today the royal compounds are called after one or another of the early European explorers to probe the ruins. *Ciudadela Rivero* was built during the reign of one of Chimor's last sovereign potentates (Plan 2). Sacked by the Inca and then mined by the Spanish, little of the artwork that ornamented the royal compound survives. However, excavation of the palace gateway by archaeologist Kent Day (1973) revealed two

Fig. 1. Wooden guardian figure flanking the main entrance of *Ciudadela Rivero,* Chan Chan. The staff the figure once held in its right hand is now missing. Note the bilobed helmet.

wooden statues in their original positions, as last beheld by Rivero's royalty centuries ago. There was one statue on each side of the narrow but long passage through the thick palace wall. Each figure—standing at attention in military garb—symmetrically faced the other from a narrow guard booth or niche built into the passage wall (Fig. 1). Originally, nine such booths had been built into each side of the passage, and a figure had been mounted in each. When the royalty of Rivero departed and closed the *ciudadela,* a narrow brick wall was erected across the passage. This transverse wall completely sealed in and hid the two surviving statues.

Each statue had held a staff or spear in its raised arm that had been carefully removed before the figures, and their booths, were bricked over. The two figures are largely identical in formal stance and costume. They can be interpreted as "gateway guardians" from a squad of 18 such centurions that once flanked the palace entrance. It is not clear whether these guardians represent a figure from the Chimor pantheon, such as the Janus deity that protected Roman gateways, or whether the statues simply represent palace guards. Whether from the ranks of men or gods, the Rivero guardians were not common folk: they wear large earspools, befitting high rank. Equally distinctive is the bipointed helmet that peaks over the right and left sides of each guardian's head. Just as earspools called out rank and class in Chimor, helmet form and headgear type called out ethnic—if not military—affiliations. Discovery of the Rivero guardians is significant because it identifies, for the first time, specific affiliations within Chimor for a particular type of headgear.

Bipointed guardian helmets are worn by modeled, bustlike figures on two Imperial Chimú libation vessels in the Sackler Collection (Nos. 82 and 83). The busts were both mold-made, but each from a different mold, as their garments indicate. One figure wears a robe with geometric designs, while the garment of the other is richly ornamented with marine motifs. These motifs are not casual design elements; rather, they are heraldic. Many of the *ciudadela* walls were embellished with ornate friezes sculpted in adobe plaster. Sea life and maritime motifs comprise the thematic content of much of this wall art.Crested ocean waves are a common frieze element, and this motif is prominently depicted in the central, vertical panel of the garment worn by the ceramic figure. (Indeed, in more stylized, geometric form, crested waves form the sole design element embellishing App. no. 53). On each side of the garment, two marine birds are depicted, beaks open, and in flight. Sea fowl are likewise a recurrent element in the palace friezes, as well as on many Imperial Chimú vessels (such as No.79). Fish were no less important symbols in the arts of Chan Chan. In the complex iconography press-molded on Number 85, a large fish, captured by hook-and-line, is held high by a richly garbed figure who grasps a ceremonial staff of office in his other hand.

In overview, the thematic concern of the Chimor artisans with the sea is not surprising. The world's driest desert supports impoverished wildlife because there is little forage for either bird or beast. Alternatively, the richest fishery of the Western oceans supports a prodigious and varied chain of life. Whereas the bleak desert presents a static vista, rolling waves are dynamic and teem with schooling fish, while overhead the sky is alive with flights of gulls, diving cormorants, and stately pelicans. It was this dynamic scene, this life that permeated the art, lore and pantheon of Chimor and its imperial capital.

It is interesting that domesticated plants (No. 68) and animals—even a strange breed of hairless Chimú dogs (App. nos. 56 and 58)—appear in the ceramic arts, but never in the friezes embellishing Chan Chan's *ciudadelas.* The land animal most frequently depicted upon the walls of the royal quarters is the monkey, and monkeys are not native to the bleak desert of the Chimú heartland. Rather, they were imported from tropical forests across the Andes and kept as valued pets, often secured by a leash attached to a belt around the animal's waist. Such a pet monkey forms the body of Number 80, a so-called stirrup-spout libation vessel. On this vessel where the spout joins the arc of the stirrup, artisans fashioned in relief a second small monkey as an *adorno.* This convention is repeated on the spouts of other libation vessels, such as Number 81. Birds or simple nodes (App. no. 82) were also employed as spout *adornos.* Stirrup-spout libation vessels are distinctly Imperial Chimú and enjoyed great popularity during the later stages of the empire. Presumably, the different classes of spout *adornos,* such as monkeys, birds, or nodes, identified the affiliations of either producers or users of the vessels.

Excavations in the artisans' quarters of Chan Chan produced little evidence of ceramic production, although other crafts—metalworking in particular—were ubiquitous. This suggests that the state did not monopolize the ceramic arts to the degree it did the production of commodities such as gold and silver jewelry or fine fabrics. If the ceramic arts were not so centrally controlled, then this may underlie the rich variability of form and design captured in the Sackler Collection.

The Ancestor Cult

The Andean peoples' concept of death was influenced by their concept of time, and time was viewed less as a linear phenomenon than as a cyclical one, akin to the annual solar cycle. The solar cycle was divided into the journey of the "young sun" and the journey of the "mature sun."[22] The young sun rose with the distant winter solstice, then gradually traveled down the Andes bringing first Spring, and then eventually, when overhead, the warm growing season. With the summer solstice, the young sun became the mature sun gradually traveling back up the Cordillera, bringing first the bounty of harvest season, but then finally the cold stillness of winter. Yet, with the winter solstice the old sun became the new, and the cycle, the journey through time and space, began again.

Because the life cycle of man was presumed to operate in accord with this solar cycle of rejuvenation, youth and maturity, death was regarded more as a state of suspended animation (but not perception) than as any sort of final separation from the world of the living. This concept, or ones broadly analogous, underlie a widespread pattern of ancestor veneration in the Andes. The wealth and resources of the hereditary nobility supported very elaborate rituals of veneration that saw their culmination in the ruling dynasties at Chan Chan and subsequently at Cuzco. A dead emperor's body was mummified and carefully preserved. Although inanimate, the deceased potentate continued to reside in his former palace, attended, garbed and "fed" by surviving members of the former king's lineage. On important state occasions the royal mummies were removed from their palace mausoleums, placed on litters to be ritually paraded through the city, then seated in assembly with other imperial ancestors to attend and oversee the ceremonies of the living.

The pomp and ceremony attendant upon the ancestor cult required tremendous resources. Great expenditures of treasure and fine arts were required in addition to the monumental architecture that transformed palaces into mausoleums. Ritual related to death and ancestry had to be played out with progressively less elaboration at successively lower rungs of the social hierarchy. The convention of "symbolic substitution" allowed ceremonies of the same structure and effect to be acted out on modest scales by use of surrogate offerings. This practice has great antiquity in the Andes. Recent excavations in coastal temples dating to the third millennium BC indicate that a certain amount of human sacrifice was attendant to building and remodeling sacred sanctuaries.[23] However, in some cases clay figurines, rather than people, were placed in offering deposits.

Within the Sackler Collection, many splendid ceramic works of the Chancay Style are sensitive reflections of ancestor veneration, and symbolic substitution. At Chan Chan, ossuaries of sacrified llamas are associated with the royal mausoleums.[24] Bones of camelids are the most commonly occurring animal grave accompaniment in cemeteries outside the city.[25] Comparable remains apparently accompany some Chancay graves, but others produce symbolic substitutes: llama figurines (Nos. 179 and 180).

In Chimor, and in the Andes in general, human sacrifice was never practiced on a scale comparable to that of Aztec Mexico. However, it did occur, and generally entailed young people, particularly women. The only royal mausoleum at Chan Chan to be explored by archaeologists contained within its thoroughly looted cell-like chambers the scattered remains of more than two hundred young women. Female accompaniment in the afterlife or next life was obviously a desire. Yet, only the highest royalty could command such sacrifice. Chancay people satisfied this desire with symbolic surrogates, and the Sackler Collection contains particularly fine examples of large female figurines from desert tombs, ranging from richly garbed women (App. no. 85) through figures nude except for their distinctive facial paints (No. 169).

Most vessels comprising the Chancay collection show little evidence of use prior to internment, and they were no doubt produced principally as tomb accompaniments. While some—the figurines of llamas and humans—can be identified as symbolic surrogates, others served different functions. Two are double-chambered libation vessels, one ornamented with a bird (No. 182) and the other with a standing man bedecked with an elaborate necklace (No. 181). Chancay libation vessels included a distinctive form of beaker (No. 173) not found in the Lambayeque and Imperial Chimú styles. Such beakers, in miniature, are held by large human effigy vessels, which themselves may have served as *chicha* containers to supply ritual toasting. To judge from the crownlike headgear, face paint, and general attire these effigies (App. nos. 79, 80, 83, and 84) depict males. Still other vessels have more utilitarian form; yet their ornate geometric designs, executed in the distinctive black-and-white patterning of Chancay, suggest that they were produced to accompany some venerated ancestor on his journey to the final solstice.

Conclusion

Upon their conquest of Chimor, the Inca dissolved the desert empire into a series of petty states under local or imposed rulers loyal to the Cuzco royalty. This subjugation transpired more than two generations before the arrival of Pizarro's conquistadors. The Spanish found Chan Chan without inhabitants and showed little curiosity about the old empire. What has shaped understanding of Chimor and the polities and peoples it incorporated is the fact that it played out the pomp and ceremony of ancestor veneration with such finery, arts and quantities of precious metal that for centuries of European occupation, returns from the looting of ancient tombs matched or surpassed what people could earn from commercial mining. This situation yielded a wealth of magnificent works reflecting upon the rich aesthetics of Chimor. However, it has only been within the last decade that archaeologists have begun to address the formidable task of identifying the specific cities, palace-courts, shrines, mausoleums, tombs, workshops and artisans' quarters specifically associated with the heirs of Tacayanamo and Naymlap and the polities these dynasties governed. The great size and sophistication of the hydraulic states involved make this a complex undertaking. Yet, when even the tentative results from the first decade of serious exploration are joined with a fine representative collection of Lambayeque and Imperial Chimú, as well as Chancay, ceramic arts such as the Sackler Collection embodies, new avenues emerge in understanding the symbolism, heraldry and cosmology of a formidable and alien desert empire. Herein lies a fresh yet fundamental appreciation of the arts of Chimor.

Footnotes

1. Moseley and Day 1982.
2. Letteau and Letteau 1978; Zeil 1979.
3. Hartline 1980.
4. Moseley and Mackey 1974.
5. Rowe 1948; Conrad 1974.
6. Conrad 1982; Kolata 1982.
7. Kosok 1965.
8. Ortloff *et al.* 1982.
9. Steward 1955; Wittfogel 1957.
10. Downing and Gibson 1974.
11. Moseley 1982.
12. Klymyshyn 1982.
13. Rowe 1948.
14. Neatherly 1977.
15. Lathrap n.d.; Moseley n.d.
16. Moseley 1975; Engel 1963.
17. Donnan 1978, figs. 183, 239.
18. Kroeber 1930.
19. Topic 1977; 1982.
20. Topic 1982; Kolata 1978.
21. Topic 1982.
22. Demarest 1981.
23. Feldman 1980.
24. Pozoroski 1979; Conrad 1982.
25. Donnan and Mackey 1978.

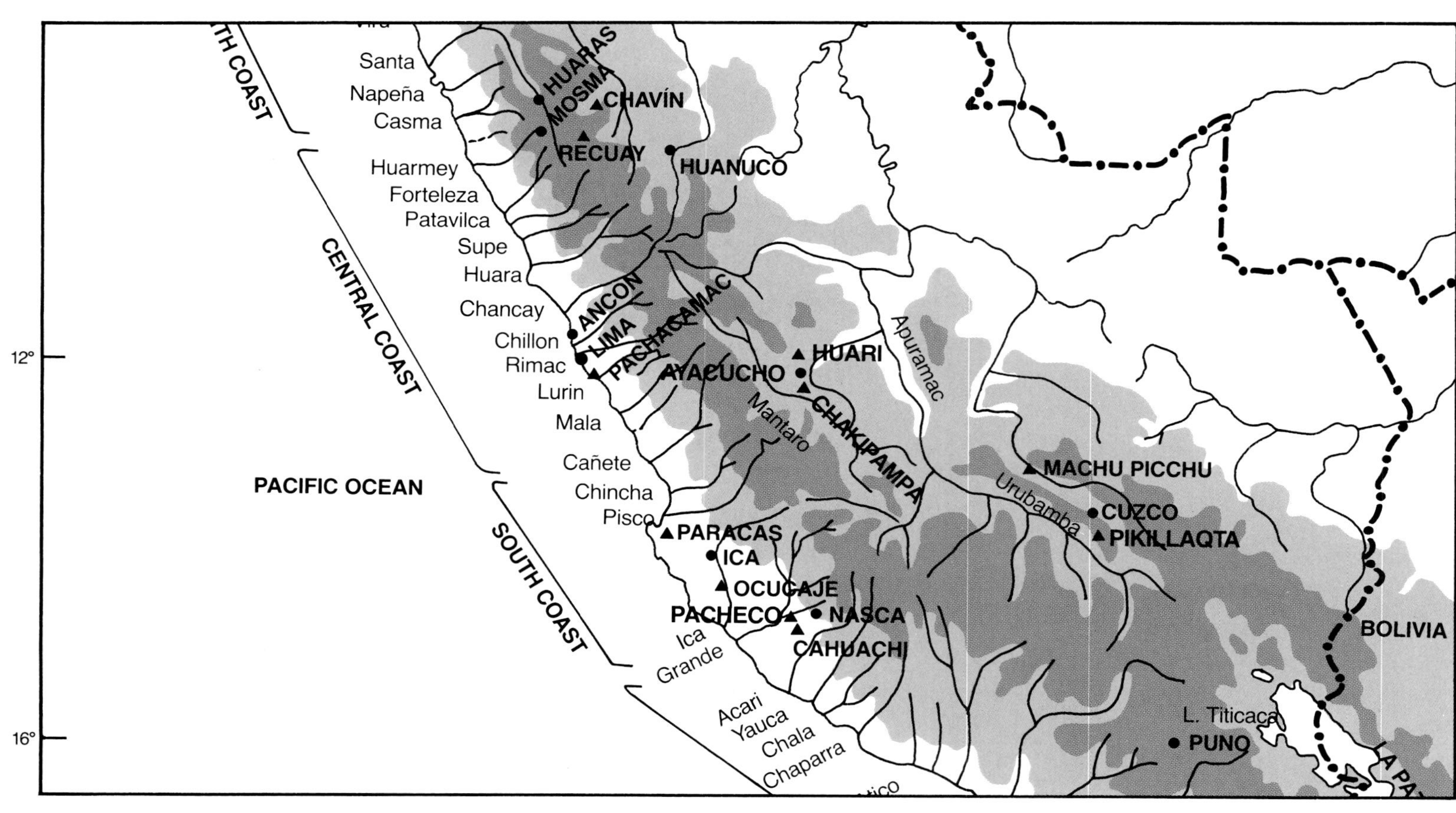

Santa
Napeña
Casma
Huarmey
Forteleza
Patavilca
Supe
Huara
Chancay
Chillon
Rimac
Lurin
Mala
Cañete
Chincha
Pisco
Ica
Grande
Acari
Yauca
Chala
Chaparra
HUARAS
MOSMA
CHAVÍN
RECUAY
HUANUCO
ANCON
LIMA
PACHACAMAC
HUARI
AYACUCHO
CHAKIPAMPA
Mantaro
Apurimac
MACHU PICCHU
Urubamba
CUZCO
PIKILLAQTA
PARACAS
ICA
OCUCAJE
PACHECO
NASCA
CAHUACHI
BOLIVIA
L. Titicaca
PUNO
CENTRAL COAST
SOUTH COAST
PACIFIC OCEAN
12°
16°

The Nasca Style

DONALD A. PROULX

THE NASCA CULTURE was a regional state that flourished on the south coast of Peru during the Early Intermediate Period (370 BC to AD 540 —see Map 1). Its art included finely woven textiles, elaborate featherwork, objects of gold and copper, pyroengraved gourds, and wooden and shell objects. But Nasca is best known for its exceptional polychrome painted pottery, and it is this art form that will be the subject of this essay.

The Nasca Style evolved directly out of the Paracas (or Ocucaje) Style of the preceding Early Horizon (1300 to 370 BC), and in many ways is simply a continuation of that style. Many of the iconographic themes so prominent in Nasca art, such as the Anthropomorphic Mythical Being, the Mythical Killer Whale, felines, foxes, trophy heads and falcons, have their roots in Paracas iconography.[1] The beginning of the Nasca sequence is not marked by a sharp break with past traditions, but is distinguished by two new artistic conventions: (1) postfired resin paints on pottery are replaced by slip paints that are baked on the vessels, and (2) pottery replaces textiles as the major medium for displaying religious iconography. Archaeologists use these rather arbitrary distinctions to separate the two cultural traditions.

Nasca pottery is painted with naturalistic motifs (plants, animals, birds, fish), mythological creatures or geometric designs in slip paints using as many as eleven colors on a single vessel. Major vessel shapes include double-spout and bridge bottles, bowls, jars and effigy forms. Although modeling is present in the Nasca Style, especially on the effigy vessel, it was not a major decorative technique, as was the case with the contemporary Moche Culture of the north coast. Indeed, there appears to have been surprisingly little influence of the Moche Style on the Nasca Style, or vice versa, during the approximately 900 years of contemporaneity shared by the two cultures.

The Discovery of the Nasca Style

Scholars have long been attracted to the Nasca Style because of its artistic beauty and its rich iconographic content. The first Nasca vessels known to have been taken from Peru were collected in 1842 by a Frenchman, Captain François Joseph Amedée de Campe de Rosamel. He acquired a collection of pottery from the Ica Valley on the south coast of Peru, including five vessels in what later was to be called the Nasca Style. The collection was deposited later that same year in the provincial museum at Boulogne-sur-Mer in France, where it remained unnoticed until 1898, when it was first described in an article by Jules Hamy.[2]

The first illustration of a Nasca vessel appeared in Charles Wiener's *Pérou et Bolivie*, but the provenience was given as Recuay, and the true source of the vessel escaped detection.[3] In 1881, a collection of pottery accumulated by Dr. José Mariano Macedo of Peru was sent to Europe with the intention of finding a buyer. Included in this collection were three Nasca Style vessels that were listed in the catalogue of the collection.[4] In the following year, this new style of pottery was again mentioned in an article on the collection by Jules Hamy, and one of the vessels was illustrated.[5]

In 1884 the Macedo Collection was purchased by the Museum für Völkerkunde in Berlin. Two more Nasca vessels (one of them doubtful) were acquired by the museum in 1888 as part of the Centeno Collection. Four of these vessels in Berlin were illustrated by Seler.[6] It was at the Museum für Völkerkunde that a young scholar named Max Uhle first saw the attractive painted pottery and became fascinated by it. He became obsessed with finding the source of this style, a feat he finally accomplished in 1901.

Max Uhle was born in Dresden, Germany, in 1856.[7] His background was in linguistics, and he earned his Ph.D. in this field in 1880. His interests quickly shifted to anthropology, and in 1888 he took a position at the Königliches Museum für Völkerkunde in Berlin where he saw the Nasca pottery. In 1892 he made his first trip to South America, where he collected ethnographic and archaeological specimens for the museum. He severed his ties with the Berlin museum in 1895 and was sponsored for the next four years by the University of Pennsylvania. During this period he made his first trip to Peru, working among other places at Pachacamac, where he undertook the first stratigraphic excavations in that country.

In 1899 Uhle began working for the University of California under the sponsorship of Mrs. Phoebe Apperson Hearst, the mother of William Randolph

	Periods	Estimated Dates	Uncorrected C-14 Dates	Equivalent Thermoluminescence Dates*	Stylistic Strains	Dawson's Phases	Sawyer's Phases	Kroeber (1956) Phases	Gayton & Kroeber (1927) Phases
AD				*See Entries					
	Middle Horizon		N-9 AD 403 ± 49 (P 511)			9	Nasca-Wari	Coast Tiahuanaco	Y-3 Y-2
500					Disjunctive				
		AD 540						Y	Y-1
375			N-8 AD 756 ± 90			8			
			N-7 AD 639 ± 60	No. 138 AD 483-993	Proliferous	7 6	Late Nasca	B	B
250									
125					Transitional	5	Middle Nasca	AB	X
0		AD 65	N-5 AD 526 ± 90 N-4 145 BC ± 53	No. 126 AD 373-933	Monumental	4 3	Early Nasca	A	A
125									
		175 BC	N-3 AD 336 ± 100 AD 273 ± 100 192 BC ± 56	No. 107 427 BC-AD 383		2			
250									
375		370 BC		No. 104 before AD 683		1	Proto-Nasca		
BC									

Table I. Correlation of Dates to Nasca Stylistic Phases

Hearst. Between 1899 and 1905, he put together major collections for the University from many parts of Peru. In February of 1901, while working in the Ica Valley on the south coast, Uhle finally realized his dream. He found a complete cemetery containing Nasca Style pottery. A total of 32 gravelots containing 146 vessels were eventually excavated from the cemeteries on the Ocucaje Hacienda, the best documented collection of Nasca pottery ever made in Peru.

Four years later, in 1905, Uhle made a collection of 660 Nasca Style vessels in the Nasca Valley, located just to the south of the Ica Valley on the south coast. Atypically, Uhle left no report or explanatory notes on how he acquired these vessels—whether by excavation or by purchase. His field catalogue lists 18 separate locations where the vessels were collected, but we are offered none of the gravelot associations that Uhle had so carefully recorded in the Ica Valley. The discovery of the style in the Nasca Valley was important, and it paved the way for later work in the region by Julio C. Tello and Alfred Kroeber.

Thomas Joyce was the first to use the term "Nasca" to describe the polychrome pottery from the south coast in his book *South American Archaeology,* published in 1912. In the following year, he also wrote an article discussing the new style.[8] Not much further scientific fieldwork occurred until 1926 when Alfred Kroeber undertook major excavations in the Nasca Valley and collected 20 gravelots with 112 vessels, which are now in the collections of the Field Museum of Natural History in Chicago. It was argued that because of the greater variety of iconographic themes and pottery shapes of the vessels from the Nasca Valley as compared to those of the Ica Valley, and because of the association of the pottery with monumental architecture at the large site of Cahuachi in the Nasca Valley, the Nasca Valley was the most likely center of the culture which produced the pottery. Joyce's term "Nasca" was therefore accepted by Kroeber and has been used to designate the style ever since.

Chronology

Uhle was unable to use stratigraphy to establish his sequence of cultures in the Ica Valley. Instead, he developed the technique of stylistic seriation based on changes of vessel form and decoration. Seriation involves the ordering of a sequence based on closest similarity. To use a modern analogy, automobiles made in the years 1957 and 1959 would share more similar traits than automobiles made in 1965 and 1952. Arrangement of the styles found in the Ica Valley in 1901 led Uhle to propose the following sequence:

Inca
Chincha
Epigonal
"New Found Style of Ica"

Uhle's "New Found Style of Ica" was the oldest he recognized for the valley, the style we now call Nasca. By 1913, he was using the term "Proto-Nasca" to refer to the style.

Uhle never undertook a study of the ceramic collections he had made in the Ica Valley. This task was left to the faculty and students of the University of California at Berkeley, where the collections were deposited. During the 1920's, Alfred Louis Kroeber directed a major study of the Uhle collections, including a seriation of 660 ceramic vessels collected by Uhle in the Nasca drainage in 1905.[9] The study was primarily a quantitative one consisting of a numerical analysis of shape, color and design attributes. Gayton and Kroeber were able to subdivide the Nasca Style into four phases, labeled A, X, B and Y (see Table 1). During the 1950's, Kroeber reevaluated the seriation of 1927 in light of both his own excavations of Nasca gravelots from the Nasca Valley made in 1926 and his restudy of the Ica Valley gravelots collected by Uhle.[10] Although he felt the original sequence to be essentially correct, he argued that his Phase X was given too much importance as a separate phase; it should be seen as a transition between Phases A and B. It should either be eliminated or at least be called Phase AB. Similarly, his Phase Y was seen as being more complex than originally thought, and instead of subdividing it into Y-1, Y-2 and Y-3, it should be represented by a Phase Y followed by Coast Tiahuanaco (see Table 1).

Meanwhile, during the 1950's, Lawrence E. Dawson of the University of California began a more thorough study of the Nasca Style under the direction of John H. Rowe. Dawson's seriation was based on principles that differed from the evolutionary or quantitative seriation of Gayton and Kroeber. Gayton and Kroeber had used a relatively small sample of unassociated pottery from the Nasca Valley for their initial study. Their four phases, A, X, B and Y, were based on a statistical analysis of the correlation of 25 shape categories with 40 design categories. The unconscious assumption was that the designs evolved from simple-naturalistic to complex-abstract.

Dawson's analysis was based on the use of similiary seriation, which correlates the associations of minute changes in shape and design features on a vessel. This type of seriation is a qualitative, rather than a quantitative, one; i.e., the presence or absence of a trait at a particular point in the sequence is more important than its frequency in the sample. Dawson utilized a much larger sample than had any previous investigator, including all the gravelots from the Ica and Nasca valleys. A gravelot consists of all the artifacts found in a single distinguishable tomb; in the case of the Nasca gravelots, the size ranges from one to fifteen vessels in each. The assumption can be made that all the vessels in a gravelot are approximately contemporary, having been made during the lifetime of the deceased and buried at the same time upon his or her death. The vessels in a gravelot, therefore, represent a unit of contemporaneity. The shapes and designs illustrate the range of variability present at a particular point in time. Using the associations of shape, design and variability within a gravelot, other unassociated vessels can be tied into the sequence. As in all seriations, the similiary seriation arranges the ceramic style in a relative order, based on closest similarity. The correct order of the sequence must be obtained by linking one or the other end of the sequence into a known temporal event. In the case of the Nasca sequence, Dawson's earliest phase could be shown to derive directly out of the Paracas Style, while the other end of the sequence was linked to the introduction of Huari stylistic influences onto the south coast of Peru at the beginning of the Middle Horizon.

Dawson developed a nine-phase sequence for the Nasca ceramic style, which is far superior to the earlier sequences discussed above (Table 1). Radiocarbon dates from the site of Cahuachi in the Nasca Valley, as well as stratigraphic test excavations conducted by Dawson in the Ica Valley, have confirmed the accuracy of his phases.[11] Unfortunately, Dawson never published the details of his sequence, making it all but impossible for many specialists to use it effectively. Alan Sawyer, for example, continues to use a scheme he developed that divides the sequence into Proto-Nasca, Early, Middle and Late Nasca, and Nasca-Wari (Table 1).

Beginning in the 1960's, other students of John Rowe elaborated on Dawson's sequence, and some of these studies have been published. Richard Roark studied Phases 5 and 6 of the style,[12] while Donald Proulx worked on Phases 3 and 4, subdividing Phase 3 into four subphases.[13] More recently, Elizabeth Farkass Wolfe published a study of the iconography of the Spotted Cat and Horrible Bird, two major themes in the art, from Phases 1 through 5.[14] Many other studies have been undertaken by Rowe's students, but remain unpublished.[15] It is hoped that someday the entire sequence can be published so that all the evidence for this excellent seriation can be presented.

Another classification paralleling Dawson's phases is the use of the terms "Monumental" and "Proliferous." The Monumental Nasca substyle or strain refers to the representation of natural or mythological themes by painted figures executed in a relatively depictive or naturalistic technique.[16] The Monumental strain corresponds to Dawson's Phases 2 through 4 of the Nasca Style. Phase 5 is seen as a transition between the Monumental and Proliferous strains. "In the Proliferous substyle the proportion of geometric designs is greater, and representational themes often include abstract elements as part of the design. Large numbers of rays and tassels are appended to many of the designs, particularly those depicting mythical subjects, producing a visual impression of almost infinitely multiplied subjects...."[17] The Proliferous strain corresponds to Dawson's Phases 6 and 7. Finally, the term "Disjunctive" has been applied to the end of the sequence, which corresponds to Dawson's Phases 8 and 9. At this time, there is a breakdown of the style due to outside influences coming from the Huari Culture of the highlands (see Table 1). The use of Monumental and Proliferous to describe the Nasca Style goes back to Uhle and has been used (and abused) by specialists ever since that time.

Thus far, we have been discussing the *relative* chronology of the Nasca Style, or the orderly development of the style through time. It is, however, much more difficult to derive an exact date or *absolute* date for the style. Among the more accurate absolute dating techniques is Carbon-14 dating, which measures the decay of the radioactive isotope Carbon-14, present in all living matter. There are many problems associated with Carbon-14 dating: contamination of specimens; use of different half-lives; and the recently discovered fact that the amount of Carbon-14 present in the atmosphere varied from time to time, necessitating a recalibration of all dates. The technique must be used with caution, but, nevertheless, several Carbon-14 dates are available for our Nasca phases (see Table 1).[18] The dates support Dawson's relative sequence and suggest that the bulk of the Nasca sequence falls between the beginning of the first century AD and the ninth century AD. For a number of reasons—including the small number of Nasca dates processed, the large plus and minus factors associated with them, and variable dates obtained for the preceding Paracas and succeeding Huari cultures—the more commonly used dates for the Early Intermediate Period (corresponding to Nasca Phases 1 through 8) are 370 BC to AD 540 (see Table 1). Although these dates may be shifted forward by a century or two when further dates are collected and analyzed, the time span seems to be accurate, based on our present evidence.

Another absolute dating technique is thermoluminescence dating, a technique based on the effect of radiation on certain minerals found in the clay of pottery. The minerals are exposed to radiation coming from the decay of uranium, thorium and potassium, which are present in all materials of geological origin. The result of this exposure is that the minerals emit light—known as thermoluminescence—when the clay is heated; the amount of glow is proportional to the age of the sample. Comparisons of the glow curve are made with natural amounts of beta, alpha and gamma radiation in the specimen, and the date is thus determined. In the case of pottery, the date refers to the last time that the object was heated to a temperature high enough to erase its last thermoluminescence signal. In other words, the date would pertain to the time the vessel was baked or fired. The accuracy of this technique is not as high as Carbon-14 dating. The usual range of error is ± 20%, but new procedures can reduce that to ± 10%. Several of the Nasca specimens in the exhibit were subjected to thermoluminescence dating. The results are provided in Table 1.

Distribution of the Style

Nasca was a strictly regional culture confined to the fertile valleys of the desert south coast of Peru. The greatest concentrations of Nasca sites and cemeteries are in the Ica and Nasca drainages, an area of barren desert transected by river valleys carrying water from the mountains to the east (Map 1). The Nasca River, with its five major tributaries, appears to have been the central focus of the style. The large ceremonial center of Cahuachi, occupied initially in Paracas times, grew in population, reaching its peak during Nasca Phase 3. It is likely that this site was the "capital" of a primitive state during the early Nasca phases. At that time other fortified sites suddenly appeared in the Pisco, Ica and Acari valleys. In Phase 4, Cahuachi was abandoned, and ceramics in adjacent valleys became more heterogeneous, reflecting loss of a centralizing influence.[19]

The distribution of the style varied from time to time. Phase 1 and 2 ceramics are found almost exclusively in the Ica and Nasca valleys—the heartland of the style. There appears to have been some influence on the late Paracas and early Nasca phases coming from the Chincha and Cañete Valley areas during this time, in the form of the Topara Style. During Nasca Phase 3, there was a major expansion, probably military in nature, which spread the Nasca Style north to the Pisco Valley and south to the Acari Valley. A shrinkage occurred during Phases 4 and 5, when the expansion collapsed and Cahuachi was abandoned. During Phase 7 there is evidence of a climatic shift, with wetter weather occurring. This set the stage for a second expansion,

Fig. 1. Bowl with trophy heads (after Seler).

this time carrying the style up into the highlands, affecting the local cultures in the area around Ayacucho. There also appears to have been an expansion on the coast as well, with the style moving back into the Pisco and Acari valleys, and perhaps an extension northward to Chincha and southward to the Yauca Valley. Indirect contact with the Moche Culture on the north coast may have taken place at this time, for some new ideas, including running human figures, appear for the first time in Nasca art. Finally, highland influences from the emerging Huari state begin to transform the waning Nasca state during Phases 8 and 9, and these changes are reflected in the art style.

Iconography

Iconography is that discipline which concerns itself with the subject matter or meaning of works of art, as opposed to their form.[20] Some art historians and anthropologists study ancient art to discover and record the conventions, techniques and mannerisms of an art style in order to place the work of art in space and time. This is not an iconographic exercise, but rather an analysis of the form of the art style. Others turn their attention to iconography *per se,* combing the art for whatever anthropological information it may contain about the people and their societies.

There are several levels of iconographic analysis, as well as various techniques or models used to interpret the form of the art. Panofsky describes three levels of iconographic interpretation:[21] (1) *Primary or natural subject matter,* which is comprehended by identifying pure forms. In the case of the Nasca pottery, this level of analysis would consist of an enumeration of the motifs present on the pottery and their relationships to one another, without any interpretive discussion. (2) *Secondary or conventional subject matter* connects artistic motifs or combinations of artistic motifs with themes and concepts. The motifs are recognized as carrying secondary or conventional meanings, and the identification of these images, stories or allegories is called iconography. Again in the case of the Nasca pottery, the association of a particular mythical being with plants could suggest that the creature has some function of fertility in ancient Nasca society. (3) *Intrinsic meaning or content,* which can be gained by ascertaining those underlying principles that reveal the basic attitude of a nation, a period, a class, a religious or philosophical persuasion—qualified by one personality and condensed into one work.[22] In the example of the Nasca pottery, this level would seek to explain the changes in religious iconography throughout the various phases and the basic nature of the religious and secular thought.

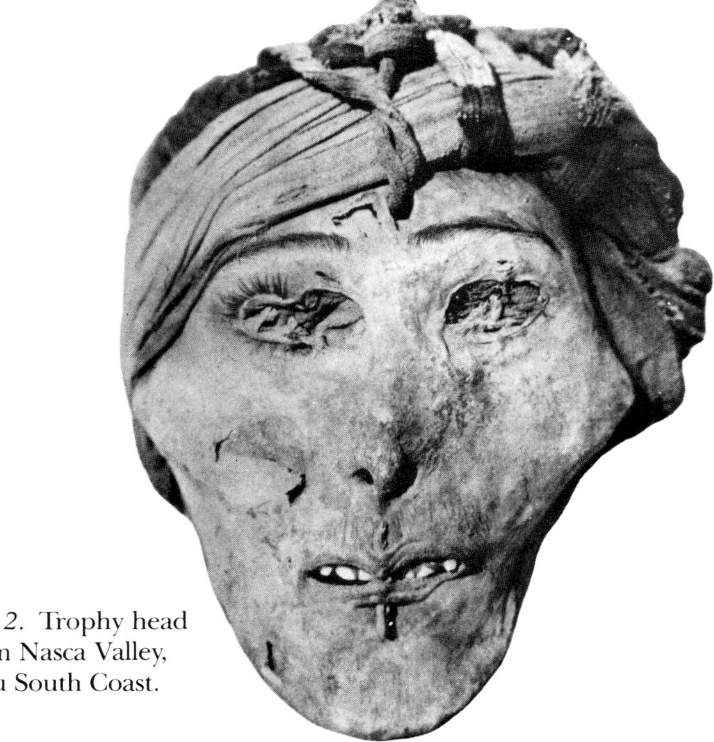

Fig. 2. Trophy head from Nasca Valley, Peru South Coast.

In applying Panofsky's three levels of iconographic analysis to an ancient civilization, like Nasca, which lacks written records, many problems emerge. In moving from the level of primary or natural subject matter to the secondary or conventional subject matter, we are apt to apply modern Western values and meanings to a completely alien society separated from us by almost fifteen hundred years. Is it possible to understand the "stories" symbolized in the complex images on the pottery? The answer, clearly, is that we will never be able to completely understand all the nuances and sometimes even the basic meanings of the themes. There are, however, several techniques for gaining some understanding of the meaning of the motifs.

One of the best methods for determining the meaning of Nasca art is through the use of the archaeological record. One of the most common themes in Nasca art is a disarticulated human head sometimes carried in the hand of a mythical creature (No. 131), being eaten by a bird demon (No. 123), modeled in the form of a jar (No. 128), or drawn as a separate motif (Fig. 1). Features of the motif suggest that it is the severed head of a corpse: closed eyes, lips pinned shut, and carrying a rope attached through the forehead. Archaeological excavations in Nasca cemeteries have revealed caches of actual trophy heads. These speci-

Fig. 3. Headdress ornament, gold. Excavated from a Nasca cemetery (from Sawyer).

Fig. 4. Mouth mask, gold. Excavated from a Nasca cemetery (from Sawyer).

Fig. 5. Shrunken head with carrying rope. Jivaro Indians, Eastern Ecuador. American Museum of Natural History.

mens have had their brains and soft tissues removed through a hole at the base of the skull, cotton carrying ropes attached through a hole in the forehead, and the lips pinned shut with thorns from a local bush (Fig. 2). More will be said about these heads later.

Archaeology has also demonstrated that certain headdresses, forehead ornaments and mouth masks made of gold, and other accessories commonly depicted on several forms of Anthropomorphic Mythical Beings in Nasca art, were actually worn by upper-class males in Nasca society. Bodies buried in Nasca cemeteries have been found wearing these headdresses (Fig. 3) and mouth masks (Fig. 4), suggesting that Nasca priests in this culture dressed in the image of their mythical heroes or deities.

Another aid in interpreting Nasca iconography is the ethnographic record. Much can be learned by examining the objects used by present-day primitive peoples in the Andean area and through the study of their customs, rituals and value systems. Elsewhere, I have argued that the reason the ancient Nasca Culture took trophy heads may be analogous to the motivations of the Jivaro Indians of eastern Peru and Ecuador.[23] The Jivaro take the heads of their dead enemies and shrink them in order to prevent the avenging spirit of the dead person from harming the killer. The Jivaro sew the lips of the trophy in a way similar to that of the pinned lips of the Nasca examples, and they, like the Nasca, insert a carrying rope through the head (Fig. 5).

Ethnographic analogy has its limitations, of course. Many anthropologists assume that local traditions continue over long periods of time with little change. While this is, to a certain degree, true, factors such as outside cultural contacts and internal historic circumstances can affect these traditions over time. Ideally, there should be continuity between the modern practices and those to which they are being compared, such as is the case with some of the Indian tribes in the American Southwest. With Nasca the continuity is only of a generalized type, since many different and distinct cultures lie between it and the historic period.

Finally, the historic record may aid the anthropologist and art historian in the interpretation of iconography. In the art of the Moche Culture from the north coast of Peru, for example, numerous modeled representations of long-haired women are seen in the pottery with insects drawn or modeled on their clothing and hair. Early Spanish chroniclers described witches or sorcerers on the north coast as having long unkempt hair covered with lice. Thus it seems plausible that the Moche representations may also be depicting witches.

All in all, Panofsky's levels of iconographic interpretation are useful constructs but work best for societies having adequate documentary records—such as Western Europe during the Renaissance. When applied to ancient civilizations without writing, other evidence, such as the archaeological record, ethnographic analogy and the historic record, can be used to elucidate the concepts.

Some anthropologists and art historians have made use of structuralist and semiotic models as alternatives to Panofsky's scheme. The theory behind this approach is the extension of linguistic concepts to nonlinguistic phenomena, such as art. Proponents of this method argue that images are structured in much the same fashion as a linguistic system, and that the interpreter can recognize meaningful contrasts by isolating discrete, recurrent units, much in the same way that significant auditory contrasts were uncovered in phonemic analysis. In a pioneering study, Kubler analyzed the art of Teotihuacan in Mexico by codifying the signs and images in the art and comparing them to nouns, verbs and adjectives in a language.[24] Donnan makes a similar argument in discussing his interpretation of Moche iconography from Peru:

> "Inherent in Moche art is a symbolic system that follows consistent rules of expression. In many respects, this system is similar to the symbolic system of a language. In language the speaker can modify what he is saying about an object (noun) by selecting a set of modifiers (adjectives and adverbs) and inserting them in their proper place in the message according to a set of rules (grammar).
>
> In art, the communication is between the artist and the viewer. The artist conveys information about objects such as houses, men or ceremonies—we might call these 'artistic nouns'—by using a set of stylistic modifiers or 'artistic adjectives.' Individuals can, therefore, be recognized as being rich or poor, high or low status, warriors, gods, or servants depending on the modifiers the artist chooses to make in the way he depicts them....
>
> Similarly, the artist uses what we might call 'artistic adverbs' to modify the action shown, and thus be able to convey the speed of a given runner, the force of a mace blow, or the intensity of a battle by the way he arranges the scene and the various details he adds to the representation." [25]

Donnan uses what he calls the "thematic approach" to his study of Moche art. Interpretation is possible by studying the consistent correlation of details in the representations, the patterns that result from the artist's working according to culturally defined rules of expression. As modern examples, he uses the nativity scene in Christian art and the representation of Santa Claus with all his associated attributes: beard, red suit, black belt, etc. Someone familiar with these representations can understand what is signified even when only parts of the theme are depicted. He feels that the same is true in ancient art as well.

Donnan's "thematic approach" has some utility when applied to Nasca art, as I will attempt to demonstrate shortly. It is best used to demonstrate variations on a theme and to understand the relationships between attributes depicted within a scene. The problem with all structuralist and semiotic models, however, is that we can never completely understand the true "meaning" of the scene depicted in the art. We might be able to identify a human figure as having high status, or perhaps being a priest or warrior. But even here we are begining to make judgmental assumptions based on Western ethnocentric biases. The more complicated the iconography, the more difficult the task becomes.

Of the two approaches to iconography, Panofsky's approach is more objective, especially when it is supported by archaeological, ethnographic and historic data. It is greatly limited, however, when used to understand the iconography of a preliterate society. The structuralist and semiotic approaches, such as those used by Kubler and Donnan, provide a more methodical way of examining an art style, and they can be applied equally well to preliterate as well as literate societies. Their main liability is that any interpretation of the meaning is highly subjective and prone to ethnocentric bias. In Nasca art, both approaches have been used to a certain extent, but our understanding of Nasca iconography is still in its infancy. Naturalistic motifs—and even species of plants, animals and birds—can be identified. Although other thematic motifs also have been identified and described, the true interpretation of the values, symbols and ritual has remained outside our grasp.

Nasca has a rich and varied iconography centering on mythological creatures, naturalistic plants, animals, birds and geometric designs. Over the past 60 years many attempts have been made to analyze and interpret this iconography. In 1923, Eduard Seler published the first major analysis of Nasca iconography.[26] He concentrated on the mythological themes that he saw as emphasizing fertility and vegetation: (1) the Spotted Cat, bearer of the resources of life; (2) the Demon Cat; (3) the Demon Cat as a bird; (4) other winged demons; (5) other demons and figures of vegetation; and (6) the demon of the jagged staff. Seler also studied some of the naturalistic motifs: humans and heads, females, animals, vegetables and objects. One of his major contributions was the excellent drawings and rollouts of the Nasca motifs that were reproduced in his book. They have formed a major corpus of the iconography for the specialist.

In the early 1930's the Peruvian Eugenio Yacovleff wrote a series of articles on selected themes in the Nasca Style. The most important of these was an article on "The Primitive Deity of Nasca."[27] In it he argued that the most important of the mythical creatures depicted in Nasca art was the Killer Whale, and that Nasca religious orientation was toward the sea. His other studies dealt with evolution of specific Nasca art motifs such as the blackbird (a swift or *vencejo*),[28] falcons and other raptorial birds,[29] the Jiquima plant,[30] and other plants.[31] Like Seler, Yacovleff illustrated his articles with excellent drawings of the motifs taken from collections in Peru.

Gayton and Kroeber[32] and Kroeber[33] also dealt with iconographic themes as part of their attempt to develop a chronological seriation for the style. Beginning in 1961, the interest in iconographic studies for their own sake returned with the publication of Alan Sawyer's article on Paracas and Nasca iconography, which traced many of the major motifs from their origins in Paracas art through the Nasca sequence.[34] Further studies were stimulated through Dawson's work, and many of John Rowe's students at the University of California at Berkeley began chronological and iconographic studies of vessels in the Uhle Collection. Richard Roark studied the iconography of themes in Nasca Phases 5 and 6.[35] Donald Proulx did a similar study on motifs in Nasca Phases 3 and 4;[36] and Elizabeth Wolfe has recently completed an analysis of the Spotted Cat and Horrible Bird motif in Nasca Phases 1 through 5.[37] Other important recent studies of Nasca iconography are those of Zuidema,[38] Eisleb,[39] Ramos and Blasco,[40] and Blasco and Ramos.[41] The latter study is a major new book on the Nasca Style, containing an excellent summary of the chronology and iconography based on collections in the Museo de América in Madrid.

For a modern attempt to understand Nasca iconography, several points should be made. Iconographic themes or motifs change throughout the nine Nasca phases, both in respect to their frequency of appearance as well as in the details of their depiction. Some themes appear only in the earlier phases, such as solid-colored fruits (No. 113), while others, like the "Harvester," appear suddenly in the sequence and last only a short period of time. The depiction of birds, plants and certain animals (Nos. 109, 110, 120 and 122) all but disappears as a primary motif after Phase 5, while such new motifs as female faces (No. 138), head jars (Nos. 128 and 135) and human stick figures make their debut. Each motif can be traced through the sequence, and minute changes in its depiction observed. These changes can be used for chronological purposes as well as for recognizing the identity of a motif that may have become quite abstracted and proliferated through time.

The arrangement of the themes on the vessel surfaces also changes through time. In the earlier Nasca phases, only one frieze is normally depicted on any single vessel. In the later phases, multiple friezes, separated from one another by horizontal bands of paint (No. 126), are common. This change is in part related to the evolution of certain vessel forms into tall jars or vases suitable for this new method of depiction.

There is a general trend in Nasca iconography to move from rather naturalistic and depictive representations (Phases 1 through 4) to abbreviated, geometricized and proliferated motifs (Phases 5 through 7). This Proliferous strain involves the addition of volutes, scrolls, tassels and other appendages to what were once rather straightforward mythical or naturalistic motifs. At the same time, these complex primary motifs are reduced in size and greatly abbreviated; often so much so, that unless one is aware of the earlier prototype, it would be impossible to identify the new representation (compare No. 131 with its later derivative in No. 134). In Phases 8 and 9, the majority of the motifs have become simple geometric elements, carelessly drawn and under heavy influence from the emerging Huari Culture of the highlands. The collapse of the Nasca polity is reflected in the poor quality of the ceramics in these last two phases.

Various specialists have classified the Nasca iconographic motifs in a variety of schemes.[42] In the following sections, I shall discuss my own classification, pointing out the main features of each, some of the changes in form that occur through time, and any interpretation of the meaning of the themes that may be possible.

Fig. 6. Drawing of Anthropomorphic Mythical Being with annotated parts. Nasca Phase 3.

Mythical Creatures

A good portion of Nasca art consists of motifs of a religious or mythical nature. The term "mythical creature" is applied to any anthropomorphic animal or human with special characteristics that suggest it is supernatural. Included in this category are the Anthropomorphic Mythical Being, the Horrible Bird, the Mythical Killer Whale, the Harpy, the Spotted Cat, and the Serpentine Creature. Seler was the first to suggest that these mythical creatures were connected with fertility and vegetation, and a study of the features associated with the seven categories still supports this argument.[43]

Taking a thematic approach to mythical representations, the mythical creatures appear to fall into two categories: those associated with trophy heads (and warfare?) and those associated with plants and vegetation. The distribution is as follows:

Trophy Head Associations	*Plant/Vegetable Associations*
Anthropomorphic Mythical Being	Mythical Spotted Cat
Mythical Killer Whale	Serpentine Creature
Horrible Bird	
Harpy	

Nasca religion incorporated the most powerful creatures of the earth, sea and air: the jaguar (*Panthera onca*), found only in the tropical forests to the east, along with smaller local felines from the coast like the Pampas Cat (*Felis colocolo*); raptorial birds, especially the condor (*Vultur gryphus*); and the Killer Whale (*Orca gladiador Lac.*). Although nothing in the art suggests much importance given to celestial phenomena, such as the sun, moon and star constellations, we must not dismiss the possibility that the Nasca people were well aware of celestial bodies and may have incorporated them into their religion. Ethnohistoric data from the Chimu kingdom of the north coast of Peru indicate the importance of the moon in that people's religion, yet few representations of the moon appear in Chimu art. The huge ground drawings on the pampas of the Nasca drainage suggest at least some familiarity with celestial phenomena. We are, however, still very limited in our ability to interpret these iconographic themes.

THE ANTHROPOMORPHIC MYTHICAL BEING

Judging from its complexity of design and frequency of depiction, the Anthropomorphic Mythical Being was one of the most important religious themes in Nasca art. The term applies to at least five varieties of a semi-human masked creature commonly found on double-spout and bridge bottles, cup bowls and, less frequently, on other-shape categories. The Anthropomorphic Mythical Being has a human body clothed with shirt and breechcloth and is characterized by a distinctive mouth mask and forehead ornament (Fig. 6). Seler called it a "cat demon," arguing that it was primarily an animal form with human characteristics.[44] Others, such as Blasco and Ramos, label it as a "fantastic human" form, emphasizing the human qualities and suggesting that the representation is that of a human with added supernatural elements.[45] An analogy would be a picture of Christ depicted with a halo surrounding his head. Actual gold mouth masks and forehead ornaments found on mummies from the south coast suggest that high-status males, probably priests, were at least partly dressed in the image of these mythical beings.

The most common type of Anthropomorphic Mythical Being is drawn horizontally around the circumference of a vessel, regardless of its shape, with most examples appearing on double-spout bottles (No.131). The body is human in form with legs either pointed

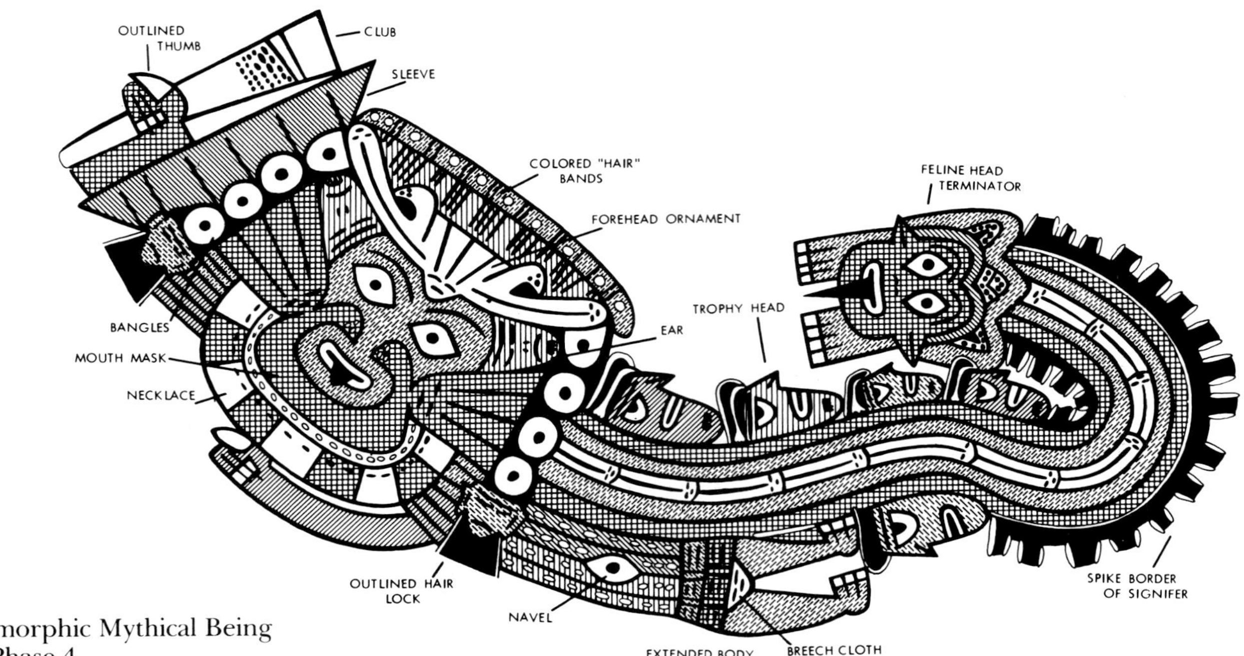

Fig. 7. Drawing of Anthropomorphic Mythical Being with annotated parts. Nasca Phase 4.

Fig. 8. Drawing of Anthropomorphic Being.

down or in an extended position (Fig. 7). On the face are found a mouth mask, forehead ornament, hair bangles and below it a necklace. A club is usually found in one hand and a trophy head in the other. A cloak or "signifer" flows from the back of the creature's head.[46] The signifer is usually spiked along the border, with trophy heads placed between the projections. The terminator or end of the signifer can take many forms. Most often, the terminator is a feline head and paws, but it may be a bird, fish, trophy head, or other form (Fig. 8). The term "signifer" suggests that this particular part of the image may denote the character or identity of the particular variation painted on the vessel, much as St. Michael might be differentiated from St. George by their associated elements in Christian art.

Details of the drawing of Anthropomorphic Mythical Beings change over time. Compare the Phase 3 example in Fig. 6 with its counterpart in Phase 4, shown in Fig. 7. Among the changes that occur are white-outlined hair hanks, multicolored necklaces, outlined thumbs, slit eyes and faces on mouth masks, and forehead ornaments, etc. By Nasca Phase 6, the body has become greatly abbreviated, with much proliferation in the area of the mouth and head (Fig. 9).

A second type of Anthropomorphic Mythical Being, not present in the exhibit, is drawn draped over the top of a double-spout bottle, in what one might call the "standing position" (Fig. 10). The body is drawn in human form. A striped shirt is characteristic of this variation. It has no signifer but often has snakes along the sides of the body and some form of attached elements at the top of the head such as arrows, snakes or fruits. Like the primary form, this variation is also holding a club and trophy head.

A third type of Anthropomorphic Mythical Being is also draped over the top of a double-spout bottle and seems to be an avian version of this creature, since it is always endowed with wings. This creature is always shown clutching a trophy head by the hair in both of its hands, and its protruding tongue is sticking into the trophy head (Fig. 11). Wolfe has dubbed this variety the "Trophy Head Taster."[47]

THE MYTHICAL KILLER WHALE

The "Mythical Killer Whale" personifies the power of the most powerful sea creature known to the ancient Nasca people. The mythical version is depicted with a fishlike body (curvilinear, with dorsal and ventral fins),

Fig. 9. Drawing of Anthropomorphic Mythical Being, Nasca Phase 6 (after Roark).

Fig. 11. Anthropomorphic Mythical Being, "Trophy Head Taster" winged avian version (after Seler).

Fig. 10. Anthropomorphic Mythical Being in "standing position" (after Seler).

Fig. 12. Mythical Killer Whale with single human arm (after Seler).

Fig. 13. Mythical Killer Whale as jawed "Bloody Mouth," Nasca 6 (after Seler).

large-toothed jaws—often with whiskers along the edge and with blood on the jaw—and a single human arm and hand that holds a trophy head and/or knife (Fig. 12). In Phase 6 this motif is reduced to a large-jawed head with blood drawn in the mouth cavity (Fig. 13). Roark refers to this latter type as "Bloody Mouth." A curved appendage is often found below the head on the more naturalistic versions.

Although not as frequently depicted as the Anthropomorphic Mythical Being, the Mythical Killer Whale also had its origin in the Paracas Style and continues throughout Nasca Phases 6 and 7 in the form of "Bloody Mouth." Yacovleff considered the Mythical Killer Whale as the primary deity of the Nasca people, a view that is not accepted by most present-day specialists.[48] A gigantic version of the Mythical Killer Whale is present among the ground drawings on the desert outside Nasca (Fig. 14).

Fig. 14. Desert drawing of Killer Whale, Nasca Valley.

THE HORRIBLE BIRD

The "Horrible Bird" is another anthropomorphized mythical creature, this time in the form of a carrion-eating bird, most likely a condor.[49] Elizabeth Wolfe, who has recently studied the motif, notes that the main char-

Fig. 15. Drawing of "Horrible Bird" eating a trophy head with trophy heads on his body (after Seler).

Fig. 17. "Harpy" with human head and avian body (after Wolfe).

Fig. 16. Drawing of "Horrible Bird" with human legs and falcon eye markings (after Seler).

Fig. 18. Mythical spotted cat, Nasca Phase 2 (after Seler).

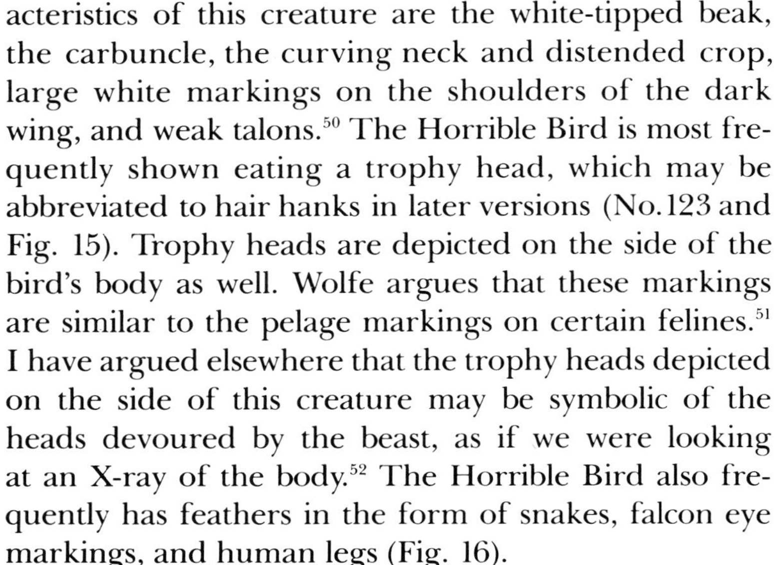

acteristics of this creature are the white-tipped beak, the carbuncle, the curving neck and distended crop, large white markings on the shoulders of the dark wing, and weak talons.[50] The Horrible Bird is most frequently shown eating a trophy head, which may be abbreviated to hair hanks in later versions (No.123 and Fig. 15). Trophy heads are depicted on the side of the bird's body as well. Wolfe argues that these markings are similar to the pelage markings on certain felines.[51] I have argued elsewhere that the trophy heads depicted on the side of this creature may be symbolic of the heads devoured by the beast, as if we were looking at an X-ray of the body.[52] The Horrible Bird also frequently has feathers in the form of snakes, falcon eye markings, and human legs (Fig. 16).

The Horrible Bird appears in the sequence for the first time in Phase 3, probably developing out of more naturalistic versions of the condor from earlier phases. The motif appears on a wide variety of vessel shapes, including double-spout bottles, cup bowls, effigy vessels and collared jars. The Horrible Bird, like most other mythological figures, decreases significantly in frequency after the end of Phase 6.

THE HARPY

The term "Harpy" comes from Greek mythology where it is used to refer to "a loathsome, voracious monster, having a woman's head and trunk and a bird's tail, wings and talons."[53] Lawrence Dawson applied the term to a motif in the Nasca art style having similar characteristics. As the Classical Harpy, Nasca harpies have a human head and avian body (Fig. 17). They are frequently associated with trophy heads, have hawk or falcon eye markings, and are portrayed wearing a headdress of from two to five lobes. On either side of the unmasked face are thick black strands of hair.

Harpies first appear in the sequence during Phase 4 and seem to last only a short time, through Phase 5.[54] They appear mainly on cup bowls, collared jars and tall vases.

THE MYTHICAL SPOTTED CAT

The "Mythical Spotted Cat" can be traced back to its naturalistic prototype in the Paracas Style, where it appears as a naturalistic rendering of the Pampas Cat (*Felis colocolo*) found locally in the valleys of the south coast of Peru.[55] The mythical version of the cat appears in Nasca Phase 2 where it is commonly depicted with mouth mask, pelage markings, ears separated by a "cap," and a thick, upturned tail (Fig. 18). Beginning in Phase 3, fruits are often appended to the body of this creature, and sometimes the protruding tongue is replaced by a plant (Fig. 19).

Earlier scholars identified the Spotted Cat as a river otter, or "gato de agua" as it is known locally.[56] Yacovleff used this identification to support his contention that ancient Nasca religion was oriented toward the sea. However, modern specialists have no doubt

Fig. 19. Mythical spotted cat, Nasca Phase 3 (after Seler).

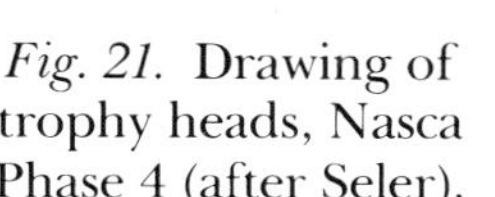

Fig. 21. Drawing of trophy heads, Nasca Phase 4 (after Seler).

Fig. 20. Drawing of cup with trophy heads, Nasca Phase 2-4. (after Seler).

Fig. 22. Drawing of warrior with breech cloth in form of trophy head (after Roark).

that the model for this mythical being was a feline, most likely the Pampas Cat. The Mythical Spotted Cat appears on many vessel forms including the double-spout bottle, the cup bowl and the collared jar.

THE SERPENTINE CREATURE

This type of mythical being is drawn with a feline head attached to a long, snakelike body (Nos. 114 and 115) The head form is quite similar to those found on Mythical Spotted Cats; a mouth mask may or may not be present, and the same is true for a protruding tongue. The band within the body is usually decorated with geometric elements, but plants and other themes have also been noted. The most distinguishing feature of this motif is the scalloped spikes that encircle the body. This creature is closely associated with vegetation, for many examples occur in which fruits are attached to the body.

The origin of the "Serpentine Creature" may be in the signifer of the Anthropomorphic Mythical Being or in the snakelike appendages that flank the second type of Anthropomorphic Mythical Being described above. Because of its unique form, the Mythical Serpentine Creature is drawn primarily on bowls, to take advantage of the long horizontal design space (No.114), but examples occur on other shapes as well (No.115).

Trophy Heads

In addition to their association with certain mythical creatures, trophy heads are an important independent motif in Nasca art. In Phases 2 through 4, trophy heads are usually painted in multiple numbers on the exteriors of bowls, jars and double-spout bottles. Trophy heads are easily identified by the carrying rope attached to the forehead, the pinned lips, closed eyes and/or bodyless form (Fig. 20). The manner in which painted trophy heads are depicted varies from one end of the sequence to the other. Beginning in Phase 4, noses often disappear, and the head becomes more geometricized (Fig. 21). The nose also migrates up and down the face, depending on the phase to which it dates.

Another form of trophy head representation is what is known as a "head jar." These are tall, cylindrical-shaped jars that portray a single trophy head (Nos. 128 and 130). The nose, and often the ears, are modeled, but the remainder of the representation is painted. In some phases, the upper part of the jar above the face is decorated with wide, colored bands. A variant of the head jar is a completely modeled trophy head, some examples of which are known from the later Nasca phases (5 through 7).

In addition to their independent portrayal, trophy heads are frequently used as substitutes for natural objects. The breechcloth of males are often in trophy-head form (Fig. 22), as are the ears of many Anthropomorphic Mythical Beings. Trophy heads are attached to the signifers of Anthropomorphic Mythical Beings, to their hair hanks, and to their shirts. It is a complex theme with a multitude of possible interpretations.

Fig. 23. Drawing of llamas from a Nasca vessel (after Roark).

Fig. 24. Drawing of spiders and other insects from a Nasca ceramic vessel (after Seler).

Fig. 25. Drawing of monkey depicted on Nasca textile (after Seler).

Naturalistic Animal Forms

The world of the ancient Nasca people centered on the ocean, the desert and the narrow oasislike river valleys where the life-sustaining crops were grown. The desert was home to the small fox *(Canis azarae)* that preyed on rodents and birds found in these sandy wastelands (No. 122). A small feline, the Pampas Cat *(Felis colocolo),* also inhabited this zone (No. 105) along with a variety of lizards and snakes. Closer to the river were found frogs and toads (No. 121), and in the thicker vegetation of the valley bottom was a wide variety of birds, ranging from parrots to swifts (Nos. 109 and 110). The llama, a camelid indigenous to the Andes Mountains, had been domesticated for over a thousand years and was then commonly herded in the coastal valleys (Fig. 23). Among the more common insects were spiders and ants (Fig. 24).

The people were also familiar with some animals not found in their local area. The jaguar, a principal component of their religious iconography, was introduced into their artistic repertory at a much earlier time. This theme can be traced back to the Chavín Culture of the Early Horizon, often called Peru's first civilization. Chavín developed its religious iconography partially as a result of contacts with the tropical forest area. Jaguars, caymans and snakes all became part of the Chavín artistic tradition, which eventually spread southward and influenced the Paracas Culture of the south coast—the immediate precursor of Nasca. The presence of jaguar elements in Nasca art, therefore, is simply a continuation of religious iconography coming from Paracas.

Monkeys, also a tropical forest mammal, are commonly depicted in Nasca art (No. 104). This theme, too, can be traced back to the earlier Paracas art style where monkeylike humans are frequently depicted in the iconography of textiles (Fig. 25). The significance of the monkey to the coastal people is not completely understood; perhaps the humanlike qualities of this primate endeared it to the peoples of the south.

The ocean waters off the coast of Peru are some of the best fishing grounds in the world. The Humboldt Current, whose cold Antarctic waters are rich in plankton, is the feeding ground for numerous varieties of fish, mammals and crustaceans. Whales, sea lions, penguins and dolphins abound in its waters. Of this group, interestingly, the Nasca artists portrayed only the killer whale, and usually in its mythological form. It is not known why the other life forms were neglected.

Fish are a common theme in Nasca art, and rightly so, for coastal peoples made ample use of fish for protein. Nasca fishing techniques can be seen on a large sample of effigy pots showing a fisherman straddling an inflated skin that he is using as a boat, along with the nets used to catch the fish (Fig. 26). Numerous varieties of fish are portrayed (Figs. 27 and 28), the smaller ones probably representing anchovies, while the larger may be corvina, bonita or other local types. Interlocking fish appear in the middle Nasca phases (No. 124). Also associated with the sea are various crustaceans; however, the Nasca artists illustrated only a few of these, including snails and chitons.

No animal form is drawn with more detail as to

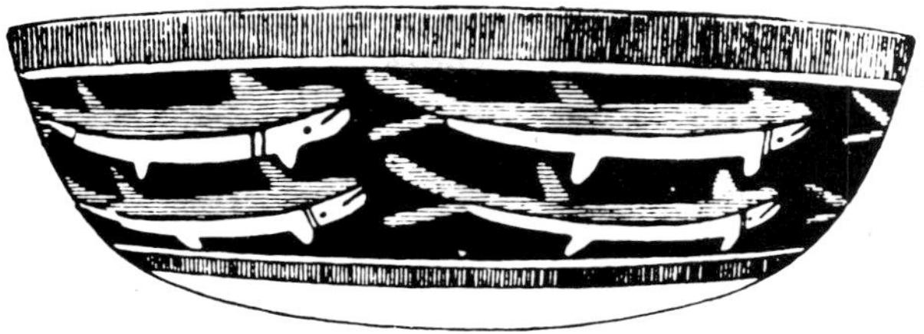

Fig. 27. Drawing of fish on Nasca bowl (after Seler).

Fig. 29. Drawing of hummingbird (after Seler).

Fig. 26. Drawing of fisherman straddling inflated skin used as a boat (after Seler).

Fig. 28. Drawing of double fish from interior of Nasca bowl (after Seler).

Fig. 30. Drawing of swift (after Seler).

Fig. 31. Drawing of egret (after Seler).

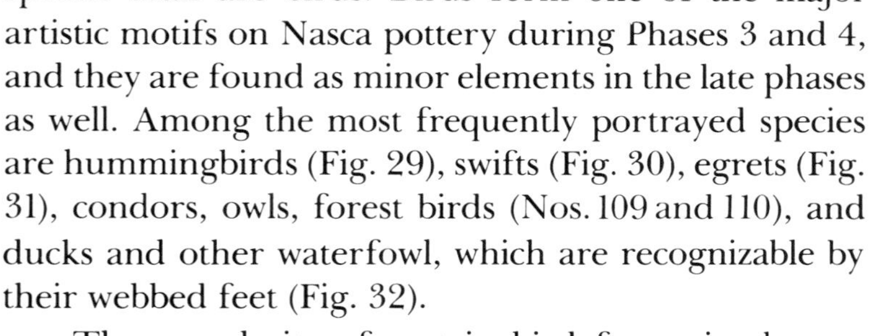

species than are birds. Birds form one of the major artistic motifs on Nasca pottery during Phases 3 and 4, and they are found as minor elements in the late phases as well. Among the most frequently portrayed species are hummingbirds (Fig. 29), swifts (Fig. 30), egrets (Fig. 31), condors, owls, forest birds (Nos. 109 and 110), and ducks and other waterfowl, which are recognizable by their webbed feet (Fig. 32).

The popularity of certain bird forms in the art changes through time. Hummingbirds, for example, are most common in Phase 3, and they are also represented in the giant ground drawings on the desert flanking the Nasca Valley (Fig. 33). The white-collared swift (*vencejo*), also makes an early appearance, but by Phase 5 it has become so stylized as to be almost unrecognizable (No. 126). The parrot is one of the few birds left in the art by Phase 7. At this time the bird is almost always associated with warriors and is depicted perched on a spear thrower (Fig. 34). The significance of this symbolism is not known.

Plants

Nasca civilization was based on a well-developed economy that centered on irrigation agriculture. The major domestic plants of this culture are portrayed in its art, perhaps for purposes of fertility: corn or maize, usually drawn in the form of an ear with tassels protruding from the top (Fig. 35); the aji pepper, major condiment of the Andean region, is depicted either as individual peppers with stripes in the interior (Fig. 36) or in multiple form hanging from its plant; beans of several

Fig. 32. Drawing of water fowl catching a fish (after Seler).

Fig. 34. Drawing of parrot perched on a spear thrower, Nasca Phase 7 (after Seler).

Fig. 33. Desert drawing of hummingbird, Nasca Valley (from M. Reiche).

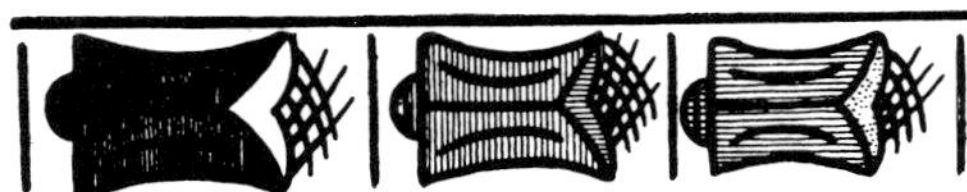

Fig. 35. Drawing of maize (after Seler).

Fig. 36. Drawing of the *aji* pepper (after Seler).

Fig. 37. Drawing of pear shaped tuber *Jiquima* (after Seler).

Fig. 38. Drawing of manioc or yucca (after Roark)

Fig. 39. Drawing of human figure wearing a fox skin headdress (after Wolfe).

types, including the common bean (*Phaseolus vulgaris*), most often depicted in its pod, and the lima bean (*Phaseolus lunatus*), drawn as an individual motif with striped interior (No. 120).

Other native Andean plants such as the Jiquima (*Pachyrrizus tuberosus*) and the Lucuma (*Lucuma bifera*) are commonly depicted in Nasca art. The Jiquima is a pear-shaped tuber that is usually drawn with stripes and attached to a stalk containing seed pods (Fig. 37). The Lucuma is a fruit that is heart shaped; it is drawn in a solid color, with two dots representing seeds or pits.

Another important crop of tropical forest origin is manioc or yucca (*Manihot esculenta*). A fibrous tuber, manioc was usually peeled and boiled by the peoples on the coast of Peru, but in other areas it was shredded and turned into flour. On the pottery, it is drawn as a stalk, with three or more carrotlike tubers attached at the bottom (Fig. 38).

It is interesting to note which plants are not portrayed in the art style. Aside from cactus, which is relatively rare, no trees or bushes are represented. Other principal plants such as gourds or squash do not appear to be represented, nor is the potato, a highland domesticate.

There are a number of unidentified objects, including solid-color geometric forms from early in the sequence (No.113), which may be plants or fruits. From the repertory of plants represented on the pottery, we get a glimpse of which plants were considered most important to the ancient Nasca peoples.

Human Figures

The depiction of human figures in the Nasca art style is one of the most interesting motifs to trace through the sequence. In the earliest phases (1 through 4), painted human figures are extremely rare on the pottery; instead, modeled effigy vessels are the major form of human representation. The most common form is a male portrayed in a seated position with legs drawn or modeled in bent form in front of the body. The head is highly modeled and may or may not be represented with a mouth mask. Usually this figure is wearing a fox-skin headdress, with the features of the animal's head and pelt clearly distinguishable (Fig. 39). In other instances, the figure wears a cap with a projection in front, perhaps a stylized version of the animal skin (Nos. 106 and 107). A single spout protrudes from the back of the head, connected by a handle to the body of the vessel. This figure is often holding fruits or vegetables in its hands and seems to have something to do with agriculture or fertility.

Another clearly effigy-vessel type is the fisherman bottle, which has been mentioned earlier. Here a human has been cleverly drawn on the top portion of a bottle representing an inflated skin used as a boat. Draped over the figure and down the sides of the jar are nets with fish (Fig. 40). A few other miscellaneous modeled human figures also come from this time period. Several examples of a "one-man band," depicting a man playing several musical instruments at the same time, are known. There is some historic confirmation of such musical abilities, and musicians in the Andes today often play a drum and blow a flute at the same time.

Beginning in Phase 5—the transition from the Monumental to the Proliferous strain in the art style—painted humans became common on the pottery. A few

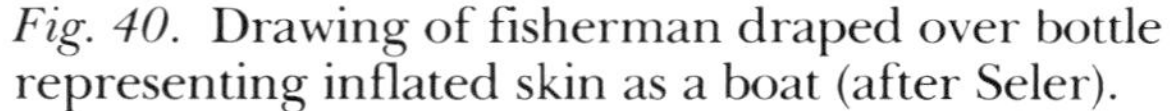

Fig. 40. Drawing of fisherman draped over bottle representing inflated skin as a boat (after Seler).

Fig. 41. Drawing of "woman form bottle" (from Wolfe).

Fig. 42. Drawing of agriculturist in profile holding digging sticks (after Roark)

early examples are known, including one from the present exhibition (No.117), but most begin at this time. Phase 5 witnessed the introduction of an interesting human motif which Roark called the "Harvester."[57] This individual appears rather suddenly in the style and then disappears almost as rapidly at the end of Phase 6. The Harvester is drawn from a frontal perspective and holds stalks with plants in his two outstretched hands (Figs. 22 and 38). A characteristic feature of this figure is a conical hat, possibly made of skins or leather, which is stitched up the front. He is often wearing a trophy-head breechcloth. The Harvester is included in this section on human images rather than with the mythical beings because he lacks the animal characteristics of other mythical beings. Whether this image represents more than merely a farmer with plants is not known at this time.

A form of modeled human head is also found in Phases 4 and 5 in the form of head jars. The trophy-head form of modeled jar has been described elsewhere, but there are also head jars representing living persons. These can be distinguished from the trophy-head jars by the presence of open eyes and the lack of pinned lips and other features associated with the latter (No.129). Some head jars have modeled turban headdresses like those actually found in graves. These turbans are composed of textiles around which has been wound a sling (No. 127).

An innovation found in Phase 5 is the appearance of another effigy form of vessel that Roark calls the "woman-form bottle." Though similar to double-spout and bridge bottles, this variation has a modeled female head in place of one of the spouts (Fig. 41). This head is then connected to the single spout opposite it by a handle or bridge. This bottle form continues through Phase 8, and in this latter phase the bottle portion of the vessel frequently has concave indentations on either side with designs painted within them.

Another Phase 5 novelty is the use of multiple painted and/or partially modeled female faces. These faces are often found in horizontal bands around the periphery of tall vases characteristic of the later phases (Nos. 137, 138). Female faces are distinguishable by the curved hair hanks on either side of the face that tend to frame the face. The eyes are usually more elongated and slant more than those of males. These, along with the sudden appearance of clay female figurines, mark a significant shift in Nasca iconography, reflecting important changes in cultural values and thought. The reason for the sudden popularity of women in the art style is not understood at this time.

In Phases 6 and 7 human forms are very common in Nasca art. Females continue to be represented in the form of multiple faces, the woman-form bottle and figurines. Men are depicted engaged in two major activities: warfare and agriculture. Warrior figures are usually drawn in profile, the figures holding spears, spear throwers and trophy heads in their hands. Often a parrot surmounts the spear thrower (Fig. 34). For the first time in Nasca art, the figures take on the appearance of motion—a trait that perhaps was derived from the indirect influence of the Moche Style of the north coast. However, in contrast to Moche warriors, the Nasca examples exhibit no fancy uniforms, armor, or insignia of rank. They are dressed only in breechcloths.

Agriculturalists also are mostly drawn in profile

Fig. 43. Drawing of multiple friezes of proliferous elements and geometric fillers (from Roark).

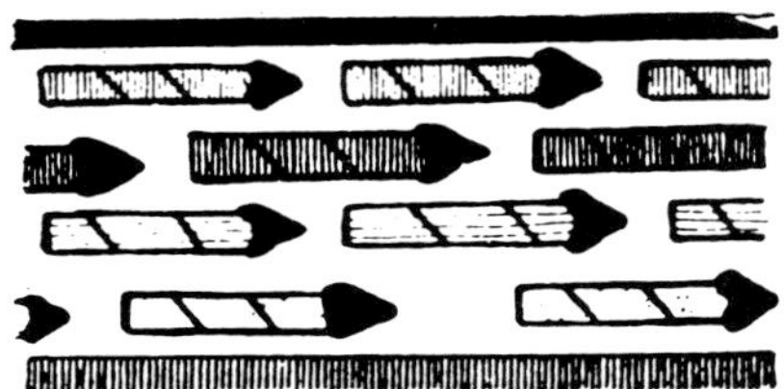

Fig. 44. Drawing of multiple spears, Nasca Phase 5-7 (after Seler 1923, fig. 417).

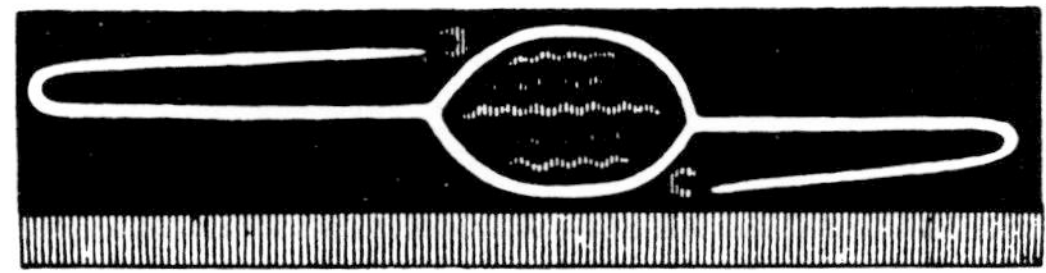

Fig. 45. Drawing of a sling motif, Nasca Phase 5-7 (after Seler 1923, fig. 425).

and holding digging sticks in their hands (Fig. 42). The "Harvester" changes form in Phase 6; he has lost his conical cap and is drawn with jagged staffs that Roark feels are no longer associated with agricultural products.[58] The humans with digging sticks seem to have taken his place. Overall, there is a tendency for human figures to take on a "stick-man" appearance in Phase 7.

Geometric Designs

Geometric designs are present throughout the entire Nasca sequence and represent one of the more conservative elements in the style. In Phases 2 through 4, geometric designs are often the primary motif on a vessel. Large in size, these solid-colored, black-and-red designs are found on bowls and on the lower half of double-spout bottles in the earliest phases (No.113). These motifs can be circular, crescent shaped, in the form of a footprint, or take a multitude of other forms. In some cases, these designs may be stylistic representations of certain fruits or other naturalistic objects; in other cases, they are purely geometric.

Other early geometric motifs include: the step fret (Nos.112 and 126), circles, ovals, diamond shapes with internal hatching, stars, wavy lines (No.119), fish-scale semicircular elements and concentric boxes (No.118)–to name just a few. Roark suggests that in Phase 6, geometric designs become the single most important design element on the pottery, comprising twice the number seen in Phase 5. This shift goes hand in hand with other innovations discussed earlier: the introduction of proliferous elements into the style, the reduction in the size of motifs, the increase in height of vases and other vessel forms, and the use of multiple friezes. This last element—multiple friezes—provided an ideal format for the use of geometric fillers, often in horizontal bands on the pottery (Fig. 43).

In Phases 8 and 9, multicolored chevron designs appear in the style at a time when the style is radically changing due to contacts with highland cultures. Many of the design elements of the last two phases represent the geometrization of mythical beings and other naturalistic forms, while others are purely geometric space fillers.

MISCELLANEOUS OBJECTS

A small category of motifs falls under the rubric of miscellaneous objects. For the most part, these motifs date to Phases 5 through 7. The most frequently represented objects are spears (Fig. 44), which are always drawn in multiples. Another frequently encountered motif is the sling, easily recognizable by its oval central section with attached cords (Fig. 45). Other motifs are tied sacks (of beans?) and panpipes.

Epilogue

Lack of space prevents us from describing the wide range of materials, other than ceramics, on which Nasca art is portrayed. Textiles were an important medium on which much religious iconography was depicted in the Paracas Culture, and this continued into the first phase of the Nasca Culture, when ceramics replaced textiles. Pyroengraved gourds, wood, gold and featherwork are other materials used by the ancient Nasca people to express themselves. Like leafing through the pages of an ancient book, looking at the pottery of the Nasca people offers us a glimpse into their natural world and religious beliefs. But Nasca art is like a picture book without words, and thus we can only dream about what its creators are trying to tell us.

1. Sawyer, 1961
2. Hamy, 1898
3. Wiener, 1880, p. 627
4. Macedo, 1881
5. Hamy, 1882
6. Seler, 1893
7. For a detailed biography of the life and achievements of Max Uhle, see Rowe, 1954
8. Joyce, 1913
9. Gayton and Kroeber, 1927
10. Kroeber, 1956
11. Rowe, 1960
12. Roark, 1965
13. Proulx, 1968, 1970
14. Wolfe, 1981
15. Wegner, MS 1975; MS 1976
16. Roark, 1965, p. 2
17. Roark, 1965, p. 2
18. See Rowe, 1960, p. 42 for a listing of the most relevant dates, and Ravines and Alvarez, 1967, for a detailed description of the specimens tested along with the scientific data.
19. See Proulx, 1968, pp. 96-100 for a lengthier discussion of the evidence
20. Panofsky, 1955, p. 26
21. Panofsky, 1955
22. Panofsky, 1955, p. 30
23. Proulx, 1971
24. Kubler, 1967
25. Donnan, 1978, p. 8
26. Seler, 1923
27. Yacovleff, 1932b
28. Yacovleff, 1931
29. Yacovleff, 1932a
30. Yacovleff, 1933
31. Yacovleff and Herrera, 1934
32. Gayton and Kroeber, 1927
33. Kroeber, 1956
34. Sawyer, 1961
35. Roark, 1965
36. Proulx, 1968
37. Wolfe, 1981
38. Zuidema, 1972
39. Eisleb, 1977
40. Ramos and Blasco, 1977
41. Blasco and Ramos, 1980
42. Seler, 1923
43. Seler, 1923
44. Seler, 1923
45. Blasco and Ramos, 1980
46. Roark, 1965
47. Wolfe, 1981
48. Yacovleff, 1932b
49. So named by Lawrence Dawson
50. Wolfe, 1981, p. 8
51. Wolfe, 1981, p. 14
52. Proulx, 1971, p. 19
53. The American Heritage Dictionary, New College Edition, 1978
54. Wolfe, 1981, p. 15
55. Wolfe, 1981, p. 2
56. Valcarcel, 1932, pp. 16-23; Yacovleff, 1932b
57. Roark, 1965
58. Roark, 1965

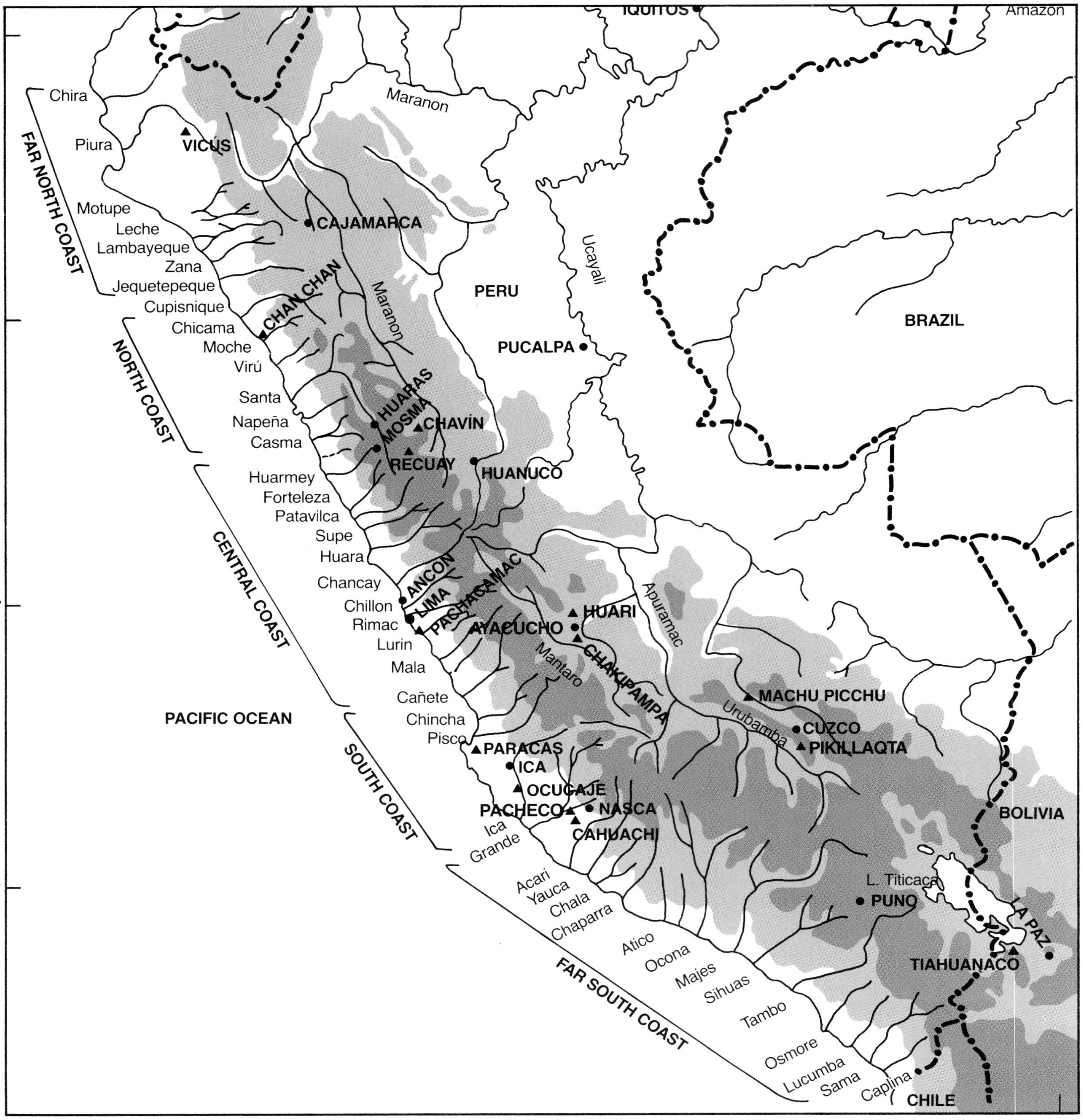

IQUITOS
Amazon
4°
Chira
Piura
VICÚS
FAR NORTH COAST
Maranon
Motupe
Leche
Lambayeque
Zana
Jequetepeque
Cupisnique
Chicama
Moche
Virú
CAJAMARCA
CHAN CHAN
Maranon
PERU
Ucayali
BRAZIL
8°
PUCALPA
NORTH COAST
Santa
Napeña
Casma
HUARAS
MOSMA
CHAVÍN
RECUAY
HUANUCO
Huarmey
Forteleza
Patavilca
Supe
Huara
Chancay
Chillon
Rimac
Lurin
Mala
Cañete
Chincha
Pisco
ANCON
LIMA
PACHACAMAC
CENTRAL COAST
12°
HUARI
AYACUCHO
Apuramac
Mantaro
CHAKIPAMPA
MACHU PICCHU
Urubamba
CUZCO
PIKILLAQTA
PACIFIC OCEAN
SOUTH COAST
PARACAS
ICA
OCUCAJE
PACHECO
NASCA
CAHUACHI
Ica
Grande
BOLIVIA
L. Titicaca
PUNO
LA PAZ
TIAHUANACO
16°
Acari
Yauca
Chala
Chaparra
Atico
Ocona
Majes
Sihuas
Tambo
Osmore
Lucumba
Sama
Caplina
CHILE
FAR SOUTH COAST

Plan of Tiahuanaco.

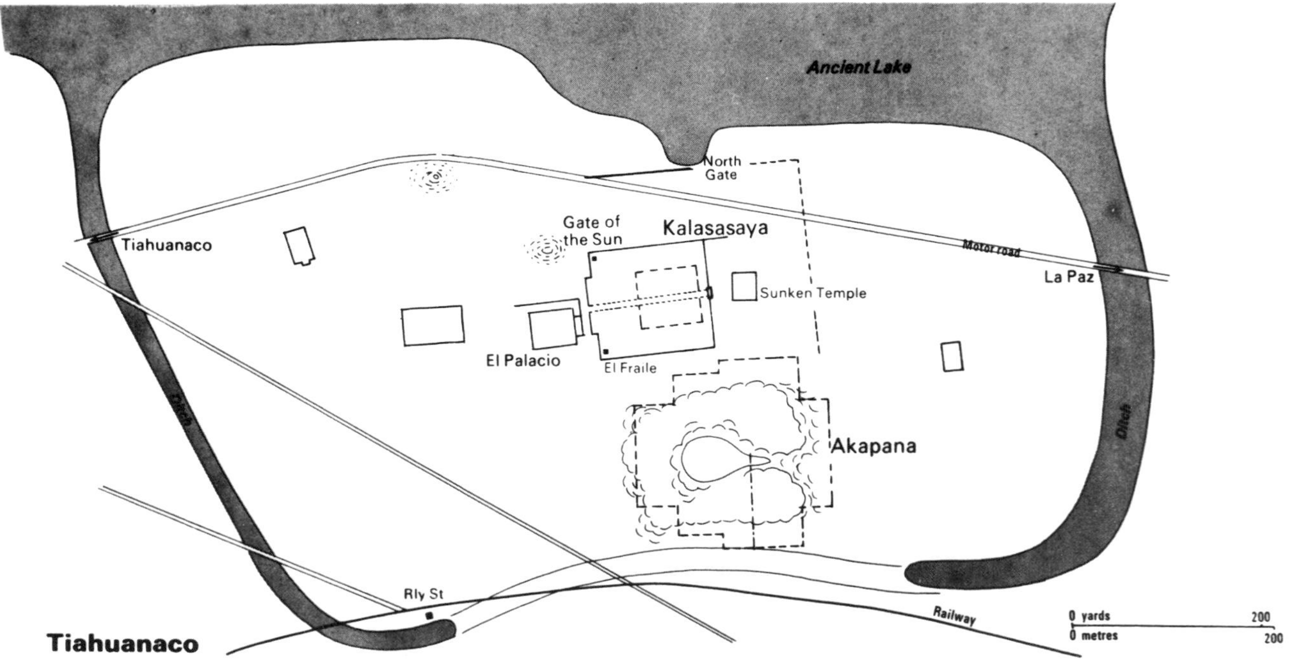

Tiahuanaco and Huari

DONALD A. PROULX

Fig. 1. Drawing of the Gateway God or Staff God at Tiahuanaco (after Alarco).

HIGH ON THE BOLIVIAN ALTIPLANO, outside the city of La Paz, is a spectacular ruin known as Tiahuanaco (see map). The central core of the site, containing ceremonial structures, occupies an area 3600 feet by 2100 feet, but the distribution of the refuse beyond this zone suggests that the site was once a major urban center with a population of between 5,000 and 20,000 people.[1] The major architectural features of the site are a stone-faced pyramid, 650 feet square and 50 feet high, called the Akapana; a large rectangular platform with a sunken internal courtyard called the Kalasasaya; a semisubterranean temple; and another enclosure called El Palacio (see plan).

Tiahuanaco was constructed of finely cut stone blocks in a pattern of large upright monoliths that are separated by wall sections made up of smaller worked stones. Tenon heads form part of the architecture of the semisubterranean temple. Much stone sculpture has been found at the site, including a monolithic portal located in the northwestern corner of the Kalasasaya known as the "Gateway of the Sun." The central figure portrayed on this gateway is a human with staffs, perhaps weapons, in his hands (Fig. 1). This figure, which represents the principal deity or mythical figure in Tiahuanaco art, has been named the "Gateway God." Surrounding the Gateway God are smaller anthropomorphic figures, some with human, others with bird heads. These figures have been named "angels" or "messengers" because of their ancillary role to the central figure (Fig. 1).

The ruins of Tiahuanaco have been known to the outside world since the Spanish Conquest in the 1530's. At a time when all ruins were being attributed to the Incas, the Spanish chronicler Pedro de Cieza de León recognized stylistic differences between the architecture of Tiahuanaco and that of Cuzco, the Inca capital, and suggested Tiahuanaco represented an earlier culture.

Max Uhle, the "father of Peruvian archaeology," had studied Tiahuanaco in the 1890's, and later, while conducting his first stratigraphic excavations at Pachacamac on the Peruvian central coast, discovered pottery with similar stylistic attributes there. He subsequently discovered this Tiahuanaco-like style on the south coast of Peru in the Ica and Nasca valleys, but felt it was different enough from the highland manifestation to be considered a variant style. He called it "Epigonal." His colleague and successor at the University of California at Berkeley, Alfred Kroeber, called the style "Tiahuanacoid." Both scholars believed that Tiahuanaco was the source of these stylistic elements.

In 1931 the Peruvian archaeologist Julio C. Tello investigated the site of Huari near the present-day city of Ayacucho in the upper Mantaro Basin of Peru (Map 1). There he found pottery and stone statues similar in style to those of Tiahuanaco. He also found local pottery styles that reflected strong influences coming from the Nasca Culture of Peru's south coast. Stylistically these local cultures seemed to immediately predate the introduction of Tiahuanaco elements into the Ayacucho area.

Along with the highland and coastal sites previously described, the new discovery of Tiahuanacoid stylistic elements in the Callejón de Huaylas of the northern Peruvian sierra suggested to some that there existed a Tiahuanaco empire, similar to, but predating, the later Inca empire.[2] The widespread distribution of these stylistic elements was considered proof of a military expansion from the Bolivian altiplano into the Peruvian region. Kroeber[3] and Gordon Willey[4] considered Tiahuanaco to be a "horizon style" which spread widely over a short period of time. John Rowe later placed Tiahuanaco in his Middle Horizon, in this case using the term "horizon" to refer to a time period in which cultural unity prevailed, as opposed to a "period" in which regional cultures predominated.[5]

It was not until 1958 that the true complexity of the Middle Horizon styles was realized. Dorothy Menzel is credited with sorting out the various local styles of the Middle Horizon and with recognizing the existence of two separate political entities, the Tiahuanaco empire and the Huari empire.[6] Using an extremely detailed ceramic analysis, Menzel was able to trace the spread of Tiahuanaco iconographic concepts from the Bolivian altiplano into the Peruvian area. In the Ayacucho area of Peru, this religious iconography was first manifested in elite ceremonial pottery associated with the local culture. Only later did these concepts filter down to the common people. These religious ideas seem to have been introduced peacefully into the local culture, not through conquest. The mechanism of the interaction between the Tiahuanaco center and the local culture of Ayacucho is not completely known, but it may have involved pilgrimage.

With the introduction of these religious concepts into the Ayacucho area of Peru, the local cultures underwent a rapid evolution. A huge new site, known as Huari, was established, and from this center a military expansion took place, involving much of the highland area of Peru and the south and central coastal areas as well.

The Tiahuanaco empire, on the other hand, was southern in its distribution. It was centered in the Lake Titicaca Basin but expanded southward through the Bolivian altiplano as far as the Cochabamba region and westerly to the southernmost part of Peru and the Atacama Desert region of Chile (Map 1). Its influence was felt indirectly as far as northwestern Argentina. Thus two major spheres of power emerged during the Middle Horizon: the Huari empire, confined to the Central Andes (Peru) and the Tiahuanacao empire, located in the Southern Andes (Bolivia and Chile). The two shared a common religious tie but were independent political entities.

The Tiahuanaco Style

Wendell Bennett was the first to systematically study the Tiahuanaco ceramic style following his excavations at the site in 1932.[7] He proposed a three-phase sequence: Early Tiahuanaco, Classic Tiahuanaco and Decadent Tiahuanaco based on stratigraphic evidence from his ten test pits. Carlos Ponce Sangines, who carried out extensive excavations at Tiahuanaco in the late 1950's, expanded Bennett's original sequence by adding two phases to the lower end of the sequence. Ponce Sangines numbers his phases Tiahuanaco I through V (Table 1). His sequence carried the roots of the Tiahuanaco pottery tradition back to the Early Horizon where it was influenced by the contemporary Pucara and Chiripa styles of the Lake Titicaca Basin.

Tiahuanaco pottery comes in a variety of standardized shapes. One of the most frequently encountered forms is a flaring rimmed cup called a kero. Other major shapes are hollow-based libation bowls with handles on the sides, flaring-rim bowls, vases, and small flaring-sided bowls. Modeling is common in the Tiahuanaco Style, particularly of animals and animal heads (No. 146), but the primary means of decoration is in the form of polychrome slip paints in up to six

Table 1. Correlation of Dates with the Cultural Sequence from Tiahuanaco.

Periods	*Estimated Dates*	*Bennett's Sequence*	*Ponce's Sequence*	*Ponce Phase Sangines's Names*
Late Horizon				
	A.D. 1476			
Late Intermediate Period				
	AD 900	Decadent	5	
Middle Horizon		Classic	4	Tiwanaku
	AD 540	Early	3	Qalasasaya
Early Intermediate Period			2	Qeya
	370 BC		1	
Early Horizon				
	1300 BC			
Initial Period				
	2050 BC			

Fig. 3. Drawings of pottery depictions of the Gateway God (after Bennett).

Fig. 4. Drawing of geometric motifs and abstracted and geometricized versions of pumas, birds and heads (after Bennett).

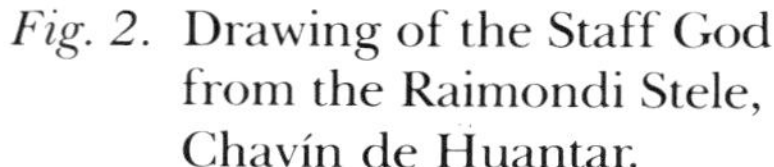

Fig. 2. Drawing of the Staff God from the Raimondi Stele, Chavín de Huantar.

colors per vessel. It is a long tradition of polychrome which has its roots in the Paracas and Nasca styles of the south coast and the Pucara and Chiripa styles of the southern highlands.

Turning to the iconography of the Tiahuanaco Style, the most significant motif in the art is the "Gateway God" or "Staff God" represented on the lintel of the Gateway of the Sun (Fig. 1). In this sculptured rendition, the figure is human in form, has a halo surrounding his head with rays, some of which end in feline heads, tear lines in the form of pumas, and trophy heads appended to his shirt. In his hands this figure holds what appears to be a stylized spear thrower in one and spears in the other. It is quite likely that the Gateway God evolved indirectly out of the Staff God of the Chavín Culture of the Early Horizon, as depicted on the famous Raimondi Stone (Fig. 2). Chavín influenced the south coast and highlands during the Early Horizon, and the motif may have been transmitted to Tiahuanaco via the Pucara and Chiripa styles of the Lake Titicaca Basin. This hypothesis is further strengthened by the depiction of canine teeth on some of the representations of the Gateway God in the Huari Style.

Arthur Posnansky, a Bolivian engineer and amateur archaeologist, claimed that the Gateway of the Sun with its figures represented an elaborate calendar, with the 11 figures on the bottom register plus the central Gateway God representing the 12 months of the year and the angels surrounding it depicting the days of the months.[9] Posnansky manipulated the evidence to support his views, and there appears to be no basis for a calendric interpretation of the portal. There is also no direct evidence, archaeological or ethnohistorical, to link the gateway with the sun. The Gateway God is sometimes given a solar identity because of the halo around its head which suggests to some people the sun with its rays. We cannot at this time support any iconographic identification of the motif except to describe it and its associations.

Full-figure representations of the Gateway God are virtually nonexistent on Tiahuanaco Style pottery; stone sculpture seems to be the major medium on

	PERIODS	*Nasca Drainage*	*Ica Valley*	*South-central Coast*	*Central Coast*	*North Coast*	*Northern Highlands*	*Central Highlands*
	c. AD 900							
MIDDLE HORIZON	Epoch 4	Nasca Epigonal	Ica Epigonal					
	Epoch 3	Soisongo	Pinilla		Huara	Huari Norteño B	? Cajamarca IV	
	Epoch 2B	Atarco B	Ica-Pachacamac		Pachacamac B	Huari Norteño A		
	Epoch 2A	Atarco A			Pachacamac A		Cajamarca III	Viñaque
	Epoch 1B	Robles Moqo Nasca 9		Cerro del Oro	Nievería			Robles Moqo Chakipampa B
	Epoch 1A	Nasca 9	Nasca 9		Lima	Moche V	[Cajamarca II?]	Conchopata Chakipampa A
	c. AD 600							
EARLY INTERMEDIATE PERIOD	Epoch 8	Nasca 8	Nasca 8	Lima (Interlocking)	Lima (Interlocking)			Huarpa
	Epoch 7	Nasca 7	Nasca 7			Moche IV		

Table 2. Chronological Chart with Local Variants of the Huari Style.

which full portrayals of this theme were executed. The pottery does include depictions of the deity's head as well as many of the elements associated with the scene on the Gateway of the Sun: angels, felines, condors and snakes in various combinations (Fig. 3). Modeled libation bowls are frequently decorated with the head of a feline, bird or llama on the rim, protruding from a square-shaped collar (No. 146).

Wendell Bennett claimed that, of the decorated pottery from his excavations at Tiahuanaco, 81 percent was painted with geometric designs. Indeed, there are many geometric motifs present in the art, especially in Phase V or what Bennett called Decadent Tiahuanaco. Many of these geometric elements are in fact abstracted and geometricized versions of the earlier naturalistic pumas, birds and heads (Fig. 4). It is unclear whether Bennett was including these abstractions in the percentages of the truly geometric motifs.

Tiahuanaco art is represented in many mediums: stone, pottery, textiles, metals, featherwork and wood. The pottery medium was somewhat restricted in the range of iconography present, but it does provide us with a tantalizing sample of the major religious concepts. Unlike some of the other styles present in this exhibit, secular elements are rare in the art. It is a somewhat stiff and formal style (to project our ethnocentric bias on it) which served the needs of a conquest state.

The Huari Style

What might be called the "Huari Style" is in reality a heterogeneous grouping of local styles that are linked together by certain elements of religious iconography which can ultimately be traced back to Tiahuanaco. Because of the complexity of these local styles, a complete description will not be attempted here. The reader is referred to Menzel[10] for an in-depth study of the interrelationships of these substyles.

Menzel divides the Middle Horizon into four epochs, dating roughly from AD 600 to 900 (Table 2). During Epoch 1, a new style of ceremonial pottery suddenly appeared in the Ayacucho area at the site of Conchopata. In an offering deposit, huge urns were found that had mythological representations painted on them (Figs. 5 and 6). These were closely related to iconographic representations from Tiahuanaco, particularly the Gateway God represented in the stone sculpture of

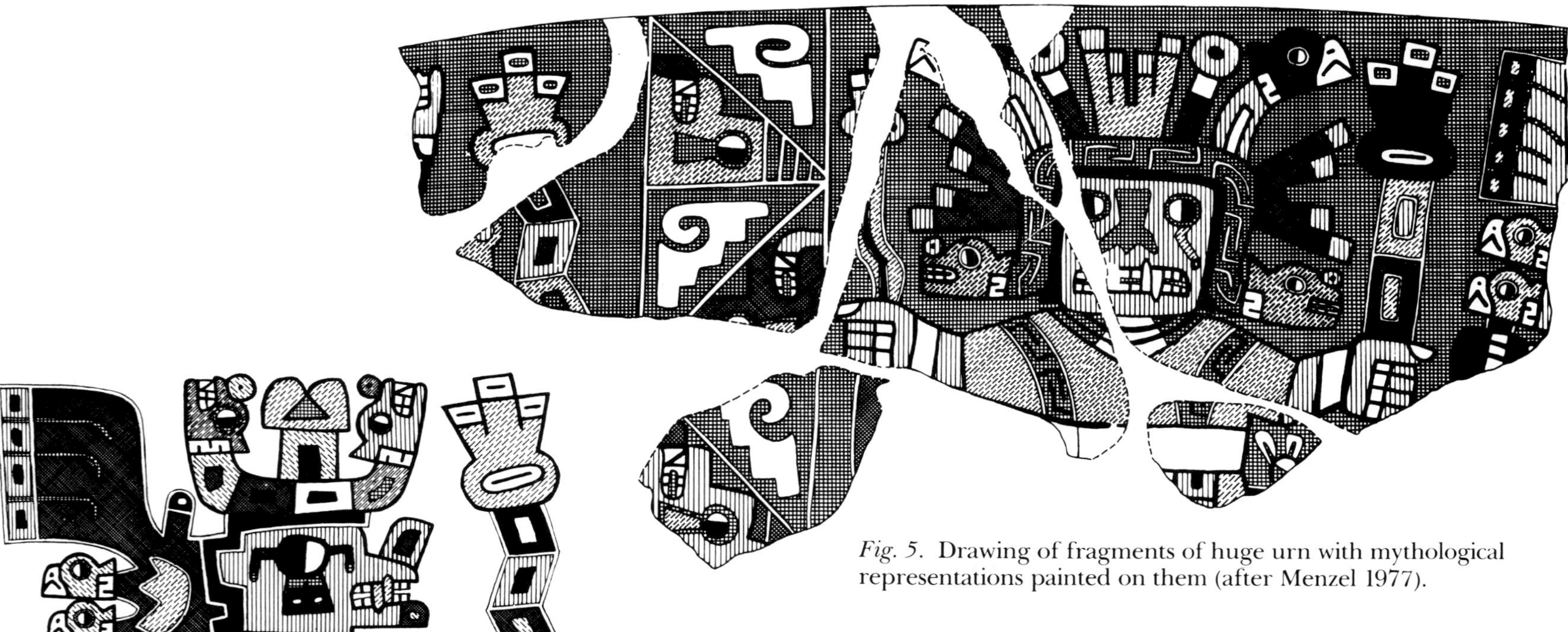

Fig. 5. Drawing of fragments of huge urn with mythological representations painted on them (after Menzel 1977).

Fig. 6. Drawing of feline-headed Angel from urn found at Conchopata (after Menzel).

the monolithic gateway. These urns, painted on the upper one-third, had been ritually smashed as an offering. The iconography on these urns was completely new to the Ayacucho area and had been introduced in a peaceful manner by means of contacts with the Tiahuanaco Culture in Bolivia. A local style of pottery, known as Chakipampa, existed side by side with the new ceremonial style in the Ayacucho area during the first half of Epoch 1.

In the second half of Epoch 1, the new religion percolated down to the masses in the Ayacucho area, with religious motifs now appearing in the local style, Chakipampa. A vigorous new style, Robles Moqo, is also found in the highlands, continuing the tradition of large urns first seen in the Conchopata Style. The new religious cult spread to the south coast for the first time. At Pacheco, in the Nasca Valley, large urns, similar to those from Conchopata, were found, painted with both male and female versions of the Gateway God in the new Robles Moqo Style (Fig. 7). These large urns also have representations of plants depicted on them along with the mythical creatures: maize, ullucu, quinoa, potatoes, añu and tarwi—all highland crops and an

Fig. 7. Exterior and interior of large urn with version of Gateway God, Robles Moqo Style, Pacheco, Nasca Valley. American Museum of Natural History.

Fig. 8. Large modeled llama, Robles Moqo Style, found at Pacheco. Museo Nacional de Antropología y Arqueología, Lima.

indication of the origin of the religious influence. Large modeled llamas are also present with these ceremonial offerings (Fig. 8).

The mythical figures depicted on Robles Moqo pottery (and some of the other substyles) have a number of distinguishing features. The eyes of the figures are commonly split in half with a vertical line, with one-half painted white and the other black. Tear lines, sometimes in the form of a puma or condor, are drawn below the eyes. The Gateway God, as well as his angels, is frequently depicted with crossed canine teeth in this style, and many of the figures depicted are associated with trophy heads, either as appendages to the costumes or held in the hand. Bird feathers, sometimes terminating in puma heads, are part of the makeup of the figures. Staffs held by the Gateway God and his attendants also have puma heads or bird heads at one end. In general, the art style makes use of a combination of bird, feline, snake and human characteristics.

During Epoch 2 the site of Huari was established near Ayacucho, and from this center a military expansion was directed north through the highlands as far as Cajamarca, and down to the coast, extending from Ocoña in the south to the north coast. The existence of this military expansion is evidenced by the presence of warehouses and army barracks at Pikillaqta in the Cuzco Valley and at Viracochapampa in the northern highlands. Huari flourished as the center of this new empire, controlling much of the production and distribution in the southern highlands. Pachacamac on the central coast became a secondary center of the empire, the seat of an important oracle and a place of pilgrimage. The Nasca Valley was also an important political center during this time period.

The important substyles of Epoch 2 were the Viñaque Style of the Ayacucho area, the Atarco Style of the Nasca Valley, and the Pachacamac Style of the central coast. Viñaque pottery shapes include flaring-sided tumblers (keros), a high vase with straight-sided walls, a small cup with lyre-shaped profile, face neck jars and several bowl forms. The most common iconographic representations are a bodyless mythical front-faced head with elaborate headdress, a bodyless profile head and a full-bodied mythical human figure. A modified form of the split-face design, as well as painted representations of skulls, is found. Many geometric designs, including fret bands, are present.

Among the best known of the Huari substyles is the Atarco Style of the south coast. A number of pottery shape categories seem to be derived from the earlier Nasca Style. These include a single-spout or necked bottle, sometimes having a small lug (No. 149). Some of these jars now have a face neck. The double-spout bottle now reappears (having been absent in Nasca Phases 8 and 9). These bottles have long, tapering spouts that flare out toward the sides, a trait that seems to have been influenced by Pachacamac on the central coast (Fig. 9). Single-spout bottles with large strap handles also continue from the Nasca Style.

Double-chambered whistling bottles are a new innovation that also represent influences coming from the north (No. 150). Some urns are also present along with vertical-sided dishes, flasks (sometimes canteen-shaped) and collared jars.

The Atarco Style incorporates a number of mythological themes in its iconography. A bodyless profile "angel" head with feline attributes is common, as is a bodyless front-faced deity head. The full-bodied male

Fig. 9. Double spout bottle missing its bridge handle, Provincial Huari, Atarco Substyle. Robert H. Lowie Museum, Berkeley, California.

Fig. 10. Drawing of running "angel" or "messenger" figures, Provincial Huari, Atarco Sub-style (after Menzel).

Fig. 11. Drawing of mythical animal, Provincial Huari, Atarco Sub-style (after Menzel).

deity is somewhat rarer. The "angel" or "messenger" derived from the flanking figures on the Gateway of the Sun at Tiahuanaco is usually depicted in a running position (Fig. 10). A mythical animal figure is also seen (Fig. 11). Another motif is a double-ended band with a profile feline head at one end and tail feathers at the other. On the secular side, bodyless human heads form one of the themes in this category (No. 149).

The Pachacamac Style of the central coast incorporates many of the same vessel shape categories as were found in the Atarco Style. The most distinctive mythical figure in the style is a griffin with a winged, feline body and an eagle head. A bodyless mythical eagle head is a variant of this figure and is confined to this style (Fig. 9). A double-headed serpentine band with feline heads and trophy heads is also found in Epoch 2. Geometric fillers consisting of "S"-shaped elements, painted circles with dots, sausage-shaped cream-colored bands with black dots, and others are common.

On the north coast Huari expansion met head-on with the Moche Culture, which had now consolidated its territories and had switched its seat of power northward to the Lambayeque River system. The presence of a strong Moche tradition prevented Huari stylistic traits from completely submerging the style in many of the north coast valleys, but in the areas which had been abandoned by the Moche, such as the Nepeña, Santa and Virú valleys, a new local style emerged called Huari Norteño. Along with the introduction of these Huari stylistic traits came a population explosion, suggesting a movement of people as well as ideas into these valleys. It is claimed by some scholars that the Huari empire introduced urbanism to Peru's central and north coasts along with a shift from extended to seated burials.

For reasons not completely understood, the site of Huari collapsed at the end of Epoch 2 and was abandoned. The empire did not fall apart at this time, for the secondary center of Pachacamac continued to exert power and influence, and a new power center was established as well in the Huarmay and Supe areas of the central coast. However, the loss of a strong centralizing political control did affect the overall prestige and power of the empire, and this is reflected in the pottery during Epoch 3.

During Epoch 3, the fancy pottery that characterized the substyles of Atarco, Pachacamac and Viñaque disappeared and was replaced by poorly executed derivatives expressed in a multitude of local styles. One such style was Huari Norteño B. Common vessel forms are face neck jars, interior painted bowls, bowls with press-molded exteriors, various jar forms, and a few examples of double-spout bottles. In place of the fancy polychrome painting of Epoch 2, Huari Norteño B used three main colors: black, white and red. Vessels are decorated with geometric elements such as scallops, circles, parallel lines, "S"-shaped elements and others (Fig. 12). Few mythical scenes occur on the pottery, and those that do are usually derived from the north coast influences and are executed in press molding rather than in traditional Huari painted format (Fig. 13). Another variant, the Huara Style from the central coast valleys of Chancay and Huara are represented by four specimens in the exhibit (Nos. 153, 155-157).

In Epoch 4 the local styles derived from Huari persisted on the central and south coasts of Peru without much change, perhaps due to the power and influence exerted by the oracle at Pachacamac, which may have acted as a unifying element. The pottery that Uhle found in the Ica Valley that he called "Epigonal" dates mainly to this time period. Huari themes are still evident as seen in the example from the exhibit (No. 152). Soon, however, regional cultures emerge in the Late Intermediate Period beginning about AD 900 that eclipse the vestiges of the Huari Style with new styles emanating from these local polities.

Tiahuanaco and Huari art are closely related in content and manner of execution. The styles are rich in religious iconography, which is difficult to interpret unless we resort to highly subjective and speculative judgments. One profitable way to investigate the styles in the future is to apply a thematic approach to the art in order to understand the nature of the disembodied heads and other motifs so frequently seen in the style. Perhaps someday, through a combination of archaeological, ethnohistoric and ethnographic research, we will be better able to understand the true meaning behind the Gateway God and his retinue.

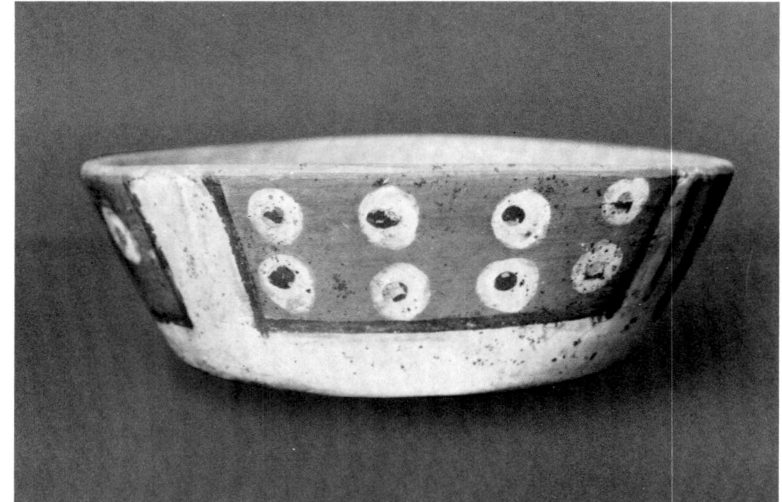

Fig. 12. Bowl with circle design, Huari Norteño B Style.

Fig. 13. Jar with mythical scene, press-molded design, Huari Norteño B Style, Chimú Capac. Robert H. Lowie Museum, Berkeley, California.

1. Hawkes 1974, p. 260
2. Bennett 1934
3. Kroeber 1944
4. Willey 1945
5. Rowe 1962
6. Menzel 1958, 1964
7. Bennett 1934
8. Ponce Sangines 1961
9. Posnansky 1945
10. Menzel 1958, 1964

A note about conservation

For over fifteen years the majority of the Pre-Columbian ceramics in the Arthur M. Sackler Collections was on loan to the Museum of the American Indian, The Heye Foundation, New York. During that time, no systematic cleaning of the vessels was undertaken. Conditions in the storage area in which they were kept included very dry heat in the winter months and very warm temperatures and high humidity during the spring and summer.

Pre-Columbian Peruvian ceramic bodies have been affected by the high salt content in the lowland or coastal soils in which they were buried, causing saltpetre to form. Wares thus affected exhibit bright white crystals that humidify as soon as there is an increase in relative humidity. Depending on the salt concentrations, saltpetre rot untreated will eventually destroy an object. Tensions are created beneath the painted and/or burnished vessel surface. Its surface will ultimately crack and break off just as its body will ultimately break up until it entirely disintegrates.

Consequently, at Dr. Moseley's suggestion, before the Sackler ceramics could be allowed to travel for exhibition, treatment was undertaken to remove all salt or saltpetre that had already formed on them. The treatment consisted in immersing each piece in distilled water for several days or weeks, depending on the vessel's need, and changing the water daily. The saltpetre was evacuated from the clay body by dissolving it in the water. Treatment continued until the water remained soft, or was no longer saline. By applying an electric current to the water, a voltmeter indicated if the current passed, that is, if the water was still saline. If it was, the soaking continued; otherwise, it ended.

During or after their immersion in the distilled water, many of the vessels became externally friable and required consolidating. On some, old and poorly done restorations were revealed and came undone. These had to be taken apart completely and reassembled properly. In the course of some of the re-restoration there was opportunity to do a better job this time around. Occasionally, original painting was revealed under an older layer of restoration, or, in certain instances, the removal of the salt allowed the paint or slip decoration to emerge brighter and truer to its original hues.

In the condition reports included with each catalogue entry, there is a brief description of the extent to which an object had been restored or re-restored as a result of the immersion required and the consequent disintegration of surface or formerly glued joins. Treatment was conducted during a seven-month period, and it is due to the enormous efforts, patience, cooperation and talent of Toby and Robert Stoetzer and their staff that the vessels could be properly treated in time for exhibition.

Thermoluminescence Testing

Whereas most archaeologists make use of Carbon-14 dating for material from excavation sites, for ceramics of mostly unknown provenience a method of relative dating is thermoluminescence (TL) analysis, as described in Donald Proulx's essay. A large number of ceramics in this exhibition (35) have been sampled and tested, some more than once, not only to establish authenticity but to attempt to verify the vessels in a relative chronology. Many of the clay samples tested indicated significant radiation fading and additional testing and sampling were necessary to determine the percentage of fading and its consequent effect on age determination. Because fading of the TL signal takes place continuously during the lifetime of the object and because it can only be measured over a very short time, the only conclusion that could be drawn was that the object must be older than the quoted age, in which case an estimate of minimum age was provided by the laboratory which did the testing.

Catalogue

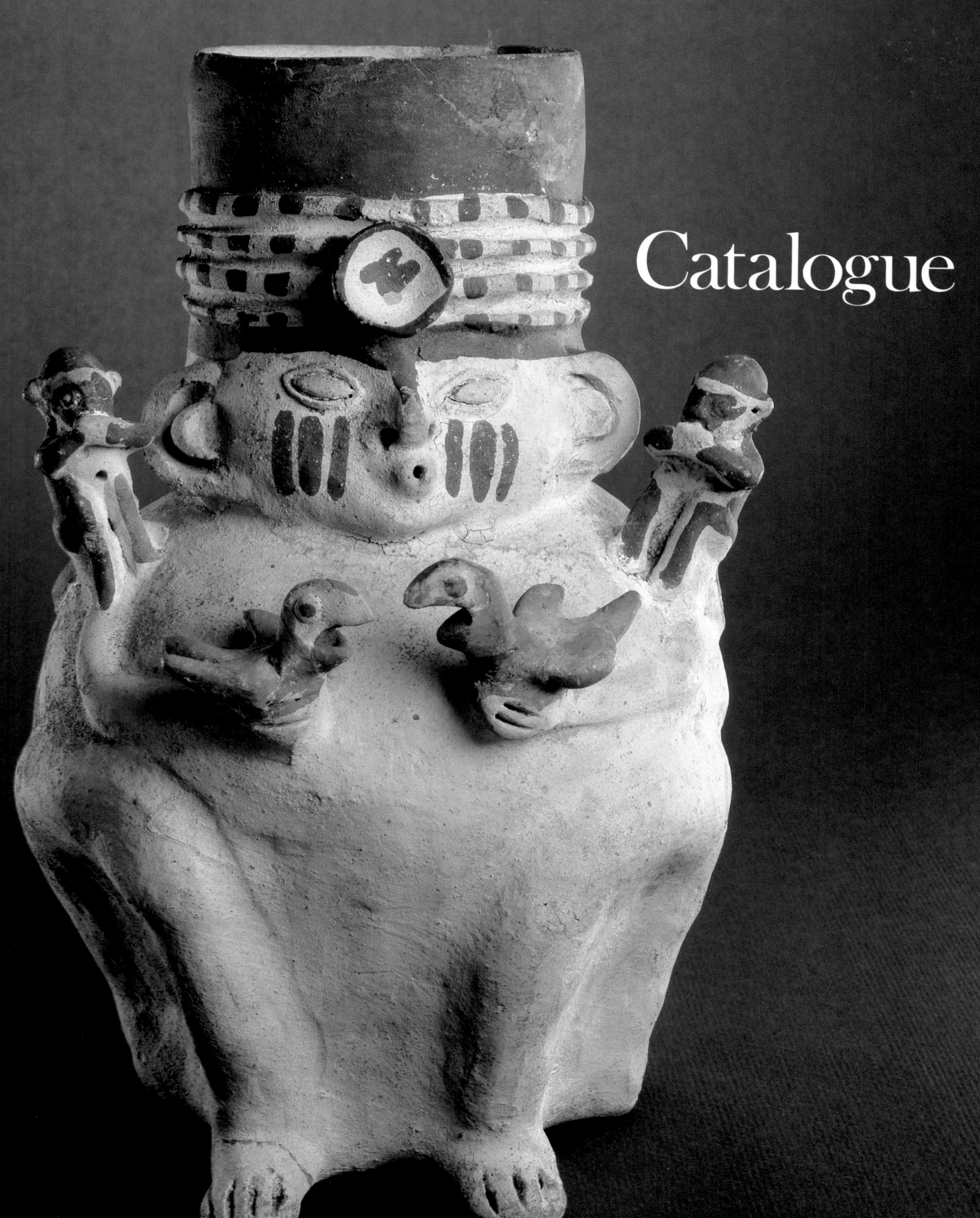

1. BOTTLE with spread-winged rapacious birds

Earthenware, burnished blackware
Late Chavín Period
Peru, North Highlands or North Coast
*400–200 BC**
Height 9½" (24.1 cm)   Width 7³⁄₁₆" (18.3 cm)
Accession no. 82.6.5

In shape, this vessel with finely turned and finished mouth rim, is a composite of two forms, a bottle in the upper section, and a dish shape for the base. The heaviness of its potting and its relief decoration recall Chavín stone carving. Two abstract designs of feline raptorial spread-winged birds in strapwork on the side of the body are repeated in miniature on the neck of the bottle.

cf. Sawyer and Maitland essay, no. 24a and Larco Hoyle 1963, fig. 40 for Chavín vessels with similar designs; see also similar type of head design in Sotheby's London, May 12-13, 1983, lot no. 137.

*Because of its pristine condition and its unusual shape for a Chavín bottle, a thermoluminescence test was done on this vessel by the Daybreak Nuclear and Medical Systems, Inc. Laboratory in Connecticut, sample no. 14a21, 12/21/81. The sample was taken from the neck of the bottle, with the results indicating that it had been last fired between 2640 and 1200 years ago, for a mean age of about 2020 years. Since the sample was taken from the neck of the bottle, there was still a question of the authenticity of the body, especially of the unusual base. Through radiography it was determined that no major repair or restoration had taken place which would explain the strange base, nor had two distinct vessels been joined together to form the unusual shape of this vessel. In fact, the radiography demonstrated that the entire vessel was made at the same time from a clay material consistent from neck to base, showing the same mineral impurities in the form of tiny white specks in the clay body. The latter evidence in itself should have dispelled any doubts there might have existed that this unusual bottle form was made from two distinct vessels, or that the neck from which the original TL sample was taken, might have been part of another vessel. Nevertheless, a second sample for thermoluminescence testing was taken from a point where the base and lower section of the body join, and was sent to the Oxford Research Laboratory for Archaeology and the History of Art (ref. no. 381f53, 4/83), with the results indicating that the vessel was fired between 1850 and 2800 years ago. In any case, there can be no doubt that this vessel was produced in antiquity by a potter living during the Late Chavin Period. *Reports of thermoluminescence tests by the Oxford Laboratory will hereafter be referred to as OX-TL ref. no.*

Fig. 1. X-ray showing similar impurities in the clay throughout the vessel and firing cracks but no repairs.

2. STIRRUP SPOUT BOTTLE with appliquéd serpent

Earthenware, burnished blackware with incised designs on the sides
Late Chavín Period
Peru, North Coast
400–200 BC
Height 7⅝" (19.4 cm)   Diameter 5½" (14 cm)
Condition: repaired spout; tail on serpent a recent replacement
Accession no. 82.6.18

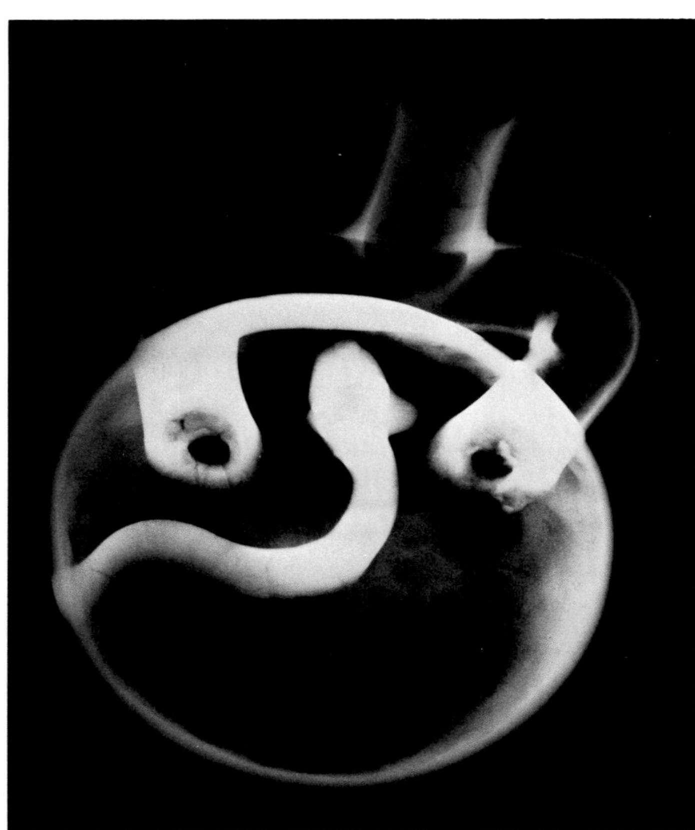

Fig. 1. X-ray of vessel showing later restoration as a darker area of tail of appliquéd snake.

The flat-bottomed, globular body of this stirrup spout vessel is slightly concave on the top. A thin, delicate, and slightly flaring stirrup rises from the lightly swelling curve of the top of the vessel and is surmounted by a spout with concave sides and a thin rim. A serpent, decorated with incised details and having a feline head with interlocked teeth, is appliquéd across the concave top of the bottle and along one side, with its head beneath the stirrup spout. Such different characteristics in one zoomorphic creature is typical of Chavín ornamentation. In fact, incised on the sides of the bottle are creatures which combine bird, serpent and feline motifs. They are almost identical to the designs of a so-called "glyph" panel on a stirrup spout vessel in the collection of Dr. Francis Robiscek, Charlotte, North Carolina. The Robiscek vessel was attributed to the Late Chavín Period, 700-400 BC, and was purported to be from Tembladera in the Jequetepeque Valley.[1] It is of similar body and spout shape to the vessel here, but each side of the stirrup spout emanates from a modeled deer head. The nature of its incised design suggests that it was executed by the same hand that cut the one on the Sackler vessel.[2]

1. See Lapiner 1976, figs. 85 and 86, and Mint Museum, 1970, no. 3-frontispiece. See also Lapiner 1976, no. 103, for a vessel of similar shape and with appliquéd twist across the top under the spout, purported to be from Tembladera, and attributed to the Late Chavín Period; and no. 44 for a feline-headed snake on another vessel purported to be from Tembladera, Jequetepeque Valley, Late Chavín Period, in The Metropolitan Museum of Art, 67.239.17.
2. A thermoluminescence test by the Labor für Fälschungserkennung, Stuttgart (ref. no. 6811021, 10/21/81), from a sample taken from the base of the body indicated a date of ca. 600 BC, with a ±20% error note. While combined zoomorphic characteristics are typical of Chavín ornamentation, Alan Sawyer questioned the authenticity of the appliquéd feline serpent appearing on this bottle. Since examination under ultraviolet failed to reveal evidence of restoration on the serpent body or the vessel body, radiographs were taken to determine if the clay of the serpent's body was different from the rest of the vessel and therefore, in fact, a later addition. From the x-ray (left) it was clear that the snake's tail was different. Additional samples for thermoluminescence testing were therefore taken from the upper part of the serpent's body and from its tail and, at the same time, another sample was taken from the base of the vessel. These samples were sent to the Oxford Research Laboratory for Archaeology and the History of Art. Results of their tests indicated the last firing between 1900 and 3000 years ago for the vessel body (ref. no. 381f53.2, 4/11/83) and between 1800 and 2800 years ago for the upper half of the serpent (ref. no. 381f53.1, 4/11/83). The analysis of the sample taken from the tail of the snake demonstrated that it had been fired less than sixty years ago (ref. no. 381f7-2/83). The snake's tail obviously had been repaired, but the remainder of its body was indeed appliquéd onto the vessel and fired with it in antiquity.

3. STIRRUP SPOUT BOTTLE with eating rodent

Earthenware, grey-brown ware
Late Chavín Period
Peru, North Coast, Upper Lambayeque Valley (?)[1]
400-200 BC
Height 9 1/4" (23.5 cm) Width 4 3/8" (11.1 cm)
Condition: intact
Accession no. 82.5.1

A seated rat-like animal eating with its paws to its mouth is modeled on one side of this stirrup spout bottle. The modeling is largely restricted to the head and front feet: the haunches and hind feet are summarily indicated. In contrast to the burnished heavy stirrup with its turned lip, the body of the animal is stippled, indicating fur. Its eyes, nose and ears are burnished. The surface and stippled area appear to have been painted in a light postfired color.

1. A scored and punctated ceramic blackware seated rat in the Chongoyape Style from the Upper Lambayeque Valley, illustrated both by Alan Sawyer and Alan Lapiner is closely comparable to the vessel here, suggesting that both may have come from the same area (Sawyer 1968, no. 42, and Lapiner 1976, nos. 81 and 82). Sawyer associated the other one with Chongoyape, whose ceramics are characterized by the skillful use of surface texture, and are usually not religious in subject matter. They were tentatively dated Middle Chavín by Sawyer in 1968 because of their close association with Chavín Style gold objects found in the vicinity of Chongoyape. The gold objects are comparable to Highland Chavín stone monuments of the Middle Chavín Period. Lapiner, following Sawyer's earlier designation, also attributed the other bottle with seated rat, which he republished in 1976, to the Middle Chavín Period. In his essay in this catalogue, however, Sawyer has reassessed that earlier attribution and now associates the Chongoyape Style ceramics with Late Chavín. See also a mouse effigy vessel in the Museum of the American Indian, with similar punctate surface and shape of stirrup spout, which was found in association with gold ornaments from Chongoyape, ill. Dockstader 1967, no. 89.

4. BOTTLE with modeled animal head

Earthenware, burnished orangeware
Late Chavín Period
Peru, North Coast
600–400 BC
Height 7 1/8" (18.1 cm) Diameter 5 1/2" (14 cm)
Condition: intact
Accession no. 82.5.4

A bottle, composed of a globular lower body and a long, slightly concave neck topped by a turned rim, has one side protruding outward to form the face of an animal. The modeled nostrils suggest that it represents a grass-eating animal. Its head is defined on the bottle wall by a circular incised line with round button eyes, small tab ears and incised brows.

cf. Kauffman-Doig 1973, p. 230.

5. STIRRUP SPOUT EFFIGY VESSEL in form of a baby animal

Earthenware, red-orangeware with black painted and incised design
Late Chavín Period
Peru, North Coast, Regional Style
700–100 BC
Height 7¾" (19.8 cm) Length 7½" (19 cm) Depth 4¼" (10.7 cm)
Condition: spout has been filed down at top; pock-marked from leaching out of salt
Accession no. 83.6.1

The animal in this effigy vessel seems to be a baby, but the species is not clear. The wide body stands on four stubby block-like legs, and the small head is turned up and partly back on itself. A black painted decoration, possibly indicating the marking of the animal's fur or coloring, is bordered by incised lines. The rounded stirrup emerging from the animal's broad back includes a short spout whose mouth rim has been ground down.

The provenience of this vessel is not known. Its incised and painted designs, however, suggest an association with vessels of similar design and decorative technique which have been attributed to the Late Chavín Period. One in a private New York collection described as having incised "glyph" decorations is attributed to "Tembladera (?), Late Chavín, Cupisnique Style, 700–400 BC." (Fig. 1).[1] Another vessel in the form of a monkey effigy, decorated with the same manner of incised and painted designs or "glyphs," is in the Museo Raphael Larco Herrera and allegedly came from Pacasmayo.[2] Both Tembladera and Pacasmayo are in the Jequetepeque Valley. The majority of Tembladera ceramics have formerly been considered as representing late phases of the coastal Chavín or Cupisnique Style when "the hold of Chavín religion over subject peoples was waning rapidly [and] the highland feline cult themes were largely being abandoned in favor of coastal subjects drawn from nature."[3] In the Sawyer and Maitland essay in this catalogue, however, the term "Cupisnique style" for so-called "coastal Chavín" ceramics has been called into question, and ceramics from coastal areas of the Late Chavín Period are being considered as regional styles of the time. Another monkey bottle illustrated as Figure 23b in the Maitland and Sawyer essay has a similar design technique and is designated "probably post-Chavín."

1. Lapiner 1976, no. 91.
2. Larco Hoyle 1963, fig. 39, p. 36.
3. Sawyer 1975b, no. 1.

Fig. 1 Stirrup spout vessel with incised and painted decoration, Tembladera (?), Jequetepeque Valley, Peru, North Coast.

6. EFFIGY BOTTLE
in the form of a pouncing feline

Earthenware, burnished redware
Salinar
Peru, North Coast
500 BC-300 BC
Height 8"(20.3cm) Length 9" (22.8 cm)
Condition: intact
Accession no. 82.6.7

This effigy bottle in the form of a pouncing feline is made so that the body appears to arch from the front paws to the hind ones. The rounded head has large, lunate, flanged ears and large button eyes with a round incision where they meet the face. The nostrils are hollowed out and the tongue protrudes from the open mouth. Large interlocking fangs are modeled on each side. A curling tail is indicated on the rump. An arched tubular handle stretches from the back of the head to the base of the diagonal, tapered spout which issues from the rump.

cf. Lapiner 1976, nos. 228, 231.

7. DOUBLE WHISTLING BOTTLE with modeled macaw head

Earthenware, cream on burnished redware
Virú
Peru, North Coast
*ca. 300 BC-AD 100**
Height 6" (15.2 cm)   Length 9" (22.9cm)
Condition: intact
Accession no. 82.6.17

A double whistling bottle with the blind spout containing the whistle modeled as a macaw's head. The pouring bottle of this vessel has a long, tapered spout and is connected to the effigy bottle by a tube and arched tubular handle. The well-modeled macaw's head has a long, curving, open beak and protruding button eyes. Feathered areas are painted on both sides of the head and there are holes where the bottle begins to swell. Details of the bird's head are picked out in cream slip paint.

cf. Schmidt 1929, p. 183; Lehmann 1938, nos. 240f, 245ff; Tello 1938, p. 159; Donnan 1978, no. 97.

**OX-TL ref. no. 381e90, 2/28/83 and 5/26/83, estimates that the sample tested has a minimum age of 1160 years according to results of two TL tests, one to analyze fading.*

8. DOUBLE WHISTLING BOTTLE with modeled house and bird

Earthenware, cream on burnished redware
Virú
Peru, North Coast, Vicús, Piura River Valley
300 BC-AD 100
Height 6″ (15 cm)   Length 8½″ (21.6 cm)
Condition: cleaned of salt deposits; original cream slip decoration mostly worn off
Accession no. N-621

This double whistling bottle, with the blind spout containing the whistle, is modeled as a house and a bird. The pouring bottle has a long, tapered spout and is connected to the effigy bottle by a tube and arched tubular handle. House walls form the effigy bottle and have two lunate windows to admit air at the top. The roof is formed by the spread wings of the nesting bird whose long neck is turned backward so that the beak rests on its back.

When acquired, this vessel was purported to have come from "Ayabaca," the site originally named as the source for objects actually excavated, it was subsequently learned, from cemeteries near a hill called Cerro Vicús in upper Piura River Valley in the far north of Peru. The Virú Culture, which appeared on the north coast of Peru at the close of the Chavín period, was displaced in the Chicama and Moche River valleys by the Moche Culture. Pure Virú Style ceramics, however, have been found at Vicús, further north, and exhibit their typical simplified modeling, long-tapering spout and arched tubular handle as on the vessel here. They are tentatively dated to circa 100 BC to AD 100.

9. SPOUTED VESSEL with bird and tubular handle

Earthenware, with cream and red slip
Virú (?)
Peru, North Coast, Virú River Valley (?)
300 BC-AD 100
Height 6 9/16" (16.6 cm) Width 5 1/4" (13.4 cm)
Condition: cleaned of salt deposits and iron stains on slip painted surface; small chips on spout and foot repaired; cracks in body sealed
Accession no. N-276

Alan Sawyer suggests that this vessel is an example of Virú-influenced Moche-stage vessels during the interaction of the Moche and Virú in the Virú River Valley. The bird was a prominent element in Virú art. Attachments, like the bird here with its head turned to its side, were often used in Virú ceramics. On this footed vessel the tubular handle connects the bird to the tapered, outward-splaying spout. The entire vessel is painted in cream slip with red slip over it on either side of the slightly convex top of the vessel body. The manner of forming the vessel foot and the nature of the modeled bird seem to relate it to vessels which Larco Hoyle associates with those of Phase I or II from the Lambayeque Valley.[1]

1. Larco Hoyle n.d.(a), figs. 39-49.

10. EFFIGY BOTTLE in the form of a seated flute player

Earthenware, red slip on kaolin body
Recuay
Peru, North Coast and Highlands, Santa River Valley
*AD 100-700**
Height 5⅝" (14.3 cm)   Width 3⅝" (9.2 cm)
Condition: intact
Accession no. 82.6.23

This globular bottle has a slightly flaring spout. Superimposed on it is a sketchily modeled seated figure with a freestanding head. The figure wears a hat with a lunate crest and large ear ornaments. Details of clothing, the hat and the face are painted in red slip on the naturally white kaolin body. The figure holds a *quena,* a type of flute, to his mouth, which forms a spout for pouring out the liquid in the vessel. This type of vessel, called a *pacha,* is used for ritual libations.

cf. Lumbreras 1974, no. 125; Walker 1971, no. 21.

**Results of thermoluminescence analysis at the Berlin Museum in 1981 while in a former collection indicated that the vessel was originally fired 1500 years ago. A second analysis was done at the Oxford Research Laboratory for Archaeology and The History of Art from a sample taken from a site adjacent to the former drilling on the base (ref. no. 381f3, 2/28/83). The result of the second analysis indicates that the vessel was last fired between 940 and 1420 years ago, or between the sixth and eleventh centuries.*

11. EFFIGY BOTTLE in the form of a man carrying a bottle

Earthenware, red, white and black slip on brown slip ground
Recuay
Peru, North Coast and Highlands, Santa River Valley
*AD 100-700**
Height 8 3/16" (20.8 cm)   Diameter 7 3/4" (19.7 cm)
Condition: mouth has been broken and repaired
Accession no. 82.6.25

The bottle is ovoid with a short, narrow neck and a wide, cup-shaped flaring mouth. Appliquéd just below the mouth rim is a human head and two strap arms raised so that the fingers grasp a tump strap on the forehead. The rest of the body and garment are painted in red, white and brilliant black over a brown slip ground. The expanding tump strap circles the bottle to give the impression that the bottle itself is on the figure's back. At the bottom of the garment is an "S" figure with reed circles within the loops.

cf. the decoration on the back of Number 17; see also Lumbreras 1974, nos. 124-127; and Larco Hoyle n.d.(b).

**OX-TL ref. no. 381e99.2/28/83, estimates that the sample tested from this vessel was last fired between 1600 and 2450 years ago.*

12. CEREMONIAL DIPPER

Earthenware, cream and black on orangeware
Recuay
Peru, North Coast and Highlands, Santa River Valley
AD 100-700
Height 3¾" (9.5 cm) Length 12¾" (32.4 cm)
Diameter of Chamber 9½" (24 cm)
Condition: some paint has rubbed off
Accession no. 82.7.1

An oblate, neckless chamber with a large horn-shaped handle extends horizontally from the middle of one side of the dipper. Its precise function is not known although this form is sometimes referred to as a "corn popper." The type is also found during the Moche III and V periods. The painting here is unusually fine with one-half slip painted in cream over the orange clay body. The solid zones and belt of the Greek key, step-fret and sun-symbol designs are in a brilliant black paint over the cream slip.

13. STIRRUP SPOUT BOTTLE in the form of a seated warrior

Earthenware, brownware
Negative Vicús
Peru, North Coast, Vicús, Piura River Valley
400-100 BC (?)
Height 7¾" (19.5 cm) Diameter 4½" (11.5 cm)
Condition: small chip on lip of spout and chip on left ear plug have been repaired; manganese oxide deposits from burial appear on the surface; remaining cream slip, visible after soaking, has been strengthened on hat and shoulders
Accession no. N-202

This stirrup spout bottle is modeled in the form of an alert, seated warrior wearing a conical helmet. His face is well-defined with a strong nose, jutting chin, and large ears containing tubular ear ornaments through the lobes. His hands rest on his chest and his fingers are separated by punctates. The small doughnut-shaped stirrup is attached to his back and the spout is turned at the top as are early Moche I and II spouts. The vessel is purported to have come from the cemeteries near Cerro Vicús in the Piura River Valley.

cf. Larco Hoyle n.d.(a), p. 92 and 95,for line drawings of similarly shaped vessels excavated at Vicús; 1965a, no. 5 for a similar kneeling figure but with hands tied behind his back; and 1966, no. 117.

14. BOTTLE in the form of a kneeling prisoner

Earthenware, brownware with black resist paint
Negative Vicús
Peru, North Coast, Vicús, Piura Valley
AD 300-700
Height 8¼" (21 cm) Diameter 4½" (11.5 cm)
Condition: the faint outline of the resist black design, which appeared more clearly after soaking, has been strengthened in restoration
Accession no. N-200

The bottle is modeled in the form of a kneeling prisoner with his arms tied in front of him. The modeled head forms a blind spout containing a whistle. Ears and nose are modeled and the diamond-shaped eyes and mouth are incised. A rounded cap juts out over the brow line. The short spout issues at an angle from the back and is attached to the back of the neck by a bridge handle. Traces of fugitive black resist paint are found on the cap and body.

This vessel, along with others in the collection, purportedly came from "Ayabaca," the site originally named as the source for the Negative Vicús ware when it was excavated in 1961. Subsequently it was learned that the actual site from which such wares derived was the cemetery near Cerro Vicús in the Piura River Valley.

cf. Disselhoff 1971, no. 38; Walker 1971, no. 36.

15. STIRRUP SPOUT BOTTLE in the form of an anthropomorphic warrior

Earthenware, brownware with traces of black resist paint
Negative Vicús
Peru, North Coast, Vicús, Piura River Valley
AD 300-700
Height 10½" (26 cm)   Width 5" (12.7 cm)
Condition: stirrup spout has been broken and repaired; after soaking in distilled water traces of resist black painted design became more obvious and were strengthened in restoration.
Accession no. N-275

This bottle is in the form of an anthropomorphic warrior kneeling on a hollow square platform. The figure is squat and, probably resulting from the way in which the breech clout falls from the figure's waist as he kneels, in profile his lower back resembles the tail of a bird. The warrior holds a shield in his left hand. His ears and nose are modeled and his mouth and eyes are incised. A rounded cap juts over his brows. A small, heavy stirrup joins the top of the cap with the figure's back. There are remnants of black resist decoration on the figure and base. This vessel was also alleged to have been excavated at "Ayabaca" before the identity of the excavation site was recognized as Cerro Vicús in the Piura River Valley.

cf. Larco Hoyle 1965a, fig. 4, for similar face and negative design, and figs. 6 and 7 for examples of similar stirrup spouts.

16. FIGURAL BOTTLE in the form of a predator's head

Earthenware, brownware with cream slip and black resist paint
Negative Vicús
Peru, North Coast
AD 300-700
Height 7" (17.4 cm)   Length 9" (22.9 cm)
Condition: the cream slip design around the sides of the vessel was revealed more clearly after soaking and was strengthened in restoration
Accession no. N-620

This elongated sausage-shaped bottle is modeled in the form of a predator's head. The short spout which issues from the top of the head between the button eyes has a handle attached to the muzzle. The long, incised jaws are open to show a row of teeth. There are traces of black resist paint and a streak of cream slip from below the ear to the nose and around the teeth. The clay body shows some fire clouding. Like previous numbers, this vessel is believed to have come from the cemeteries at Cerro Vicús in the Piura River Valley.

cf. Larco Hoyle, n.d.(a), p. 103, for a line drawing of a similarly shaped predator's head, but with a stirrup spout handle rather than the short spout and handle seen here.

17. EFFIGY HEAD BOTTLE

Earthenware, black resist on tanware body with cream and red slip paint
Negative Vicús
Peru, North Coast, Vicús, Piura River Valley
AD 300-700
Height 6" (15.2 cm)   Width 6⅛" (15.9 cm)
Condition: intact
Accession no. 83.3.1

The bottle is modeled in the form of a man's head whose eyes are incised ovals above a small appliqué nose. His mouth is a wide rectangle with a double row of incised teeth. Buttons or plugs are incised and covered in cream slip in the "B"-shaped ear ornaments. The face is banded, mask-like, to indicate face painting, in resist black, with one band covering the cheeks and the other across the eyes and over the nose. A fringed band of double undulating lines in red slip covers the head below the spout. A strap handle loops from the spout at the back.

cf. a larger version in the Museum of the American Indian, The Heye Foundation, New York, Accession no. 24/3526 also Disselhoff 1971, pl. 44B.

18. CUP in the form of a human head

Earthenware, black resist and cream slip decoration
Negative Vicús (?) or North Coast Virú
Peru, North Coast
ca. AD 300–AD 700
Height 5" (13 cm) Width 5¼" (13.3 cm) Depth 4¾" (12 cm)
Condition: cleaned of salt deposits; back of head, base, restored cracks on rim
Accession no. N-3

The face of this footed cup modeled in the form of a human head is spade shaped with a prominent chin, modeled tab ears, and sharply ridged nose; eyes are indicated by slight raised edges around a sunken oval, and the mouth is a deeply incised curving line. Hair is represented on both the front, above the face, and back, by black resist lines on the cream slip of the vessel. An elegant band of cream and black horizontal figure-8's containing reed circles decorates the back of the neck, perhaps to represent a scarf or body paint. Like Numbers 13, 14, 15 and 16, this vessel, when acquired, was said to have come from "Ayabaca," or what is now known to have been the cemeteries at Cerro Vicús in the Piura River Valley. Alan Sawyer, however, has suggested a North Coast Virú attribution rather than Vicús. Yet the closest parallels can be found in the shapes of faces on Recuay vessels.[1]

1. see Schmidt 1929, p. 238 and Lapiner 1976, nos. 409-442.

19. INCENSE BURNER in the form of a human head

Earthenware, brownware body with cream slip and black resist paint
Negative Vicús ware
Peru, North Coast, Vicús, Piura River Valley
ca. AD 300–700
Height 5 1/2" (14 cm) Width 5 1/2" (14 cm)
Condition: has been broken and repaired; cleaned of salt deposits; traces of black resist and cream slip have been strengthened
Accession no. N-211

This open-bottom incense burner is in the form of a human head with a charming "jack-o'-lantern" face. Its slightly spreading cone shape is topped with an everted dish-shaped flange which becomes a hat for the face. The ears are rectangular flanges and the hooked nose is modeled. The mouth and eyes are cut through to the interior in the shape of crosses and the top of the vessel inside the cap is perforated. Ear flanges, face and the back of the head are decorated with streaks of cream slip and the remains of negative black.

cf. Larco Hoyle n.d.(a) frontispiece.

20. EFFIGY STIRRUP SPOUT BOTTLE in the form of a supernatural figure

Earthenware, red on cream slip
Moche I
Peru, North Coast
*300-100 BC**
Height 8½" (21.5 cm)   Width 5¼" (13.3 cm)
Condition: intact, some flaking of surface paint
Accession no. 82.6.22

This effigy bottle is modeled in the form of a seated supernatural figure, whose head is animal-like and has flaring nostrils, wide-open mouth, large fangs and protruding tongue. Stylized angular curls rise from the top of the head and muzzle. The figure is seated with its hands on its knees and wears a wide, segmented collar and bracelets. The entire bottle is slip painted in cream with details of the head, collar and bracelets accented in red.

Moche art represents a variety of supernatural figures who can be recognized by their physical appearance like the figure here, or by garments and/or activities. In the absence of any historical documentation however, it is very difficult to reconstruct the supernatural realm of the Moche or the importance of the figures in it. A similar figure published by Alan Lapiner has a slightly more detailed headdress with what appears to be two stepped thrones on either side of it.[1] The latter sits in the same pose and is similarly ornamented with necklace and bracelets. That vessel, which is in the Domingo Seminario Collection, Lima, purportedly comes from Cerro Vicús, in the Piura Valley. Another almost identical figure is published by Donnan, differing from the Seminario piece in that it has only one stepped throne on either side of the headdress.[2] Lapiner describes the Seminario vessel as one with a seated figure wearing a feline helmet. This may be the case for all three vessels, that is, each figure is wearing a large feline helmet or mask. Another vessel illustrated by Donnan shows a supernatural figure with such a feline head or head mask decapitating a human. The head on it is more naturalistically feline but down the center of the snout are two sets of stepped thrones.

1. Lapiner 1976, no. 252.
2. Donnan 1978, no. 149.
3. *Ibid.*, no. 151.

**OX-TL ref. no. 381e79, 1/31/83, estimates that the sample tested was last fired between 1200 and 1850 years ago.*

21. EFFIGY STIRRUP SPOUT VESSEL in the form of a frog

Earthenware, brownish-cream ceramic, burnished
Moche I
Peru, North Coast, Vicús, Piura Valley
ca. 300-100 BC
Height 6¼" (15.9 cm)   Width 4⅝" (11.8 cm)
Condition: has been cleaned of salt deposits and repaired on body
Accession no. N-77

The degree of realism in Moche iconography is apparent in this frog effigy with stirrup spout. Its general form with bulging eyes and slit mouth has appeared often in Moche ceramics. Frogs in Moche I form have been found in Cerro Vicús, Piura Valley as well as in the centers of Moche Culture in the Chicama and Moche River valleys and other areas south of Vicús. The frog here, however, is purported to have come from "Ayabaca," i.e., the Vicús cemeteries in the Piura River Valley.

cf. Larco Hoyle 1965a, fig. 31, for another Vicús frog with Moche I type spout, and Donnan 1978, no. 81, for a Moche I frog almost identical to the one here.

22. EFFIGY STIRRUP SPOUT BOTTLE in the form of a llama with burden

Earthenware, brownware
Moche I
Peru, North Coast
*300-100 BC**
Height 6½" (16.5 cm)   Width 3⅞" (9.8 cm)
Condition: the bars of the pack bags have been broken and the miniature vessels inside have been lost
Accession no. 82.6.9

This stirrup spout bottle is modeled in the form of a standing llama carrying matched pack bags slung over its back. Its head is strongly modeled with deep-set eyes, flaring nostrils and laid-back ears. There is an incised symbol on the forehead. The braided tether is attached through a hole in the right ear and lies over the animal's back. The sides of the containers are incised to suggest basketry patterning with the interior divided by bars across the opening. An identical effigy vessel, but larger in size, although of the same body clay and decoration, is in the Museum of the American Indian. This larger vessel still retains the miniature bottles or round-bodied jars that fitted inside the middle section of each pack bag, the dividing bars in the bag serving to hold the bottles in the packs.

cf. Donnan 1978, no. 176, for the llama from the Museum of the American Indian, and no. 178, for a reclining llama vessel with the llama's ear notched and the llama carrying similar woolen pack bags with ceramic vessels inside them. The three llamas, including the one here, are similar enough to have come from one workshop.

**OX-TL ref. no. 381f6, 2/28/83 and 5/26/83, estimates that the sample tested has a minimum age of 1200 years according to results of two TL tests, one to analyze fading.*

23. EFFIGY STIRRUP SPOUT BOTTLE in the form of a seated man

Earthenware, burnished redware
Moche I
Peru, North Coast
*300-100 BC**
Height 8" (20.3 cm)   Width 5" (12.7 cm)
Condition: intact
Accession no. 82.6.20

This effigy bottle is modeled in the form of a seated man clasping his knees. His heavily lined face, chest and back suggest great age. Hair is represented by five striations on his head. The deep-set almond eyes may once have been inlaid with pigment or shell. The ears are large and convoluted and the fingers and toes are separated by deep incisions. Two very similar faces appear on figures from two vessels, one in a private collection and one in the Linden Museum, Stuttgart, but the faces are fanged and more deeply wrinkled and the body is more completely modeled than in the figure here.[1] The fanged figure in the private collection is purported to have come from Vicús, Piura Valley.

1. see Lapiner 1976, no. 247, and Donnan 1978, no. 155.
**OX-TL ref. no. 381e78, 1/31/83, estimates that the sample tested was last fired between 1350 and 2050 years ago.*

24. EFFIGY STIRRUP SPOUT BOTTLE in the form of a seated woman

Earthenware, white and dull and bright red on burnished redware
Moche I
Peru, North Coast
*300–100 BC**
Height 7¼" (18.4 cm)   Width 5 1/16" (12.8 cm)
Condition: intact
Accession no. 82.6.21

This effigy stirrup spout bottle is modeled in the form of a seated woman whose long dress covers her from neck to feet. Her hands rest on her knees which are pulled up under her dress. Her deep-set almond-shaped eyes are heavy-lidded and have curved brows which meet the bridge of her nose. She has square-cut, striated hair which falls down her back and she wears a heavy zoned collar and bracelets, both painted in alternating panels of white and dark red. Her hands, arms and face are painted red and her fingernails and eyes are painted white. The bottom of the vessel is fully modeled and shows the drawn-up legs, feet and genitals.

cf. Donnan 1978, no. 37.

**OX-TL ref. no. 381f1-5/26/83, estimates that the sample tested has a minimum age of 1120 years according to results of two TL tests, one to analyze fading.*

25. EFFIGY STIRRUP SPOUT BOTTLE in the form of a man chewing coca

Earthenware, cream on burnished redware
Moche I
Peru, North Coast
*300-100 BC**
Height 7 1/8" (18.1 cm) Width 5 1/4" (13.3 cm) Depth 6 3/16" (15.7 cm)
Condition: intact
Accession no. 82.6.13

An effigy stirrup spout bottle modeled in the form of a man. The figure is seated cross-legged with his arms out of his tunic and his hands resting on his knees. His expressive face has deep-set, almond-shaped, white eyes and large ears pierced along the edge. His hair is striated and his colorful tunic has red and white bands with "S" designs on the flapping sleeves. He carries a coca pouch on his back with the braided cord around his neck, and his cheek is distended by a large chew of coca leaves.

Individuals chewing coca leaves frequently appear in Moche art. A handful of dry coca leaves was chewed until they formed a quid. The quid was kept in the cheek and lime was added as the chewing continued. Lime served as a catalyst to free the cocaine from the leaves. The figure here has the quid of coca leaves in his mouth, as evidenced by the bulge in his cheek.[1]

cf. Lehmann 1938, no. 435; Sawyer 1966, no. 23; Donnan 1978, no. 181; Bird et al. 1981, p. 37.

1. For a description of the method and paraphernalia, see Donnan 1978, p. 117.

**OX-TL ref. no. 381e92, 2/28/83 and 5/26/83, estimates that the sample tested has a minimum age of 980 years according to results of two TL tests, one to analyze fading.*

26. EFFIGY STIRRUP SPOUT BOTTLE in form of a monkey with mortar and pestle

Earthenware, burnished redware
Moche I
Peru, North Coast
*300-100 BC**
Height 7 5/8" (19.3 cm) Width 3 7/8" (9.8 cm)
Condition: possible repair to the pestle and right arm
Accession no. 82.6.10

This effigy stirrup spout bottle is modeled in the form of a seated anthropomorphic monkey who holds a mortar between his feet and a pestle with both hands. His round face has large, almond-shaped eyes, a splayed nose, an open mouth with double feline teeth and large, convoluted ears. His long tail curls up on his foot and there is an incised belt around his waist.

cf. Lapiner 1976, no. 239 and no. 242, for Salinar monkey vessels represented with the conventionalized mouth and teeth of a feline.

**OX-TL ref. no. 381e91, 2/28/83 and 5/26/83, estimates that the sample tested has a minimum age of 1490 years according to results of two TL tests, one to analyze fading.*

Fig. 1. Form of the vessel when acquired (left), and during dismantling of the earlier restoration.

27. JAR OR CUP in the form of a portrait head

Earthenware, dark grey, reduction fired body, burnished
Vicús Moche or Early Moche I or II
Peru, North Coast, Vicús, Piura River Valley
*ca. 300 BC–AD 600**
Height 8½" (21 cm) Width 5" (12.8 cm) Depth 5¼" (13.4 cm)
Accession no. N-205

This head jar is said to have come from "Ayabaca," or what is now recognized to be Cerro Vicús in the Piura Valley. When originally acquired it had a closed cranium and a tubular spout and handle. But when recently selected for exhibition, it was obvious that the top of the vessel was heavily restored. Black paint from an earlier restoration began to chip off around the band above the forehead, leading some to believe the piece was a fake. Alan Sawyer, however, suggested that originally it might in fact have been designed with an open cranium, somewhat like the vessels in Number 48.

In soaking it to remove saline deposits from the surface, the earlier restoration was clearly revealed indicating that the top with spout and handle indeed did not belong to it and that it was originally designed with an open cranium. Ultimately it became clear that the mouth of the cup was slightly bevelled with a finished interior rim. Figure 1 illustrates the vessel before and during dismantling.

The cup form is seen in an inlaid metal Moche IV example and in other ceremonial vessels of open-cranium type.[1] The face is also similar to ceramic and copper face masks associated with the Late Moche Period from Pampa Grande.[2] On the other hand, the profile and face are typical of faces on vessels from the Early Moche Periods at Vicús and on a mask of patinated green copper from Loma Negra, attributed to the Early or Middle Moche Period.[3]

1. Sawyer 1968, no. 308, Nicholson/Cordy-Collins 1979, no. 195; Lapiner 1976, no. 334.
2. AD 500-700, Lapiner 1976, nos. 321, 322, 323, 333; see also Sawyer 1968, No. 309
3. Lapiner 1976, no. 258 and no. 349; see also Dockstader 1967, no. 121.

**OX-TL ref. no. 381g30 indicates that the sample tested was last fired between 1400 and 2200 years ago.*

28. EFFIGY STIRRUP SPOUT BOTTLE in the form of a seated man

Earthenware, burnished blackware
Moche I
Peru, North Coast
*ca. 300-100 BC**
Height 7¾" (19.7 cm) Width 4½" (11.4 cm)
Condition: intact
Accession no. 82.6.1

This vessel is modeled in the form of a seated man with his hands resting on his knees. His strong facial features include almond-shaped eyes set between heavy lids and a slightly hooked nose. He wears circular ear ornaments and a neckband. His fingers and toes are incised, and his hair is parted and decorated in zones of circular depressions suggesting a sexual symbolism. A figure of similar form in the Arthur M. Sackler Collections in the Museum of the American Indian is illustrated in the *Introduction.*[1] It too has the hair parted and decorated in zones of circular depressions. The facial features, however, are different, with eye pupils appliquéd in relief. He holds a cup in his right hand and resting on his shoulder, and his body is decorated with the same punctate markings or circular depressions as on his hair and the hair on the figure here. An almost identical vessel form is in a private collection in Florida. The latter depicts the same figure but with his head slightly more forward, the cup raised onto his left shoulder and with a rope around his neck, indicating a prisoner. Apparently a similar mold, perhaps standard for a particular potter, was used for the latter two forms and the figure here.

cf. Donnan 1978, nos. 12-13, for other figures with the same face but seated in a cross-legged position and with bodies in more sculptured form rather than retaining the essential form of a vessel as in Number 28 here; in Donnan's catalogue, no. 12 has the same parted hair form but with parallel lines, rather than depressed circles, indicating hair; see also Larco Hoyle 1965a, fig. 39, for another Moche I effigy vessel almost identical to no. 12 in Donnan 1978, and fig. 40, for a Moche I figure in the same body form as the figure here and the two described above in the Museum of the American Indian and in a private collection in Florida. Alan Sawyer included a similar vessel from Vicús in the 1968 Guggenheim exhibition (no. 91) from the Domingo Seminario Collection.

1. Plate XIX and App. no. 25

**OX-TL ref. no. 381f5, 2/28/83, estimates that the sample tested was last fired at least 1600 years ago.*

29. EFFIGY STIRRUP SPOUT VESSEL with male figure seated on a throne

Earthenware, with cream and red slip painting
Moche I or II
Peru, North Coast, Vicús, Piura River Valley
ca. 300 BC–AD 100
Height 6" (15.2 cm) Width 3¼" (8.3 cm) Depth 4¼" (10.8 cm)
Condition: cleaned of salt deposits; arms broken and repaired; edges of ear lobes chipped and repaired; stirrup spout is a restoration
Accession no. N-161

A man with mask-like head, with large eyes sunken to receive inlaid decoration, a large hooked nose and large ears with perforations meant to have received ear plugs, sits on a stepped platform, arms now extended forward and legs resting on the lowest step. He wears a breechclout or loincloth and a flat-topped headdress. The platform on which he sits, probably a throne, is decorated with red resist circular forms like the spots on an animal's skin.

There are numerous representations in Moche art of small stepped platforms that look like thrones. Sometimes they were built on the top of circular bases reached by a ramp or steps.[1] The throne, like the one here, may consist of a series of two or four steps, or be a simple bench on which a person sits. A litter, rather than a throne, with similar painted decor is depicted on a Moche painted vessel with an example of the Presentation Theme.[2]

The face on the seated figure here is reminiscent of masks in clay and copper as well as the features of other figural Moche vessels from the Piura River Valley at Vicús and Loma Negra.[3] It is not clear what the figure was doing with his arms since they had already been restored when the vessel was acquired. It is possible however that they were in a different position and could have been holding a variety of implements.

1. For description of throne types, see Donnan 1978, p. 83.
2. Donnan 1978, fig. 239b.
3. See Lapiner 1976, no. 354, for gilded copper head from Loma Negra near Cerro Vicús; no. 349, a mask of a man with ear disks and similar ears to the ones on the figure here; nos. 321, 322, and 334, for various masks from Pampa Grande, Cajamarca, or copper ones in nos. 323 and 333 also from Pampa Grande, as well as in a Moche figural vessel from Vicús in no. 258; also a copper face mask in the Museo Arqueologico Bruning, Lambayeque, ill. in Sawyer 1968, fig. 309.

30. STIRRUP SPOUT BOTTLE with painted design

Earthenware, cream slip on burnished orangeware
Moche I
Peru, North Coast
ca. 300-100 BC
Height 8" (19.5 cm) Diameter 5" (12.7 cm)
Condition: cleaned of salt deposits; one side of body and a chip in the mouth rim of the spout have been repaired
Accession no. N-43

This bottle with nearly straight walls and a slightly convex curved crown top, from which a heavy stirrup spout rises, has burnished orangeware walls with vertical stripes and a row of reed circles placed above the stripes all painted in cream slip. Two lines of cream slip circle the crown of the bottle. The design is in the form of a head-dress.

cf. Donnan 1978, no. 72, for a Phase I Moche vessel with painted decoration.

31. STIRRUP SPOUT EFFIGY VESSEL in the form of a kneeling warrior

Earthenware, dark greyware, burnished and inlaid with turquoise for earplugs and shells for eyes
Moche II
Peru, North Coast, Vicús, Piura River Valley
ca. 300–100 BC
Height 7 1/16" (18 cm) Width 4" (12 cm) Depth 5 3/8" (13.7 cm)
Condition: the shell inlay of the eyes has been reattached; burnish on proper left hand rubbed off and hand was possibly repaired; traces of cream slip appear on headdress, shield and body
Accession no. 83.5.1

Fig. 1. Kneeling warrior, orangeware, mauve and cream slip, inlaid eyes, Vicús, Piura Valley, Domingo Seminario Collection, Lima.

This kneeling warrior, with stone and shell inlay in place for eyes and earplugs, probably originally had a gold nose ring and was equipped with a miniature copper mace held in his right hand which rests on his right knee. He kneels on his left knee; on his left forearm is a circular shield with spiral decoration. On his head he wears a helmet with two stepped peaks emanating from the cap-like crown and extending slightly to right and left. The spiral design on the shield is reminiscent of the decoration on the earplugs of a seated man with feline fangs and strongly Chavinoid features on a stirrup spout vessel also from Vicús but attributed to the earlier Chavinoid Phase of perhaps 400-300 BC.[1]

The warrior figure here, however, is almost a mirror image, except for the headdress, of another kneeling warrior in orangeware which comes from Vicús (Fig. 1).[2] Both the Chavinoid feline-fanged effigy vessel and the vessel with the kneeling warrior are in the Domingo Seminario Collection from the hacienda Pabur, Piura. It is on this hacienda that the hill called Cerro Vicús, where a vast ancient cemetery was uncovered in 1961, is located. Ceramics from the graves there have been assigned to two cultural periods: one referred to as Classic Vicús or Vicús Moche, circa 400 BC–AD 100; the other as Negative Vicús, circa AD 100–700. The face of the warrior here is not unlike that on the portrait cup in Number 27, which was also originally purported to have come from "Ayabaca" or what is actually now known to have been Cerro Vicús. The headdress on the figure here, however, is similar to the type which appears on two gilded copper, striding warriors, with shell inlay eyes and holding battle maces, said to have been excavated at Loma Negra (also called Lomas Negras or Pampa de los Ovejeros), a site near Cerro Vicús, in the Department of Piura, where hundreds of tombs yielded quantities of jewelry, turban ornaments and plaques of copper, silver, silvered copper, gold and gilded copper. Ceramic sherds from the site gave virtually no evidence of Early Moche pottery. A claim was made by *huaqueros*, however, that twenty-one complete or nearly complete ceramic versions of a kneeling warrior in full regalia came from it.[3] The Loma Negra site has been tentatively dated 300 BC–AD 300, although a carbon 14 date of AD 200–390 was secured from the remnants of a wooden form inside a copper object there, suggesting the Middle Moche Period (AD 200-300) as the date for the site.

1. Sawyer 1968, no. 86, pp. 25 and 26.
2. Sawyer 1968, no. 96, pp. 26 and 27.
3. Lapiner 1976, p. 114.

32. EFFIGY VESSEL in seated monkey (?) or male skeletal form as Death

Earthenware, black negative wash on redware
Moche II
Peru, North Coast, Vicús, Piura River Valley
100 BC–AD 100
Height 7½" (19.4 cm)   Width 4½" (11.5 cm)
Condition: cleaned of salt deposits; chips on spout, arm and ears of monkey restored; root marks remain on body throughout
Accession no. N-191

This stirrup spout effigy vessel is in the form of a seated Death deity (?) wearing a triple necklace. The arms, with elbows akimbo, are separated from the body. The upper lip is outlined to represent the lack of skin covering over the mouth, giving the figure a skeletal appearance. Similar outlining of the upper lip appears on a Moche vessel in the Linden Museum, Stuttgart, with a skeleton carrying a deer on its back, and on a Moche skull vessel in a private collection.[1] The depiction of Death can also be seen in the skull cup in Number 59.

1. see Lapiner 1976, nos. 287 and 288; for other Moche vessels with Death figures, see Donnan 1978, nos. 171, 172 and 173.

33. EFFIGY STIRRUP SPOUT BOTTLE in the form of a man with dipper

Earthenware, burnished blackware
Moche II
Peru, North Coast, Vicús, Piura River Valley
100 BC–AD 100
Height 7" (16 cm)
Condition: cleaned of salt deposits; chips on spout restored; the rim of the spout, now restored, had been broken and filed down when the vessel was acquired, but the thickened interior of the mouth and the remains of a flange on one side indicated a Moche II type flange
Accession no. N-199

This effigy stirrup spout bottle is modeled in the form of a seated man wearing a cape with a collar and a conical roll-brimmed hat. His eyes are deep-set and have heavy brows; his cheeks are wrinkled or scarred. A deep groove in his upper lip represents a harelip. In his right hand he holds a dipper and in his left, what probably is a melon or a rolled-up mat. The stirrup spout end connected to the figure's back is threaded into his sash. Betty Benson describes such vessels as Vicús Moche Style. It is an interesting variant of a subject shared between Moche and Vicús wares.

34. EFFIGY STIRRUP SPOUT BOTTLE in the form of a blind man

Earthenware, cream on burnished redware
Moche II
Peru, North Coast
*100 BC-AD 100**
Height 6" (15.2 cm) Width 4 1/16" (10.3 cm)
Condition: some of cream slip has rubbed off; spots of iron staining
Accession no. 82.6.19

An effigy stirrup spout bottle modeled in the form of a seated blind man with his knees drawn up. The figure's head is hunched into his shoulders with his face raised. His hands meet on his breast. The artist has powerfully modeled the face, emphasizing the sharp cheekbones, the deep lines beside the nose and the empty eye sockets. The flowing head cloth is slip-painted in cream. Many individuals depicted in Moche art appear to have physical defects or to be suffering from illness. Blind people seem to be frequently represented.

cf. Lehmann 1938, no. 385; Tello 1938, p. 64; Lapiner 1976, no. 246, for a blind man holding a fox, from Vicús, Piura River Valley; and a portrait head jar of a blind individual in Donnan 1978, no. 186.

**OX-TL ref. no. 381f2, 2/28/83, and 5/26/83 estimates that the sample tested has a minimum age of 1380 years according to results of two TL tests, one to analyze fading.*

35. EFFIGY STIRRUP SPOUT BOTTLE in the form of a crouching feline cub

Earthenware, cream and black slip on burnished redware
Moche II
Peru, North Coast
100 BC-AD 100
Height 7½" (19 cm) Width 3¾" (9.5 cm) Depth 6¾" (17.3 cm)
Condition: tip of nose and proper left ear repaired
Accession no. N-208

The effigy stirrup spout bottle is very realistically modeled in the form of a crouching feline. The slight turn at the top of the spout places it in the Moche II Period. Body markings are in cream and lustrous black paint.

Like others in this collection, when acquired, this vessel allegedly came from "Ayabaca" or what was subsequently learned to be the cemeteries around Cerro Vicús in the Piura River Valley. A number of Early Moche felines have been associated with the same site.[1] Felines are frequently depicted in Moche art, with feline attributes such as fangs, claws and pelage markings commonly used in Moche dress and ornament.[2] In contemporary Moche folk belief, the cat is valued for its sharp eyesight, symbolic of visionary insight, for its swiftness and agility, significant in chasing away supernatural dangers, and for its force and valor, important in attacking and defending against evil spirits.

1. Lapiner 1976, nos. 282, 283, 284 and 285; also Donnan 1976, no. 89.
2. See Donnan 1978, p. 139, for the discussion of the cat symbolism in contemporary Moche folk healing.

36. STIRRUP SPOUT BOTTLE

Earthenware, cream slip and negative black on redware body
Moche II
Peru, North Coast Vicús, Piura Valley
ca. 100 BC–AD 100
Height 9" (23 cm) Diameter 6" (15.5 cm)
Condition: after soaking for removal of salt deposits, the resist design became more apparent and was strengthened
Accession no. N-44

The vessel allegedly was excavated at Cerro Vicús in the Piura Valley. The form of the stirrup spout places it in the Formative Moche Period when Moche ceramics from the Vicús area demonstrate cultural mixtures. The painting on the rounded, oblate body is divided into four triangular or wedge-shaped zones: two are painted with cream slip reed circles against a black negative ground; the two alternate zones have a design in negative resist of which only traces remain, but enough to indicate a design in the form of a bean(?) with elliptical dots surrounding it, comparable to motifs on so-called Negative Vicús wares from the same area.

The negative technique consisted of a motif first painted on the pot with a clay mixture that acted as a resist. The vessel was then dipped in a resinous substance and allowed to dry. After drying, it was held in a fire, causing the resin to char and creating a carbon-black impregnation on the exposed surface. A negative of the painted design remained when the clay was removed. The negative technique was rarely used by the Moche, but was employed by the Virú, Recuay, and the later Vicús Culture, designated in this catalogue as Negative Vicús. The form of the spout on stirrup spout bottles of the Moche Period is one of the most characteristic aspects of the ceramic phase of a vessel. Here, the wide, short spout is similar to those of Moche Phase I bottles but the lip is considerably reduced in size as in Moche II spouts. It is also slightly flared at the rim, however, which would seem to put it in a Moche III category. Yet the negative painting on the vessel and its oblate body form make it more compatible with Moche Phase I or II vessels. An example of a similarly shaped bottle with organic black ground surrounding a circle design in red slip in two zones, alternating with white slip in two others, was excavated in 1972 from a Moche I burial at the pyramids in the Moche Valley.[1]

1. Donnan/Mackey 1978, burial M-11, trench c, pp. 60-61.

37. STIRRUP SPOUT BOTTLE with painted design

Earthenware, with cream slip and black resist decoration on burnished orangeware body
Moche II
Peru, North Coast
ca. 100 BC–AD 100
Height 8" (19.5 cm) Diameter 5 1/2" (14 cm)
Condition: has been cleaned and cracks repaired
Accession no. N-46

A squat, round bottle with a stirrup spout rising from the curved crown, the slight turn on the spout rim places it in the Moche Phase II. A continuous wave or interlocking hook design is painted in cream slip on the burnished orangeware walls and is framed with a resist black border. Areas outside the wave design are filled with resist black circles. Much of the fugitive black has disappeared.

cf. Schmidt 1929, p. 188; Lumbreras 1974, no. 118, and Donnan 1978, no. 73, for painted bottles of Phase II Style.

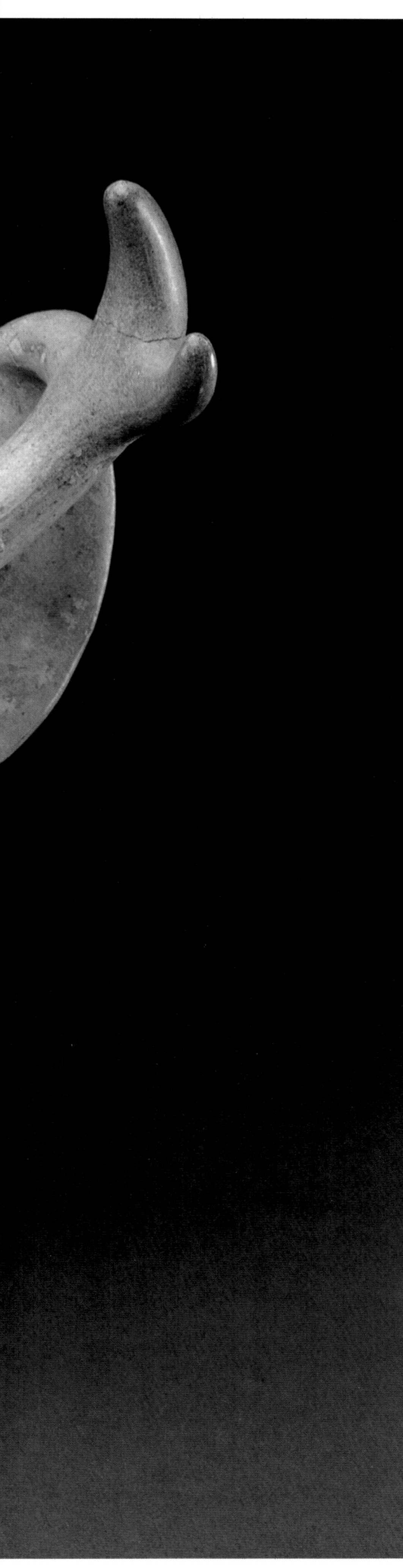

38. VASE in the form of a deer's head with antlers

Earthenware, cream slip on red-brown ceramic
Moche III
Peru, North Coast
ca. AD 100–200
Height 9½" (24.1 cm) Width 11½" (29.2 cm)
Condition: one antler has been broken and repaired; much of the cream slip has rubbed off
Accession no. 82.5.3

The proportions and sculptural rendering of this large vase modeled in the form of a deer's head are exquisite. The large, folded ears and realistic bowed antlers spread out from the head. The eyes are large and round with eyelashes painted on in cream slip. The nostrils flare and the lips are slightly parted.

The deer in Moche art apparently had significance beyond the mere representation of familiar fauna. Most Moche hunting scenes, painted or in relief, show humans in pursuit of deer, fox or felines, and many vessels include deer heads or complete animals. Since the attire of the hunters, seen on vessels with hunting scenes, appears to be too elaborate for a secular, everyday activity, it would seem that the hunt of the deer was ritualistic, engaged in by elite members of society on specific occasions.

cf. Sawyer 1966, no. 79, for a vessel in the form of an antlered deer holding its young in its arms; Lapiner 1976, no. 262, reclining deer from Vicús; and Donnan 1978, no. 85, for a vessel in the form of a deer head without antlers. See other examples in Lehmann 1938, no. 119f; Larco Hoyle 1966, no. 43f; Bird et al. 1981, p. 51.

39. EFFIGY VESSEL in the form of a reclining deer

Earthenware, cream slip on red unburnished ware
Moche III
Peru, North Coast
*AD 100-200**
Length 15" (38.1 cm)
Condition: intact
Accession no. 82.6.12

An effigy vessel beautifully modeled in the form of a deer reclining on its side with its head tilted upward. The large, folded ears spread out from the head and the round eyes are deep and expressive. The deer is slip-painted in red but its head is dappled with white and it has a white rectangle on its belly and white ears, neck, feet and tail.

cf. Lehmann 1938, no. 119ff; Tello 1938, p. 168; Lapiner 1976, no. 262, for a stirrup spout vessel in the form of a reclining deer from Vicús, Piura Valley.

**OX-TL ref. no. 381e77, 1/31/83, estimates that the sample tested was last fired between 1250 and 1900 years ago.*

40. EFFIGY VESSEL in crouching dog form

Earthenware, cream on burnished redware
Moche III
Peru, North Coast
ca. AD 100-200
Height 9½" (23.8 cm)   Width 11" (27.9 cm)
Condition: saline deposits removed by immersion in distilled water
Accession no. N-615

A stirrup spout vessel in the form of a crouching dog deity with head thrust forward. His mouth is open and snarling with the fangs showing. The teeth, shoulder ruff and tail are cream slip on burnished redware. The stirrup issues from the back.

Single animal representations, as the dog here, are probably symbols that carried nonsecular meaning in Moche Culture. Dogs are depicted as minor players in the Presentation Theme in Moche art. The Presentation Theme is one of the basic themes in Moche art and involves the presentation of a goblet to a major figure. It is not known what the goblet contains but there is reason to suspect it may have contained human blood taken from prisoners usually seen in such scenes. The dog usually appears at the feet of one of the major figures presenting the goblet.[1] Dogs also appear in scenes of the hunt.[2]

cf. Tello 1938, no. 170ff; Lapiner 1976, no. 283; Donnan/Mackey 1978, no. 9.

1. See Donnan 1978, nos. 239b and 240, for dogs in the Presentation Theme.
2. Donnan 1978, no. 262, for a dog in a deer hunt painted on a Moche bottle.

41. EFFIGY URN in human form

Earthenware, cream on burnished redware
Moche III-IV (?)
Peru, North Coast
ca. AD 200
Height 10" (25.4 cm) Width 7½" (19.1 cm)
Condition: intact; after cleaning off saline deposits, the cream slip on the figure's proper left was strengthened
Accession no. N-5

This large, ovoid urn is in human effigy form with the face and hat modeled on the neck. Ears are in loop form. The arms and hands, pushing out in low relief from the bottle form, rest on the figure's chest. Broad, striped hat ornamentation and garment patterning are painted in cream on the burnished redware body. Although not necessarily a Moche type of vessel, this head neck jar is a rather early Moche ceramic. It continues a form popular in the earlier Gallinazo or Virú Period. Another example of this form but with an owl head on the vessel's neck has been excavated from a grave in the Moche Valley at the site of the pyramids at Moche and assigned to Moche Phase I.[1]

cf. Benson 1972, nos. 5-24; Donnan 1976, nos. 34-5.
1. see Donnan/Mackey 1978, p. 61, burial M-I1.

42. EFFIGY JAR in the form of a prisoner

Earthenware, cream slip on redware
Moche III
Peru, North Coast
ca. AD 100–200
Height 13¼" (33.5 cm)   Width 6½" (16.5 cm)
Condition: after soaking to remove salt deposits, the cream slip decoration was strengthened
Accession no. N-371

This tall jar is in the form of a captured prisoner with his head modeled on the spout. He wears a helmet and a tunic, both decorated with circle patterns in cream on redware. His arms, outlined in cream, are behind his back.

cf. Donnan 1978, nos. 60 and 247, for ceramic jars in the form of prisoners with hands tied behind their backs but more plastically rendered in their modeled form; also Schmidt 1929, p. 134; Benson 1972, nos. 6-18; Donnan/Mackey 1978, no. 8.

43. STIRRUP SPOUT VESSEL with painted scene

Earthenware, maroon-red slip on cream slip ground
Moche III
Peru, North Coast
ca. AD 100–200
Height 10¹/₁₆" (28.5 cm)   Width 6¹/₄" (16 cm)
Condition: cleaned of salt deposits
Accession no. N-89

This ovoid flat-bottomed vessel is painted with a repeated scene of a stylized plumed puma (?) and a warrior (?) with a *tumi* in his headdress. Birds and stars are interspersed and the dots may indicate the starry heavens.

Alan Sawyer has suggested a "Formative Moche," that is, Moche Phases I or II, attribution for the vessel. Painted Moche pottery of this period is relatively rare and is usually decorated with geometric designs or in patterns borrowed from textiles. Recuay-derived figure motifs, however, do appear occasionally, as in this vessel which Sawyer believes depicts Recuay-influenced sky beings. In early Moche pottery there is fairly frequent representation of a "moon monster" on both painted and modeled pots. [1] Usually it is a dark, sleek, curving creature that rarely has feline dentition—although it sometimes has a forked tongue. The creature is also a Recuay motif.

cf. Schmidt 1929, p. 189; Kutscher 1954, nos. 41f, 44ff; Sawyer 1966, fig 21, for Recuay-derived figure motifs on Moche I ceramics; and Donnan 1978, no. 138, for the so-called plumed puma as a decoration on a house wall.

1. See Benson 1972, p. 38, fig. 2-15 for a stirrup spout vessel with moon monster and explanation of moon monster, p. 44; Menzel 1977, fig. 139.

44. PORTRAIT HEAD VESSEL with stirrup spout

Earthenware, maroon on cream
Moche III-IV
Peru, North Coast
*ca. AD 200**
Height 11⅜" (28.8 cm)   Width 6⅝" (16.8 cm)
Condition: cleaned of salt deposits; spout restored, and left ear repaired, iron stains on spout and face
Accession no. N-4

The portrait head on this vessel has powerfully modeled features and is wearing full headcovering with textile patterning painted in maroon on cream. The ear ornaments are inserted plugs and the stirrup spout issues from the top of the head.

cf. Schmidt 1929, pp. 125ff; Tello 1938, nos. 1-12 and passim; Bennett 1951, no. 44; Sawyer 1966, nos. 37-40; Walker 1971, no. 36; Benson 1972, nos. 1-17, 4-18, 5-25, 6-30; Lumbreras 1974, no. 119; Donnan 1978, nos. 1-9, 26, 51; Sawyer 1975a, no. 34; Sawyer 1975b, no. 6f; Donnan 1978, nos. 1ff, 26; and Bowden-Conrad 1982, no. 8.

* Two samples for thermoluminescence tests were taken from the base of the vessel and sent to two laboratories, the Alpha Analytic Laboratory, Miami, Florida, and the Research Laboratory for Archaeology and the History of Art, Oxford, England. The results of both tests indicate the vessel was indeed fi. ed in antiquity: *OX-TL ref. no. 381f61, 3/17/83 and 6/27/83, results indicate a last firing between 1600 and 2450 years ago; Alpha Analytic Inc., Miami, Florida, ref. no. Alpha-539, 3/3/83, indicates the thermoluminescence properties measured are characteristic of ceramic materials of the age range 240 BC to AD 850.*

45. STIRRUP SPOUT EFFIGY VESSEL in the form of a feline deity (?) head

Earthenware, burnished redware
Moche III-IV
Peru, North Coast
ca. AD 200
Height 9½" (23.2 cm)   Width 6½" (16.5 cm)
Condition: cleaned of salt deposits; traces of cream slip
Accession no. N-613

This very striking and finely modeled stirrup spout vessel is in the form of a feline deity (?) head. The head rises from a round base and has large, erect ears, wide-open eyes and snarling mouth. The mouth exhibits the typical deity fangs. The stirrup spout, typical of Moche III -IV, rises from the top of the head.

Felines are frequently depicted in Moche art. The attributes of the cat, its sharp eyesight, swiftness and agility, and its force and valor must have impressed the Moche people to consider it as a symbolic defender against evil spirits. Long before the Moche Culture developed, however, feline motifs were significant design elements in ancient Peru.

cf. Tello 1938, no. 177ff; Lehmann 1938, no. 177; and Lapiner 1976, no. 285, for a Moche I or II example of such a feline head vessel with red and cream slip.

46. STIRRUP SPOUT EFFIGY VESSEL in form of a marine deity

Earthenware, cream slip on maroon slip
Moche III-IV
Peru, North Coast
ca. AD 200
Height 9" (24 cm)   Width 5½" (14 cm)
Condition: cleaned of salt deposits; chips on head ornament and spout repaired
Accession no. N-263

This basically globular-shaped, footed vessel on rounded base becomes somewhat irregular as it terminates in the head of a deity with jaguar fangs, who appears to be lying on a rock in the ocean. He wears a half-moon head ornament attached to a headband, beads and ear ornaments. Seals and sea birds gambol around the lower half of the body. The stirrup spout leans in the opposite direction from the deity head, helping to create the well-balanced form of the vessel.

The sea lion is another significant animal in Moche art. Sea lions were and are hunted on the offshore islands of Peru, and are, among contemporary folk-healers, considered to have symbolic medicinal qualities. Stones or common beach pebbles swallowed by sea lions are, after their capture, extracted from their intestines and ground down into powders used to cure heart trouble and epilepsy. Christopher Donnan has suggested that "representations of sea lion hunting in Moche art are most likely to be depictions of a ritual activity—the quest for the magical sea lion stones."[1]

cf. Kutscher 1955, no. 72; Benson 1972, nos. 2-7; and Donnan 1978, no. 55, for a fine line drawing of a sea lion hunt on a ceramic bottle.

1. Donnan 1978, p. 178.

47. STIRRUP SPOUT VESSEL with monkeys tied to a rack

Earthenware, cream slip on burnished redware
Moche III-IV
Peru, North Coast
ca. AD 200
Height 9½" (22 cm) Width 5½" (14 cm)
Condition: cleaned of salt deposits; paint chips filled in near base
Accession no. N-26

The rounded body of this vessel has a flat bottom and a slightly flared stirrup issuing from its crown. On either side the vessel walls are modeled with monkeys in relief, with their heads rising above the vessel's shoulder. The monkeys are tied to a rack painted onto the vessel's surface.

cf. Tello 1938, no. 135; Benson 1972, nos. 2-21; Donnan 1976, nos. 68-69; Menzel 1977, no. 44B; Donnan 1978, no. 146.

48. HEAD VASES, pair

Earthenware, cream slip on redware body
Moche III-IV
Peru, North Coast
ca. AD 200
Height 5½" (14 cm) Width 5½" (14 cm)
Condition: cleaned of salt deposits; chips and cracks repaired
Accession no. N-1A and N-1B

Although formed in molds, the sculptural quality of this pair of vases modeled in human head form is strong. A headdress falls around the back of each head and over the ears. Eyes are outlined in cream slip on the redware body. The particular face depicted on this pair is encountered frequently in Moche art.

cf. Lehmann 1938; no. 301; Bolz 1975, no. 9; Donnan 1978, no. 61; Nicholson/Cordy-Collins 1979, no. 195.

49. MOLD-MADE STANDING FEMALE FIGURINE

Earthenware, fire clouded redware with traces of cream slip details
Moche III or IV
Peru, North Coast
ca. AD 200-AD 500
Height 7⅝" (19.3 cm) *Diameter 4 11/16" (12 cm)*
Condition: cleaned of salt deposits; surface abraded
Accession no. N-457

This standing female figurine is mold-made and hollow. It exhibits strongly modeled features – large, almond-shaped eyes, large, hooked nose and large ears – reminiscent of similar faces on male effigy vessels. The figure here is wearing dangles through her ears and holds her hands on her chest.

A mold-made standing figurine of the type seen here, but with hands extended outward, was excavated in 1972 from a Moche IV burial at the site of the Pyramids at Moche in the Moche River Valley.[1] The excavated figurine however – found in a double grave of a female, aged 30-40, and a child, aged 4-6, apparently interred at the same time – is considerably larger than the figure here.[2] Its hand position is similar to that of another Moche figurine in a seated position, now in a private collection, which is also larger than this.[3] The nature of our figure, with overlarge head compared to the compact, squat body, suggests that it is a female dwarf. Dwarfs were often depicted in Moche art (see Pl.XXIX), although their actual significance is not known.

There are additional symbolic possibilities for the figure here. Another Moche ceramic figurine has been associated by Christopher Donnan with the Presentation Theme.[4] The latter figurine, although more appropriately dressed for that ritual as a warrior, holds its hands in the same position on its chest as the figure here, but the hands, done in higher relief, are holding a goblet and a disc relevant to the Presentation Theme ritual. It is conceivable that the proper paraphernalia were painted on to the body of the figure here, as a necklace and other details of ornament once were, and that the figure represented an individual from a specific ritual. Women are known to appear in preparation-for-death and afterlife scenes both in elaborate painted and relief pottery and on modeled pots.[5] On the other hand, as a female image, she may have been carrying implements in her hands appropriate to women in Moche society, for instance a needle case or a spindle whorl.[6]

Christopher Donnan also describes the use of a Single Woman Staff by contemporary Peruvian folk healers.[7] "It is used to invoke the spirit of sacred lagoons in the northern Andes of Peru for the cure of love spells." According to local folklore, these lagoons are places where the most powerful magical herbs used in folk healing are to be found. The spirit governing these lagoons, as described by the folk healer Donnan names as Eduardo Calderon, "is a female guardian wearing a shawl and carrying a bouquet of flowers symbolic of the curative herbs over which she has domain. She is also conceptualized as an ancient spinster, a sort of wise old lady whom Eduardo associates with the traditional herbal lore and wisdom of the pre-Columbian people."

cf. Lehmann 1938, nos. 358 and 359, said to be from Chimbote.

1. Donnan/Mackey 1978, pl. 8, Moche burial M-IV 14, 15:16, pp. 168-174.
2. Ceramic no. 16 from the burial is approximately 13" (or 36 cm.) high.
3. Donnan 1978, frontispiece, 28.6 cm high.
4. *Ibid.*, fig. 250, from the Nathan Cummings Collection, The Metropolitan Museum of Art, 14.2 cm high.
5. Benson 1975, p. 109.
6. See an Early Huari South Coast spouted vessel with a seated woman holding a needle case in Lapiner 1976, no. 539.
7. Donnan 1978, p. 127

50. STIRRUP SPOUT EFFIGY VESSEL in form of seated man with lime gourd

Earthenware, cream slip on redware
Moche III or IV
Peru, North Coast
ca. AD 200-AD 500
Height 8" (20 cm) *Width 5½" (14 cm)*
Condition: cleaned of salt deposits; crack from left shoulder to base repaired
Accession no. N-262

The face is strongly modeled with the mouth turned down at the corners. The figure wears dangles which are attached to his earlobes. His headdress appears to be tied with a braided sling which stands out in relief. A cream slip-painted robe hangs from one shoulder down to his feet. Two hair braids hang over his shoulders down his back. In his right hand he holds a lime container which identifies him with the coca ritual.

Lime, used as a catalyst to free cocaine from the coca leaves, was kept in a small, narrow-necked gourd, and transferred in small quantities to the mouth with a stick. The lime gourds, as in the one here, have a thick mouth, probably resulting from the practice of rubbing the stick around the neck of the gourd and creating, with the buildup of lime in hardened form, a thick rim.[1]

1. Donnan 1978, nos. 180-185, and p. 117; also Donnan 1976, no. 17.

51. STIRRUP SPOUT EFFIGY VESSEL in form of a blind man

Earthenware, cream and deep red slip on burnished redware
Moche IV
Peru, North Coast
ca. AD 200-500
Height 7½" (19 cm) *Width 4½" (11.5 cm)*
Condition: cleaned of salt deposits and restored
Accession no. N-255

This finely executed vessel is in the form of a blind man with forlorn expression, seated cross-legged and with hands resting on his legs. He wears a cream slip-painted headdress and tunic. His face, hands and legs are burnished red, while the stirrup spout is a deeper red.

According to Elizabeth Benson, figures on modeled pots which have physical deformities or disabilities such as blindness, lameness, old age or traces of disease, are representations of priests chosen for their office because they had a physical deformity. They were, in other words, associated with the dead by a sympathetic magic.[1] In the canons of Moche art, depictions of humans or anthropomorphized creatures involve a standard enlargement of hands and head as seen in this effigy vessel, and in Number 50, which has nothing to do with specific deformity.[2]

This vessel, as indicated with earlier catalogue numbers, allegedly came from "Ayabaca," or what eventually was recognized to be the site of Cerro Vicús in the Piura River Valley.

cf. Schmidt 1929, pl. 142, for the same face on a blind man playing a musical instrument; Tello 1938, no. 57ff; Donnan 1978, no. 186; and Bird et al. 1981, p. 47.

1. Benson 1975, p. 114.
2. Donnan 1978, p. 30.

52. STIRRUP SPOUT EFFIGY VESSEL in form of a seated dignitary or warrior

Earthenware, cream on burnished redware
Moche IV
Peru, North Coast
AD 200-500
Height 9½" (24 cm)   Width 5½" (14 cm)
Condition: cleaned of salt deposits; cracks on body repaired
Accession no. N-271

On the top of this stirrup spout vessel, which is ovoid with a flat bottom, a ruler, dignitary or warrior is seated cross-legged with his hands on his knees. He wears a conical headdress with conical prongs or projections and large ornate ear spools. His headdress ties under his chin and he wears a square-collared tunic and a belt.

Headdress varies widely in form and elaboration in Moche art and was apparently an important aspect of Moche iconography, symbolic of an individual's status or role. The headdress with conical prongs worn on the figure here may represent the setting of five mountain peaks, and mountains played an important role in the ideology of the Moche people. To present-day folk-healers in Peru, mountains are where the magical herbs grow and are believed to be inhabited by guardian spirits.[1] The figure here may represent such a guardian spirit.

cf. Schmidt 1929, p. 134, for an effigy bottle in the form of a kneeling warrior wearing the same type of crown and carrying a mace; and Menzel 1977, no. 80.

1. See Donnan 1978, pp. 144-151.

53. STIRRUP SPOUT EFFIGY VESSEL in form of a warrior

Earthenware, cream slip painted on redware
Moche IV
Peru, North Coast
AD 200–AD 500
Height 8¼" (21 cm) Width 4⅝" (11.8 cm)
Condition: surface chips on spout rim have been repaired; after removal of salt leaching, cream slip decoration was strengthened
Accession no. N-266

The ovoid vessel here is in the form of a warrior wearing a conical warrior's hat and ear spools. His hands are raised in relief on his breast. Details of cuffs, fingernails, necklace and hat decoration are cream on redware, as is the stirrup.

Warriors played a significant role in the ceremonial life of the Moche people, as well as in the defense of their territory. Their status may have been similar to European medieval knights since their apparel bore distinctive heraldic devices of order and rank. Their most common helmets, an easy means of their identification, were either conical in form, as on the figure here, with an armored neckpiece and chin strap to which ornamental ear protectors were attached, or turban-like and covered with ocelot or bird skin and other embellishments. Another type is represented in Number 31. Warriors also wore wide protective collars and cuffs as seen painted on the figure here.

cf. Kutscher 1955, no. 72.; Sawyer 1966, pp. 44ff.; Donnan 1976, no. 35.

54. EFFIGY STIRRUP SPOUT VESSEL in the form of a man with coca bag

Earthenware, cream and red slip on redware body
Moche IV
Peru, North Coast
*ca. AD 200–500**
Height 8⅞" (22.5 cm)   Width 4 5/16" (11 cm)
Condition: cracks on body and chips on nose and cheek repaired.
Accession no. N-192

This effigy stirrup spout vessel is in the form of a standing man dressed in a long robe, multiple belts and a fine head cloth with tassels. His face is well-modeled with deep age lines. He carries a pack on his back suspended by a tumpline. In one hand he holds his coca-leaf pouch; in the other his lime container. Details of dress are picked out in cream slip. Alan Sawyer has suggested an Early Middle Horizon date, that is, Early Chimu, for this unusual vessel, since he believes the long spout is characteristic of Chimu.

1. Elizabeth Benson has indicated that a similar piece is in The National Museum, Lima.

**OX-TL ref. no. 381g29, 6/27/83, estimates that the sample tested has a minimum age of 1100 years according to results of two TL tests, one to analyze fading. Another sample, tested at Alpha Analytic Inc., Florida, ref. no. Alpha-686, 6/15/83, indicates that the thermoluminescence properties measured are characteristic of ceramic materials of the age range AD 100 to 700.*

55. EFFIGY VESSEL in the form of a closed bottle with bat head top

Earthenware, painted in red-brown on white slip
Moche IV
Peru, North Coast
ca. AD 200–500
Height 8¼" (21 cm) Width 4⅛" (10.5 cm)
Condition: cleaned of salt deposits and repaired
Accession no. N-611

A stirrup spout vessel in bottle form with a slight flare at the base. The closed top of the bottle is modeled in the form of a diety head with an open mouth and with the fangs and tongue showing. The ears, mouth, eyes and basal flange are tipped with red-brown and the vessel is slipped white with vertical groove striping. The type IV stirrup issues from the back of the head and stretches to the back of the vessel.

56. EFFIGY VESSEL in the form of a bird of prey

Earthenware, redware with traces of cream slip
Moche IV
Peru, North Coast
ca. AD 200–500
Height 8 1/4" (21.0 cm) Diameter 5 1/2" (14.0 cm)
Condition: cleaned of salt deposits; only traces of the original coloring remain.
Accession no. N-609

An ovoid stirrup spout vessel surmounted by a crouching bird of prey pecking at game (?) held in its talons. The type IV stirrup extends from the back of the bird to the shoulder of the vessel.

The possibility exists that the bird represented here is a hawk. It has lost its surface markings, but a very similar form of bird appears on a ceramic bottle in the Krannert Museum, University of Illinois.[1] In it, a large hawk is seated upon the body of a soldier, still dressed in his full battle regalia, apparently tearing at his chest. The bird is identifiable as the same as the one here. Alan Sawyer has written about the Krannert vessel that although the hawk is not a carrion eating bird, the scene on the vessel "is probably a symbolic representation of the totem," of the hawk clan of warriors, "reclaiming the soul of the fallen warrior so that his strength will not be lost to the clan."

cf. Tello 1938, no. 145ff.

1. Sawyer, 1975a, no. 40.

57. PAINTED BOTTLE

Earthenware, a redware body with red slip on a cream slip ground
Moche IV
Peru, North Coast
ca. AD 200 - 500
Height 9½" (24 cm) Width 7" (17.7 cm)
Condition: cleaned of salt deposits
Accession no. N-27

This ovoid bottle has a flat bottom and a long slender spout. A solid rounded handle arches from the upper third of the spout to the vessel's shoulder. There is a ring of dark red at the base of the neck and around the median of the vessel. Between the two rings fan out fine-line petaloid forms in red on a cream ground. The bottom portion of the vessel, the spout and the handle are left the natural redware.

cf. Lehmann 1938, no. 9; Benson 1972, nos. 4-12; Donnan 1976, no. 31; Donnan/Mackey 1978, pp. 86, 88, 109 and passim.

58. STIRRUP SPOUT VESSEL with fine line drawing

Earthenware, maroon-red slip on a cream slip ground
Moche IV
Peru, North Coast
ca. AD 200-500
Height 12" (30 cm)   Diameter 6½" (16.5 cm)
Condition: cleaned of salt deposits; chip in mouth rim repaired; flaked slip on surface restored
Accession no. N-38

This large, flat-bottomed, ovoid vessel has a stirrup which flares and straight spout walls. Two serpent warriors, running and carrying shields, are painted on the cream-slipped walls of the vessel. The fine line painting and the wave motifs on the stirrup are in maroon red slip.

Although it is dangerous to attempt to identify the work of a single painter, there are some instances in which two or more drawings show enough characteristics to be almost certainly by the same artist or at least produced in the same workshop. It is particularly in the drawing of the line that valid comparisons may be made. The drawing here of the serpent warrior holding a shield and mace is reminiscent of the drawing of a monster decoration on a pot in the Museum of the American Indian,[1] as well as that of another warrior on a pot in the Museum of Cultural History, University of California, Los Angeles.[2] All, including the one here, have similarly decorated stirrups as well as spouts of the same vintage.

There can be no doubt, however, that the painter of the Sackler vessel painted two others whose provenience is given as Chimbote in the Santa Valley: one, in the Macedo Collection, differs in shape from that of the Sackler vessel in that it has a short foot, however, the serpents drawn on it, with human arms and legs, have spots identical to the trefoils seen in the space around the same serpentine creatures in the Sackler vessel; the other, in the Gretzer Collection, has the serpent demons marked with trefoils with solid dots in each of the three petal forms, identical to the design on this serpent demon body.[3]

cf. Schmidt 1929, no. 191ff; Benson 1972, nos. 3-3, 4-9; Lumbreras 1974, no. 120; Donnan 1976, nos. 18-23, 29b; Donnan 1978, nos. 62-4, 75, 113.

1. Dockstader 1973, no. 208.
2. Donnan 1978, no. 75.
3. Kutscher 1954, 41A, B and C.

59. JAR in the form of a skull

Earthenware, cream and red slip on reddish body
Moche, Phase IV
Peru, North Coast, Vicús, Piura Valley
ca. AD 300–500
Height 7⅛" (18.0 cm) Width 4" (10.2 cm) Depth 4¾" (12.1 cm)
Condition: cleaned of salt deposits; cracks on base and rim repaired; iron stains throughout; pockmarks in surface
Accession no. N-8

This is a cup in the form of a skull or flayed head with the neck forming the base. The eyes and nostrils are sunken. The lipless mouth shows the teeth sharply defined. The shape of the mouth and teeth are outlined in red with a red slash extending on to the left cheek.

Alan Sawyer has described this as an example of the Moche flayed face.[1] Larco Hoyle believed that flaying was a form of punishment.[2] Elizabeth Benson believes that faces may have been flayed as punishment although there is little pictorial evidence in the Moche art for it. That it was not a sign of punishment she feels is made clear by a step motif often found on the cheeks of such skeletal figures. The step motif she believes is evidence of the importance of the dead after they no longer wore garments to identify their status.[3] On the left cheek of the skull here the slash-mark seems to resemble a step motif similar to such marks appearing on other pots with skeletal figures in their design.[4] Benson believes step motifs also appear on the faces of the important dead to "signify something like "mountains" and all that implies" indicating that the important dead are still stamped as "mountain people," or inheritors of the importance or divinity of mountains.[5] This head jar when purchased was said to come from "Ayabaca."

1. Personal communication.
2. Larco Hoyle 1965, p. 87.
3. Benson 1975, p. 119.
4. *Ibid*, p. 118, fig. 11 and 12.
5. *Ibid*, p. 119.

60. BOTTLE with deity figure

Earthenware, cream on redware
Moche V
Peru, North Coast
AD 500–750
Height 11½" (30 cm)   Width 9½" (24.8 cm)
Condition: cleaned of salt deposits; serpent head, proper left, restored
Accession no. N-508

This large bottle, whose wide spout protrudes from the top, is modeled in the form of mountains with peaks. Hanging from the two lower peaks is a deity figure with fangs. A serpent emerges from a peak on either side above his head. The figure on this vessel has been referred to as the principal deity of the Moche and their descendants, the Chimú. At the time of the Spanish conquest, the Chimú referred to this deity as *Ai-Apec.* He is shown here against a background of mountain peaks. *Ai-Apec,* a warrior god, was guardian of agriculture, domestic animals, and of the food of the sea, fighting all threats to the survival of his people.[1] An identical vessel, probably from the same mold, is in the Museum of the American Indian.[2]

cf. Donnan 1978, no. 222; Schmidt 1929, p. 165; Sawyer 1966, pp. 52-54, nos. 71, 72, 73, 74.

1. Sawyer 1966, pp. 52-53.
2. Accession no. 23/4865.

61. WIDE-NECKED BOTTLE with impressed "Dance of Death"

Earthenware, cream slip on unburnished redware
Moche III
Peru, North Coast
ca. AD 100–200
Height 9" (22.9 cm) *Diameter 7 1/8" (18 cm)*
Condition: cleaned of salt deposits; much slip worn off
Accession no. N-530

On the side of this large mold-made bottle with a wide neck is impressed a procession of many personages engaged in the "Dance of Death." Cream slip accents the details of the design.

The "Dance of Death" motif is a recurring theme in late Moche art. It is usually found in relief on bottles with central spouts or with central spout and tubular side handle. On one side of the scene here there is a figure, dressed in a warrior's helmet, playing a flute. A man in front of him is beating a drum. Another man with a helmet, behind the figure beating the drum, is also playing on a *quena,* a reed flute, or on panpipes. Behind one of the flute-playing figures is another figure with a rope (?) around his neck, followed by others, presumably dancers. All the figures in the scene have hollow eye sockets and are skeletal-looking, although they are clothed.

cf. Schmidt 1929, pp. 221ff; also Sawyer 1975b, no. 11.

62. BOTTLE with impressed procession of "Dance of Death" motif on sides

Earthenware, cream slip on redware
Moche V
Peru, North Coast
AD 500–750
Height 9 15/16" (22.7 cm) *Diameter 6 3/4" (17.1 cm)*
Condition: cleaned of salt deposits; surface worn and pitted; some slip worn off
Accession no. N-353

This large bottle with flaring spout is impressed on the sides with a procession of anthropomorphic figures with cat features and tails in the "Dance of Death" motif. Highlights of faces, breechcloths and tails are in cream slip. There is a painted band with geometric designs around the neck and circles around the rim.

The figures on this vessel, like those on Number 59, have the sunken or hollow eye sockets, although not the emaciated aspect, of those other skeletal figures. These hollow-eye figures may have lost their eyes through disease. It is possible, as Alan Sawyer has indicated, that such figures, whether they lost their eyesight through punitive causes or natural causes, were made to perform in funeral rituals.[1]

The figures here are playing panpipes and seem to have a stepped design on their cheeks. According to Elizabeth Benson, musical instruments appear in almost every afterlife scene: "They are frequently held or played by priest figures. The evidence is strong that they are death-associated and that at least some of them indicate the other world, or the preparation for it."[2] Instruments also seem to be indicated in a status order, with the deity usually shown playing panpipes.[3] Benson believes that "panpipes existed as a symbol, almost like a word, perhaps signifying death as well as status."[4]

1. Sawyer 1975a, p. 36; see also Sawyer 1975b, no. 11; Schmidt 1929, p. 221ff.
2. Benson 1975, p. 116.
3. *Ibid.*
4. *Ibid,* p. 117.

63. EFFIGY VESSEL in the form of a llama giving birth

Earthenware, blackware
Early Chimú
Peru, North Coast
*ca. 8th century**
Height 7" (17.8 cm) Length 8½" (21 cm) Width 3¼" (8.3 cm)
Condition: cleaned of salt deposits; cracks have been repaired
Accession no. N-570

The vessel here stands on a short ring base or foot and has a tapered spout and flat bridge handle with a whistling hole revealed just behind the llama head which forms the blind spout in which the whistling element is placed and to which the bridge handle is connected. The tapered spout and flat bridge handle is a typically Huari influenced element although tapered spouts and rounded bridge handles trace back to the Virú ceramics of the north coast and were, except for the rounded bridge, very similar to the later tapered spout and bridge handle.

On the north coast following the demise of the Moche culture, modeled ceramics were still being produced in the Early Chimú style. The term Early Chimú refers to the style evolved by the Chimú people on the north coast during the Middle Horizon Period, apparently before the establishment of the Kingdom of Chimor. Yet the stylistic breakdown between Early Chimú and Chimú has not yet been clearly established archaeologically.

The emphasis in this vessel seems to be the genre subject itself, indicating the attention of the Early Chimú people to matters of every day living and their rejection of the religious pre-occupation of both their Moche predecessors and the later intrusive Huari priesthood.

**OX-TL ref. no. 381e97, 1/17/83, estimates that the sample tested was last fired 1230 years ago.*

64. EFFIGY VESSEL in monkey form

Earthenware, blackware
Early Chimú
Peru, North Coast
AD 1000-2000
Height 9" (23 cm)   Width 4" (10 cm)   Depth 8⅝" (22 cm)
Condition: cleaned of salt deposits
Accession no. N-581

A characteristic example of Chimú ware, this mold-made stirrup spout effigy vessel is in the form of a crouching monkey. The stirrup has a long concave spout in the manner of late Moche vessels. The monkey is tied with a banding over his back. He is represented in an awkward crouching position on a pedestal-type base with a slightly convex bottom. The monkey has appeared continuously in Pre-Columbian Peruvian art. An earlier Moche example in Number 26 shows him with a mortar and pestle.[1] As other writers have pointed out, certain types of fauna are not native to north coast Peru and the monkey is among those which are not.[2] It is, however, native to the coast of Ecuador farther north. The presumption is that monkeys may have been imported from that area. As seen here and in Number 80, monkeys often wore leashes. They also wore collars and earrings.

The monkeys on the vessel here and in Number 80 have identical faces and indicate the Chimú practice of interchangeable mold parts, in this case using the head of the monkey with different body renderings. The same head appears on another monkey in the Museo Nacional de Antropología y Arqueología, Pueblo Libre, Peru.[3]

1. see Lapiner 1976, nos. 259 and 260, for Early Moche- and Salinar-style monkey vessels from Vicús, Piura Valley.
2. Donnan 1978, p. 62 and nos. 95 and 96 for other Moche monkey vessels.
3. Sawyer 1968, no. 648.

65. STIRRUP SPOUT VESSEL with impressed crabs

Earthenware with molded design enhanced with slip paint in red and cream
Early Chimú, Middle Horizon
Peru, North Coast
AD 1000-1200
Height 6½" (16.3 cm)   Width 4¾" (12 cm)
Condition: cleaned of salt deposits
Accession no. N-49

Fig. 1. Crab, gilded copper with green patination. Early to Middle Moche, Loma Negra, Vicús. From the Arthur M. Sackler Collections.

A mold-made vessel with each side completely filled with a pressed crab in low relief, the body of the vessel is a redware with the stirrup spout slip painted in dark red. The crab on this vessel is identical to a Moche crab in hammered metal with shell eyes in the Arnold and Jane Goldberg Collection, New York.[1] Another, minus its tail, still adhering to a stone, is in the Arthur M. Sackler Collections (Fig. 1). Apparently, the crab played an important role in Moche ritual. Elizabeth Benson has referred to a fanged-mouth deity fighting a crab that has a deity face on its shell.[2] The vessel here allegedly came from "Ayabaca," or, as described earlier, what came to be realized as the site of Cerro Vicús in the Piura Valley. The Vicús site included objects of the later Lambayeque and Chimú cultures.[3]

1. Donnan 1978, no. 19; see also Lapiner 1976, no. 378, for crabs alleged to have come from Loma Negra.
2. See Benson essay, Moche and Vicús, in this catalogue, p. 69.
3. Larco Hoyle 1965(a), pp. 34-35.

66. STIRRUP SPOUT BOTTLE in the form of an architectural model

Earthenware, with red and cream slip
Early Chimú
Peru, North Coast
AD 1000–1200
Height 6¾" (17.5 cm) Width 5¼" (13.4 cm)
Condition: cleaned of salt deposits and restored
Accession no. N-88

The bottle is mold-made in the form of an open-fronted temple on a high oblong base. The flat roof slants somewhat toward the back and is supported by the two side walls and back wall of the structure. The stirrup rises from the roof. Impressed and painted within the front opening is a representation of a crab (?) deity with flowing hair. The vessel is slip painted in cream with crab (?) motifs in red around the base. The columns at the front and the back walls are decorated with red geometric designs; the stirrup is also painted red.

The figure in the temple appears to wear no headdress; his long hair spreads out above his head. Although it is rather unusual to see individuals not wearing at least simple head coverings, supernatural figures are sometimes shown without headgear, their long tresses left exposed. The design at the base of the bottle is reminiscent of decoration on a fragment of a Chimú textile which may have ornamented a temple or public building. In the field of that design there are rows of human heads with four scroll-like appendages, similar to the scroll-like appendages seen here.[1] Adobe reliefs at Chan Chan also depict a bird with such scroll-like appendages for wings and legs.

1. Sawyer 1975a, fig. 78 for the Chan Chan adobe reliefs and fig. 80 for the textile design.

67. STIRRUP SPOUT VESSEL with four joined fruits

Earthenware, cream and black on burnished brownware
Early Chimú
Peru, North Coast
AD 1000–1200
Height 7½" (19.1 cm) Width 8 7/16" (21.4 cm)
Condition: cleaned of salt deposits and restored
Accession no. N-28

This vessel is composed of four fruits forming four chambers and joined at the top with a stemmed node. The flaring stirrup, which has a short spout, emerges from the top of the fruit cluster. Each fruit is painted with lateral cream and black stripes to resemble the natural markings of the fruit. The vessel illustrates the continuation of the early Moche Style, particularly in the bi-chrome color combinations.[1] Such coloring and design are also found on vessels from the Lambayeque Valley.[2] The less restrained shape and the stirrup proportions place this piece in the Late Intermediate Period.

1. see Larco Hoyle n.d.(a), fig. 31.
2. *Ibid.*, figs. 29 and 30.

68. EFFIGY VESSEL in fruit form

Earthenware, black lines on a cream slip ground
Early Chimú
North Coast
AD 1000–1200
Length 9" (23.8 cm) Diameter 3½" (9 cm)
Condition: cleaned of salt deposits and restored
Accession no. N-511

This mold-made vessel has a wide mouth with short flared neck and its body is formed of rippling bulges from the neck and tapers to a point at the other end, resembling a *pacae* fruit (*Inga feuillei*). It is covered with a cream slip and painted with fine black lines.

The *pacae*, a bean-shaped fruit of a tree grown on the north coast of Peru, was cultivated in abundance in Pre-Columbian times. It was often represented during the Chimú-Inca Period, as well as in the earlier Moche Period. In the latter period, it was among the native north coast flora represented in Moche art and has been excavated from Moche habitation refuse along with corn, beans, squash, peanuts, *pepino*, and manioc.[1]

Sometimes in the Chimú-Inca Period it appeared in a ceramic form known as a *pacha*, an object used in an Inca water cult. Water was revered by the Inca as symbolic of life force. In a *pacha*, liquid poured into the vessel at the top, flowed through it and exited out a vent at the other end. *Pacae*-shaped ceramics used as *pachas* symbolized the capacity of water to produce the life-giving power of food.[2]

1. For a Moche example, see Donnan 1978, no. 93.
2. A Chimú-Inca Period example appears in Sawyer 1975a, no. 88; see also Schmidt 1929, pl. 184, for a Chimú (?) *pacae* supposedly excavated at Chimbote, and Tello 1923, p. 109.

69. ORNAMENTAL HEAD

Earthenware, black and white pigment on buffware
Lambayeque-Chimú
Peru, North Coast
AD 700-1200
Height 8½" (21.6 cm)
Condition: surface paint worn throughout; decoration on headdress has been repaired
Accession no. 82.5.7

This free-standing ornamental head of a deity comes from a tomb near Chiclayo in the upper Lambayeque Valley. The mask-like face is surmounted by a crescent headdress with a horned-moon ornament. Its bulging eyes have moon crescents below them and are slip painted in white. The nose extends over a bowed mouth. Stylized ear and ornament flanges jut out on either side of the head. The headdress has a wide groove filled with black. The rest of the headdress, eyes, ears and mouth are slip painted in white.

Eight of these heads are purported to have come from the same tomb. Each surmounted a post at the four corners, with two on each of the long sides of the tomb. A palm ceiling or canopy was said to have rested above the tomb posts which the heads surmounted. One of the eight was exhibited in 1968 in the Guggenheim exhibition "Mastercraftsmen of Ancient Peru."[1] Another was formerly in a New York private collection.

1. Sawyer 1968, no. 608.

70. DOUBLE SPOUT VESSEL with bridge handle

Earthenware, painted in black on a whitish cream slip ground
Lambayeque-Chimú
Peru, North Coast
AD 700–1200
Height 7¼" (18.4 cm) Diameter 8½" (21.6 cm)
Condition: cleaned of salt deposits and reassembled; cleaning revealed more of the original design; left spout is a restoration
Accession no. N-931

The footed vessel here has three sharply divided areas of ring base, lower body and upper body crown with a sharp ridge at the shoulder. Two long, tapered and slanted spouts rise from the shoulder. The arched bridge handle, with triangular indentations, is topped by a modeled deity head flanked on either side by prone adoration figures or "swimmers." Beneath either spout is a projecting serpent head. A cursive black line design on the shoulder includes a step pattern in a zone around the neck as well as a lively bird pattern in panels around the base of the shoulder. A circle pattern decorates the lower body and foot. The basic form and design of this vessel, suggest an influence derived from the nearby Huari center of Cajamarca. But the projecting feline heads jutting from the base of the spouts are a Lambayeque trait, a heraldic emblem of Naymlap, his heirs and the Lambayeque-Chimú Style.

According to imperial lore, Naymlap, as a revered old man, evaded mortal death by having the ability to fly, and leaving his realm in prosperous order, he flew into heaven at the end of his reign. This theme is encapsulated in this vessel, where the central figure flanked by two smaller attendants, rides atop the crest of the rayed, double-headed rainbow symbolizing ritual flight. The theme of a central "heroic" figure flanked by two attendants of smaller stature is a carryover from earlier Moche art style. In Lambayeque Style renderings, the central hero is distinguished by unusual headgear, particularly the laterally projecting ear ornamentation as seen here. The bird ornamentation on the shoulder band may refer to the hero's flight into heaven.

cf. Sawyer 1975a, fig. 52.

71. DOUBLE SPOUT VESSEL

Earthenware, reduction-fired blackware with remains of burnishing
Lambayeque-Chimú
Peru, North Coast
AD 700–1200
Height 6 1/8" (15.5 cm)   Diameter 7 9/16" (19.3 cm)
Condition: cleaned of salt deposits; burnished surface has been eroded in spots
Accession no. N-32

This mold-made, footed vessel, has two slanted and tapered spouts connected by a twisted "rope" handle. The upper sides are mold-pressed with figures with arms upraised and wearing noble attire against a stippled ground. The figures wear the *tumi* headdress, a form adapted from the crescent-shaped ceremonial knife, as well as an abbreviated tunic or kilt, and large ear ornaments. Their activity is uncertain, but the frontal stance with bent and upraised arms is reminiscent of staff-bearing figures seen elsewhere in Chimú art. The serpent-head projections from beneath each spout, typical on Lambayeque pottery, appear here as on Number 70.

The double-headed serpent represented a celestial symbol in Moche art but was a heraldic emblem of Naymlap and the Lambayeque-Chimú Style. The association of the double-headed serpent and Lambayeque royalty had its foundations in recent excavation of adobe friezes with celestial serpents at Naymlap's shrine of Chotuna. Michael Moseley has indicated the spherical vessels of the type here were used for ceremonial libations.[1]

cf. Larco Hoyle 1966, no. 70; Larco Hoyle n.d. (c); Walker 1971, no. 132; Kauffmann-Doig 1973, p. 393; Sawyer 1975b, no. 16; Bawden/Conrad 1982, p. 64.

1. Moseley essay in this catalogue, p. 77.

72. BOTTLE with deity head spout

Earthenware, burnished blackware
Lambayeque-Chimú
Peru, North Coast
AD 700–1200
Height 6 11/16" (17 cm)   Width 4 11/16" (11.9 cm)
Condition: cleaned of salt deposits; top of spout restored
Accession no. N-576

This mold-made globular, footed or ring-based bottle with a single spout and strap handle and a modeled head of a deity on the lower portion of the spout is a common Lambayeque ceramic type. The eyes of the deity are upward-slanted, elongated, teardrop shapes, a diagnostic Lambayeque eye stylization. The hat band is ridged and the ear ornaments have long tassels which fall to the shoulder of the vessel and are another characteristic feature of the Lambayeque Style. The arched strap handle at the rear supports two prone adoration figures which face each other.

The notable eye feature of the Lambayeque Style was allegedly introduced by Naymlap, the legendary Lambayeque king who purportedly unified the Lambayeque people after arriving in the area in a fleet of boats. The date of Naymlap's arrival is not known, but he established a dynasty and was succeeded by twelve of his descendants whose names have been preserved.[1] The eye form becomes one of the most distinctive traits of Lambayeque Style. It may portray a physical characteristic of Naymlap and his descendants or some form of face or eye decoration of the time. Its first appearance, however, can be traced to Moche Phase IV,[2] after which it continues in the Middle Horizon, and then into the Late Intermediate Period in Early Chimú examples.[3]

1. See essay in this catalogue by Michael Moseley.
2. Donnan 1976, pl. 2b.
3. Donnan 1972, front cover; Schaedel 1978, no. 32; Donnan/Mackey 1978, pl. 11; Keatinge 1978, no. 33; Larco Hoyle n.d. (c); Walker 1971, no. 135; Sawyer 1975a, no. 55f; Menzel 1977, no. 81B; Nicholson/Cordy-Collins 1979, no. 207.

73. BOTTLE with deity head spout

Earthenware, burnished blackware
Lambayeque-Chimú
Peru, North Coast
AD 700–1200
Height 6 1/4" (16 cm)   Width 4 5/8" (11.8 cm)
Condition: cleaned of salt deposits and repaired
Accession no. N-593

This mold-made, globular, footed or ring-based bottle with a single spout and a modeled head of a deity on the lower portion of the spout is another example of this common Lambayeque ceramic form. The eyes on the head here are also upwardly slanted, elongated teardrop shapes. The face is marked as if tatooed and the ornate ear ornaments have long tassels which fall to the surface of the vessel. An arched strap handle at the rear supports two prone adoration figures facing each other. At either side of the spout is a projecting serpent head.

The same cast of Chimú cosmic characters appears on the libation vessel here. The head of the central hero is flanked by the heads of the celestial serpent, while attendant figures ride on the handle of the vessel. In Number 72 and Appendix nos. 44, 45 and 48, the serpent heads are dropped, while attendant figures are retained and elaborated upon.

74. BOTTLE with fruit

Earthenware, slip painted and with negative resist design
Lambayeque-Chimú
Peru, North Coast
AD 700-1200
Height 7¾" (19.5 cm) *Width 4½" (11.5 cm)*
Condition: cleaned of salt deposits and restored
Accession no. N-34

A mold-made vessel, this footed bottle has a long, tapered spout and a solid, round handle which arches from the spout to the shoulder of the vessel. Two modeled fruits are attached to the sides of the vessel and connected by their stems to the spout. The foot is impressed with geometric motifs and the tan slip-painted surface is decorated with red slip paint and resist black lines and bands. Wave motifs are part of the linear decoration on the shoulder, formed by a stepped cresting, i.e., a step motif and a sweeping C configuration. They are probably an indication of lingering Moche traditions. Four stepped motifs around a circle form part of the panel decoration on the curve of the shoulder. The fruits on the sides of the vessel are striped and their stems decorated with circles. An almost identical bottle is in the Krannert Art Museum, University of Illinois, Urbana-Champaign.[1]

1. see Sawyer 1975a, no. 53.

75. BOTTLE with corn deity

Earthenware, burnished blackware
Lambayeque-Chimú
Peru, North Coast
AD 700–1200
Height 8" (20.3 cm)   Width 5½" (14 cm)
Condition: handle which once existed on the reverse of this vessel came off when cleaned of salt deposits and proved to be a later addition
Accession no. N-569

The head of a deity, emerging from a heaped pile of ears of corn which he holds in his arms, decorates this mold-made, footed or ring-based, single spout bottle. The seated deity wears ear spools, a collar and a pendant, and his rounded face—with its long, slanting eyes in elongated teardrop shape—is topped by a double half-moon crested helmet. It is apparently a popular vessel form of the period, since others of almost identical form are found in many collections, either as a single bottle or as part of a double bottle shape.

76. STIRRUP SPOUT VESSEL in the form of a duck

Earthenware, orangeware with designs painted in red on cream slip ground
Early Chimú (?), Middle Horizon
Peru, North Coast
AD 1000-1300
Height 6⁵⁄₈" (17 cm) Length 8¹⁄₄" (21 cm)
Condition: cleaned of salt deposits; surface slip worn in spots
On loan to Columbia University
Accession no. N-610

The predilection for modeled ceramics among inhabitants of the Peruvian north coast, even after the demise of Moche cultural traditions, is illustrated in this Early Chimú (?) duck vessel. The sculptured form of the mold made vessel here, however, is more simplified, in contrast to the realism in Moche examples.[1] The orangeware body is decorated with red slip on a cream ground in simple linear designs with a zigzag pattern on the sides probably imitating feathers. The spout here turns inward at the rim and is more consistent with Chimú spouted vessels, although such spouts also appear on Inca-Tallan examples.[2] A Chimú duck in the Museum of the American Indian is of a different form from the one here.[3] But a spouted vessel attributed to the Middle Chimú Period, with strap handle and "Tin Woodman" figure spout, has two similar ducks on either side of the spout figure and they are also painted red and black on a cream slip ground.[4] The duck figures on the latter Lambayeque-Chimú vessel has the round eye form seen on the duck here.

1. see Moche example of Muscovy duck in Donnan 1978, no. 91.
2. see Sawyer 1975a, no. 95.
3. 23/6883 Dockstader 1967, no. 143; another duck from an earlier north coast culture is in Larco Hoyle 1965 (a) fig. 34, red orangeware with Virú traits.
4. Lapiner 1976, no. 652.

77. EFFIGY STIRRUP SPOUT portrait vessel

Earthenware, orangeware, molded, with traces of cream slip
Early Chimú
Peru, North Coast
AD 1000-1300
Height 9½" (24 cm) Width 5" (13 cm)
Condition: cleaned of salt deposits
Accession no. N-41

The stirrup spout vessel here is modeled in the form of a man's portrait with a smiling face. Deep laughter wrinkles are impressed on either side of the eyes and the mouth is open showing teeth. While similar in concept to early Moche portrait vessels, the simpler lines, squared stirrup, and knob at the joint of the stirrup and spout are diagnostic of the Chimú Period, although orangeware is relatively rare during this period. Chimú ceramics were predominantly blackware. They were mold-made and were mass produced in large workshops.

This smiling face was apparently a popular motif. Another vessel, apparently from the same mold and workshop as the one here, is in the Museum of Mankind, London.[1] It too is in orangeware. The same face appears on another vessel in black burnished ware of tall bottle form in the L.K. Land Collection, California, described as a Chimú-Inca vessel. The face is molded into the lower body of the bottle.[2]

cf. Schmidt 1929, p. 129; Tello 1938, no. 1ff., especially no. 7; Benson 1972, nos. 5-25.

1. Accession no. S333c or St. 3331.
2. Nicholson/Cordy-Collins 1979, no. 216.

78. DECORATED BOTTLE with two spouts

Earthenware, burnished blackware
Middle Chimú
Peru, North Coast
*AD 700–1470**
Height 8¼" (21.1 cm) Diameter 8" (20 cm)
Condition: cleaned of salt deposits; small hole repaired bottom right [1]
Accession no. N-528

This football-shaped bottle has a flared spout in the center and another on the shoulder. Birds or foxes or "wrinkled" dogs and whorls (see drawing), in a dotted or stippled ground decorate a band on each of the ends. Plant forms, which may represent *pacae* or maize, surround the spouts. The design was incorporated directly into the mold and was then pressed on the exterior of the clay body. Press-molding, as the technique is known, is a very efficient method of rapidly producing designs on pottery. The Chimú perfected it although it was begun in Late Moche times.

When acquired, the vessel was given a Patavilca attribution. The Patavilca Complex was located in the Fortaleza, Patavilca and Supe River valleys. Patavilca vessels are impressed with various floral and geometric designs, but the ones published by Kosak are quite distinct from the vessel here in shape and design.[2] Designs of the type found on this bottle, however, appear on Middle Chimú vessels of similar shape excavated in the Moche River Valley.[3] They are decorated with clearly recognizable seabirds and whorls, or whorls and plants. The creature on this bottle, however, is not so easily distinguished, and the drawing, taken from a rubbing, does not clarify its identity. On another Middle Chimú football-shaped bottle excavated in the Moche Valley, a long-tailed creature with wrinkled body decorates either side of its shoulder below the spout.[4] Dogs with deeply wrinkled skin were raised by the inhabitants of the Andes and Middle America for food. Frequently represented on ceramics, they were probably pets while still remaining a source of food.

Whorls may represent the sea waves into which birds dove to catch food. The combination of motifs, therefore, seems to express the idea of fertility or fecundity. The form of the vessel suggests that it was a *pacha* used for ritual libation, with the water poured into one spout while being emitted from the other, symbolizing a continuous flow of the life-giving essence.

1. The post-fired perforation was probably the result of a rod used to probe for graves by *huaqueros*, or grave robbers.
2. Kosak 1965, pp. 217-226.
3. Donnan/Mackey 1978, MC 11-1 and MC14-2, pp. 321, 332.
4. *Ibid.*, MC14-4, p. 333.

**OX-TL ref. no. 381f96, 5/26/83, estimates that the sample tested has a minimum age of 1000 years according to results of two TL tests, one to analyze fading.*

Fig. 1. Detail of decorative band showing similar sea birds. Chimú embossed silver disk, AD 1300–1400. The Arthur M. Sackler Collections, the Museum of the American Indian, New York.

79. BOTTLE with modeled bird head spout

Earthenware, burnished blackware
Imperial Chimú
Peru, North Coast
AD 1300–1400
Height 9¾" (25 cm) Diameter 6⅞" (17.5 cm)
Condition: cleaned of salt deposits; old repairs reglued; surface worn around lower body
Accession no. N-545

This mold-made bottle with an impressed band of pelican-like birds around the middle is an unusual form. The *oya* body is surmounted by a spout that swells towards the top, where an appliquéd beak and reed-circle eyes form a bird's head.

Similar pelican-like birds with turned-back heads appear on the first band of decoration on a group of embossed silver disks. One, alleged to have come from the Lambayeque Valley, is in the Sackler Collections in the Museum of the American Indian (Fig. 1).[1] Another, published by Lapiner, is reported to have come from a pyramid on the Hacienda Mocollope along with the Sackler disk.[2] In all, there were alleged to have been 25 (?) repoussé silver disks from the tomb or tombs from this site.

1. Dockstader 1967, no. 150, accession no. 23/6190.
2. Lapiner 1976, no. 601 and p. 447; see also Schmidt 1929, p. 313, for a pelican band on the shoulder of an Ica vessel; and Kroeber 1925a, pl. 61K; Menzel 1977, p. 28.

80. STIRRUP SPOUT VESSEL in monkey form

Earthenware, burnished blackware
Imperial Chimú
Peru, North Coast
AD 1400-1450
Height: 9 11/16" (24.6 cm) Width 4 7/16" (11.2 cm) Depth 9 1/16" (23 cm)
Condition: cleaned of salt deposits; top of spout restored
Accession no. N-614

This effigy vessel in the form of a standing monkey has a squared stirrup, diagnostic of Middle to Late Chimú, issuing from its back. As mentioned in the description of Number 78, a standing monkey effigy vessel in the Museo Nacional de Antropología y Arqueología, in Peru, is identical to the vessel here.[1] The body of this monkey vessel, however, as described for the head form on this vessel and on Number 78, was from the same mold used in the representation of other animals, particularly the puma, as can be seen in vessels in the Krannert Art Museum, the University of Illinois, and the Museum of the American Indian.[2] This particular body form as a continuation of the standing monkey vessels mentioned in Number 79 as being of Early Moche and Salinar Style of at least one thousand years earlier from Vicús, Piura Valley, which is in the far north of Peru and close to the Ecuadorian border.

1. Sawyer 1968, no. 648.
2. Sawyer 1975a, no. 66 (acc. no. 67-29-237) and Dockstader 1967, no. 143 (acc. no. 15/197); see also Kroeber 1926-30, I, pl. 7.

81. STIRRUP SPOUT VESSEL with a figure on a litter or throne

Earthenware, burnished blackware
Imperial Chimú
Peru, North Coast
AD 1300-1400
Height 6½" (16.5 cm)   Width 5½" (14 cm)
Condition: cleaned of salt deposits; spout repaired
Accession no. N-564

The mold-made vessel here is in the form of a litter or throne with a square base and square backrest. A ruler (?) sits cross-legged on it. The stirrup is joined to the back of the throne and a small monkey stands at the joining of stirrup and spout. The square base is fairly common on Chimú ceramics. In the Amano Museum, Lima, figures of musicians appear on a group of stirrup spout vessels with square bases as on this vessel.[1] Their headdresses, however, are different from the small pill-box-type hat form worn by the seated figure here, and none of them sits against a vertical backrest; rather, the stirrups emerge from their own backs instead. Another vessel with square base and a figure similar to the musicians and wearing a similar headdress but without a musical instrument is published by Luis Lumbreras.[2]

1. Bird et al. 1981, pp. 98-99, from the Amano Museum, Lima.
2. Lumbreras 1974, fig. 191; see other square-based Chimú vessels in Sawyer 1975a, nos. 70 and 71.

82. DOUBLE BOTTLE whistling vessel with guardian head

Earthenware, press-molded burnished blackware
Imperial Chimú
Peru, North Coast
AD 1300–1400
Height 7¼" (18.4 cm)   Length 7¼" (18.4 cm)
Condition: cleaned of salt deposits, surface abrasions in spots
Accession no. NN-2

Two mold-pressed bottles, one with a spout and the other modeled as a guardian head with a double-peaked helmet, are connected by a tube and a strap handle. The bottle with the guardian head has on its front face a stippled panel divided by an unstippled vertical bar adorned with scrolls, and two stylized seabirds on the stippled ground on either side of the divider. The bottle with the spout includes on its outer face a panel decorated with a large, shark-like fish on a stippled ground. The interior sides of each bottle also include a stippled ground.

Double-chambered vessels have a long history on Peru's north coast, but those with whistles occur first in the Chavínoid phase of Paracas Culture on the south coast. Double-chambered whistling vessels seem to appear in the north at the end of the Chavín Period, when they were presumably introduced by the Virú Culture. Vicús vessels were also double-chambered as well as whistling, but such vessels were used by the Moche Culture only occasionally. In the Huari Period on the central coast, interest in double-chambered whistling vessels was renewed and continued to be popular in the Chimú Period and afterwards. Two Chimú vessels are included in the present exhibition: this one and the one in Number 83. A third, also in the Sackler Collection, is illustrated in Appendix no. 49.

83. DOUBLE BOTTLE whistling vessel with guardian head

Earthenware, press-molded burnished blackware
Imperial Chimú
Peru, North Coast
AD 1300–1400
Height 7 3/8" (18.7 cm) Width 5 3/8" (13.6 cm)
Condition: cleaned of salt deposits, burnishing has worn off in spots
Accession no. N-574

The vessel here, with two mold-made bottles, one with spout and the other with a blind spout modeled as a woman's head, connected by a tube and a flat handle, is similar to the one in Number 82. Here, however, the bottles are impressed with a textile design in the form of zigzags set on diagonals, patterning which Michael Moseley believes is also an heraldic device. The double-peaked helmet or flaring headdress on the figure on this vessel and Number 82 appears often in Chimú ceramics, generally worn by females.[1]

In his essay Moseley has indicated that bipointed helmets may have specific affiliations. The archaeologist Kent Day, excavating the palace gateway of the Ciudadela Rivero in Chan Chan in 1973, revealed two wooden statues in their original position on each side of a narrow passage. Each figure stands at attention in military garb in a guard booth or niche built into the passage wall. These statues presumably held a staff or spear in their raised arms. They have been interpreted as from a squad of eighteen that once flanked the palace entrance. They wear large earspools, indicative of high rank. Distinctive also are the bipointed helmets indicating ethnic, if not military, affiliations.

1. Sawyer 1968, no. 616; Sawyer 1975a, no. 50; see also Kroeber 1926-30, I, 9; Schmidt 1929, p. 214; Proulx 1973, pl. 16g; Lumbreras 1974, no. 191; Bird et al. 1981, p. 101.

84. EFFIGY BOTTLE with sky god mask

Earthenware, press-molded burnished blackware
Chimú-Inca
Peru, North Coast
AD 1470–1532
Height 8½" (21.5 cm) Width 7¼" (18.8 cm)
Condition: cleaned of salt deposits; edges of spout rim and hole on body repaired
Accession no. N-577

The canteen-shaped, pressed-ware bottle here with wide, flaring spout, suspension lugs on the shoulder on either side of the spout, and almost completely stippled on its main surfaces, is impressed on one side with a sky god mask similar to earlier Lambayeque gold masks used for attachment to mummy bundles. Its mouth is ridged and bird-head ear ornaments with round dangles flank it on each side. A ridge extends from the top corners of the mask around the back of the bottle in a crescent shape and may represent a carrying sling. Arms and legs, as well as the mask, are in relief. The Lambayeque Style mask has upturned, pear-shaped eyes and angular ear flaps which may have been a part of the headdress, as on Lambayeque ceramics with the so-called "tin woodsman" type on the spout, Numbers 72 and 73. A very similar Lambayeque Style mask in depletion-gilded copper is in the L.K. Land Collection, California, and is attributed to the Chimú Period.[1]

1. Nicholson/Cordy-Collins 1979, no. 215; see also Dockstader 1967, fig. 151; Schmidt 1929, p. 224; Sawyer 1975a, no. 174.

85. BOTTLE, with sky deity

Earthenware, press-molded burnished blackware
Chimú-Inca
Peru, North Coast
AD 1470–1532
Height 6¼" (16 cm) Width 5" (12.8 cm)
Condition: cleaned of salt deposits; chips on rim and cracks on sides repaired
Accession no. N-572

This pressed-ware bottle also has a funnel-shaped spout and two suspension lugs on either side of it. Its iconography is complex. Pressed on one side is a large panel containing a richly garbed figure, perhaps a version of the sky deity, who with one hand is capturing a large fish with a hook and line. In his other hand he grasps a ceremonial staff of office. He is surrounded by birds and sea life. On the other side, the large panel is decorated with a centralized sky deity grasping weapons and flanked on each side by an anthropomorphic monkey, which has one paw on the weapons. The ground of both panels is stippled.

86. BOTTLE with impressed sky deity

Earthenware, press-molded burnished blackware
Imperial Chimú
Peru, North Coast
ca. AD 1000-1300
Height 6 7/16" (16.4 cm) Diameter 5 3/8" (13.7 cm)
Condition: cleaned of salt deposits; cracks repaired
Accession no. N-557

This pressed-ware molded bottle in canteen form has a short neck and two lugs for suspension cords on either side of it. Impressed on the sides is a panel on stippled ground with a sky deity figure holding two vertical scarves and flanked by two others. The simple abstract treatment of this figure is typical of Chimú art, in contrast to the realism and naturalism of earlier Moche art.

cf. Schmidt 1929, p. 224; Sawyer 1975a, no. 74.

87. BOTTLE with human head

Earthenware, burnished blackware
Chimú-Inca
Peru, North Coast
*AD 1470-1532**
Height 7½" (19.1 cm)   Width 6¼" (16 cm)
Condition: cleaned of salt deposits
Accession no. N-580

This unusual pressed-ware bottle with a flaring spout is shaped in the form of the head of a dignitary. His bulging eyes have ridged lids; his brows join a narrow nose with flaring nostrils; and his ears extend out from the sides of the vessel. The open mouth reveals his teeth. An intricate coiffure surrounds the face with areas of fine braiding above the forehead and an incised representation of a woven cap above the braids. The bulge in his cheek indicates that he is chewing coca.

An almost identical bottle, but with the flaring rim of the spout broken, is in the Musées Royaux d'Art et d'Histoire, Brussels, and another, in the Baessler Collection, Germany, was illustrated by Max Schmidt in 1929. Both have as their provenience Guadalupe, the main town of the irrigated plain to the north of the Jequetepeque River.[1] The head jar or bottle illustrated in Schmidt has slightly different decorative details on the cap, but the face is identical to that on the Sackler bottle and the one in Brussels.

From the central coast, in the so-called Teatino Style—which was influenced by Huari pottery and persisted as a style into post-Huari times, there is a head jar of very similar facial features although in a red color.[2] A mummy mask of flat sheet silver in the Museum of the American Indian bears a repoussé design of the same face.[3] Whether this face represented a specific personage or was ritualistically significant is not possible to know, but that it was important in burial is obvious from its frequent appearance on grave goods.

In shape, the Sackler bottle and the Brussels and Baessler bottles are typical of Chimú-Inca forms. An example of a similar form, but with the smiling face of our Number 70, is in the L. K. Land Collection, California.[4] The pronounced flaring lip is a specific feature of the new, prestige ware of the Inca elite evident in Chimú ceramics from the Late Horizon on the north coast.[5]

1. Schmidt 1929, p. 219; see also Kroeber 1925a, no. 68e; for the Brussels head see Santa 1963, pl. XXXVI.
2. Larco Hoyle 1963, no. 131.
3. Dockstader 1973, fig. 226, with a Supe Valley provenience.
4. Nicholson/Cordy-Collins 1979, no. 216.
5. Donnan/Mackey 1978, no. 357.

**OX-TL ref. no. 381e96, 1/17/83 and 5/26/83; last fired at least 380 years ago, according to the results of two TL tests, one of which was to analyze fading.*

88. BOTTLE in the form of a celestial house

Earthenware, partly slip painted in cream on orangeware with black painted details
Chimú-Inca
Peru, North Coast
AD 1470-1532
Height 10" (25.3 cm) Width 5½" (14 cm) Depth 5¼" (13.3 cm)
Condition: mouth rim chips repaired
Accession no. N-18

On this oblong, mold-made bottle representing a celestial house, the upper portion slants to a peak like a roof gable. Two suspension loops are attached on the sides of the flaring spout where it is joined to the roof. A double panel is impressed on both sides of the roof gable. The top panel contains two stylized cats face to face, while the bottom panel has two large sea birds back to back. The two triangular or wedge-shapes above their backs may be tails of each bird joining a large, double-bird head or may instead represent two stylized fishtails at the end of a double fish-design. Each bird has a smaller bird at the edge of its beak, and the beaks of the smaller birds are touching the top of the double-bird head or pair of fish.

The style of the excised or carved design on the bottle here is reminiscent of the designs found in the Chimú capital at Chan-Chan, at the extreme northwest of the Moche Valley, with its palace and temple walls decorated with relief friezes carved in clay. Some of the clay reliefs are composed of geometric designs and others depict complicated mythical figures that probably related to a cult. The design on the bottle here appears on other Chimú pottery, usually in raised relief formed from press molds. It depicts two confronting, hunched felines ready to pounce, watching aquatic birds, possibly pelicans, dive for fish. A globular grey vessel excavated from a site in the Viru Valley shows flocks of aquatic birds of similar type driven by the same four-footed animals around the borders.[1]

The same feline forms appear on a Chimú bottle in the L.K. Land Collection, California, as a pierced wall decoration of a gabled structure. The designs below the felines on the Land bottle have been described as geometric, but in comparison to the design on the Sackler bottle, they may actually be more abstracted forms of the fish motif seen here.[2]

The gabled roof form which appears on the upper part of this bottle occurs in Chimú art but can also be traced back to Early Horizon cultures. Christopher Donnan referred to the anomalous appearance of gabled roofs in Moche art, which is produced in an essentially rainless area.[3] The geographical area of the Chimú was the same; consequently, the likelihood is that such a structure was for ceremonial rather than functional use. Supernatural events apparently took place within gabled structures. Notable is a series of bottles depicting a copulating couple inside a building with a gabled roof.[4]

1. Ubbelohde-Doering 1967, fig. 154.
2. Nicholson/Cordy-Collins 1979, no. 205.
3. Donnan 1976, p. 75.
4. See one in Menzel 1977, no. 64.

89. FIGURAL VESSEL in the form of a llama head

Earthenware, burnished blackware
Chimú-Inca
Peru, North Coast
AD 1470–1532
Height 4" (10.2 cm) Length 7 1/2" (19.1 cm)
Condition: intact
Accession no. 82.6.26

The charming realism of this llama head is reminiscent of the naturalism of earlier Moche ceramics. Yet, as the vessel here attests, Chimú artisans were also capable of rendering rich portrayals of animal life. The two-part mold in which this vessel was made is indicated by the mold lines apparent on the muzzle and over the chin of the animal. The eyes are ridged ovals, the nostrils are well delineated, and the open mouth shows the llama's teeth. A restraining tie crosses the muzzle in the form of a serrated ridge.

cf. d'Harcourt 1948, no. 133.

90. STIRRUP SPOUT BOTTLE with anthropomorphic figure

Earthenware, burnished and slip-painted in a pinkish red, cream-white and black on orangeware body
Inca-Tallan
Peru, Far North Coast, Piura area
ca. AD 1450
Height 7" (17.8 cm) Diameter 4½" (11.5 cm)
Condition: cleaned of salt deposits and chips on spout repaired
Accession no. N-21

Flat-bottomed with outward-slanted sides on the lower body, this vessel includes a crown top from which the stirrup rises. One part of the stirrup is in the form of an anthropomorphic figure with its arms spread wide. Its heavy features with round eyes and wide mouth are animal-like. The hat or crown has projecting spikes and the top of the vessel's chamber is decorated with radiating white slip lines and black dots on a pinkish-red slip over the burnished orange body.

The style of the vessel is a blending of late north coast styles. The jutting lower jaw and broad mouth of the figure seem to be typical Tallan characteristics, while the spiky headdress is reminiscent of earlier Vicús headdresses, as seen, for instance, in a Sackler vessel in the Museum of the American Indian.[1] The Tallan Style, found in the far north coast valleys of the Chira and Piura rivers, developed in the same region that had produced the earlier Vicús wares. The area, dominated by the Chimú for a relatively short time before the Inca conquest, produced a style which was a regional variant of the Chimú-Inca Style. The vessel here has a variation of the standard Chimú-type stirrup spout, but the polychrome treatment is typical of Tallan ceramics, although unusual here because of the colors used.[2]

1. see *Introduction*, Plate XVb and Appendix no. 18.
2. Sawyer 1975a, no. 95.

91. BOWL with incised and painted face

Earthenware, blackware with red, white and yellow pigments
Paracas, Formative Phase 3
Peru, South Coast, Chiquerillo (?)
900-700 BC
Height 3" (7.6 cm) Diameter 5 1/2" (14 cm)
Condition: excellent
Accession no. 82.6.2

The incised areas of decoration on this straight-sided, heavily potted bowl with a human face design are filled with a thick, shiny, postfired paint. The face is yellow and has U-shaped eyes and oblong lips with wavy side lines. Its Chavinoid eyes are white with black pupils and the mouth is filled with a single row of rectangular white teeth. Interior and exterior walls are black. Three rows of multiple reed circles are painted in red on the exterior except for the pouring area. A similar vessel from a gravelot of two bowls with well-preserved resinous paint, is now in the Metropolitan Museum of Art.[1] The latter was said to have come from Chiquerillo, a small early site between Ocucaje and Callango in the Lower Ica Valley, but shows several typical traits of the time range associated with the Cerrillos site, in the Upper Ica Valley, excavated by Dwight T. Wallace. The bowl here has the same incised and painted face.

1. Sawyer 1966, no. 95, and a line design of the same mask in Menzel et al. 1964, no. 28.

92. BOWL with incised and painted owl

Earthenware, black-brown ware with red and yellow pigments
Paracas, Formative Phase 3
Peru, South Coast, possibly from Carhua
900–700 BC
Height 3 3/8" Diameter 6 3/4"
Condition: intact; paint has worn off
Accession no. 82.6.28

This small, round-bottomed bowl with convex sides, curving in at the mouth rim, and a dark, carbon-blackened body, is in the form of an owl's head, incised and painted with resinous red and yellow postfired paint. The round eyes with raised pupils give this object a whimsical and pleasing appearance. A very similar design on a flat-bottomed bowl of Late Chavín date, apparently from the Jequetepeque Valley on Peru's north coast, demonstrates the force of Chavín influence on south coast ceramics such as the vessel here.[1] Recent discoveries on the coast below the Paracas peninsula, at a site called Carhua, indicate that emissaries arrived from the north with painted textiles exhibiting Chavín religious iconography. They apparently established religious centers in south coast communities, unified the people of the area, and influenced the rapid cultural advance which followed.[1]

1. See Fig. 13 in *Introduction*.
2. Sawyer 1975b, no. 25.

93. MELON-SHAPED BOTTLE

Earthenware, black-brown ware with red and white pigments
Paracas, Formative Phase 3, probably Juan Pablo Style
Peru, South Coast
900-700 BC
Height 14" (35.6 cm) Length 17½" (44.5 cm)
Condition: only traces of postfired red and white resinous paint remain
Accession no. 82.5.5

This unusual, large, melon-shaped bottle with a wide, short neck has a highly abstract feline design incised on it across the top and down the shoulders. A simplified feline mask confined to the limits of a rectangular panel and a longer rectangular panel representing a feline body next to it are a common decoration on Juan Pablo bowls. It is rather unusual, however, on this bottle whose shape is a Juan Pablo Early Paracas innovation.[1] The brow, whiskers, ear and pelt markings of the feline mask appear in the rectangle at the lowest end of the shoulder on each side of the neck. A stylized body extends above it. The feline mask associated with the earlier Chavín Culture has lost the fierce vitality of the jaguar and has become instead a benign ocelot under disciplined control.

1. Sawyer 1966, no. 184.

94. BOWL with incised and painted bird and feline motifs

Earthenware, black-brown ware with red, white, yellow and grey pigments
Paracas, Early Phase 5-6, Juan Pablo Style
Peru, South Coast, Upper Ica Valley, Cerro Teojate
700–600 BC
Height $2^{5}/_{16}$" (5.8 cm) Diameter 8" (20.3 cm)
Condition: much of the postfired resinous paint has flaked off
Accession no. 82.6.16

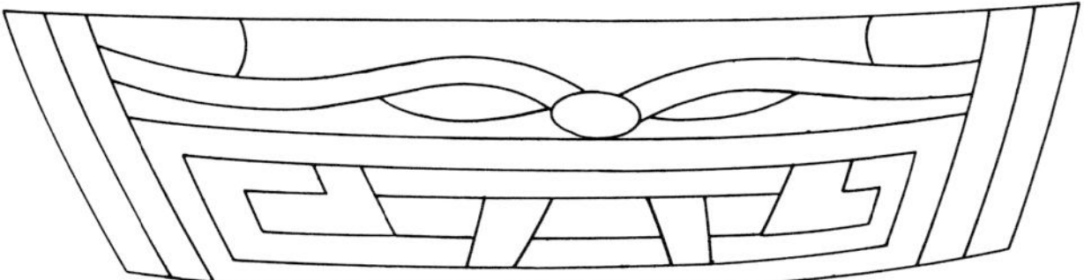

This incised, round-bottomed, black-brown bowl painted with postfired resinous pigments in red, white, yellow and grey has as its main motif a feline mask and body. Another incised motif is an abstract, rectangular representation of the *vencejo,* a bird like the whippoorwill. The large, double circle eye and the whisker-like elements circling to meet the beak, place this vessel in the style of the Late Formative to Early Paracas periods. Wings, body and tail of the bird are reduced to horizontal geometric components. A panel containing a row of three reed circles connected by short lines reveals another secondary motif.

cf. Sawyer 1966, no. 176.

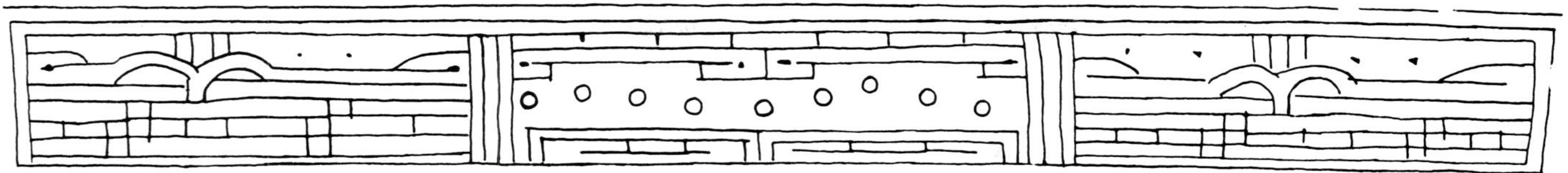

95. BOWL with incised and painted feline motif

Earthenware, black-brown ware with red and white pigments
Paracas, Early Phase 5-6, Juan Pablo Style
Peru, South Coast, Upper Ica Valley, Cerro Teojate
700–600 BC
Height 2⅝" (7 cm) Diameter 7" (17.8 cm)
Condition: has been treated to remove salts and restored
Accession no. N-322

The round-bottomed, straight-sided bowl here has a burnished red interior, and its sides are incised and painted with postfired red and white resinous pigments. The incised motif is a representation of the feline mask and body in abstract rendering in two rectangular panels side by side. The mask has eyes, brow and whiskers, and the teeth have been reduced to brick-like renderings between two parallel lines except for the fangs which extend above and below them. The ears are rendered as two loops at the end of the brow. The pelt markings on the body are represented by circles. Two Chavinoid eye patterns appear below the body between the legs, and the tail may be the two hooked ends at the top. The mask and body here relates to Sawyer's second-phase version of the feline figure motif at Juan Pablo.[1]

1. Sawyer 1966, no. 155.

96. NECKED BOTTLE incised and painted with "God's Eye" motif

Earthenware, black-brown ware with red pigment
Paracas, Early Phase 7
Peru, South Coast, Upper Ica Valley (?)
600–500 BC
Height 10¾" (27.2 cm) Diameter 9⅝" (24.5 cm)
Condition: has been restored after removal of salt deposits; postfired pigments remain as traces only
Accession no. N-359

A bottle with a spherical body and a spool-shaped neck, this vessel has as decoration two so-called "God's Eye" motifs, composed of an inner trapezoid shape and the lines immediately surrounding it. It resembles the earlier Chavinoid feline eye. The other lines composing the outer edges of the design may be specially modified representational features of the feline mouth band. The degree of abstraction among Paracas designs make all speculations possible.

cf. Menzel et al. 1964, nos. 13–14.

97. NECKED BOTTLE with incised and painted step-fret motif

Earthenware, black-brown ware with red pigment and resist black
Paracas, Early Phase 7, Juan Pablo Style
Peru, South Coast, Upper Ica Valley, probably from Cerro Teojate
600–500 BC
Height 9¾" (24.6 cm) Diameter 8¼" (21 cm)
Condition: restored after cleaning of salt deposits; traces of negative design
Accession no. N-364

This bottle with spherical body and spool-shaped neck is decorated with step-fret motifs incised and painted with postfired red resinous pigment high on the shoulder. There are still traces of black resist circles on the body of the vessel.

cf. Menzel et al. 1964, nos. 13-14.

98. BOWL with incised and painted geometric designs

Earthenware, black-brown ware with red and white pigments
Paracas, Middle Phase 9
Peru, South Coast
500–300 BC
Height 3¾" (9.6 cm) Diameter 8¼" (21.1 cm)
Condition: cleaned of salt deposits; cracks repaired
Accession no. N-325

This typical Paracas round-bottomed bowl, with a wide incised exterior rim band painted with postfired red and white resinous pigments, is decorated with a geometric design consisting of a form of the diagonal step motif with multiple zigzags and vertical bars. The step motifs are filled in with a resinous red pigment and the vertical bars with white. Although the significance of this design is not clear in this early culture, it continues as a major design motif in the later periods in the north and south coasts and in the highlands.

cf. Menzel et al. 1964, no. 53d, h.

99. BOWL with incised and painted geometric designs

Earthenware, blackware with red, white, and yellow pigments
Paracas, Middle Phase 9
Peru, South Coast
500–300 BC
Height 3 1/8" (8 cm) Diameter 7 3/4" (19.5 cm)
Condition: cleaned of salt deposits; cracks repaired; interior restored and stabilized
Accession no. N-223

On this round-bottomed bowl, black inside and out, there is a wide, exterior incised rim band painted with postfired, red, white, and yellow resinous pigments. Its geometric design consists of a form of the diagonal step motif with multiple zigzags and vertical bars. Alternate designs are painted red or yellow outlined with white.

cf. Menzel et al. 1964, no. 53d, h.

100. BOTTLE with pouring spout

Earthenware, burnished blackware, undecorated
Paracas, Late Phase 9 or 10
Peru, South Coast, Callango, Ica Valley (?)
300–200 BC
Height 5 1/2" (14.1 cm) Diameter 6 3/4" (17.7 cm)
Condition: cleaned of salt deposits
Accession no. N-583

This squat, ovoid jar, with its short spout with thickened rim and a pouring spout on the shoulder, exhibits a certain elegance in its very simplicity. Unornamented on its burnished surface, it was probably a utilitarian vessel as well as a funerary one. The Callango attribution was suggested by Alan Sawyer. Bottles of similar shape but highly decorated with postfired resinous paint have been found at Chucho, south of the Pisco River drainage.

101. BOWL

Earthenware, with cream postfired resinous paint
Paracas, Late Phase 9 or 10
Peru, South Coast, Callango, Ica Valley (?)
300–200 BC
Height 2⁷⁄₈" (7.2 cm) Diameter 7⁵⁄₈" (19.4 cm)
Condition: cleaned of salt deposits; cracks repaired
Accession no. N-346

The simple zigzag decoration in postfired resinous cream paint is the only apparent decoration on the simple, burnished blackware body of this bowl. As in Number 100, the surface is severe, but the elegance of the shape and thinness of the potting indicate the sensitivity of the potter. Alan Sawyer has identified this bowl as being from Callango at the southern end of the Ica Valley. Callango was fertile and densely populated in Paracas times. Although large collections of Callango ceramics exist in Peru, comparatively few have reached this country. They exhibit distinctive regional characteristics, particularly in their decorated wares. Their undecorated wares, such as the bottle in Number 100, and the relatively undecorated bowl here, may have been produced for daily use or for the burial of a less important person.

102. PANPIPES

Earthenware, burnished blackware
Paracas, Phase 9
Peru, South Coast
ca. 300-200 BC
Length 10½" (26 cm)   Width 2⅞" (7.4 cm)
Condition: cleaned of salt deposits; cracks repaired
Accession no. N-398

A set of four tubes of varying length have been bound together with clay and fired in a reducing atmosphere to produce blackware. The earlier panpipes differ from later periods of Paracas and Nasca by the addition of a thickened band just below the mouthpiece to resemble the lashing of the tubes on reed panpipes.

cf. Menzel et al 1964, p. 187.

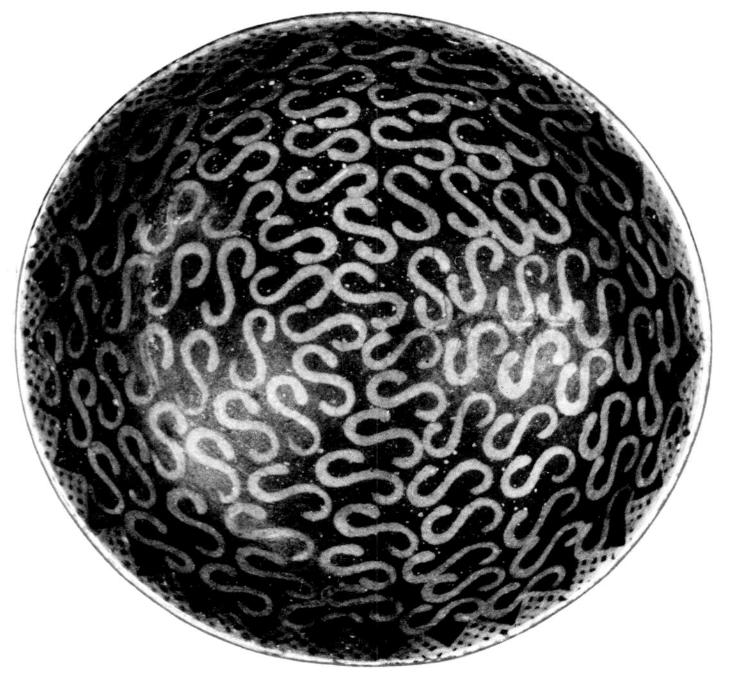

103. BOWL with negative resist geometric designs

Earthenware, negative black on red-orange ware
Paracas, Late Phase 10
Peru, South Coast
300–200 BC
Height 2½" (6.4 cm) Diameter 7½" (19.1 cm)
Condition: excellent
Accession no. 82.6.4

This hemispherical bowl is decorated with geometric patterns in a negative resist technique. On the exterior below the rim there are multiple zones formed by two narrow diagonal blocks of four lines each which cross each other and form an X. Near the rim of the interior walls are multiple triangles filled with tiny cross-hatching. The rest of the interior is filled with tightly curled S-shaped figures.

cf. Menzel et al. 1964, pl. 14b, no. 64c; Sawyer 1966, p. 95.

104. EFFIGY BOTTLE in monkey form

Earthenware, slip painted in white, black, and red
Nasca, Phase 2
Peru, South Coast
250 BC–AD 125
Height 6½" (16.5 cm) Diameter 3¹⁵⁄₁₆" (10 cm)
Condition: cleaned of salt deposits; flaking painted areas strengthened and restored
Accession no. N-52

The upper portion of the bottle is modeled as a monkey's head, with a round, flattened, concave face and relieved ears, nose, and mouth. The spout issues from the top of the head, and an arched strap handle joins the rear of the head to the back of the vessel. The body of the vessel is painted in a white slip, but the spout, and the head and long bent arms of the monkey are painted in black slip. Under the handle, on the reverse, the back of the monkey's body is painted with its tail coiled in concentric circles. The handle is painted in red slip.

As Donald Proulx has noted, monkeys are commonly depicted in Nasca art, but the theme can be traced back to earlier Paracas art, where monkey-like humans are depicted in the iconography of their textiles.[1] Yet monkeys are a typical forest mammal not native to the coastal people, and thus their significance to them is not completely understood. As we have seen on the north coast, monkeys there were apparently imported from the tropical forests of Ecuador.

cf. Martin-Vegue 1949, no. XL and other monkey vessels of Early Nasca (Proto-Nasca) in Lapiner 1976, nos. 471 and 472.

1. Proulx essay, p.87

105. BOWL in form of a feline head

Earthenware, slip painted in tan, orange, red, white and black
Nasca, Phases 2-3
Peru, South Coast
250 BC–AD 125
Height 3½" (9.1 cm) Diameter 4¾" (12.2 cm)
Condition: cleaned of salt deposits
Accession no. N-394

The ovoid bowl in-curving to the rim is in the form of a feline head with modeled ears and nostrils. Both eyes and pupils are semi-circles with arched double brows. The open mouth shows teeth, fangs and protruding tongue. Whiskers in wing form stretch sideways from either side of the mouth. Black pelt marks appear on the back of the head. The feline represented is probably the Pampas Cat (*Felis colocola*). Alan Lapiner published a mask, described as that of a fox, which has similar features, particularly the nose, ears and whiskers.[1]

1. Lapiner 1976, no. 470.

106. FIGURAL BOTTLE of a panpipe player

Earthenware, slip painted in brown, red, white and black and burnished
Nasca, Phase 2–Early 3
Peru, South Coast
250 BC-AD 125
Height 8 13/16" (22.4 cm) Diameter 5 3/4" (14.5 cm)
Condition: cleaned of salt deposits; surface chips repaired; top and right side of spout repaired
Accession no. N-260

This ovoid bottle is modeled in the form of a seated man playing panpipes held to his mouth. Such figural forms are relatively rare in Nasca art. While most of the detail is painted, the panpipes and the head, sporting a horned hat, are modeled. The eyes are outlined with bird-head markings. A spout rises from the back of the vessel and is attached to the back of the head by an arched strap handle.

cf. Schmidt 1929, fig. 329; Wolfe 1981, no. 186.

107. FIGURAL BOTTLE of a seated man

Earthenware, slip painted in red-brown, black and white
Nasca, Phase 2–Early 3
Peru, South Coast
250 BC-AD 125
Height 10¼″ (26 cm) Diameter 5⅜″ (13.5 cm)
Condition: cleaned of salt deposits; chip under left arm repaired; hole over right knee
Accession no. N-268

The cylindrically shaped body with rudimentary modeling of arms and legs and a superimposed head on this vessel is similar to the form of the effigy bottle in Number 106 and is equally rare in Nasca ceramics. The figure here also wears a brimmed hat with frontal projection. A pouring spout is at the rear of the head. An arched strap handle joins the brim of the hat to the back of the figure.

cf. Wolfe 1981, no. 186.

108. DOUBLE SPOUT BOTTLE with birds in flight

Earthenware, slip painted in red-orange, black, white, grey and brown
Nasca, Phase 3
Peru, South Coast
250 BC–AD 125
Height 6¾" (17.2 cm) Width 5½" (14 cm)
Condition: cleaned of salt deposits and restored
Accession no. N-357

A family of birds in flight is painted on a red ground in the main design register on both sides of this bulbous bottle below the double spout and bridge handle. A row of butterflies decorates a lower register near the base and is painted on a creamy white ground.

As Donald Proulx has noted, nothing is drawn with more detail as to species than birds. Among the most frequently portrayed species are the hummingbirds, depicted here. Birds are one of the major artistic motifs in Nasca pottery during Phases 3 and 4 and are found as minor elements in late phases as well. Hummingbirds are most popularly represented in Phase 3.

The hummingbird flying about San Pedro cactus, which is a hallucinogenic, is represented on a Chavín textile from the south coast.[1] A double spout and bridge bottle in the L.K. Land Collection, California, depicts hummingbirds extracting a substance from a rayed circular object, like a slice of multi-ribbed San Pedro cactus.[2] Hummingbirds and San Pedro figure in the curing practices of present-day Peruvians. Such an association may suggest the reason for the popularity of the hummingbird in Nasca art.

1. Cordy-Collins 1977, fig. 6.
2. Nicholson/Cordy-Collins 1979, no. 199 or 200.

109. BOWL with band of painted birds

Earthenware, slip painted in red, brown, grey, orange, black and white
Nasca, Phase 3
Peru, South Coast
250 BC–AD 125
Height 3 1/8" (8 cm)   Diameter 7 7/8" (20 cm)
Condition: cleaned of salt deposits and repaired
Accession no. N-436

A round-bottomed bowl with a wide, white-slipped exterior band on which is painted a row of birds, possibly Forest Birds. While each bird is nearly identical in shape, the color combinations differ from bird to bird. The interior is painted in red slip.

cf. Putnam 1914, no. III; Lehmann 1938, no. 577; Lumbreras 1974, p. 128.

110. BOWL with band of painted birds

Earthenware, slip painted in red, grey, tan, lavender, black and white
Nasca, Late Phase 3
Peru, South Coast
250 BC–AD 125
Height 2½" (6.4 cm) Diameter 5½" (14 cm)
Condition: cleaned of salt deposits and restored
Accession no. N-437

A round-bottomed bowl with a white-slipped exterior and a red-slipped rim band and interior. Painted around the exterior is a row of birds, possibly parrots. While each bird is nearly identical in shape, the color combinations differ from bird to bird. Spacing is uneven.

cf. Putnam 1914, no. 111; Lumbreras 1974, p. 128.

111. BOWL with band of painted birds

Earthenware, slip painted in red, grey, tan, black and white
Nasca, Late Phase 3
Peru, South Coast
250 BC–AD 125
Height 3⅞" (9.8 cm) Diameter 7" (17.8 cm)
Condition: cleaned of salt deposits and restored
On loan to Columbia University
Accession no. N-431

This round-bottomed bowl with slightly concave sides rising to the outward-flaring mouth has white-slipped exterior sides with a red-slipped mouth rim. Painted in a row around the exterior are birds, possibly Forest Birds, with diamond-shaped eyes, protruding breasts, wedge-shaped tails and oblong, white wing blocks tipped with three triangular feathers. While the birds are nearly identical in shape, the color combination differs from bird to bird, and the spacing between them is uneven.

cf. Putnam 1914, no. 111; Lumbreras 1974, p. 128.

112. BOWL with step-fret pattern

Earthenware, slip painted in white, reddish-brown, red and black
Nasca, Phase 3
Peru, South Coast
250 BC-AD 125
Height 3 1/8" (8 cm)   Diameter 9 1/8" (23.3 cm)
Condition: cleaned of salt deposits and repaired
Accession no. N-313

The bowl here with rounded bottom and slightly outflaring sides has a wide, white slip painted band, decorated with a row of reddish-brown step-fret motifs outlined in black. The interior is slip painted in red with black rim and basal bands.

113. BOWL with painted floral motifs

Earthenware, slip painted in red, black, white and orange
Nasca, Phase 3
Peru, South Coast
250 BC–AD 125
Height 4 1/16" (10.5 cm) Diameter 8 1/2" (21.6 cm)
Condition: cleaned of salt deposits and restored
Accession no. N-381

The conical-bottomed bowl here has white slip ground on the upper exterior wall, on which is painted, in zones delineated by vertical black lines, alternating red and black blossoms placed horizontally. One zone contains a small vertical blossom to fill extra space. Such space fillers are often used in Nasca art. The narrow rim border is painted in tiny blocks of red, white and orange.

cf. Schmidt 1929, p. 337; Martin-Vegue 1949, no. LIV-XLV.

114. DOUBLE SPOUT BOTTLE with Serpentine Creature

Earthenware, slip painted in browns, tan, orange, black and white
Nasca, Phase 3
Peru, South Coast
250 BC–AD 125
Height 7 1/4" (18.5 cm) Diameter 5 3/4" (14 cm)
Condition: cleaned of salt deposits and restored
Accession no. N-374

The globular bottle here has double spouts connected by a flat bridge handle. It is slip painted in chestnut brown with black spouts and handle. Painted around the circumference is the so-called Serpentine Creature wearing a feline mouth mask and with tongue protruding. The most distinguishing feature of this motif is the scalloped spikes which encircle the body. Such creatures are closely associated with agriculture and are drawn primarily on bowls to take advantage of the long horizontal design space, as on Numbers 115 and 116.

cf. Sawyer 1966, nos. 202, 206; Walker 1971, no. 70; Parsons 1974, no. 47; Wolfe 1981, p. 44ff.

115. BOWL with Serpentine Creature

Earthenware, slip painted in red, dark brown, grey, orange, black and white
Nasca, Phase 3
Peru, South Coast
250 BC–AD 125
Height 5 1/2" (14 cm) Diameter 9 3/8" (23.8 cm)
Condition: cleaned of salt deposits and restored
Accession no. N-425

The cup bowl here, with sides painted a deep red, has undulating around the exterior wall a Serpentine Creature wearing a feline mouth mask, double ear ornaments and a head ornament similar to those depicted in Numbers 114 and 116. The long serpent body is segmented, and the tongue protrudes.

cf. Putnam 1914, nos. IV, V; Lumbreras 1974, p. 128; Nicholson/Cordy-Collins 1979, no. 202; Wolfe 1981, p. 56.

116. BOWL with Serpentine Creature

Earthenware, with chestnut, orange, white and black pigments on red slip ground
Nasca, Phase 3
Peru, South Coast
250 BC–AD 125
Height 4 1/8" (10.5 cm) Diameter 8 1/2" (21.6 cm)
Condition: cleaned of salt deposits and restored
Accession no. N-427

This deep, round-bottomed bowl is painted in red slip on the exterior and interior. A polygrooved Serpentine Creature is painted around the exterior. The creature wears a feline mouth mask with upturned whiskers, a stylized face ornament, and has a protruding tongue in the form of a vegetable. Its forepaws are feline. The segmented body is filled with stylized trophy heads.

cf. Wolfe 1981, p. 57.

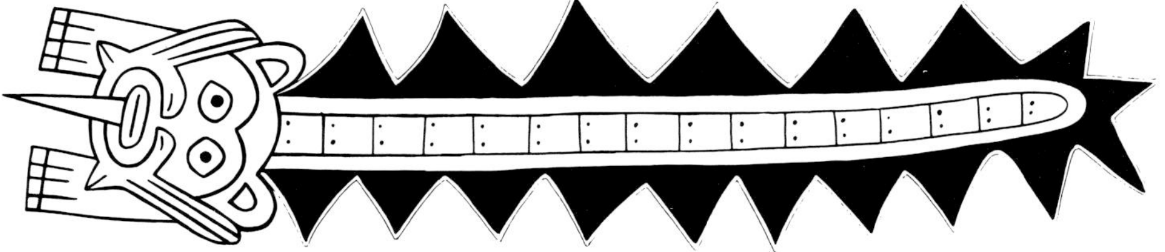

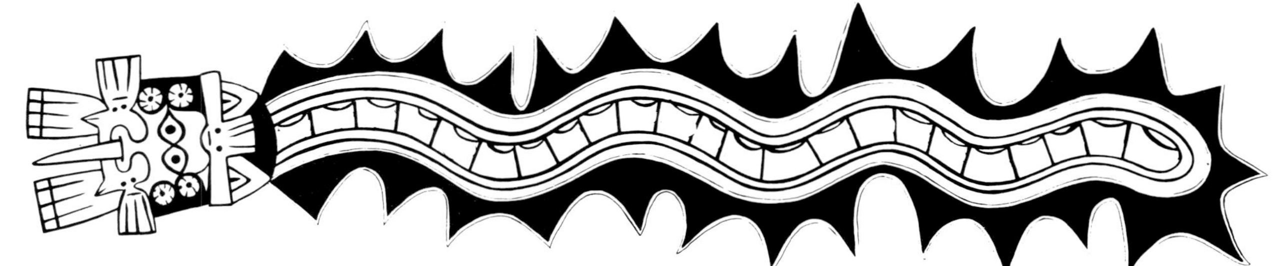

117. BOWL with warriors

Earthenware, slip painted in browns, orange, red, grey, black and white
Nasca, Phase 3
Peru, South Coast
250 BC–AD 125
Height 4 1/8" (10.7 cm) Diameter 6 1/4" (16 cm)
Condition: cleaned of salt deposits and restored
Accession no. N-383

The cup bowl here has a wide white exterior band painted with three warriors, each holding a spear thrower in one hand and darts in the other. Each warrior also wears a net hat with tassel. Their facial painting differs, however, being either stripes or dots.

cf. Putnam 1914, no. VIII; Disselhoff 1967, p. 19; Nicholson/Cordy-Collins 1979, no. 202.

118. BOWL with geometric motifs

Earthenware, slip painted in red, white, and black
Nasca, Late Phase 3
Peru, South Coast
250 BC–AD 125
Height 3¾" (9.5 cm) Diameter 7¹¹⁄₁₆" (19.5 cm)
Condition: cleaned of salt deposits and chips on rim repaired
Accession no. N-316

This conical-bottomed bowl is slip painted red with a wide, white exterior wall band painted with a repeat motif of multiple concentric black squares. Each motif is separated by one or more vertical black lines.

cf. Putnam 1914, nos. III, IV, IX; Schmidt 1929, p. 326; Martin-Vegue 1949, nos. XLIV, XLV.

119. BOWL with wave patterning

Earthenware, slip painted in white, orange, grey and red on a black ground
Peru, South Coast
250 BC–AD 125
Height 3⅛" (8 cm) Diameter 5½" (14 cm)
Condition: cleaned of salt deposits
Accession no. N-393

A cup bowl which has the interior slipped in red. Covering nearly the entire side walls of this cup bowl is a painted textile or multiple-wave patterning. The design is framed by white lines which are connected to the outer wave motifs by short vertical lines.

cf. Putnam 1914, no. IV; Martin-Vegue 1949, no. XLV.

120. BOWL with half-bean design

Earthenware, slip painted in white, red, yellow, and black
Nasca, Late Phase 3–Early Phase 4
Peru, South Coast
250 BC–AD 125
Height 4¾" (12 cm) Diameter 8⅛" (20.7 cm)
Condition: cleaned of salt deposits; crack from rim to center has been repaired
Accession no. N-317

This bowl with its conical bottom is slip painted red in its interior with a black rim band. On a wide exterior band, with a red slip ground, is painted a series of half-beans in various color combinations. The half-bean rather than the full-bean design is unusual.

cf. Putnam 1914, no. III; Schmidt 1929, no. 336; Martin-Vegue 1949, nos. XLIV, XLV; Lumbreras 1974, p. 128.

121. BOWL with toad or frog motif

Earthenware, painted with dark brownish-red, orange, white, black, gray and tan slip
Nasca, Phases 3-4
Peru, South Coast
250 BC–AD 125
Height: 3⅞" (9.8 cm) Diameter 6½" (16.5 cm)
Condition: cracks in body and chips on rim repaired; cleaned of salt deposits
Accession no. N-171

This cup bowl is slip painted red on the interior and exterior and has a narrow black rim band. Around the exterior wall is a row of stylized frogs.

cf. Putnam 1914, no. V; Martin-Vegue 1949, nos. XLII, XLVI; Sawyer 1966, no. 201; Lumbreras 1974, p. 128; Nicholson/Cordy-Collins 1979, no. 202.

122. JAR with foxes

Earthenware, slip painted in red, black and white
Nasca, Phases 3-4
Peru, South Coast
250 BC-AD 125
Height 5¾" (14.6 cm) Diameter 7⁷⁄₁₆" (19 cm)
Condition: cleaned of salt deposits and restored
Accession no. N-396

Painted on the white slip-painted ground of this collared jar is a procession of foxes. The lead fox stands with one paw on a representation of the Serpentine Creature. The animals are quite realistic, done in solid color with details in black and white. Foxes are not common subjects during this period.[1]

cf. Schmidt 1929, pp. 321, 338; Parsons 1974, no. 132.
1. Proulx 1968b.

123. DOUBLE SPOUT BOTTLE with Horrible Bird

Earthenware, slip painted in yellow, brown, tan, grey, red, black and white
Nasca, Phase 4
Peru, South Coast
250 BC-AD 125
Height 4¾" (12 cm) Diameter 4¼" (10.7 cm)
Condition: cleaned of salt deposits and restored
Accession no. N-440

A double spout bottle with a bridge handle which is slipped white on the upper walls above a wide red band. The spouts and bridge handle of this bulbous bottle are slip painted in red. On the white slip ground of the body are two representations of the Horrible Bird. Series of trophy heads decorate the backs of the birds and are intermingled in the feathers.

cf. Schmidt 1929, pp. 332,342; Proulx 1968b, p. 158, pl. 9b.

124. BOWL painted with interlocking snake patterns

Earthenware, slip painted
Nasca, Phase 5
Peru, South Coast
250 BC–AD 125
Height 2¹⁵⁄₁₆" (7.4 cm)   Diameter 6⅞" (17.5 cm)
Condition: cleaned of salt deposits and restored
Accession no. N-433

Slip painted in red on the interior, and with a narrow black rim band, this round-bottom bowl has exterior walls of slipped white, painted with an abstract textile patterning of double snakes in brown and black interlocking with a single snake in white and black.

cf. Putnam 1914, no. 111.

125. BOWL with stylized trophy heads

Earthenware, slip painted in white and black
Nasca, Phase 5
Peru, South Coast
AD 125–250
Height 3¼" (8.3 cm)   Diameter 3⁹⁄₁₆" (9.1 cm)
Condition: some iron staining on the white ground; has been cleaned of salt deposits and chip on rim repaired
Accession no. N-246

The exterior wall of this cup bowl is painted on a white slip ground with double rows, in alternating spaces, of trophy heads sketched in black with their half-moon heads bordered by feather patterns. A narrow black band lines the mouth rim.

Trophy heads are an important independent motif in Nasca art, as their representation here implies. They are depicted in various ways from the beginning of the Nasca sequence to the end. They are also often used as substitutes for natural objects. It is a complex theme with many possible interpretations. Donald Proulx has argued that among the ancient Nasca, the reason for taking trophy heads might be analogous to the motivations of the historic Jivaro Indians of Eastern Peru and Ecuador, who take heads of their dead enemies (and shrink them) in order to prevent the avenging spirit of the dead person from harming the killer.

cf. Martin-Vegue 1949, nos. XLIV, XLiii.

126. BEAKER with bird and step-fret motif

Earthenware, slip painted in brown, dark red, tan, yellow, grey, black and white
Nasca, Phase 5
Peru, South Coast
AD 125-250
Height 6 1/16" (15.5 cm) Diameter 4 1/8" (10.6 cm)
Condition: cleaned of salt deposits and restored
Accession no. N-382

The beaker, rising from a slightly curved base, bulges in a soft curve on the lower body. Surface decoration is divided into horizontal bands from the base to the mouth.

The wide lower band is undecorated but painted brown. Above it is a band of step-fret or throne or litter motifs on a white ground set between two black bounding lines. The step-fret band is separated from the uppermost level of decor by two encircling bands, one grey-blue, the other brown-red. A series of white banner-like panels seem to hang from the brown-black line around the mouth rim: they are set on orange ground; each panel contains a bird facing downward and in profile, in alternating colors of brown-red, orange-red and yellow. The white panels are interconnected near the mouth rim as if imitating a hanging or drapery used in an architectural setting, perhaps a temple precinct. The key to the identity of the bird, possibly a white-collared swift, may be more naturalistic birds appearing on a painted panpipe in the Regional Museum of Ica. The birds' heads and bodies on the vessel here, however, are in more abstract forms.[1] On the other hand, a cup in the Krannert Art Museum at the University of Illinois has similar birds, as well as general organization of decor, and Alan Sawyer has described them as abstracted *vencejo* motifs.[2] The *vencejo*, already seen in abstract form on Number 9, is one of the most ancient south coast motifs. Undoubtedly, it had a special ancient religious significance.

1. Bird et al. 1981, p. 69.
2. Sawyer 1975a, fig. 137, see also Putnam 1914, nos. 11, IX; Parsons 1974, no. 142.

127. HEAD JAR

Earthenware, slip painted in white, black, red and brownish-red
Nasca, Phase 5
Peru, South Coast
AD 125-250
Height 6¼" (16 cm) Diameter 7½" (19 cm)
Condition: has been cleaned of salt deposits; cracks and chips near the rim have been restored
Accession no. N-9

This bulbous jar has been formed and decorated to depict a head with the swell at the top forming a turban bound with slings. The thin, beak-like nose is modeled and extends from the surface. Eyes are almond-shaped with dot pupils and multiple brows. The face is painted in white slip, but the rest of the vessel is black with faint red sling lines on the turban. Large, leaf-shaped areas of red-brown are painted below the eyes, which have three lines above as brows. The mouth is a lighter red oblong. Conical holes have been drilled into the top of the jar near the rim and were probably meant for the passage of a carrying cord or thong.

Nasca Culture spread over the south coast by military means. Trophy heads were presumably made from the decapitated heads of prisoners. Yet, in Nasca Culture, trophy heads are frequently associated with so-called mythical beings, and it is therefore probable that the main purpose for headhunting was ritualistic: possibly the heads were meant as offerings to the Mythical Being.

"Head jars" modeled by Nasca potters in the form of trophy heads are found in many Nasca burials. They "may represent imitations of the ritually powerful heads which the buried individual may not have been fortunate to have collected himself, or they may have served as replacements for heads which had been taken."[1] The head jar here is distinguished from trophy head jars by the presence of open eyes and the lack of pinned lips and other features associated with the latter.[2] It is modeled with a turban headdress like those, actually found in graves, composed of textiles around which a sling was wound.

cf. Schmidt 1929, pl. V; Lehman 1938, no. 553; Martin-Vegue 1949, nos. XLII, XLVI; Disselhoff 1967, p. 129; Proulx 1968, no. 29a; Wolfe 1981, nos. 239-40.
1. Proulx 1971, p. 20.
2. Proulx essay in this catalogue, p. 33.

128. JAR in the form of a trophy head

Earthenware, slip painted in tan, red, black and white
Nasca, Phase 5
Peru, South Coast
AD 125–250
Height 7 1/16" (18 cm) Diameter 4 3/4" (12 cm)
Condition: cleaned of salt deposits and areas of paint loss restored
Accession no. N-380

The "head jar" here bulges in the lower section and narrows at the neck. It is modeled and painted as a trophy head. The ears are mere bulges in the sides of the head, the eyelids have a fringe of lashes on them, the modeled nose is thin and straight, and the mouth is elongated and filled with black dots. Pins hold the lips closed. There is triangular face paint below the closed eyes. Two wide horizontal bands, one red, one black, circle the neck of the jar above the stylized black hair. Mummified specimens of trophy heads date back to the pre-ceramic period in ancient Peru. The most extensive occurrence of head hunting, however, appears to be on the south coast, especially in the Ica and Nasca valleys where the Early Paracas and the succeeding Nasca cultures were located. Their pattern of warfare and their religious mythology were intricately involved in head-taking. Certainly the head was something powerful to the Paracas and Nasca peoples. Archaeology has substantiated frequent depictions of trophy heads in the religious art. Their mythical beings seem to have thrived on them. A skillful warrior could gain stature and power by his military prowess in capturing prisoners for head-taking.

The fact that the lips of trophy heads are pinned shut, as on the jar here, implies that head-taking might mean the acquisition of a slain enemy's power or the prevention of his soul or spirit from harming the killer. Pinning lips shut on the trophy head could inhibit the loss of the soul or power embodied within the head.[1]

A very similar head jar from the Uhle Collection at University of California was excavated from the Nasca Valley.[2]

cf. Putnam 1914, no. IX; Schmidt 1929, pl. V; Martin-Vegue 1949, nos. XL, XLI, XLIII; Sawyer 1968, no. 402; Proulx 1968b, pl. 29b; Parsons 1974, no. 102; Sawyer 1975a, no. 138; Wolfe 1981, no. 239.

1. Proulx 1971.
2. Proulx 1968b, pl. 29b, then associated with Nasca Phase 4.

129. HEAD JAR

Earthenware, slip painted in cream, tan, red, black and white
Nasca, Phase 5
Peru, South Coast
AD 125–250
Height 5 1/2" (14 cm) Diameter 6 1/4" (16 cm)
Condition: cleaned of salt deposits and spots of paint loss restored
Accession no. N-388

The jar here is bulbous and squat with a round base and sides curving in towards the mouth rim. Painted and modeled in the form of a human head, it gives the appearance of having full, fleshy cheeks. Its almond-shaped eyes have pupils attached to the upper eyelids, with a single curved brow above them and wide red bands below the lower lids and over the nose, which is modeled. The mouth is a rectangle. There are round, red dots on the cheeks. The hair is black with long sideburns and is tied with a zigzag band, possibly a sling.

"Head jars," judging just from the ones illustrated here, were obviously important in burial, perhaps, as the head itself, a repository of the life force. It was the precious energy of the head that was sought in the taking of trophy heads, since the head was considered to be the residence of the spiritual power of the individual. The jar here, however, represents a living person and is distinguished from the trophy head jars by the presence of open eyes and the lack of pinned lips.

cf. Martin-Vegue 1949, no. XLV; Parsons 1974, no. 132.

130. HEAD JAR

Earthenware, slip painted in tan, red, black and white
Nasca, Phase 5
Peru, South Coast
AD 125–250
Height 6 1/16" (15.5 cm) Diameter 6" (15.3 cm)
Condition: cleaned of salt deposits; nose is a restoration
Accession no. N-441

The bulbous vase here is also painted and modeled in the form of a human head. Its eyes, with eyelashes shown, are closed, and two straight lines above them indicate the brows. The nose is modeled. Markings around the oval mouth represent a moustache and beard. Red triangles on the cheeks outlined in black probably represent a form of face paint. Ears are modeled tabs. The black hair, hanging long in back, is bound with a white and black band which comes to a point over the forehead. It is not quite clear whether, with its closed eyes, a trophy head is meant. There are, however, no pins through the lips.

cf. Schmidt 1929, pp. 331, 338f; Martin-Vegue 1949, no. XLV; Parsons 1980, no. 132.

131. DOUBLE SPOUT BOTTLE with Anthropomorphic Mythical Being

Earthenware, slip painted in browns, tan, orange, yellow, black and white
Nasca, Phase 5
Peru, South Coast
AD 125–250
Height 7½" (19 cm) Diameter 7" (17.8 cm)
Condition: cleaned of salt deposits; spots of flaked paint restored; one spout lip repaired
Accession no. N-355

Of globular shape with double spouts bridged by a flat handle, this bottle is painted with two Anthropomorphic Mythical Beings on a white ground. The body parts, such as arms, legs and face are recognizable and realistically rendered. Each Being wears a feline mouth mask and grasps a trophy head in one hand and a club in the other. This creature is basically human in form with feline attributes primarily in facial characteristics. His mouth mask is shown with lateral elements in the form of cat's whiskers, which also appear to be stylized trophy heads. He wears forehead ornaments, bangles in the hair and a cloak which appears as the back and tail of an animal. He also wears a segmented necklace. Donald Proulx has indicated that Nasca religion revolved around a series of Mythical Beings, or deities who had certain functions, apparently in the cosmos.[1] As in Greek mythology, each god probably was the subject of certain myths. No written records, however, have transmitted the details of the mythology.

Several Nasca Mythical Beings are always associated with trophy heads. Others have agricultural functions. The leading figure among those associated with trophy heads is the one here. Five distinct varieties of this creature were known by early Nasca times.[2] The format here has been described by Elizabeth Farkass Wolfe as the *animal emblem format.*[4] It portrays a natural or mythical animal, often including the head, which probably originated from animal skin headdresses.

The necklace, made of pieces of spondylus shell attached to a braided cord, is frequently encountered in Nasca graves. The spondylus shell was coveted in ancient Peru. It is found from the Bay of Guayaquil in Ecuador to Baja California and was traded throughout the Andes from Chavín times to the colonial period.

cf. Sawyer 1966, no. 202; Proulx 1968, p. 152, pl. 3a; Walker 1969, no. 70; Parsons 1974, no. 47; Lapiner 1976, no. 202; Wolfe 1981, pp. 44ff.

1. Proulx 1971, p. 19.
2. *Ibid.*, p. 18.
3. Sawyer 1975a, p. 134.
4. Wolfe 1981, p. 18 and fig. 195.

132. VASE with Anthropomorphic Mythical Being

Earthenware, slip painted in browns, red, grey, black and white
Nasca, Phase 5
Peru, South Coast
AD 125–250
Height 6 1/16" (15.5 cm)   Diameter 4 1/8" (10.6 cm)
Condition: cleaned of salt deposits; crack on base and surface chips repaired
Accession no. N-170

This conical cup has a flat base and its sides splay out from the base to the midsection where they swell further and revert inwards towards the rim. Painted horizontally on the white ground of the wide band on the upper half of the cup is another example of the Anthropomorphic Mythical Being described in Number 131. The Being wears a grey feline mask, painted in the form of a trophy head, a head ornament and multiple ear ornaments. The thumbs are in the form of vegetable appendages. The signifier, whose primary function is to carry abstract symbols which may represent more than one mythical aspect of the being, ends in a spear point.

cf. Martin-Vegue 1949, no XLI.

133. BOTTLE with lug handles

Earthenware, slip painted in brown, brown-red, black, red, orange, white, grey, mauve, tan
Nasca, Phase 5
Peru, South Coast
*AD 125-250**
Height 13⅞" (34.6 cm) Diameter 12¾" (31.9 cm)
Condition: chips in slip at mouth rim; possibly repair to one lug
Accession no. 83.4.1

This large bottle, with rounded sides curving inward to a short, narrow neck and spaced around the upper walls with three loop handles, is pointed at the base. Except for the base, the vessel is fully painted. The large central figure, facing outward, appears to be an agricultural deity. His shield-shaped, yellowish-tan face is spotted with black and red; the nose is not indicated. He wears a white conical cap with stitching or lacing on it. His collar and tunic contain agricultural symbols in each hand. The body of the Serpentine Being radiates from either side of the deity's collar. Both ends of the Serpentine Being terminate in a cat-like head and paws. The complicated iconography and format of the design make the vessel extremely unusual and one which requires more time to study in order to interpret properly. The spotted face and conical cap appear on other vessels but not on any as large or as densely painted. One in the May Collection in St. Louis shows the deity holding two different plants, and vegetal motifs are attached to his arms.[1] A vessel formerly in the Wasserman-San Blas collection is similar to the May bottle: the head sports the same conical cap, but the face of the figure is not spotted and instead of vegetal forms, he carries weapons in his hands.[2] All the vessels with this figure on it seem to be painted in predominantly brown and brown-red tones.

A more detailed discussion of the iconography and style of this unusual vessel is planned as the subject of an article by Donald Proulx. The technical measurements already undertaken have confirmed its authenticity. X-rays, taken after the thermoluminescence analysis was reported on a clay sample from the base of the bottle, indicate a consistency in the clay body from neck to base with one long firing crack which, apparently, was reinforced from the inside of the vessel, possibly in antiquity, and a possible repair to one of the lugs on the shoulder.

1. See Parsons 1980, no. 445; another vessel similar to the one in the May Collection with single spout, bridge handle and effigy head wearing a conical cap, the hands of the figure painted in holding plants, is in the Museum für Volkerkunde, published in Eisleb 1977, vol. II, pl. 250, and is unusual in having the figure eating an animal; a cup with the same figure on it was published in Lehmann 1938, no. 580, and another, almost identical one by della Santa 1965, pl. 40, fig. 57.

**OX-TL ref. no. 381g25, 6/23/83 indicates that the sample tested was last fired between 1000 and 1600 years ago.*

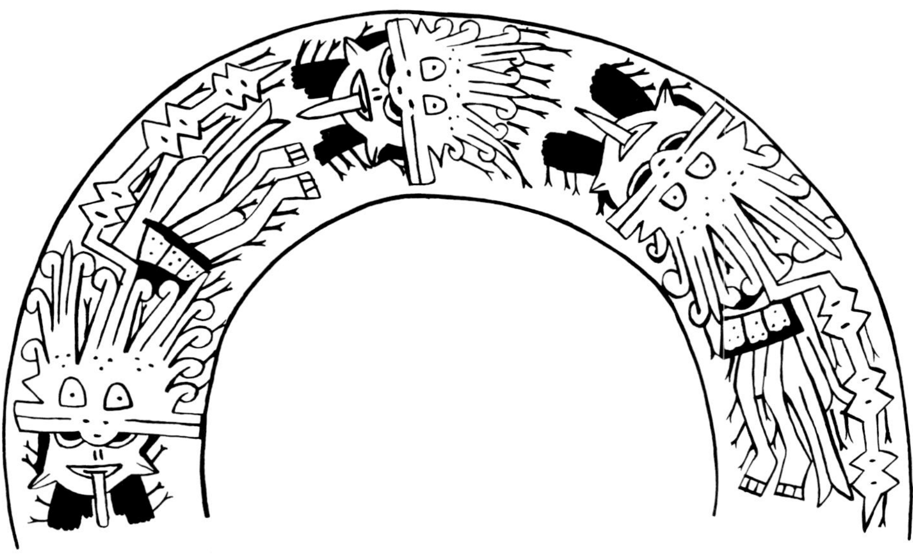

134. BOWL with row of trophy head deities

Earthenware, slip painted in tan, grey red, black and white on the white
Nasca, Phase 6
Peru, South Coast
AD 250-540
Height 4 ⅛" (10.4 cm) Diameter 9½" (23 cm)
Condition: cleaned of salt deposits and of overpainting; cracks repaired
Accession no. N-389

The bowl, flaring out from a rounded bottom, has painted on the exterior a row of proliferous trophy head deities or tasters. The small "V"-shaped grey heads with half-moon eyes and extended tongues are topped with scrolled and peaked forehead ornaments which have eyes, nose, and a spreading serpent-like finial. Bifurcated hairs project from all parts. In laying out the design on the bowl, the painter seems to have underestimated his space, since a single head appears unattached to body parts. In the rollout drawing it is possible to see what the figures include. As the Nasca phases progressed, there was at first a tendency towards more intricate motifs, crackling with energy. The complex style is referred to as proliferous. The faces on the figures here have elaborate whisker masks and from the complex headdress ornament a jagged streamer appears. Black, glove-like arms appear below the head. The reduced lower half of a figure, legs and loincloth decorated with trophy heads, is appended to the headdress ornament.

cf. Walker 1969, no. 103; Sawyer 1975a, no. 143.

135. HEAD JAR

Earthenware, slip painted in browns, grey, yellow, tan, red, black and white
Nasca, Phase 6
Peru, South Coast
AD 250-540
Height 5¼" (13.3 cm)   Diameter 6¼" (16 cm)
Condition: intact
Accession no. 82.6.27

A variation of the head jars already seen, the lower portion of this vessel is rounded and sharply constricted below the flaring upper portion. It has the shape of a spittoon. The lower portion is painted to represent a trophy head. Below stylized black hair the oval eyes contain round pupils, and have simple arched brows and stepped face painting below them, typical of Nasca Phase 4. The mouth, with flanking moustachios and a chin beard, is pinned with thorns. Above multiple horizontal lines the flared upper portion is painted with a band of repeat interlocked proliferous trophy head deities or tasters.

This deity or trophy head taster is an even more abstract version of the proliferous deity in Number 134. Here the face, whiskers and forehead ornament are simplified, but heads or masks are interconnected, with the tongue of one joining the brow of the next, giving the motif the appearance of a bizarre string of beads. The face mask and forehead elements of deities grow in complexity from the time of their introduction in the Late Paracas Period until they become a primary motif with tightly curled and sharply angular lines.

cf. Proulx 1968b, p. 77; Sawyer 1975a, no. 144.

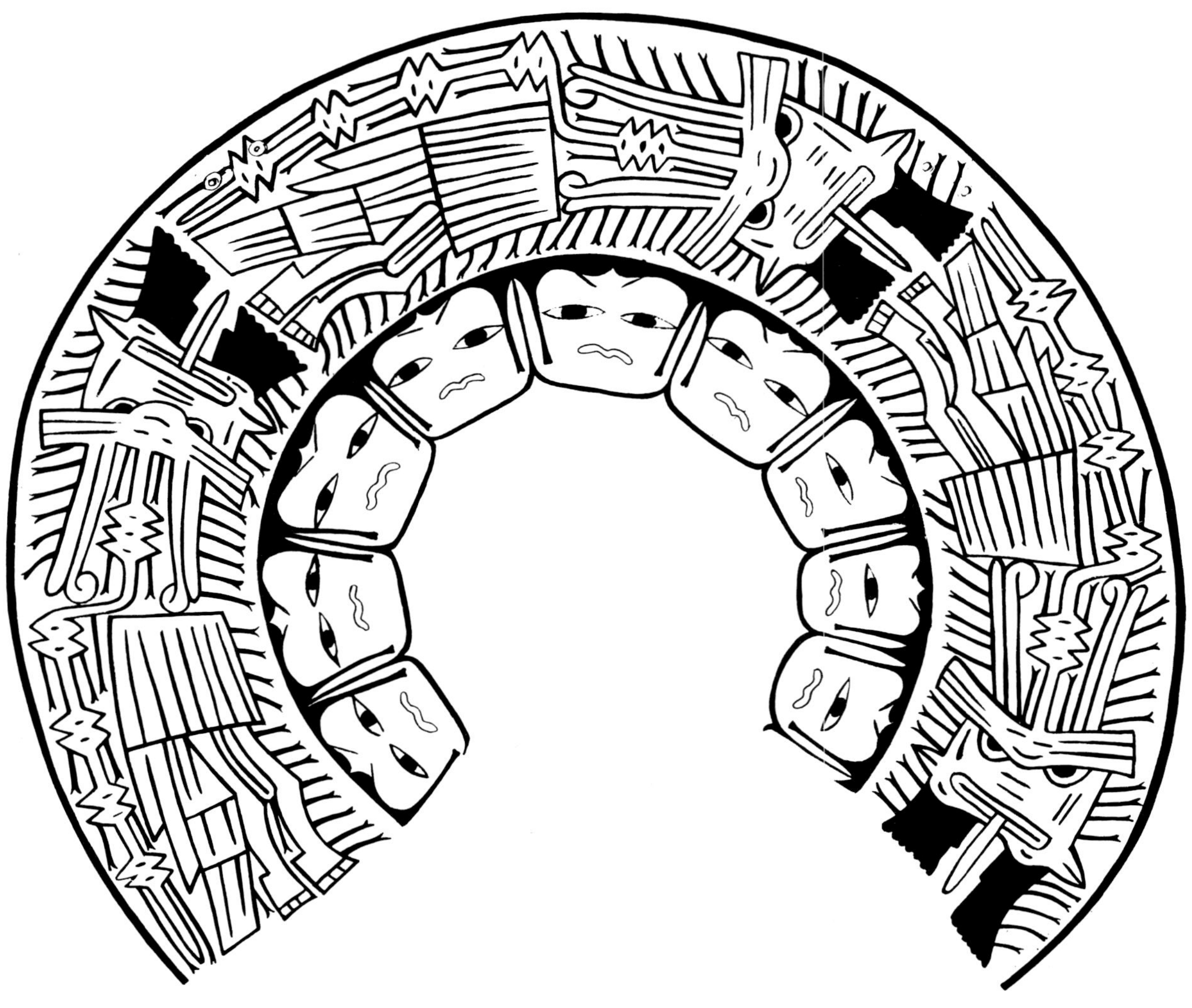

136. LARGE BOWL with painted figures

Earthenware with orange, red, white and black pigments
Nasca–Huari (?), Phase 6
Peru, South Coast
AD 250–540
Height 5⁷⁄₁₆" (13.8 cm)   Diameter 15⅝" (39.6 cm)
Condition: cleaned of salt deposits; there are two large cracks on the sides with conical holes made in antiquity on either side of each crack to hold it together
Accession no. 83.2.1

This very large bowl flares out from a rounded bottom. Painted on a wide band below the rim are three stylized, elongated figures representing the Feline Guardian of agriculture (?). The forehead ornament of each consists of two tall "horns"and a central plume which falls beside the body to the feet. Their tongues protrude between the glove-like arms. Their long bodies with breechcloths are separated from their heads. Each figure is lined on both sides with elements with bifurcated ends which may represent trophy hair, and by inference the trophy head. The lowest band of decoration contains stylized female heads, three of which, for lack of space are painted with one eye only.

The figure here is less bristling than we have seen in Number 134, although some of the same elements appear on both: jagged streamer, black glove-like arms and legs with loincloth added. But the deity is altered in appearance and expressive quality. The face is simpler and the rendering of the whole is freer with a more slashing line. The design here also lacks the tight controlled complexity of Number 134.

cf. Sawyer 1975a, no. 145.

137. BEAKER with tiers of female faces

Earthenware, slip painted in red, cream, brown, black and white
Nasca, Phase 6
Peru, South Coast
AD 250–540
Height 7⁷⁄₈" (20 cm)   Diameter 4" (10.2 cm)
Condition: cleaned of salt deposits and cracks and rim chips repaired
Accession no. N-432

The tall beaker here is shaped with two convexly swelled bands, one at the bottom above the rounded base and one in the middle of the vessel, each incorporating painted rows of joined female heads. Between these bands is a concave area, slipped white, on which is painted a row of step-fret motifs. The concave walls below the rim are slipped white and painted with oblique, repeating darts and staffs.

The multiple painted and partially modeled female faces are a Phase 5 innovation, but they are often found in horizontal bands around the tall vases characteristic of later phases. The femaleness of the faces is characterized by the curved hair hanks on either side of each face which tend to frame it.

cf. Putnam 1914, nos. II, VII; Lehmann 1938, no. 584; Martin-Veque 1949, no. XL.

138. BEAKER with tiers of female heads

Earthenware, slip painted in tan, brown, red, black and white
Nasca, Phase 6
Peru, South Coast
AD 250–540
Height 7 7/8" (20 cm) Diameter 4" (10.2 cm)
Condition: cleaned of salt deposits and chips on rim repaired
Accession no. N-435

The tall beaker here differs from Number 137 in shape and design although it includes two wide bands of joined female heads. The vessel has slightly concave sides which rise to a flaring mouth and is painted in five tiers. The eyes of the female heads are oval with dot pupils; the mouths are oval or rectangular. Long, black braids hang down on either side of the head. The bands at the neck and base are narrower and contain diamond/dot motifs which differ in color combinations. The narrow central band contains a repeating geometric design consisting of a rectangle with lines emanating from either side.

139. LARGE FACE COLLAR JAR

Earthenware, slip painted in brown, tan, red, black and white
Nasca, Phase 6 or 7
Peru, South Coast
AD 250-540
Height 12¼" (31 cm) Diameter 10" (25.4 cm)
Condition: cleaned of salt deposits and restored
Published: Dockstader 1967, no. 128
Accession no. N-339

This very large ovoid jar with three lug handles has a human face painted on the collar. The eyes are almond-shaped with dot pupils and have a single curved brow. The nose is modeled; the mouth is a rectangle. Black hair surrounds the face in a severe style and long tresses flow over the shoulder of the vessel. Three lines of "tears" flow from each eye. On the shoulder two arms embrace a cluster of vegetables. Among the pottery excavated from Huaca del Loro phase burials at Cahuachi in the Moche River Valley are four polychrome effigy jars with similar faces on the necks.

1. Strong 1957, p.37; see also Putnam 1914, nos. X, XI; Martin-Veque 1949, no. XLII; Nicholson/Cordy-Collins 1979, no. 201.

140. LARGE FACE COLLAR JAR

Earthenware, slip painted in grey, tan, red, yellow, black and white
Nasca, Phase 6 or 7
Peru, South Coast
AD 250-540
Height 11¾" (30 cm) Diameter 11¾" (27.9 cm)
Condition: cleaned of salt deposits and restored
Accession no. N-340

A very large, ovoid jar with a human face painted on the collar. The eyes are almond-shaped with dot pupils and have a single curved brow. Both the nose and mouth are modeled. There is a painted cap, with crosses, and long black hair with sideburns. The upper portion of the vessel is painted as a shawl with arms and hands painted on the front. The red shawl is decorated with yellow and grey elliptical forms. A certain resemblance can also be seen on this jar with the faces of the effigy jars excavated from Huaca de Loro and referred to in Number 139.

1. Strong 1957, fig. 15d.

141. EFFIGY BOTTLE, modeled head on neck

Earthenware, brown, orange, white and black slip
Nasca, Phase 7
Peru, South Coast
AD 250–540
Height 5¾" (14.4 cm) Width 5" (12.7 cm)
Condition: cleaned of salt deposits and repaired at rim
Accession no. N-451

This small, flask-shaped vessel has been painted and modeled as a man wearing a poncho. The man's head is on the neck of the bottle with small appliqué nose and ears. A horizontal black line below the rim suggests a cap. The features are drawn in black on a white slip. The upper portion of the bottle is striped in orange, brown and white, and edged with black, suggesting a poncho. Two lugs to hold a suspension cord are attached to the shoulders.

142. SET OF PANPIPES

Earthenware, with red slip painting, and burnished
Nasca
Peru, North Coast
ca. AD 300 (?)
Height 16¼" (41 cm) *Width 6" (15.3 cm)*
Condition: cleaned of salt deposits and cracks on upper section repaired
Accession no. N-320

Ten slip cast tubes of varying length have been joined with clay into a set of panpipes. According to Lawrence Dawson, slip cast panpipes begin to appear in archaeological sites on the coast sometime in the later part of the Early Horizon, circa 50 BC–AD 50, and are associated with pottery of Phase 9 of the Paracas Ocucaje Style.[1] Laboratory examination shows no trace of contact with any object on the inner surfaces. Slip casting was not used in Europe until the eighteenth century; thus the ancient Peruvian potters can be credited with having known about it some eighteen hundred years earlier.

A study of the musical characteristics of South Coast panpipes was made by William W. Suggs in an unpublished typescript cited by Dawson. According to Suggs, panpipes being produced by Phase 3 Nasca could play several modes of the pentatonic scale. Many such pipes were made in graduated sets of two or three instruments, presumably to be played in some polyphonic combination. Suggs' study of the scales produced by these panpipes also led him to suggest that ancient Peruvian music may have been more sophisticated, in several aspects, than what was being produced at the same time in Europe.

1. Dawson 1964.

143. BOTTLE in kidney shape

Earthenware, painted in red slip
Nasca (?)
Peru, South Coast
*AD 500-600**
Height 7" (18 cm)   Width 8¾" (22 cm)
Condition: cleaned of salt deposits and chips on lip of spout repaired
Accession no. N-110

The widest area of this kidney-shaped canteen is at the top. Its short spout has a thickened rim, and loop handles are attached to the sides just below the shoulder. The entire vessel is painted with a red slip. Such a vessel shape does not appear in any of the literature, but there is a similar piece in a New York private collection known to the author.[1] The surface color and finish are comparable to the Nasca panpipes in Number 142, and the bottle is therefore included with the Nasca material, although actual provenience is not known. The minimum age indicated in the thermoluminescence analysis indicates that the piece was fired in antiquity but does not provide any basis of dating beyond that minimum age. Further technical measurements, such as trace element analysis of the clay and analysis of the slip with which the vessel was painted may, in the future, provide a method for establishing provenience, if comparisons can be made with similar analysis of other objects.

1. Seen while on loan to Duke University Museum.

**OX-TL ref. no. 381f1, 2/08/83 and 5/26/83 estimates that the sample tested has a minimum age of 470 years according to results of two TL tests, one to analyze fading.*

144. LARGE JAR with fox and birds

Earthenware, black and white on redware
Ica-Chincha
Peru, South Coast
AD 1300-1476
Height 12¼" (31.1 cm) Width 12¾" (32.3 cm)
Condition: intact
Accession no. 82.6.11

A large, kidney-shaped jar with a narrow neck and flaring rim, this vessel is decorated with a continuing motif of stylized fox-like animals chasing a flock of birds painted around the shoulder above seven black and white bands. Closer to the neck are five circling bands in black and white, the wider band containing a wavy frieze. Two wide black bands circle the neck and rim. The black and white motifs are copied from textiles.

By comparison with the splendid Nasca traditions which preceded it, the ceramics of the Ica Style have been described as competent but dull. There were a few elegant forms, like the vessel here, but the designs, like those on textiles, were mostly of small figured geometric patterns.

The crouching animal on this jar and the small shorthand drawing of the flock of birds can be seen on another vessel of the same shape and culture in the Krannert Art Museum at the University of Illinois.[1] Ica art developed in the Late Horizon Period, when people on the south coast valleys formed a confederation known as "Ica" after the name of the confederation's central valley. Their confederation was formed after the breakup of the Huari Empire and extended north to the Pisco and Chincha valleys and south through the Rio Grande de Nasca.

cf. Schmidt 1929, p. 307; Lumbreras 1974, no. 199.

1. Sawyer 1975a, no. 163.

145. KERO with modeled animal head

Earthenware, painted in cream, orange, red, grape, and black
Tiahuanaco
Bolivia, South Andean Highlands
AD 400-700
Height 11" (27.9 cm) Width 7⁵⁄₁₆" (20.1 cm) Depth 12" (30.4 cm)
Condition: the head and tail have been broken and repaired; cleaned of salt deposits
Loan to Columbia University
Accession no. N-16

The *kero* or slant-sided beaker is a classic Tiahuanaco form which remained in use for centuries in ancient Peru and diffused throughout the southern Andes during the period between AD 500 and 800. Here it is modeled with a cat's head on one side of the undulating rim, in contrast to Number 146, which has a bird's head. Painted in profile on the sides is a chunky feline. Its body, outlined in black, is reserved in gray. The animal's eyes are divided vertically black and white, typical of the highland area style. The body is filled with black spots and a red and orange symbol in reverse scrolls. The red ground of the vessel is decorated with abstract designs or symbols in orange and black. The so called "Greek" key frieze circles the base.

cf. Schmidt 1929, pp. 357-9; Dockstader 1967, no. 177; Lumbreras 1974, no. 156.

146. KERO with modeled bird's head

Earthenware, burnished redware with black pigment
Tiahuanaco
Bolivia, South Andean Highlands
AD 400-700
Height 8" (20 cm) Diameter 6" (15 cm)
Condition: cleaned of salt deposits; ruff around bird's head restored on top, proper right side and bottom; tail has been broken and repaired.
Accession no. N-14

This *kero* with undulating rim has on one side a bird's head with a square plaque ruff and on the other a spread tail. The body of the vessel and the square ruff are decorated with elegantly drawn black lines and abstract vignettes of stylized rapacious bird heads and wings. The interior is painted in black slip and the tail is barred with black.

cf. Schmidt 1929, pp. 357-9; Lumbreras 1974, no. 156.

147. EFFIGY VESSEL in the form of a llama

Earthenware, buffware slipped with white and burnished red
Tiahuanaco
Peru, Central Highlands
ca. AD 400-700
Height 6½" (16 cm)   Length 6" (15.2 cm)
Condition: cleaned of salt deposits; one ear is a restoration; cracks repaired
Accession no. N-601

This rare effigy vessel of a llama with large, flaring, burnished red spout at the rear, is delicately modeled with excellent proportions. The ears are laid back and the mouth is partly open. The body is slip painted white except for the red spout flaring up from the hindquarters. The piece is reminiscent of a large, modeled llama found on the coast and now in the Pacheco National Museum of Anthropology and Archaeology, Lima, except that the modeling on the Sackler llama is more elegant and refined.[1]

1. Bird et al. 1981, p. 85; see also Cossio 1971, p. 103.

148. HEAD SPOUT BOTTLE

Earthenware, cream slip with burnished orange, grey, black and white pigments
Coastal Huari, Atarco Style
Peru, South Coast
ca. AD 600-700
Height 6 3/8" (16.2 cm)   Diameter 4 3/4" (12 cm)
Condition: cleaned of salt deposits; spots of flaked paint restored
Accession no. N-384

This globular bottle, a popular form of the Huari Period, has a long spout modeled in the form of a man's head with the nose and ears appliquéd and the mouth ridged. Eyes and brows are painted in black on the cream face, and orange and black squares are painted on the cheeks. A narrow, painted rim band delineates the cap, which is filled with lines, blocks, and hooks. The round bottle form is painted on each side of a central vertical band with what becomes a chevron design whose colored bands get progressively smaller. The collar is decorated with frets.

cf. Schmidt 1929, pp. 282f and pl. 111; Dockstader 1967, fig 139.

149. GLOBULAR BOTTLE with tall spout

Earthenware, with dark red, tan, yellow, grey, black and white pigments and burnished
Coastal Huari, Atarco Style
Peru, South Coast
*ca. AD 600–700**
Height 7 9/16" (19.2 cm) Diameter 5 7/8" (14.9 cm)
Condition: excellent with no repairs
Accession no. 82.6.14

This flat-bottomed, round bottle with a slim, tapered neck has a row of disembodied heads in profile around the shoulder. Each headdress has trailing plumes which include a stylized feather and each head is separated by a vertical dart motif. The slender, tapered spout is encircled by a polychromed chevron motif.

cf. Schmidt 1929, p. 282; Menzel 1964, no. 20.

**OX-TL ref. no. 381e98, 2/28/83, estimates that the sample tested was last fired between 650 and 1000 years ago.*

150. DOUBLE WHISTLING BOTTLING with human effigy

Earthenware, with red, dark red, tan, black and white pigments
Coastal Huari, Atarco Style
Peru, South Coast
*ca. AD 600-700**
Height 4½" (11.4 cm) Length 6½" (16.5 cm)
Condition: excellent with no repairs
Accession no. 82.6.15

One bottle of this double whistling vessel is connected to the other by a tube and an arched strap handle. The first bottle is modeled in human form with the blind spout head containing the whistle. The face of the figure is strongly modeled and there is a large, square, red patch under each eye and across the nose. The figure wears a black tunic bordered with white and white straps over his black hair, which is depicted with long sideburns. His sleeves and hands are painted on the side of the bottle. The second bottle has the typical tapered Huari spout at the base of which is painted a garland of red and black fruit or vegetables.

cf. Schmidt 1929, p. 271; Menzel 1968b, pl. xxxix, p. 48; Lapiner 1976, nos. 575, 579 left.

**OX-TL ref. no. 381f4, 2/28/83, estimates that the sample tested was last fired between 650 and 1000 years ago.*

151. EFFIGY BOTTLE in the form of a dignitary

Fig. 1. Effigy bottle from the same gravelot as Number 151. Private Collection, New York.

Earthenware, polychrome slip
Coastal Huari, Atarco Style
Peru, South Coast
*AD 600-700**
Height 16¼" (41.2 cm) Diameter 11" (27.9 cm)
Condition: excellent with some flaking of clay on base
Accession no. 83.1.1

This large effigy bottle is in the form of a dignitary whose face appears on the modeled and painted spout. He has a triangular nose and flanged ears. Above his head the spout narrows into the form of a headdress. The face is strong: its oval eyes are surrounded by hawk wings, which form the brows and highlight the nose; the mouth is a large oval with prominent teeth. The cap is decorated in textile patterning with a woven band and a feather crest probably meant to imitate so-called "Peruvian velvet" hats made of pile cloth. Painted below the neck of the bottle is what appears to be a collar, filled with geometric designs, but is in fact the body of a snake. A large bib with concentric half-moons and curving vertical panels hangs from the neck. A wide vertical band extends from the left side of the bib to the feet and is painted to resemble a complex interlocked textile design. On the back, the black hair is pulled into a "ponytail" and intertwined with colored strings. The hands, held as if bound behind him as a prisoner, are entwined by the remaining body, tail and head of the snake seen on the front around the figure's neck. The bottle originally formed part of a pair, the two allegedly coming from the same gravelot (Fig. 1).

cf. Schmidt 1929, pl. 111; Lapiner 1976, nos. 542, 559; Bird et al. 1981, p. 92.
**OX-TL ref. no. 381g24, 6/23/83 indicates that the sample tested was last fired between 1200 and 1850 years ago.*

122. JAR with foxes

Earthenware, slip painted in red, black and white
Nasca, Phases 3-4
Peru, South Coast
250 BC-AD 125
Height 5¾" (14.6 cm)   Diameter 7⁷⁄₁₆" (19 cm)
Condition: cleaned of salt deposits and restored
Accession no. N-396

Painted on the white slip-painted ground of this collared jar is a procession of foxes. The lead fox stands with one paw on a representation of the Serpentine Creature. The animals are quite realistic, done in solid color with details in black and white. Foxes are not common subjects during this period.[1]

cf. Schmidt 1929, pp. 321, 338; Parsons 1974, no. 132.

1. Proulx 1968b.

152. BOTTLE with stylized parrot motif

Earthenware, light orange body with dark brown, chestnut, black and white slip pigments
Coastal Huari, Huara Style
Peru, South Coast
ca. AD 600–700
Height 9³/₈" (24 cm) Diameter 9¹/₈" (23 cm)
Condition: cleaned of salt deposits; paint worn in spots has been restored
Accession no. N-164

The large, ovoid bottle slants up from its shoulder to the wide, straight spout. A stylized parrot with an open beak is painted in two panels around the shoulder and sports a feather crest typical of the Huari feather motif. Circular bands around the spout are filled with black S-shaped elements. From sites in the Huara Valley ceramics show a clear relationship to Huari Style but maintain a strong regional character. Motifs often display an advanced degree of abstraction, as in the bird motifs which decorate this bottle.

cf. Schmidt 1929, pp. 267, 280 and 283; Menzel 1977, no. 106.

153. BOWL with modeled standing figure

Earthenware, red, black, grey, and white on orangeware
Coastal Huari, Huara Style
Peru, Central Coast
ca. AD 700–800
Height 4¼" (11 cm) Diameter 9" (11.8 cm)
Condition: cleaned of salt deposits; intact
Accession no. N-216

This broad hemispherical bowl has a small modeled standing figure fastened to the interior bottom. The figure's head, large in proportion to his body, is tilted up. His hands rest on his breast. He is painted in red, with details of his face, cap, and hands picked out in cream. The figure is typical of Huari figurines, as seen in Numbers 156, 157, 158 and 159. The interior wall of the bowl is painted with a zigzag band of red on a wider band of orange. Both bands are framed in black lines and decorated with dotted circle motifs painted in cream slip. A swag motif circles the interior mouth rim.

An almost identical vessel is in the Krannert Art Museum at the University of Illinois.[1] In describing the Krannert vessel, Alan Sawyer noted that the subject of its design is non-Huari, indicating the Huara stylistic independence from the Huari Style. The meaning of the figure in the bowl here and the Krannert vessel is difficult to interpret, but from the Krannert vessel liquid could be drawn by sucking on the turban-like mouthpiece ontop of its head. The latter feature does not appear on the figure in the vessel here.

1. Sawyer 1975a, no. 184.

154. GLOBULAR JAR with modeled human face

Earthenware, with dark red, cream, and black on orangeware
Coastal Huari, Huara Style
Peru, Central Coast
ca. AD 700–800
Height 7 15/16" (19.9 cm) Diameter 4 7/8" (12.4 cm)
Condition: cleaned of salt deposits and some paint loss restored
Accession no. N-517

A jar with a rounded lower section and straight, wide neck, this vessel is modeled in the lower section as a human head with tab ears on the sides. The face is slipped red and the eyes white. A thin black line frames the face and is painted down the bridge of the nose. Diagonal black lines run from the nostrils to the sides of the cheeks. The double rim band is dark red above and pale orange framed with black below. White and black eye-shaped designs are painted at intervals in the pale orange band and around the figure's forehead. The back of the head has dark red and white stripes.

cf. Larco Hoyle 1963, no. 131.

155. KERO with geometric design

Earthenware, with dark red, black, and white on orangeware
Coastal Huari, Huara Style
Peru, Central Coast
ca. AD 700–800
Height 5½" (14 cm) Diameter 6½" (16.4 cm)
Condition: cleaned of salt deposits and pressure crack has been stabilized
Accession no. N-253

This *kero* or flare-sided beaker is painted on the exterior with wide rim panels. The borders of the panels are painted dark red, black, and white. Each panel contains a central zigzag design in dark red and black with white reed circles at the points, and is interspaced with a linear design of two solid lines bordering a four-dotted line.

cf. Sawyer 1975a, no. 177, and passim.

156. ANTHROPOMORPHIC FELINE FIGURINE

Earthenware, with black, white and purple on orangeware
Coastal Huari, Huara Style
Peru, Central Coast
ca. AD 700-800
Height 5¾" (14.5 cm)   Width 4⅜" (11.2 cm)
Condition: cleaned of salt deposits; intact
Accession no. N-61

This standing figurine is in the form of an anthropomorphic feline. Its modeled nose is straight, the white eyes with black pupils are ridged and round, the white and black mouth is a raised oval, and it has black and white striped tab ears. Its modeled arms are rope-like, with hands resting on the stomach. The head is rimmed in black, and there is black and purple paint on the cheeks and chin. The back of the head has black, purple, and white stripes. Forearms and legs are painted purple and barred and dotted with white to resemble fur. The chest has a purple and white branched symbol.

cf. Number 157 (N-62).

157. JAR in the form of an anthropomorphic feline

Earthenware, purple, black, and white on orangeware
Coastal Huari, Huara Style
Peru, Central Coast
ca. AD 700-800
Height 8½" (21.5 cm) Width 4½" (11.5 cm)
Condition: cleaned of salt deposits; chips on rim of spout repaired
Accession no. N-62

This orangeware figural jar is in the form of a standing anthropomorphic feline. The figure's round, flat face is painted in vertical zones with the two outer zones in purple. It has a straight appliquéd nose painted with a black streak, round, ridged black and white eyes, and a raised oval white mouth. The tab ears are striped with black, and two white tear streaks fall from the eyes. The figure has modeled and applied rope-like arms, and carries an object in its hands. Its arms and feet are painted in purple with white markings. The chest and back are decorated with square and rectangular black symbols. A strap handle extends from the spool-shaped flaring spout to the back of the head and is decorated with purple and white geometric designs.

158. FIGURINE in the form of an anthropomorphic feline

Earthenware, dark red and white slip on orangeware body
Coastal Huari, Huara Style
Peru, Central Coast
ca. AD 700-800
Height 8 1/6" (20.5 cm) Width 4 1/2" (11.5 cm)
Condition: cleaned of salt deposits and chips on edges of feet repaired
Loan to Columbia University
Accession no. N-94

The flat face of this solid orangeware figurine in the form of an anthropomorphic feline is tilted upward. Its nose is sharp and the round eyes and oval mouth are ridged. The face is painted with dark red triangles bordered with white, and the tab ears are cat-like. Its arms are folded across its breast. The cap it wears is spotted and a decorated panel is painted down the front of its body.

159. FIGURINE in the form of a standing dignitary

Earthenware, red and white on orangeware
Coastal Huari, Huara Style
Peru, Central Coast
ca. AD 700–800
Height 7" (17.9 cm) Width 3 15/16" (10 cm)
Condition: cleaned of salt deposits and chips repaired
Accesssion no. N-456

This solid orangeware figurine is in the form of a standing dignitary. His nose is straight, his mouth a raised oval, and his ridged eyes are painted white with a double row of falling tears. The fan-like headdress he wears is painted red and white with vertical bars and dots. The figure also still wears the miniature woven cotton shawl placed around it at the time of burial. Since many miniature textile costumes are found, it is safe to assume that a number of such "dolls" were originally dressed.

cf. Schmidt 1929, p. 546.

160. RITUAL CONTAINER in the form of multiple bowls

Earthenware, white and purple paint on orangeware
Coastal Huari
Peru, Central Coast (?)
ca. AD 700- 800
Height 2⅞" (7.3 cm) Width 12¼" (32.4 cm) Depth 14½" (41.6 cm)
Condition: cleaned of salt deposits and repaired; one bowl is a restoration
Accession no. N-138

A rectangle of nine interlocked, small, rounded bowls, connected by internal tubes has a tenth pouring bowl, which is slightly taller and with inward-sloping sides, connected to the center of one side. Each of the nine bowls is banded in white at the rim. The pouring bowl has a design on the sides of small circles in white and purple within white and purple rectangles. The colors are typical of Central Coast Huari painting.

Ritual pouring vessels are called *pachas*. Another example in this catalogue, for instance, is Number 10. An object similar to the one here, however, is not known in the literature.

161. CUP with serpent stem

Earthenware, with black, white and tan slip
Coastal Huari
Peru, Central Coast
AD 700–1000
Length 8 7/16" (22 cm) Diameter 4 1/2" (10.7 cm)
Condition: cleaned of salt deposits and restored
Accession no. N-442

This cup-shaped vessel was made with a long stem which has been looped back on itself to form the body and head of a viper. The patterning on the bowl, in black and white bars, zigzags and circles duplicates the body markings of the serpent. The head is partially modeled with the horns of the viper.

162. BIRD JAR

Earthenware, brown, white and cream on orangeware
Huara
Peru, Central Coast
AD 1300-1400
Height 6¼" (14.7 cm)   Width 6" (15.3 cm)
Condition: cleaned of salt deposits and chips repaired
Accession no. N-627

The jar, probably from Supe Valley, is in the general form of a bird's body with the blind spout modeled as a bird's head. A wide, slanted pouring spout, representing the tail, is connected near the top by a flat arched handle to the back of the bird's head. The wings and head are painted in chestnut brown with white markings. The spout and handle are slipped cream.

163. LARGE BOTTLE in the form of a frog

Earthenware, cream on burnished redware
Coastal Huari
Peru, Central Coast
ca. AD 700–800
Height 10" (25.4cm) Length 10" (25.4cm)
Condition: cleaned of salt deposits and chips repaired
Accession no. N-631

A very large figural bottle in the form of a frog, this vessel of burnished redware represents an agricultural deity. It combines the general frog shape with the legs, teeth and fangs of a feline. As in the earlier Moche representation, the fangs indicate that the figure is a deity. Agricultural symbols are modeled on the sides and like the details of the eyes, teeth and throat spot are picked out in cream slip. A large flaring spout issues from the back.

cf. Schmidt 1929, p. 230; Kutscher 1955, no. 47; Hommel 1969, no. 65.

164. EFFIGY JAR, owl

Earthenware, cream slip on redware
Coastal Huari, Huara Style
Peru, Central Coast
AD 700–800
Height 7¼" (13.4 cm) Width 4⅝" (11.8 cm)
Condition: chips on the edge of the spout have been repaired
Accession no. N-602

This charming but rather crudely made bowl is typical of ceramics produced on the central coast during the decline of the Huari Culture and the beginning of the Chancay Culture's traditional black and white style. The rounded jar has a wide flaring spout emerging from the back to suggest the tail feathers of a bird. A rounded head with appliqué beak and eyes rises up from the front of the vessel to complete the owl form. Double cream circles around the face and markings on top and spout simulate its feather patterning.

165. BOTTLE with an anthropomorphic feline

Earthenware, black and white on redware
Coastal Huari, Huara Style
Peru, Central Coast
ca. AD 700–800
Height 9¾" (25 cm) Diameter 6¾" (17 cm)
Condition: cleaned of salt deposits and surface chips repaired
Accession no. N-132

This melon-shaped bottle is swollen at the neck, which has an expanding bowl-shaped rim. Two strap handles extend from the swell at the neck to the shoulder of the bottle. Each side is painted with a black and white anthropomorphic feline demon with a lunate head. The figure stands with arms and hands raised. A bifurcated streamer is attached to the top of it's head and sweeps down on both sides. The worm-like snake on the swell of the neck and the rim are both painted in black and white style. Such vessels are the forerunners of the later Chancay black and white style. The same delightful feline design appears on a jug in the Krannert Art Museum at the University of Illinois.[1]

1. Sawyer 1975a, no. 183; see also Kroeber 1926, pl. 85b.

166. FEMALE FIGURINE

Earthenware, originally slip painted
Chancay
Peru, Central Coast
AD 1000-1470
Height 11³⁄₁₆" (28.4 cm) Width 6⁵⁄₁₆" (16 cm)
Condition: cleaned of salt deposits; cracks and chips repaired
Accession no. N-327

A hollow, well-modeled figure, the female here, in gingerbread form, stands with arms raised and hands almost touching her ears. The oblong head has ridged oval eyes and mouth. At the top of the bonnet are five perforations. The textile bonnet band is incised as are bracelets on either wrist. Originally, the face of this figure probably had a red slip painted on it, a characteristic which would date it to the early transitional phase of the Chancay Period. Sexuality is expressly indicated but its blandness is characteristic of the style. The presumption is that the frequent occurrence of nude figures in Chancay ceramic art may indicate a preoccupation with fertility.[1]

Huara (also spelled Huaura), Chancay, Ancón and Chillón were the home valleys of the Chancay Culture and Style. The culture which emerged on the central coast north of Lima at the close of the Middle Horizon developed directly from the Huari. The independent trends in Huara art developed directly into Chancay art. Chancay Culture achieved a high degree of urban development as well as technological ability: large ceremonial and residential settlements can be traced throughout the valleys in which it spread; extensive agricultural works were associated with it, such as terracing, reservoirs and canals, whose hydraulic engineering manifest the culminating achievements of Pre-Columbian coastal irrigation engineering.

Possessing a very individual quality, although permeated with a degree of primitiveness, the Chancay Style is distinctive. Before the black on white mode into which Chancay Style settled, there was an interval during which red and black on white decor was predominant. The black on white decor continued during the periods of Chimú and Inca rule when, in the 15th century, Chancay was incorporated into the Inca Empire.

1. Sawyer 1975a, p. 129.

167. EFFIGY JAR

Earthenware, slip painted in white and brown
Chancay
Peru, Central Coast
*AD 1000-1470**
Height 10" (25.4 cm) Width 6" (15.2 cm)
Condition: intact
Accession no. 82.6.24

The jar here is in the form of a seated man holding a bird (parrot?) in either hand. A small monkey sits on either shoulder. The neck of the jar is modeled in the likeness of a human face, with oval eyes, large loop ears and a pursed mouth as though whistling. The upper part of the vessel neck forms the hat decorated with four ridge bands and a central medallion. Details of face, hat and monkeys are picked out in light brown slip. The monkeys appear to be holding something to their mouths, perhaps a musical instrument of some sort to accompany the whistler.

**OX-TL ref. no. 381e94, 2/28/83, indicates that the sample tested was last fired between 630 and 950 years ago.*

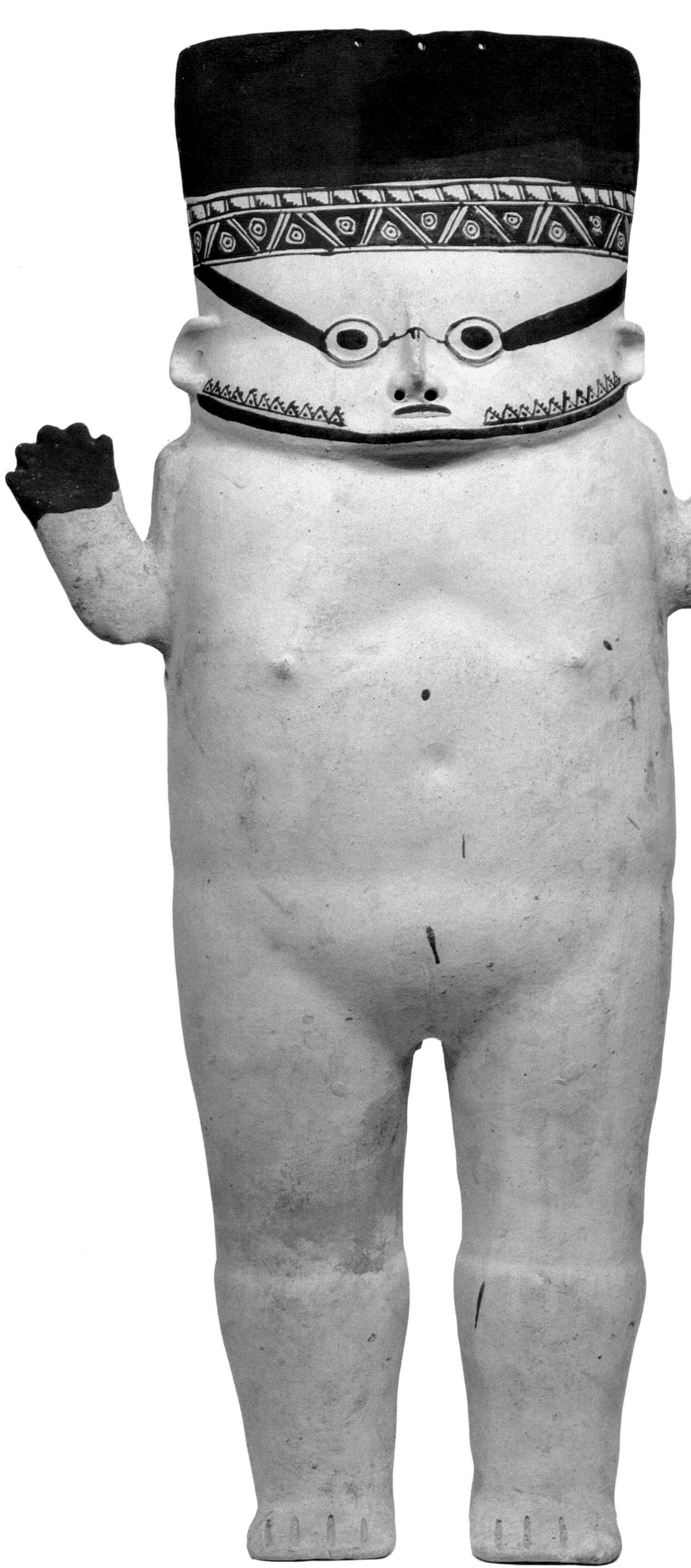

168. LARGE FEMALE FIGURE

Earthenware, slip painted in white and brown
Chancay
Peru, Central Coast
AD 1000–1470
Height 25" (63.4 cm)   Width 13 1/8" (33.3 cm)
Condition: cleaned of salt deposits and repaired in areas of surface loss.
Loan to Columbia University
Accession no. N-365

This large scale, hollow figurine of a standing female with raised stubby arms is the best known type of Chancay nude figure and is of much later date than Number 166. The eyes are raised ovals with brown pupils and brown oblique streaks running from the outside corners to the edge of the headband. The flattened oblong top of the head represents a dark brown bonnet with a textile pattern forehead band decorated with a step design, triangles, and geometrics. A dark brown stripe runs from below the modeled ears across the chin. Above it on either side of the mouth is a painted triangular motif with dots and hairs. The hands are painted dark brown. Genitalia and toes are indicated.

Such large scale Chancay figures are usually female. Others in the exhibition are Numbers 169 and 170. All have a simplified body, small vestigial arms raised to the sides and a flattened face with markings on their chin and brow and a geometric head band. The purpose of such figures is not known but it has been suggested that their frequent occurrence in Chancay graves may indicate that they may have been a symbolic female companion to accompany the deceased into the next world. On the other hand, a few paired figures, male and female, have been excavated from Chancay graves and their existence challenges the idea of symbolic female companionship.

cf. Sawyer 1975a, no. 194; Sawyer 1975b, no. 36; Lapiner 1976, no. 673.

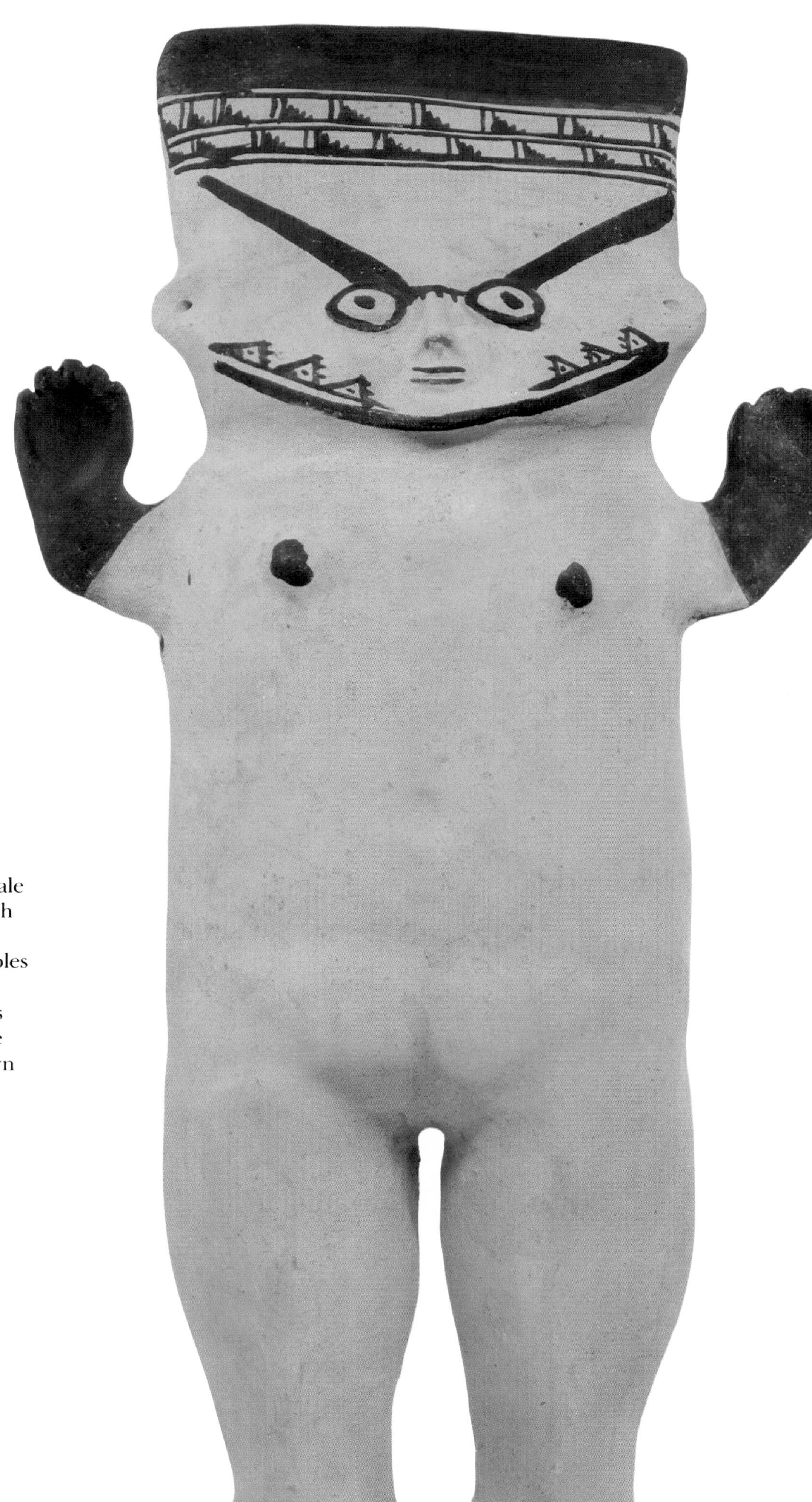

169. LARGE FEMALE FIGURE

Earthenware, slip painted in white and brown
Chancay
Peru, Central Coast
AD 1000–1470
Height 20⅛" (51 cm) Width 10¼" (26 cm)
Condition: cleaned of salt deposits; slight cracks on thighs and left arm repaired.
Accession no. N-98

This large scale hollow figure of a standing female with stubby arms raised is also painted white with details in dark brown. The eyes are ovals with oblique extensions from the corners to the temples giving the appearance of spectacles being worn. The flattened oblong top of the head represents the bonnet which is brown with a painted textile band. The line of the chin is picked out in brown with geometric design.

170. LARGE FEMALE FIGURE

Earthenware, slip painted
Chancay
Peru, Central Coast
AD 1000–1470
Height 20″ (50.5 cm) Width 7 9/16″ (19.3 cm) Depth 5 7/16″ (13.6 cm)
Condition: cleaned of salt deposits; cracks repaired.
Accession no. N-328

Another large, hollow figure of a standing female with stubby arms raised and slip painted in white with details in dark brown is seen here. The eyes are oval with long oblique extensions from the corners to the temples. The bonnet is brown, with a painted textile band, as is the tunic.

cf. Lapiner n.d., nos. 40, 42; Lapiner 1976, no. 673.

171. LARGE FIGURAL URN

Earthenware, brown and cream
Chancay
Peru, Central Coast
AD 1000–1470
Height 21" (53.3 cm)   Diameter 8½" (21.6 cm)
Condition: cleaned of salt deposits; cracks repaired.
Accession no. N-493

Another frequent type of Chancay effigy jar is this large egg-shaped urn, round bottomed and depicting a seated figure with the head of the figure modeled on the neck. Its eyes are raised ovals, the modeled nose is triangular and the mouth is a small oval. Ears are half-moon flanges extending out from the head. The top portion of the neck becomes a hat which is painted brown and has four serrated projections, probably representing animal feet. Triangular ornaments are painted on either cheek and the eyes, mouth, and chin are also touched with brown. The body of the figure is indicated on the urn by a slight modeling of the arms, which cross the breast, and the hands, which hold an offertory cup. Tiny feet and breasts protrude. The arms, large "knee" areas, and breasts are also painted brown. As with the hollow female figures, the purpose of these figural jars is not known.

cf Schmidt 1929, p. 250; Dockstadter 1967, no. 157; Lumbreras 1974, p. 195; Parsons 1974, no. 430; Parsons 1980, no. 61.

172. BOWL with cat's head appliquéd adornments

Earthenware, dark brown and cream
Chancay
Peru, Central Coast
AD 1000–1470
Height 2¼" (7 cm)   Diameter 5" (12.7 cm)
Condition: cleaned of salt deposits; small rim chips repaired
Accession no. N-214

This small round-buttomed bowl, slightly incurving to the rim, is decorated in dark brown on a cream slip ground with a panel of diagonal lines and dots. Appliquéd on opposite sides below the rim are adornments in the form of mold-made cat's heads. Most Chancay vessels display a simplicity of form and direct and spontaneous application of painted and modelled decoration as shown in this example and the following Numbers.

cf. Kroeber 1926, no. 15f; Lothrop-Mahler 1957, p. 7; Mason 1957, no. 32.

173. BEAKER with two mold-made birds appliquéd near top rim

Earthenware, slip painted
Chancay
Peru, Central Coast
AD 1000-1470
Height 7" (17.9 cm)   Diameter 4" (10.1 cm)
Condition: cleaned of salt deposits; cracks and chips repaired
Accession no. N-544

This elegantly shaped beaker is simply decorated with vertical zones of checker board and striped patterns and solid zones in dark brown on cream.

cf. Kroeber 1926, no. 82; Sawyer 1975a, no. 207.

174. LARGE BOTTLE with pods

Earthenware, slip painted in cream and brown
Chancay
Peru, Central Coast
AD 1000–1470
Height 10½" (26.6 cm) Diameter 8⅛" (20.5 cm)
Condition: cleaned of salt deposits; chips on rim repaired
Accession no. N-492

This ovoid bottle with a flaring neck and arched handles has two appliquéd pods attached to one of its handles. The cream slipped body is simply painted with brown stripes except for panels on the sides and the bottom painted in solid brown.

cf. Kroeber 1926, no. 81; Lothrop/Mahler 1957, nos. 1, 5; Mason 1957, no. 32.

175. LARGE BOTTLE with monkey adornos

Earthenware, slip painted in cream and brown
Chancay
Peru, Central Coast
AD 1000–1470
Height 13" (33 cm) Diameter 8" (20.3 cm)
Condition: cleaned of salt deposits; chips to rim repaired
Accession no. N-539

The large bottle is egg-shaped with a bulging neck and a bowl-shaped mouth as if a small bowl was resting on a flaring rim. The latter shape may be a reflection of a custom of using a bowl as a combined lid and receptacle with which to drink the liquid stored in the jar.[1] Two loop handles are attached mid-point on the sides and there are two small lugs on the neck. Modeled monkeys with raised heads and looped tails whose tips rest on the surface of the vessel are appliquéd on either side of the shoulder. The entire upper surface of the bottle from just below the handles is painted with various geometric and linear designs in dark brown on the cream surface: they include solid triangles, zigzags, and small seed-like motifs.

cf. Kroeber 1926, no. 80; Lothrop/Mahler 1957, pl. V.

1. Sawyer 1975a, no. 206.

176. BOTTLE painted with textile designs

Earthenware, slip painted in cream and brown
Chancay
Peru, Central Coast
AD 1000-1470
Height 10" (25.4 cm) Diameter 7½" (19 cm)
Condition: cleaned of salt deposits; small painting loss on sides restored.
Accession no. N-534

A canteen-shaped bottle with bowl-shaped neck and two loop handles. Slipped cream with geometric textile designs on sides and neck in dark brown. Two lugs near rim.

cf. Kroeber 1926, no. 85; Lothrop/Mahler 1957, no. 6.

177. WIDE-MOUTHED JAR with mouse effigy

Earthenware, slip painted in cream and brown
Chancay
Peru, Central Coast
AD 1000–1470
Height 5 1/2" (14 cm) Diameter 5 1/8" (13 cm)
Condition: cleaned of salt deposits; some paint loss restored.
Accession no. N-301

The bulbous jar with slightly inward slanted neck is decorated with vertical and horizontal panels of textile patterning in dark brown on the cream ground. Appliquéd on one side is a small mouse or anteater(?) painted dark brown.

cf. Kroeber 1926, no. 81f.

178. BOTTLE with animal as part of neck

Earthenware, slip painted in cream and brown
Chancay
Peru, Central Coast
AD 1000–1470
Height 6¾" (17.2 cm) Diameter 4½" (11.5 cm)
Condition: cleaned of salt deposits
Accession no. N-418

This bulbous bottle curves in to the neck which then flares out to the mouth rim. The lower part of the neck swells to form a small animal with appliquéd head, legs and tail. The vessel has two strap handles. A dark brown gadroon pattern is painted on the cream body and textile designs on the neck. The animal on the neck and the handles are dark brown.

cf. Lothrop-Mahler 1957, nos. 1, 4f.

179. ANIMAL FIGURINE in the form of a llama

Earthenware, slip painted in cream and dark brown
Chancay
Peru, Central Coast
AD 1000–1470
Height 8³⁄₁₆" (20.8 cm) Width 14³⁄₁₆" (36 cm)
Condition: cleaned of salt deposits
Accession no. N-630

The hollow figurine of a llama stands on four stubby legs. It has a large, egg-shaped body and a small head. Head details, the heavy line around the body, and the spotted back are in dark brown. It is possible that such vessels were made as toys for children.

cf. Sawyer 1975a, no. 200ff; Sawyer 1975b, no. 35.

180. ANIMAL FIGURINE in the form of a llama

Earthenware, slip painted in cream and dark brown
Chancay Culture
Peru, Central Coast
AD 1000–1470
Height 3½" (9 cm) Length 7¼" (18.4 cm)
Condition: cleaned of salt deposits; nose repaired; chips repaired; some paint loss restored
Accession no. N-280

The smaller, hollow figurine of a llama with head and tail erect also stands on four stubby legs. A heavy brown line runs from the brown head to the brown tail and the back is spotted dark brown.

cf. Sawyer 1975a, no. 200ff.

181. DOUBLE WHISTLING VESSEL with male effigy

Earthenware, slip painted in cream and black-brown
Chancay, Inca period
Peru, Central Coast
15th century AD
Height 10" (25.4 cm)   Width 8½" (21.6 cm)
Condition: cleaned of salt deposits; handle, spout and body repaired
Accession no N-81

This is another characteristic late Chancay vessel. Two globular, footed bottles are joined by a short tube and an arched strap handle between the long, tapered spout on one bottle and the effigy figure on the other. The double bottles are of inverted *olla* forms. The figure is in the form of a standing man, arms akimbo. He wears a round hat with spike ornament, multiple necklaces and a short tunic. The whistle sound emanates from a hole at the effigy shoulder and the joining of the handle. The vessel is slip painted in white with details on the effigy side in black-brown slip.

A similar hunchbacked man or warrior(?) appears on other Chancay vessels.[1] His more realistic modeling and the ridged eye convention probably indicates Chimú influence.

cf. Lapiner 1976, no. 669.

1. Sawyer 1975a, no. 199.

182. DOUBLE WHISTLING VESSEL with bird effigy

Earthenware, slip painted
Chancay, Inca Period
Peru, Central Coast
15th century AD
Height 9⅞" (25 cm)   Length 8" (20. 3 cm)
Condition: cleaned of salt deposits; cracks and chips on spout, spout rim and handle have been repaired.
Accession no. N-87

A slight variation on Number 181 is seen in this vessel. Here, two footed, drum-shaped bottles are joined by a short tube and an arched handle stretching from the base of the long, slender spout on one bottle to the wing of the bird effigy on the other. The modeled bird is hollow with a whistle built into the wing and joint of the handle. The vessel is painted over all in a cream slip with dark brown slip on the rounded edges of the bottles and for the textile patterning on the flat surfaces. Details on the bird are also picked out in brown.

cf. Larco Hoyle 1966, no. 78; Dockstader 1967, no. 155; Walker 1969, no. 183.

183. MUMMY BUNDLE FALSE HEAD

Fabric and metal
Chancay
Peru, Central Coast
AD 1000–1470
Height 25" (63. 5 cm) Width 15" (38.1 cm)
Condition: cloth and metal attachments have been cleaned separately; gilding remains in traces
Accession no. Y-001

The woven envelope in coarse, plain-weave, tan cotton also includes attachments of thin, gilded metal in the form of oval eyes with diamond cutouts, a U-shaped nose stuffed with raw cotton and a cutout oblong mouth. A narrow gilded metal head band with step pattern cutouts circles the top of the head. A large U-shaped gilded metal plaque starts at either side of the eyes and falls below the mouth. The eyelashes are coarse brown yarn. Painted below the U-shaped plaque are two red stripes duplicating the plaque. When used, the envelope would have been stuffed with cotton bolls or other material and fastened as a false head to the top of a mummy bundle.

184. MUMMY BUNDLE FALSE HEAD

Fabric and metal
Chancay
Peru, Central Coast
AD 1000-1470
Height 20½" (52 cm) Width 16" (40.6 cm)
Condition: cloth and metal attachments cleaned separately; gilding remains in traces
Accession no. Y-002

The plain-weave, tan cotton woven envelope has cutout oval eyes, U-shaped nose with dangle and oblong cutout mouth of thin, gilded metal sewn into it. Brown yarn behind the eyes gives texture and forms lashes. A gilded metal band encircles the top of the head over a blue and brown textile strip and creamy gauze. There is a textile band around the bottom of the envelope as well.

cf. Walker 1971, no. 218; Lothrop/Mahler 1957, pl. ld; Waisbard 1965, p. 66 and pl. III.

185. MUMMY BUNDLE FALSE HEAD

Fabric and metal
Chancay
Peru, Central Coast
AD 1000-1470
Height 21" (53.3 cm) Width 15½" (39.3 cm)
Condition: cloth and metal attachments cleaned separately; gilding remains in traces
Accession no. Y-003

Another woven envelope in plain-weave, white cloth has diamond-shaped cutout eyes, V-shaped nose stuffed with raw, brown cotton and oblong mouth with cutout teeth made of thin, gilded metal. A plain gilded band encircles the top of the head and a V-shaped gilded plaque starts on either cheek and falls below the mouth.

186. ARYBALLOS with geometric designs

Earthenware, brownware with red, tan, blue, and white pigments
Imperial Inca
Peru, Central Highlands
AD 1470
Height 10 1/8" (25.7 cm)   Width 9 1/4" (23.5 cm)
Condition: cleaned of salt deposits; rubbed paint from spot on neck restored
Accession no. 83.2.2

The aryballos or storage jar is a characteristic Inca ceramic shape. As seen here, it has a long neck with flared rim and low-placed handles on a round body with a pointed base. The pointed base made it possible to pour liquid easily by tilting the vessel so that the angle of the base and side would serve as a fulcrum close to the center of gravity. The flared rim has two small lugs probably used to tie on a saucer-like lid, and a node in the form of a cat's head just below the neck and midway between the two lug handles facilitate the use of a tumpline for carrying. On one side is a handsome geometric design of diamonds, squares and lozenges.

cf. Schmidt 1929, p. 349; Jones 1964, no. 1; Sawyer 1968, no. 705; Sawyer 1975a, no. 256.

187. DOUBLE BOTTLE whistling vessel

Earthenware, slip painted and burnished
Provincial Inca
Peru, Central Coast
ca. AD 1400
Height 8 1/8" (20.6 cm) Width 8 1/16" (20.4 cm)
Condition: intact
Accession no. 82.6.8

A double bottle whistling vessel consisting of two spouted bottles with flared rims connected by a tube and a vertical bridge handle. The bottles are painted in contrasting dark brown, red and yellow segments with a polychrome band of geometric designs resembling weaving patterns around their shoulders. Human faces are modeled at the base of each spout. The spouts themselves are not characteristically Inca. The bridge handle is slip painted with a stylized bird. The blind spout containing the whistle is topped with a reclining feline painted in red and yellow.

cf. Number 188.

188. DOUBLE VESSEL with bird effigy

Earthenware, slip painted and burnished
Provincial Inca
Peru, Central Coast
ca. AD 1400
Height 6" (15.3 cm)   Width 7" (17.2 cm)
Condition: cleaned of salt deposits
Accession no. N-519

A double bottle vessel consisting of two spouted bottles joined by a tube and a vertical bridge handle carved with interlocking triangles. Around the shoulder of each vessel are painted wide bands of step and checkerboard patterns in black, white and red connected by multiple fine black lines. On top of the blind spout containing the whistle is a modeled bird. Although the spout rims are not flared, the wall patterning and handle are typically Inca in style.

cf. Walker 1971, no. 50; Willey 1971, p. 178, nos. 3-113; Lapiner 1976, no. 694; Menzel 1977, no. 39f; Nicholson/Cordy-Collins 1979, no. 218; Bowden/Conrad 1982, p. 99.

189. STIRRUP SPOUT EFFIGY BOTTLE

Earthenware, slip painted in orange, black and cream, burnished
Provincial Inca
Peru, Central Coast
ca. AD 1400
Height 7⅝" (19.4 cm) Width 3⅛" (8 cm) Depth 6" (15.3 cm)
Condition: excellent
Accession no. 83.3.2

The effigy bottle here is composed of a standing man poised on one end of a rectangular bottle and holding panpipes to his mouth. His large head and face are strongly modeled with large, oval, ridged eyes, large ears and a jutting nose. He wears a sling wrapped around his head and a black tunic with an ornamented border over a cream-colored breech clout. His hair under the turban-like sling, is rendered in deeply grooved, incised lines. The stirrup, with a flattened rim on the spout, emerges from the back and curves down to the rear of the rectangular bottle. The spout and rim are ringed in black. The sides of the bottle are painted with obliques and meanders in orange reserved in black. Two black, stylized sea birds are painted on the surface of the bottle under the spout.

cf. Jones 1964, no. 46.

190. EFFIGY BOTTLE in form of seated man with llama

Earthenware, slip painted and burnished
Recuay-Inca
ca. AD 1430
Height 5 1/4" (13.3 cm)   Width 7 3/8" (18.7 cm)
Condition: intact
Accession no. 82.6.6

The effigy bottle is in the form of a seated male with a small llama held on his back by ties. The llama and the man's spout hat, eyes, beard, and belt are slip painted in black and white on burnished redware. The imposed body on the bottle and the coloration are Recuay characteristics while the flattened spout and hat decoration are Inca, thus indicating a fusion of the two styles.

cf. Jones 1964, fig. 47 for similar North Coast Inca handling of man with llama; fig. 48 for similar handling of the face.

A. DOUBLE SPOUT VESSEL with bridge handle

Earthenware, painted in cream, brown, orange, mauve and black slip
*Modern forgery in Nasca Style**
Height 5½" (14 cm)   Diameter 4½" (11.4 cm)
Condition: cleaned of salt deposits; broken and repaired
Accession no. N-438

As Alan Sawyer has described elsewhere, Nasca ceramics have been extensively forged in the twentieth century.[1] The fakes of the early twentieth century were fairly easy to detect, however, and until 1960 it was generally assumed by Peruvianists that forgers were incapable of duplicating Andean slip decoration techniques. In that year Sawyer acquired a strange loop bottle from a Lima collection displaying various technical and iconographic errors which made him recognize it as a fake. The forger, the first to fake the Nasca slip painting technique for commercial purposes, has since been identified as a potter living near the town of Nasca in Peru, and his fakes, which had "enjoyed considerable success" during the 1960's, are now well-known to archaeologists or Andean specialists.

The vessel here was acquired in the early 1960's and has been identified as his work by Sawyer. Its pale slip colors, thin walls and mixed iconography with a version of the Nasca Serpentine Creatures are features of his Nasca Style and make possible the attribution to him. The modern date has since been confirmed by thermoluminescence analysis.

1. Sawyer 1982, p. 30,

**Alpha Analytic Inc., Florida, ref. no. Alpha-677, 5/16/83, indicates that the thermoluminescence properties of the sample measured are characteristic of ceramic materials fired less than 100 years ago.*

B. DOUBLE SPOUT VESSEL with bridge handle

Earthenware, painted in cream, tan, orange, mauve and brown slip
*Modern forgery in Nasca Style**
Height 7½" (19 cm) Width 6½" (16.5 cm) Depth 6¼" (15.9 cm)
Condition: cleaned of salt deposits; broken and repaired
Accession no. N-375

This bottle is elaborately painted with a modern version of the Nasca Serpentine Creature surrounded by trophy heads. More heavily potted than A, it is also more carefully painted with precise execution and deep tones. The slip colors faithfully replicate those of ancient Nasca examples but are more varied than is usual and are thinly painted in spots, allowing the base clay to show through, as is evident in the lower part of the body on the front of this vessel. The style of the painting here does not seem to indicate that its creator was the same potter who did the vessel in A. Instead, the drawing style—the line and the colors in the design—suggest the hand of a Peruvian artist named Zenón Gallegos Ramirez, also identified by Alan Sawyer as the creator of Nasca pots that Sawyer was asked to authenticate in 1972.[1] Ramirez was a ceramic restorer in the town of Nasca, who earlier had a brief career as artist and teacher. After analyzing ancient production techniques through a study of broken Nasca pottery, diligently locating proper clays and slip materials native to the South Coast, and studying Nasca ceramics in Peruvian collections and publications, in 1971 he began to make "replicas" of ancient Nasca pottery, and made over two thousand of them by the time his own ceramics were exhibited at a Lima art gallery in 1977. The vessel here, however, was acquired in the 1960's before Ramirez allegedly began his replications of Nasca pots. Nevertheless, this vessel reveals evidence of what Sawyer characterizes as an element of Ramirez' late style (1978) as opposed to others seen earlier (1972): the colors tend to build up so that they may be seen in relief with a raking light.[2]

1. Sawyer 1982, p. 30-35.
2. *Ibid.*, fig. 14.

**Alpha Analytic Inc., Florida, ref. no. Alpha-680, indicates that the thermoluminescence properties of the sample measured are characteristic of ceramic materials that were fired less than 100 years ago.*

Appendix

1. SEATED COUPLE with child *(Plate I)*

Earthenware, painted,
Bahía Culture, ca. 500 BC–AD 300
Ecuador, Manábi Province, Los Esteros
Height 21" (53.3 cm) Width 16"(40.6 cm)
Condition: extensive remains of original painting
Arthur M. Sackler Collections, Museum of the American Indian, New York
Accession no. 23/7000
Published: Dockstader 1967, no. 44; Dockstader 1973a, no. 100
cf. Lapiner 1976, nos. 739-742, 747, 750.

2. SINGLE SPOUT BOTTLE with modeled and incised monkey head *(Plate II)*

Earthenware, black-brown body with red and green pigment in incisions
Late Chavín Period, ca. 700–400 BC
Peru, North Coast, Tembladera, Jequetepeque Valley
Height 7" (17.8 cm)
Condition: only traces of pigment remain; abraded surface
Arthur M. Sackler Collections, Museum of the American Indian
Accession no. 23/7010
Published: Dockstader 1973, no. 95

3. BOTTLE with tall, flared spout *(Plate III)*

Brownware, with textured, punctate marked globular base, and contrasting burnished neck
Late Chavín Period, ca. 750–500 BC
Peru, North Coast, Tembladera, Jequetepeque Valley
Height 7³/₄" (19.7 cm) Diameter 5" (12.7 cm)
Condition: surface scratches
Arthur M. Sackler Collections, Museum of the American Indian
Accession no. 24/1010
Published: Dockstader 1972, pl. 78

4. STIRRUP SPOUT EFFIGY VESSEL in the form of a seated figure *(Plate IV)*

Earthenware, with cream and red slip, incised and burnished
Late Chavín Period, Regional Style, 400–100 BC
Peru, North Coast
Height 8³/₄" (22cm)
Condition: head has been broken and repaired
Gift to the Museum of the American Indian, New York
Accession no. 23/8954 (N-194)
cf. Bird 1981, p. 20; Larco Hoyle 1941, fig. 124; as well as a Late Chavín Period figural vessel alleged to have come from Templadera in the Jequetepeque Valley in Lapiner, no. 2.

5. HOLLOW FIGURINE of a standing man *(Plate V)*

Earthenware, tan gray body incised with traces of white paint
Late Chavín Period, ca. 700–400 BC
Peru, North Coast, Tembladera, Jequetepeque Valley
Height 5¹/₄" (13.4 cm)
Condition: most of paint worn off
Arthur M. Sackler Collections, Museum of the American Indian
Accession no. 23/6467
Published: Dockstader 1967, no. 91; Lapiner 1976, pl. 59 and p. 438

6. STIRRUP SPOUT EFFIGY VESSEL
with feline(?) head

Earthenware, redware with incised and punctate decoration
Salinar Culture, 500–300 BC
Peru, North Coast, Chicama Valley
Height 6¾" (17 cm)
Condition: surface worn and stained with orange; chips on animal's ears and mouth
Gift to the Museum of the American Indian
Accession no. 23/8963 (N-20)
cf. Larco Hoyle 1944, pp. 7 and 8.

7. DOUBLE BOTTLE WHISTLING EFFIGY VESSEL with bald, squatting man

Earthenware, brownish-redware with cream slip
Virú Style, 400 BC–AD 100
Peru, North Coast, Vicús, Piura Valley
Height 6¾" (17 cm)
Condition: only traces of cream slip remain; surface abrasions
Gift to the Museum of the American Indian
Accession no. 23/8959 (N-257)

8. EFFIGY VESSEL with seated man

Earthenware, oxidized red and reduced black body, burnished
Moche II, 400 BC–AD 100
Peru, North Coast, Vicús, Piura Valley
Height 6¼" (16 cm)
Condition: iron stains on surface; only traces of slip remain
Gift to the Museum of the American Indian
Accession no. 23/8960 (N-193)

9. EFFIGY VESSEL in the form of a squatting man *(Plate VII)*

Earthenware, brownish-red body, burnished black hands and chin
Moche II(?), 400 BC–AD 100
Peru, North Coast, Vicús, Virú Valley
Height 7½" (19 cm)
Condition: traces of cream slip
Gift to the Museum of the American Indian
Accession no. 23/8955 (N-264)

10. EFFIGY VESSEL in the form of a kneeling prisoner *(Plate VIII)*

Earthenware, negative resist circles on body
Negative Vicús, AD 100–700
Peru, North Coast, Vicús, Piura Valley
Height 8½" (20.5 cm)
Condition: some of the resist decor has worn off
Gift to the Museum of the American Indian
Accession no. 23/8936 (N-212)
cf. Disselhoff 1971, pl. 39, for mate to this in a private collection in Buenos Aires.

11. SPOUTED STRAP HANDLE EFFIGY VESSEL in form of a squatting prisoner *(Plate IX)*

Earthenware, brownish-red body, negative resist with cream slip
Negative Vicús, AD 100–700
Peru, North Coast, Vicús, Piura Valley
Height 7¾" (19.7 cm)
Condition: resist decoration worn in spots; iron stains on surface
Gift to the Museum of the American Indian, New York
Accession no. 23/8935 (N-189)

12. SPOUT AND STRAP HANDLE EFFIGY VESSEL in form of feather-crowned squatting prisoner *(Plate X)*

Earthenware, negative resist ware
Negative Vicús, AD 300–700
Peru, North Coast, Vicús, Piura Valley
Height 10½" (26.7 cm) Width 5¼" (13.3 cm)
Condition: broken and repaired headdress, spout and lower body
Gift to the Museum of the American Indian, New York
Accession no. 23/8934 (N-265)

13. SPOUT AND STRAP HANDLE EFFIGY VESSEL in form of kneeling crowned prisoner *(Plate XI)*

Earthernware, brownish body with cream slip
Negative Vicús, AD 300–700
Peru, North Coast, Vicús, Piura Valley
Height 10½" (26.7 cm) Width 5¾" (14.4 cm)
Condition: chip on nose and crown; slip worn
Gift to the Museum of the American Indian, New York
Accession no. 23/8937 (N-463)

14. SPOUT AND STRAP HANDLE EFFIGY VESSEL in form of kneeling prisoner *(Plate XII)*

Earthenware, plainware
Negative Vicús, AD 300–700
Peru, North Coast, Vicús, Piura Valley
Height 7⅞" (20 cm) Width 4¼" (10.8 cm)
Condition: left ear chipped; feet chipped; surface cracked and peeling
Gift to the Museum of the American Indian, New York
Accession no. 23/8939 (N-269)

15. STIRRUP SPOUT EFFIGY VESSEL with two warriors in line *(Plate XIII)*

Earthenware, negative resist in black, red and cream
Negative Vicús, AD 300–700
Peru, North Coast, Vicús, Piura Valley
Height 9¾" (25 cm)
Condition: intact
Gift to the Museum of the American Indian, New York
Accession no. 23/8938 (N-206)
cf. Lapiner 1976, no. 444

16. DOUBLE BOTTLE EFFIGY VESSEL with feline *(Plate XVII)*

Earthenware, negative resist decoration in black, cream and red
Negative Vicús, AD 300–700
Peru, North Coast, Vicús, Piura Valley
Height 8½" (21.6 cm) Width 10½" (26.7 cm)
Condition: some resist decor has worn off
Arthur M. Sackler Collections, Museum of the American Indian
Accession no. 23/7098
Published: Dockstader 1967, pl. 104

17. WHISTLING EFFIGY VESSEL with turbaned female *(Plate XIVa)*

Earthenware, negative resist decoration on black, cream and red
Negative Vicús, AD 300–700
Peru, North Coast, Vicús, Piura Valley
Height 8½" (21.6 cm)
Condition: excellent
Arthur M. Sackler Collections, Museum of the American Indian
Accession no. 23/5551
Published: Dockstader 1967, pl. 123
cf. Sawyer 1966, no. 19; Disselhoff 1971, pl. 36 b and d for similar pair to this and Appendix 18.

18. WHISTLING EFFIGY VESSEL with crowned male *(Plate XIVb)*

Earthenware, negative resist decoration in red, black and cream
Negative Vicús, AD 300–700
Peru, North Coast, Vicús, Piura Valley
Height 8½" (21.6 cm)
Condition: spots on surface worn
Arthur M. Sackler Collections, Museum of the American Indian
Accession no. 23/5552
Published: Dockstader 1967, pl. 123

19. WHISTLING EFFIGY VESSEL with seated female wearing headdress *(Plate XVI)*

Earthenware, negative resist decoration in red, black and cream
Negative Vicús, AD 300–700
Peru, North Coast, Vicús, Piura Valley
Height 6¾" (17 cm)
Condition: some resist decor worn off
Gift to the Museum of the American Indian, New York
Accession no. 23/8940 (N-201)

20. WHISTLING EFFIGY VESSEL with ring handle and stylized feline

Earthenware, negative resist decor in red, black and cream
Negative Vicús, AD 300–700
Peru, North Coast, Vicús, Piura Valley
Height 12" (30.5 cm) Height 12" (3 cm)
Condition: excellent, with much of color retained
Arthur M. Sackler Collections, the Museum of the American Indian
Accession no. 23/5550
Published: Dockstader 1967, no. 126

21. VESSEL with ring handle in the form of a human arm and hand

Earthenware, negative resist decor in red, black and cream
Negative Vicús, AD 300–700
Peru, North Coast, Vicús, Piura Valley
Height 7¾" (19.7 cm) Width 10¾" (27.2 cm)
Condition: some of negative resist decor rubbed off
Gift to the Museum of the American Indian, New York
Accession no. 23/8943 (N-524)

22. STIRRUP SPOUT BOTTLE in the form of a man and woman copulating

Earthenware, negative resist decor in black and red
Negative Vicús, AD 300–700
Peru, North Coast, Vicús, Piura Valley
Height 7½" (19 cm)
Condition: most of negative decor rubbed off
Gift to the Museum of the American Indian, New York
Accession no. 23/8944 (N-6)

23. EFFIGY BOTTLE with ring handle in the form of copulating figures

Earthenware, negative resist decor
Negative Vicús, AD 300–700
Peru, North Coast, Vicús, Piura Valley
Height 8" (20.5 cm)
Condition: negative decoration worn off
Gift to the Museum of the American Indian, New York
Accession no. 23/8945 (N-7)

24. EFFIGY JAR in the form of a llama head with knobbed handles *(Plate XVIII)*

Earthenware, incised lines around top
Negative Vicús, AD 300–700
Peru, North Coast, Vicús, Piura Valley
Height 5½" (14 cm)
Condition: traces of cream slip
Gift to the Museum of the American Indian, New York
Accession no. 23/8941 (N-109)

25. EFFIGY VESSEL in the form of a squatting man holding jar on shoulder *(Plate XIX)*

Earthenware, grayware with punctate decoration on body and head
Moche II, 400 BC–AD 100
Peru, North Coast, Vicús, Piura Valley
Height 7¹⁄₁₆" (18 cm)
Condition: intact
Gift to the Museum of the American Indian, New York
Accession no. 23/8956 (N-207)
cf. Number 28.

26. EFFIGY VESSEL with seated cross-legged man with grid hatching on his chest *(Plate XX)*

Earthenware, burnished
Moche II, 400 BC–AD 100
Peru, North Coast, Vicús, Piura Valley
Height 8" (20 cm)
Condition: surface rubbed, traces of cream slip
Gift to the Museum of the American Indian, New York
Accession no. 23/8950 (N-256)

27. EFFIGY BOTTLE with seated cross-legged warrior with striped headdress *(Plate XXI)*

Earthenware, burnished, red and cream slip headdress
Moche II, 400 BC–AD 100
Peru, North Coast, Vicús, Piura Valley
Height 7½" (19 cm)
Condition: intact, some of slip worn off
Gift to the Museum of the American Indian, New York
Accession no. 23/8949 (N-261)

28. EFFIGY STIRRUP SPOUT VESSEL in the form of a kneeling prisoner *(Plate XXII)*

Earthenware, burnished with traces of cream slip in eyes and on rope
Moche II, ca. 400–100 BC
Peru, North Coast, Vicús, Piura Valley
Height 6¾" (17 cm)
Condition: abraded surface
Gift to the Museum of the American Indian
Accession no. 23/8958 (N-198)
cf. Sawyer 1975b, no. 3.

29. EFFIGY BOTTLE in the form of frog with large ears *(Plate XXIII)*

Earthenware with cream slip decoration
Moche II, 400 BC–AD 100
Peru, North Coast, Vicús, Piura Valley
Height 6¾" (17 cm)
Condition: intact
Gift to the Museum of the American Indian, New York
Accession no. 23/8957 (N-210)

30. STIRRUP SPOUT EFFIGY BOTTLE in the form of an owl

Earthenware, blackware
Moche II(?), 200 BC–AD 200
Peru, North Coast
Height 7" (18.5 cm) Width 4¼" (11 cm) Depth 5¾" (14.5 cm)
Condition: nose and toes chipped; surface poor; spout rebuilt and repainted
Accession no. N-595

31. EFFIGY BOTTLE with seated man and plate of cakes *(Plate XXIV)*

Earthenware, redware with cream slip decoration
Moche IV, AD 200–500
Peru, North Coast
Height 7½" (19 cm)
Condition: cream slip worn off in spots
Gift to the Museum of the American Indian, New York
Accession no. 23/8961 (N-190)

32. WIDE-NECKED BOTTLE with warrior hunting fox

Earthenware, cream slip on redware and molded decoration
Moche III–V, AD 100–200
Peru, North Coast
Height 9⅞" (25 cm) Width 7¾" (19.5 cm)
Condition: cleaned of salt deposits; chips repaired; cream slip strengthened
Accession no. N-533

cf. Donnan 1978, p. 182.

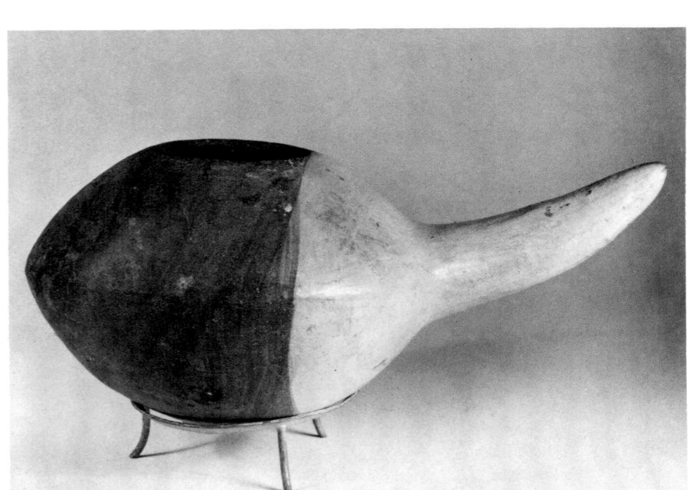

33. CEREMONIAL DIPPER

Earthenware, slipped cream and dark red-brown
Moche III-IV, ca. AD 200
Peru, North Coast
Height 5½" (13 cm) Width 7¼" (18.5 cm)
Condition: badly worn surface
Accession no. N-505

cf. Lehmann 1938, nos. 147 and 148; Tello 1938, pp. xviii, 1i ff.; no. 21; Disselhoff 1971, p. 46; Donnan 1976, p. 52; Donnan/Mackey 1978, M-IV.3-27, p. 108, M-IV.7-6, p. 135, and M-IV.7-15, p. 137.

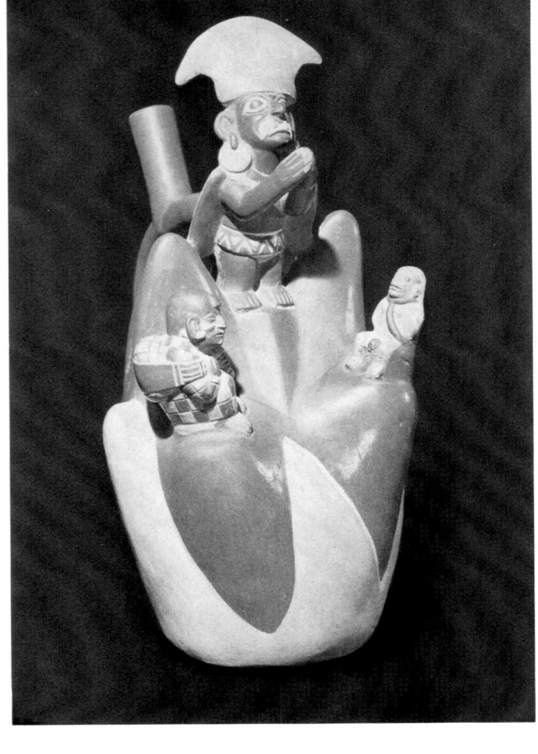

34. EFFIGY VESSEL with portrait of a warrior with face paint and helmet *(Plate XXV)*

Earthenware, burnished and with red and cream slip decoration
Moche IV, AD 200–500
Peru, North Coast
Height 12" (30.5 cm) Width 6" (15.2 cm)
Condition: slip worn in spots
Arthur M. Sackler Collections, Museum of the American Indian
Accession no. 23/6889
Published: Dockstader 1967, no. 112

35. EFFIGY VESSEL in form of five-peaked mountain with fanged deity *Ai-Apec (Plate XXVI)*

Earthenware, burnished and with red and cream slip decoration
Moche IV, AD 200–500
Peru, North Coast
Height 11¾" (29.8 cm)
Condition: excellent
The Arthur M. Sackler Collections, the Museum of the American Indian
Accession no. 23/4865
Published: Dockstader 1967, no. 118; Star Gods Exhibition 1982, to be published

36. STIRRUP SPOUT EFFIGY VESSEL with foxes in relief on sides *(Plate XXVII)*

Earthenware, burnished redware with cream slip
Moche IV, AD 200–500
Peru, North Coast
Height 9¾" (25 cm)
Condition: restored on spout and repainted; slip worn in spots
Gift to the Museum of the American Indian, New York
Accession no. 23/8953 (N-24)

37. BOWL with interior relief of reclining nude female giving birth *(Plate XXVIII)*

Earthenware, redware
Moche IV, AD 200–500
Peru, North Coast
Height 4" (10 cm)
Condition: broken and repaired
Gift to the Museum of the American Indian, New York
Accession no. 23/8952 (N-11)
cf. Lehmann 1938, no. 149; Benson 1972, 6-16; Sawyer 1975b, no. 9.

38. EFFIGY JAR in form of standing dwarf with harelip *(Plate XXIX)*

Earthenware, burnished and with red and cream slip decoration
Moche IV, AD 200–500
Peru, North Coast
Height 6¼" (15.9 cm) Width 4⅜" (10.9 cm)
Condition: chips on mouth rim; slip worn in spots
Gift to the Museum of the American Indian, New York
Accession no. 23/8952 (N-469)

39. EFFIGY JAR in shape of warrior with pronged headdress, holding shield and club *(Plate XXX)*

Earthenware, redware with cream slip on collar, cuffs and headdress
Moche IV, AD 200–500
Peru, North Coast
Height 12¼" (31 cm)
Condition: cream slip worn in spots
Gifts to the Museum of the American Indian, New York
Accession no. 23/8951 (N-113)
cf. Schmidt 1929, p. 146.

40. BOTTLE with appliquéd monkeys

Earthenware, dark red on cream on redware
Moche IV, AD 200–500
Peru, North Coast
Height 8" (10.4 cm) Width 5½" (14 cm)
Condition: crack on body, paint rubbed
Accession no. N-50
cf. Lehmann 1938, no. 9; Benson 1972, nos. 4-12; Donnan 1976, no. 31.

41. JAR with appliquéd mask

Earthenware, cream and maroon slips
Moche IV, Middle Horizon, Sausal Style, AD 200–500
Peru, North Central Coast
Height 8 1/8" (20.5 cm) Diameter 6 1/2" (16.4 cm)
Condition: chips on nose; paint flaking on lower body and rubbed throughout
Accession no. N-100

cf. Tello 1938, no. 221; Donnan/Mackey 1978, Burial M-IV.3-42, p. 111.

42. PEAR-SHAPED JAR with short, splayed neck with lugs on shoulder

Earthenware, with cream slip decor
Early Lambayeque, AD 700–1200
Peru, North Coast
Height 7 3/4" (20 cm) Width 7 1/2" (19 cm) Depth 5" (12.8 cm)
Condition: neck broken and repaired; cracks on body; hole on side repaired; slip worn
Accession no. N-105

43. LARGE ROUND SPOUTED JAR with impressed design of copulating figures *(Plate XXXI)*

Earthenware, press-molded blackware
Imperial Chimu, AD 1300–1470
Peru, North Coast, Lambayeque Valley(?)
Height 10 1/2" (27 cm)
Condition: surface abrasions in spots
Gift to the Museum of the American Indian, New York
Accession no. 23/8968 (N-369)
Published: Star Gods Exhibition 1982, to be published

cf. Anton 1972, pl. 251 for face collar jar with same design

44. BOTTLE with chieftain head spout

Earthenware, cream slip and red paint with postfired black decoration
Lambayeque-Chimú, AD 1000–1300
Peru, North Coast
Height 5 1/2" (14 cm) Width 4 1/4" (11 cm) Diameter 4 3/4" (12 cm)
Condition: handle has been replaced; crack in center of body; paint rubbed; needs to be cleaned of salt deposits
Accession no. N-120

cf. Sawyer 1975a, no. 54; Lapiner 1976, no. 652.

45. BOTTLE with deity head spout

Earthenware, burnished blackware
Lambayeque-Chimú, AD 1000–1300
Peru, North Coast
Height 5 5/16" (13.5 cm) Diameter 5" (12.8 cm)
Condition: perforation below handle, which has been broken and repaired; needs to be cleaned of salt deposits
Accession no. N-573

cf. Walker 1971, no. 135; Sawyer 1975a, no. 55f; Menzel 1977, no. 81B; Larco Hoyle n.d. (c).

46. BOTTLE with figural spout

Earthenware, burnished blackware
Lambayeque-Chimú, AD 1000–1300
Peru, North Coast
Height 6⁷⁄₁₆" (16.5 cm) Diameter 4" (10.2 cm)
Condition: top of spout formerly falsely restored; cleaned of salt deposits and restored (photographed before cleaning and repair).
Accession no. N-592

cf. Walker 1969, no. 135; Sawyer 1975a, no. 55f; Menzel 1977, no. 81B; Nicholson/Cordy-Collins 1979, no. 207; Larco Hoyle n.d.(c).

47. SPOUTED GLOBULAR VESSEL with two heads and attendant figures

Earthenware, burnished blackware
Lambayeque-Chimu, AD 100–1300
Peru, North Coast, Lambayeque Valley
Height 7" (18 cm)
Condition: figure missing on handle(?)
Gift to the Museum of the American Indian, New York
Accession no. 23/8974 (N-307)

48. BOTTLE with deity head spout

Earthenware, burnished blackware
Lambayeque-Chimú
Peru, North Coast
AD 1000–1300
Height 5" (12.8 cm) Width 4³⁄₈" (11 cm)
Condition: chipped spout rim, base, and left ear; surface abraded; to be cleaned of salt deposits
Accession no. N-594

cf. Walker 1969, no. 135; Sawyer 1975a, no. 55E; Menzel 1977, no. 81B; Nicholson/Cordy-Collins 1979, no. 207; Larco Hoyle n.d.(c).

49. DOUBLE BOTTLE with guardian head with whistle

Earthenware, burnished blackware
Imperial Chimú, AD 1300–1400
Peru, North Coast
Height 6⁷⁄₈" (17.5 cm) Depth 7³⁄₄" (19.7 cm) Width 4¹⁄₂" (11.4 cm)
Condition: cleaned of salt deposits and repaired
Accession no. N-274

cf. Kroeber 1926–30, I, 9; Schmidt 1929, p. 214; Proulx 1973, pl. 16g; Lumbreras 1974, no. 191; Bird et al. 1981, p. 101.

50. STIRRUP SPOUT VESSEL in compressed oval form with small birds

Earthenware, undecorated
Early Lambayeque, AD 700–1200
Peru, North Coast
Height 8¹⁄₂" (21.5 cm) Width 6¹⁄₄" (15.8 cm) Depth 6" (15.2 cm)
Condition: hole in base; spout rim broken on one side; broken and poorly repaired where stirrup joins body; negative painting completely worn off
Accession no. N-39

51. STIRRUP VESSEL with fruit

Earthenware, black resist decoration on orangeware body
Imperial Chimú, AD 1300–1400
Peru, North Coast
Height 7½" (19 cm) Width 5¾" (14.5 cm) Depth 4½" (11.5 cm)
Condition: chips on rim of spout; all slip paint worn off
Accession no. N-56
cf. Walker 1969, no. 156.

52. BOTTLE with impressed panels

Earthenware, burnished blackware
Imperial Chimú, AD 1300–1400
Peru, North Coast
Height 37½" (95.3 cm) Diameter 5¾" (14.7 cm)
Condition: surface abrasion; to be cleaned of salt deposits
Loan to Columbia University
Accession no. N-555
cf. Schmidt 1929, p. 224; Sawyer 1975a, no. 74.

53. STIRRUP BOTTLE with impressed designs

Earthenware, burnished blackware
Imperial Chimú, AD 1300–1400
Peru, North Coast
Height 4⅛" (10.5 cm) Diameter 6" (15.3 cm)
Condition: surface abrasions in spots on lower body and stirrup spout; cleaned of salt deposits
Accession no. NN-34
cf. Proulx 1973, pl. 16b.

54. ROUND, FLAT BOTTLE with open-mouth animal spout

Earthenware, blackware with incised hatched line
Inca, AD 1470–1532
Peru, North Coast, Pacasmayo, Lambayeque Valley
Height 5⅜" (13.8 cm) Diameter 6⅛" (15.7 cm)
Condition: unknown (vessel not located for photography)
Gift to the Museum of the American Indian, New York
Accession no. 23/8976 (N-586)
cf. Museum of American Indian 19/9290, for a similar bottle in blackware

55. EFFIGY BOTTLE in the form of a llama foot

Earthenware, burnished blackware
Chimú-Inca, AD 1470–1532
Peru, North Coast
Height 4¾" (12.1 cm) Width 3¼" (8.3 cm) Depth 4" (10.2 cm)
Condition: chip on spout rim; overpainted with lacquer; surface abrasions
Accession no. N-225

56. EFFIGY BOTTLE in form of a "wrinkled" dog

Earthenware, burnished blackware
Chimú-Inca, AD 1470–1532
Peru, North Coast
Height 5½" (14 cm) Width 3¾" (9.5 cm) Depth 6¾" (17 cm)
Condition: chips on rim and spine
Accession no. N-554
cf. Bolz 1975, no. 39.

57. EFFIGY BOTTLE in form of a "wrinkled" dog biting its phallus

Earthenware, burnished blackware
Chimú-Inca, AD 1470–1532
Peru, North Coast
Height 8 1/2" (23 cm) Width 3 1/4" (8.3 cm)
Condition: chips on spout and scratches on face
Accession no. N-125
cf. Bolz 1975, no. 39.

58. EFFIGY BOTTLE in form of a dog biting its phallus

Earthenware, burnished blackware
Chimú-Inca, AD 1470–1532
Peru, North Coast
Height 10" (25.4 cm) Width 4 1/8" (10.5 cm)
Condition: some surface scratches
Accession no. N-10
cf. Bolz 1975, no. 39.

59. CYLINDER-SHAPED HEAD CUP with slightly flared rim modeled with faces on either side

Earthenware, micaceous grayware
Inca Period
Peru, Central Coast, Lima, Rimac Valley
Height 4 3/4" (12.1 cm) Diameter 3 7/8" (7.9 cm)
Condition: surface wear
Gift to the Museum of the American Indian, New York
Accession no. 23/8927 (N-448)

60. FLASK BOTTLE with feline figure at neck, and over shoulders, cream

Earthenware, cream slip on red
Chimú-Inca, AD 1470–1532
Peru, North Coast, Lambayeque Valley
Height 5 1/2" (14.2 cm) Diameter 4 1/4" (10.8 cm)
Condition: surface cracks, paint worn in spots
Accession no. N-629

61. BOWL WITH INCISED DESIGN of feline mask and body *(Plate XXXII)*

Earthenware, blackware with red, yellow and black postfired resinous paint
Paracas
Peru, South Coast, Ocucaje, Ica Valley
Height 3 1/4" (8 cm)
Condition: some paint worn off
Gift to the Museum of the American Indian, New York
Accession no. 23/8947 (N-220)

62. SPOUTED WHISTLING VESSEL with red bird head and bridge handle *(Plate XXXIII)*

Earthenware, incised with feline mask and Vencejo *motif and with remains of red and black postfired resinous paint*
Paracas, 750–250 BC
Peru, North Coast, Ocucaje, Ica Valley
Height 5" (13 cm)
Condition: only traces of paint remain
Published: Dockstader 1973, pl. 201
Gift to the Museum of the American Indian, New York
Accession no. 23/8946 (N-321)

63. LARGE, OVOID VASE with incised design of oculate being *(Plate XXXIV)*

Earthenware, brownish body with traces of pigment
Paracas, Phase 9, 500–200 BC(?)
Peru, South Coast
Height 13½" (34.3 cm)
Condition: all post fired resinous paint worn off
Published: Dockstader 1967, pl. 100; Star Gods Exhibition 1982, to be published
The Arthur M. Sackler Collections, the Museum of the American Indian
Accession no. 23/5500
cf. Menzel 1964, p. 242-243

64. WHISTLING BOTTLE with human head, blind spout and trophy head figures *(Plate XXXV)*

Earthenware, blackware incised and with postfired resinous paint
Paracas, 750–250 BC
Peru, South Coast, Ocucaje, Ica Valley
Height 6½" (17 cm)
Condition: paint impressed with traces of cloth and worn off in spots
Accession no. 23/7093
Published: Dockstader 1973, no. 105

65. BOTTLE with short, slightly flared neck and squat oval body

Earthenware, brownware burnished with simple incised decoration around neck in white post fired resinous pigment
Paracas, 500–300 BC
Peru, South Coast
Height 7½" (19 cm)
Condition: needs to be cleaned of salt deposits
Accession no. N-363

66. SMALL, FLAT FEMALE FIGURINE, slightly modeled, arms raised, full headdress

Earthenware, black with white slip
Nasca(?), AD 500–800
Peru, South Coast, Ica Valley
Height 4½" (11.6 cm)   Width 3" (7.8 cm)
Condition: surface worn
Gift to the Museum of the American Indian, New York
Accession no. 23/8975 (N-474)

67. KERO-TYPE BEAKER with modeled lizard head on side *(Plate XXXVI)*

Earthenware, redware polychromed
Tiahuanaco, AD 100–800
Bolivia, Andean Highlands, La Paz
Height $6\frac{1}{2}$" (16.5 cm) Diameter $6\frac{1}{8}$" (15.6 cm)
Condition: painted design worn off in spots; broken and repaired
Gift to the Museum of the American Indian, New York
Accession no. 23/8964 (N-167)

68. INCENSER(?) in form of puma head and body *(Plate XXXVII)*

Earthenware, tanware with polychrome slip decoration
Tiahuanaco, AD 100–800
Bolivia, Andean Highlands, La Paz
Height 16" (40.6 cm) Width $11\frac{1}{2}$" (29.2 cm)
Condition: slip worn in spots on body and Puma face
The Arthur M. Sackler Collections, the Museum of the American Indian, New York
Accession no. 23/7095
Published: Dockstader 1973, no. 178; Star Gods Exhibition 1982, to be published

69. KERO with straight, splayed sides painted with figural and geometric designs *(Plate XXXVIII)*

Earthenware, tanware with polychrome slip
Coastal Huari, AD 700–800
Peru, Central Coast
Height $4\frac{3}{8}$" (11 cm) Width $4\frac{11}{16}$" (11.9 cm)
Condition: one chip in rim
Gift to the Museum of the American Indian, New York
Accession no. 23/8965 (N-250)

70. KERO with straight, splayed sides and staff-holding figures on sides *(Plate XXXIX)*

Earthenware, tan body with polychrome slip
Coastal Huari, AD 700–800
Peru, Central Coast
Height 5" (12.7 cm) Diameter $5\frac{3}{4}$" (14.6 cm)
Condition: has been broken and repaired
Gift to the Museum of the American Indian, New York
Accession no. 23/8966 (N-179)

71. KERO with straight, splayed sides and figural design *(Plate XL)*

Earthenware, tan body with polychrome slip
Coastal Huari, AD 700–800
Peru, Central Coast
Height $5\frac{1}{3}$" (13 cm) Diameter $5\frac{7}{8}$" (14.9 cm)
Condition: chips in rim
Gift to the Museum of the American Indian, New York
Accession no. 23/8967 (N-169)

72. EFFIGY VESSEL in form of prisoner bound at hands and feet

Earthenware, mold made, slightly modeled, painted in black, yellow and white
Huari, AD 700–800
Peru, Central Coast and Highlands
Height 7¾" (20 cm) Width 4⅞")12.4 cm) Depth 5½" (14 cm)
Condition: chips in rim; head band broken and repaired, surface pitting
Gift to the Museum of the American Indian, New York
Accession no. 23/8969 (N-112)
cf. Sawyer 1975a, nos. 171 and 172

73. STANDING FEMALE FIGURINE, slightly modeled head with pronged headdress

Earthenware, coarse red body with black, red and white slip
Chancay, AD 1000–1500
Peru, Central Coast, Huara Valley
Height 8½" (21.6 cm) Width 4⅝" (11.8 cm)
Condition: cracks through back
Gift to the Museum of the American Indian, New York
Accession no. 23/8970 (N-72)

74. EFFIGY BOTTLE in the form of an owl

Earthenware with black, white and red slip on redware body
Coastal Huari, Huara Style, . AD 700–800
Peru, Central Coast
Height 6¾" (17 cm) Diameter 5¼" (13.4 cm)
Condition: chip on back and handles
Accession no. N-122
cf. Sawyer 1975b, no. 15.

75. EFFIGY BOTTLE in the form of a feline

Earthenware, red, white and black on redware
Coastal Huari, AD 700–800
Peru, Central Coast
Height 7¾" (19.7 cm) Length 8¾" (22.3 cm)
Condition: slip eroded; cleaned of salt deposits and restored
Accession no. N-618
cf. Schmidt 1929, p. 230; Mason 1957, no. 31; Larco Hoyle 1963, no. 124.

76. SPOUTED JAR with handle in form of puma devouring its victim

Earthenware, blackware, burnished
Middle Horizon, Huara Style, AD 700–800
Peru, Central Coast
Height 5½" (14.5 cm) Width 5¾" (14.5 cm) Depth 3¼" (8 cm)
Condition: chips on left ear and handle; surface badly worn
Accession no. N-596

77. BOWL with painted design

Earthenware, painted in black-brown slip on a cream slip ground
Chancay Culture, AD 1000–1450
Peru, Central Coast
Height 2⅛" (5.4 cm) Diameter 4¹¹⁄₁₆" (12 cm)
Condition: chips on rim and slip paint worn on exterior
Accession no. N-312

78. HEMISPHERICAL BOWL with painted design

Earthenware, slip painted in cream and dark brown
Chancay, AD 1000–1450
Peru, Central Coast
Height 2" (5 cm) Diameter 7 7/8" (20 cm)
Condition: chipped and abraded surface
Accession no. N-350

cf. Krober 1926, no. 82; Lumbreras 1974, no. 195.

79. LARGE URN in form of seated figure holding votive cup

Earthenware, painted with cream and brown slip
Chancay, AD 1000–1450
Peru, Central Coast
Height 14 3/16" (36 cm) Diameter 7 7/8" (20 cm)
Condition: cracks in rim, right ear, fingers of right hand; needs to be cleaned of salt deposits
Accession no. N-96

80. LARGE, EGG-SHAPED FIGURAL URN with modeled face and holding a votive cup

Earthenware, slip painted in cream and dark red on redware
Chancay, AD 1000–1450
Peru, Central Coast
Height 14 3/16" (36 cm) Diameter 7 1/2" (19 cm)
Condition: surface badly worn; needs to be cleaned of salt deposits
Accession no. N-329

cf. Schmidt 1929, no. 250; Dockstader 1967, no. 157; Lumbreras 1974, no. 195; Parsons 1974, no. 430.

81. URN in figural form of a rounded, weighted base, suspension lugs on head

Earthenware, with brown on cream slip
Chancay, AD 1000–1450
Peru, Central Coast
Height 10 1/8" (25.5 cm) Width 6 1/4" (16 cm) Depth 6 1/8" (15.5 cm)
Condition: suspension loops broken; chips on ear; cracks on body; worn surface
Accession no. N-335

82. OVOID BOTTLE with splayed neck, two lug handles and human effigy figure

Earthenware, painted in cream and brown slip
Chancay, AD 1000–1450
Peru, Central Coast
Height 10" (25.4 cm) Width 8" (20.3 cm)
Condition: surface poor with slip worn throughout
Accession no. NN-41

83. EFFIGY JAR in the form of a hunchback who once held a votive cup

Earthenware, slip painted in cream and brown
Chancay, AD 1000–1450
Peru, Central Coast
Height 7 1/8" (18.2 cm) Width 4 1/4" (11 cm) Depth 3 7/8" (10 cm)
Condition: badly worn due to poor quality of the clay and sloppiness of decoration
Accession no. N-229
cf. The Paul A. Clifford Collection, no. 181; Walker 1969, no. 181.

84. LARGE FIGURAL URN in the form of a female(?) figure holding a votive cup

Earthenware, slip painted
Chancay, AD 1000–1450
Peru, Central Coast
Height 15 3/8" (39 cm) Width 6 1/2" (16.5 cm) Depth 6 7/8" (17.5 cm)
Condition: surface worn and chips throughout
Accession no. N-334

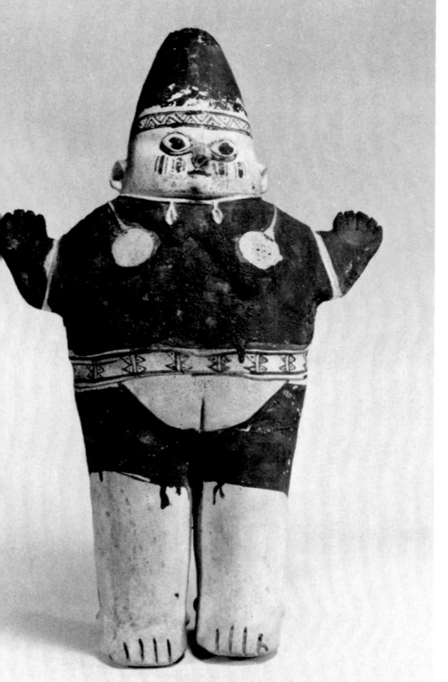

85. LARGE, HOLLOW FIGURINE in the form of standing female with conical hat

Earthenware, slip painted in cream and brown
Chancay, AD 1000–1450
Peru, Central Coast
Height 19 11/16" (50 cm) Width 11 1/4" (28.5 cm) Depth 4 7/8" (12.5 cm)
Condition: legs broken and repaired; cracks on body; needs cleaning
Accession no. N-326
cf. Bird et al. 1981, p. 121.

86. FIGURINE with raised stubby arms

Earthenware, painted in black on cream slip
Chancay, AD 1000–1450
Peru, Central Coast
Height 10 1/2" (26.5 cm) Width 5 1/8" (13 cm) Depth 3 1/2" (8.9 cm)
Condition: right arm repaired; finger chipped; surface very rough
Accession no. N-478

87. LARGE, OVOID BOTTLE with bowl-shaped neck and two strap handles

Earthenware, slip painted in cream and brown with geometric textile designs
Chancay, AD 1000–1450
Peru, Central Coast
Height 11 3/4" (29.8 cm) Diameter 9 1/2" (24.1 cm)
Condition: chips on rim and handles
Accession no. N-338
cf. Lothrop/Mahler 1957, nos. 1 and 4.

88. PENDANT in the form of a female figurine

Earthenware, slip painted in cream and brown
Chancay, AD 1000–1450
Peru, Central Coast
Height 7 1/2" (19 cm) Width 3 1/2" (9 cm) Depth 5" (12.7 cm)
Condition: chips on top of head; right ear broken off
Accession no. N-480
cf. Easby 1967, no. 537; Sawyer 1975a, no. 194; Lapiner 1976, no. 673.

89. DOUBLE DRUM-SHAPED BOTTLE WHISTLING JAR with standing musician(?)

Earthenware, cream slip
Chancay, AD 1000–1500
Peru, Central Coast
Height 9 1/8" (23.2 cm) Width 8 1/8" (20.6 cm)
Condition: broken spout; one bottle broken and repaired
Gift to the Museum of the American Indian, New York
Accession no. 23/8972 (N-73)

90. STANDING MALE FIGURINE, slightly modeled and with textile headdress

Earthenware, black and red on cream slip
Chancay, AD 1000–1500
Peru, Central Coast, Ancón Valley
Height 6 1/2" (16.5 cm) Width 3 1/2" (9.1 cm)
Condition: chips on edges
Gift to the Museum of the American Indian, New York
Accession no. 23/8971a (N-455a)

91. STANDING FEMALE FIGURINE, slightly modeled

Earthenware, black and red on cream slip
Chancay, AD 1000–1500
Peru, Central Coast, Ancón Valley
Height 6 1/2" (16.5 cm) Width 3 1/2" (9 cm)
Condition: chips on edges
Gift to the Museum of the American Indian, New York
Accession no. 23/8971b (N-455b)

Drawings and Rubbings

INTRODUCTION

Fig. 2 rubbing by Elizabeth Stockton; Fig. 8 after Donnan 1978, fig. 71; Fig. 9 after Donnan 1978, fig. 54.

A REAPPRAISAL OF CHAVÍN

Fig. 1 after Willey 1951, fig. 3-39; Fig. 3 after Carrión Cachot 1948, XXVI; Fig. 5 after Rowe 1967, fig. 2, courtesy of John H. Rowe; Fig. 6 after Tello 1960, fig. 31; Fig. 7 after Lumbreras 1970; Fig. 9 after Maitland, Mowatt, Phillips and Watson 1967, revised 1983; Fig. 10 by Jennifer McKim after Bennett 1942, fig. 9 and Tello 1960, p1. XLII; Fig. 11 by Jennifer McKim after Sawyer photos; Fig. 12 by Jennifer McKim after Lumbreras 1970 and Tello 1960, fig. 31; Fig. 13 by Jennifer McKim after Lumbreras 1970 and Tello 1943, p1. XVIIIa; Fig. 14 by Jennifer McKim after Bennett 1942, fig. 7 and Sawyer photo; Fig. 15 by Jennifer McKim after S. Watson 1975; Fig. 17 by Jennifer McKim; Fig. 29b by Jennifer McKim after Ravines and Isbell 1975.

DESERT EMPIRE AND ART: CHIMOR, CHIMÚ AND CHANCAY

Plans 1 and 2 courtesy of the author.

THE NASCA STYLE

Fig. 1 after Seler 1923, fig. 191; Fig. 9 after Roark 1965, fig. 62; Fig. 10 after Seler 1923, fig. 27; Fig. 11 after Seler 1923, fig. 74; Fig. 12 after Seler 1923, fig. 330; Fig. 13 after Seler 1923, fig 234; Fig. 15 after Seler 1923, fig. 115; Fig. 16 after Seler 1923, fig. 107; Fig. 17 after Wolfe 1981, fig. 123a; Fig. 18 after Seler 1923, fig. 8; Fig. 19 after Seler 1923, fig. 11; Fig. 20 after Seler 1923, fig. 190; Fig. 21 after Seler 1923, fig. 194; Fig. 22 after Roark 1965, fig. 56a; Fig. 23 after Roark1965, fig. 69; Fig. 24 after Seler 1923, fig. 412; Fig. 25 after Seler 1923, fig. 258a; Fig. 26 after Seler 1923, fig. 347; Fig. 27 after Seler 1923, fig. 337; Fig. 28 after Seler 1923, fig. 343; Fig. 29 after Seler 1923, fig. 282b; Fig. 30 after Seler 1923, fig. 290; Fig. 31 after Seler 1923, fig. 306; Fig. 32 after Seler 1923, fig. 304; Fig. 34 after Seler 1923, fig. 134; Fig. 35 after Seler 1923, fig. 384; Fig. 36 after Seler 1923, fig. 389; Fig. 37 after Seler 1923, fig. 379; Fig. 38 after Roark 1965, fig. 54; Fig. 39 after Wolfe 1981, fig. 186; Fig. 40 after Seler 1923, fig. 349; Fig. 41 after Wolfe 1981, fig. 89; Fig.42 after Roark 1965, fig. 64; Fig. 43 after Roark 1965, fig. 66; Fig. 44 after Seler 1923, fig. 417; Fig. 45 after Seler 1923, fig. 425.

TIAHUANACO AND HUARI

Fig. 1 after Alarco 1971, vol. 2, p. 465; Fig. 3 after Bennett 1934, fig.15; Fig.4 after Bennett 1934, fig. 17; Fig. 5 after Menzel 1977, fig. 62; Fig. 6 after Menzel 1964, fig. 13; Fig. 10 after Menzel 1964, fig. 10a; Fig. 11 after Menzel 1964, fig. 11a.

DRAWINGS IN CATALOGUE ENTRIES

No. 1 rubbing by Elizabeth Stockton; Nos. 16, 58, 61, 62, 131, 134, 528 and A by Joseph Robles; No. 95 by Nicholas Stoetzer; Nos.78, 114, 116, 117, 123, 132, 136, 145, and 146 by Janet E. Montgomery.

Photo Credits

INTRODUCTION

Fig. 1 Otto Nelson photo; Fig. 6 courtesy of The Museum of the American Indian, Heye Foundation; Fig. 7 courtesy Long Island University Press; Fig. 10 courtesy of the collector; Fig.11 author's photo; Fig.13 courtesy of The Brooklyn Museum, New York; Fig. 14 courtesy of St. Louis Art Museum, Morton D. May Collection.

A REAPPRAISAL OF CHAVÍN

Fig. 2 Pedro Rojas Ponce photo, Sawyer archive; Figs. 4, 18, 19, 20a and b, 22, 23a and b, 24a and b, 25 Sawyer photos; Fig. 8 courtesy of Dumbarton Oaks, Washington, D.C.; Fig. 16 courtesy of The Solomon Guggenheim Museum, New York; Fig. 21 courtesy of Alan Lapiner from Alana Cordy-Collins; Fig. 26 courtesy of Museo Nacional de Antropología y Arqueología, Lima, Sawyer photo; Figs.27a and b courtesy of F. Landmann, Sawyer photo; Figs.28 and 29a courtesy of Museo Nacional de Antropología y Arqueología, Lima, Maitland photos; Fig. 30 courtesy of Paul Truel Collection, Lima, Pablo Soldi photo, Sawyer archive; Figs.31 and 36 Osmond Varella photos, Sawyer archive; Fig. 32 Alfredo Rosensweig photo, Sawyer archive; Fig. 33 courtesy of Raymond Wielgus; Fig. 34 courtesy of The Textile Museum, Washington D.C., Osmond Varella photo, Sawyer archive; Fig. 35 courtesy of Louis Slavitz, Murray Shear photo; Fig. 37 courtesy of The Brooklyn Museum, New York.

DESERT EMPIRE AND ART: CHIMOR, CHIMÚ AND CHANCAY

Fig. 1 courtesy of the author.

THE NASCA STYLE

Fig. 2 courtesy of the author; Figs. 3 and 4 courtesy of The Textile Museum, Washington, D.C.; Fig. 5 courtesy of American Museum of Natural History, New York; Fig. 14 courtesy of Scientific American; Fig. 33 courtesy of Long Island University Press.

TIAHUANACO AND HUARI

Fig. 7 courtesy of American Museum of Natural History, New York; Fig. 8 courtesy Museo Nacional de Antropología y Arqueología, Lima; Figs.9 and 13 courtesy Robert H. Lowie Museum, Berkeley, California; Fig. 12 courtesy of the author.

FIGURES IN CATALOGUE ENTRIES

Fig. in No. 5 courtesy of F. Landmann, Thomas Brown photo; Fig. in No. 27 Robert Stoetzer photos; Fig. in No. 31 author's photo; Fig. in No. 79 Museum of the American Indian photo; Fig. in No. 151 Murray Shear photo.

Bibliography

Alarco 1971 — Alarco, Eugenio. *El Hombre Peruano en su Historia.* 2 vols. Lima: Editorial Ausonia Talleres Graficos. 1971.

Anton 1972 — Anton, Ferdinand. *The Art of Ancient Peru.* New York. 1972.

Arriaga 1968 — Arriaga, Pablo Joseph. *The Extirpation of Idolatry in Peru.* Lexington: University of Kentucky Press. 1968.

Baessler 1902–3 — Baessler, Arthur. *Ancient Peruvian Art.* 3 vol. New York. 1902–3.

Bandelier 1910 — Bandelier, Adolf. *The Island of Titicaca and Koati.* New York. 1910.

Bankes 1980 — Bankes, George. *Moche Pottery from Peru.* London: The Trustees of the British Museum. 1980.

Beadle 1972 — Beadle, George W. "The Mystery of Maize." *Field Museum Bulletin* 43 (10, 1972): pp. 2–11.

Bennett 1934 — Bennett, Wendell C. "Excavations at Tiahuanaco." *Anthropological Papers of the American Museum of Natural History* 34 (3, 1934). New York.

Bennett 1939 — ______. "Archaeology of the North Coast of Peru: An Account of Exploration and Excavation in Virú and Lambayeque Valleys." *Anthropological Papers of the American Museum of Natural History* 37 (1, 1939): pp. 3–153. New York.

Bennett 1942 — ______. "Chavín Stone Carving." *Yale Anthropological Studies* 3 (1942): pp. 1–9, plates 1–30. New Haven.

Bennett 1944 — ______. "The North Highlands of Peru: Excavations in the Callejón de Huayalas and of Chavín de Huantar." *Anthropological Papers of the American Museum of Natural History* 39 (1, 1944): pp. 5–116. New York.

Bennett 1946 — ______. "The Archaeology of the Central Andes." In *Handbook of South American Indians,* ed. J.H. Steward, Bureau of American Ethnology Bulletin 143 (2, 1946): pp. 61–147.

Bennett 1950 — ______. *The Gallinazo Group, Virú Valley, Peru.* Yale University Publications in Anthropology, vol. 43. New Haven. 1950.

Bennett 1954 — ______. *Ancient Arts of the Andes.* New York: Museum of Modern Art. 1954.

Bennett/Bird 1960 — ______ and Junius B. Bird. *Andean Culture History.* New York. 1960.

Benson 1972 — Benson, Elizabeth P. *The Mochica: A Culture of Peru.* New York and London. 1972.

Benson 1974 — ______. *A Man and a Feline in Mochica Art.* Dumbarton Oaks Studies in Pre-Columbian Art and Archaeology, vol. 14. Washington, D.C. 1974.

Benson 1975 — ______ "Death-Associated Figures on Mochica Pottery." In *Death and the Afterlife in Pre-Columbian America: A Conference at Dumbarton Oaks, Oct. 27, 1973,* pp. 105–144. Washington, D.C. 1975.

Benson 1976 — ______. "'Salesmen' and 'Sleeping' Warriors in Mochica Art." *Actas del XLI Congreso Internacional de Américanistas, Mexico, 1974* II (1946): pp. 26–34.

Benson 1978 — ______. "The Bag with the Ruffled Top: Some Problems of Identification in Moche Art." *Journal of Latin American Lore* 4 (1, 1978): pp. 28–47.

Benson 1979 — ______. "Garments as Symbolic Language in Mochica Art." *Actes du XLIIe Congrès International des Américanistes, Paris, 1976* VII (1979): pp. 291–299.

Benson 1982 — ______. "The Man with the V on His Headdress: A Figure in Moche III-IV Iconography." *Indiana* 7, Gedenkschrift Walter Lehmann, Teil 2 (1982): pp. 201–215.

Benson n.d. (a) — ______. *The Men Who Have Bags in Their Mouths.* Memorial volume for Gerdt Kutscher, Lateinamerika Institut, Berlin. In press.

Benson n.d. (b) — ______. "The Owl as a Symbol in the Mortuary Art of the Moche." Paper presented at the Coloquio Internacional de Historia del Arte, Mexico, October, 1980.

Benson n.d. (c) — ______. "The Well-Dressed Captives: Some Observations on Moche Iconography." *Baessler-Archiv,* Berlin. In press.

Benson, ed. 1971 — ______, ed. *Dumbarton Oaks Conference on Chavín, 1968.* Dumbarton Oaks, Washington, D.C. 1971.

Benson, ed. 1972 — ______, ed. *The Cult of the Feline: A Conference on Pre-Columbian Iconography, 1970.* Dumbarton Oaks, Washington, D.C. 1972.

Berezkin 1978 — Berezkin, Yuri E. "Dve Gruppi Inoplemennikov na Izobrajeniak Mochica. (Two Groups of Foreigners on Mochica Representations.)" *Societskaya Etnografia* 1 (1978): pp. 126–137.

Bird et al. 1981 — Bird, Junius B., E.P. Benson and W.J. Conklin. *Museums of the Andes.* Great Museums of the World. New York. 1981.

Blasco/Gomez 1980 — Blasco Bosqued, Concepcion, and Luis Ramos Gomez. *Ceramica Nasca* 13 (1980). Valladolid: Seminario Américanista de la Universidad de Valladolid.

Bolz 1975 — Bolz, Ingeborg. *Sammlung Ludwig: Altamerika.* Ethnologica, New Series, vol. 7. Recklinghausen. 1975.

Bonavía 1961 — Bonavía, Duccio. "A Mochica Painting at Panamarca, Peru." *American Antiquity* 26 (4, 1961): pp. 540–543.

Bawden/Conrad 1982 — Bawden, Garth, and Geoffrey W. Conrad. *The Andean Heritage.* Cambridge, Mass.: Peabody Museum. 1982.

Burger 1978 — Burger, Richard Lewis. "The Occupation of Chavín, Ancash, in the Initial Period and Early Horizon." Ph.D. diss., University of California, Berkeley. 1978.

Burger 1981 — ______. "The Radiocarbon Evidence for the Temporal Priority of Chavín de Huantar." *American Antiquity* 46 (3, 1981): pp. 592–602.

Buse 1981 — Buse de la Guerra, Hermann. *Actividad Perquera.* Lima. 1981.

Bushnell 1956 — Bushnell, G.H.S. *Peru.* Ancient Peoples and Places. New York. 1956.

Calancha 1638 — Calancha, Antonia de la. *Crónica moralizada del orden de San Augustín en el Perú, con sucesos exemplares vistos en esta Monarchia....* Barcelona.

Canby 1979 — Canby, Thomas Y. "The Search for the First Americans." *National Geographic* 156 (3, 1979): pp. 330–363.

Carrión 1948 — Carrión Cachot, Rebeca. "La cultura Chavín; nuevas colonias: Kuntur Wasi y Ancón." *Revista del Museo Nacional de Antropología y Arqueología* II (1, primer semestre, 1948): pp. 99–172. Lima.

Cieza 1959 — Cieza de Leon, Pedro de. *The Incas.* Norman: University of Oklahoma Press. 1959.

Cobo 1979 — Cobo, Bernabe. *History of the Inca Empire.* Austin and London: University of Texas Press. 1979.

Collier 1955 — Collier, Donald. "Cultural Chronology and Change as Reflected in the Ceramics of the Virú Valley." *Fieldiana: Anthropology* 43 (1955).

Conklin 1980 — Conklin, William J. "Elements of a North Coast Architectural Sequence." Paper presented at the 20th annual meeting of the Institute of Andean Studies, Berkeley. 1980.

Conrad 1974 — Conrad, Geoffrey W. *Burial Platforms and Related Structures on the North Coast of Peru: Some Social and Political Implications.* Ph.D. diss., Harvard University. 1974.

Conrad 1982 — ______. "The Burial Platforms of Chan Chan: Some Social and Political Implications." In *Chan Chan: Andean Desert City,* eds. Michael E. Moseley and Kent C. Day. Albuquerque: University of New Mexico Press 1982.

Cordy-Collins 1976 — Cordy-Collins, Alana. "An Iconographic Study of Chavín Textiles from the South Coast of Peru: The Discovery of a Pre-Columbian Catechism." Ph. D. diss., Institute of Archaeology, University of California, Los Angeles. 1976.

Cordy-Collins 1977 — ______. "The Moon is a Boat!: A Study in Iconographic Methodology." In *Pre-Columbian Art History: Selected Readings,* eds. Cordy-Collins, A., and J. Stern, pp. 421-434. Palo Alto. 1977.

Cossío 1971 — Cossío del Poman, Felipe. *The Art of Ancient Peru.* New York. 1971.

Dawson 1964 — Dawson, Lawrence E. "Slip Casting: A Ceramic Technique Invented in Ancient Peru." *Nawpa Pacha* 2 (1964): pp. 107–112.

Day 1973 — Day, Kent C. *Architecture of Ciudadela Rivero, Chan Chan, Peru.* Ph.D. diss., Harvard University, 1973.

della Santa n.d. — della Santa, Elisabeth. *La collection de vases mochicas des Musées Royaux d'Art et d'Histoire.* Brussels. N.d.

Demarest 1981 — Demarest, Arthur A. *Viracocha, The Nature and Antiquity of the Andean High God.* Peabody Museum Monograph no. 6, Harvard University. 1981.

d'Harcourt 1948 — d'Harcourt, Raoul. *Arts de l'Amérique.* Arts du monde. Paris. 1948.

d'Harcourt 1924 — ______, and Marie d'Harcourt. *La Céramique ancienne du Pérou.* Paris. 1924.

Disselhoff 1956 — Disselhoff, Hans D. "Hand-und Kopftrophäen in Plastischen Darstellungen der Recuay-Keramik." *Baessler-Archiv,* Band IV (1956): pp. 25–32.

Disselhoff 1967 — ______. *Daily Life in Ancient Peru.* Trans. Alisa Jaffa. New York. 1967.

Disselhoff 1971 — ______. *Vicús: Eine neu entdeckte alfperuanische Kultur.* Monumenta Americana, vol. 7. Berlin. 1971.

Dockstader 1967 — Dockstader, Frederick J. *Indian Art in South America.* Greenwich, Ct. 1967.

Dockstader 1972 — ______. *Naked Clay: 3000 Years of Unadorned Pottery of the American Indian.* New York: The Museum of the American Indian, the Heye Foundation. 1972.

Dockstader 1973 — ______. *Indian Art of the Americas.* New York: The Museum of the American Indian, the Heye Foundation. 1973.

Dockstader 1973a — ______. *Masterworks from the Museum of the American Indian.* New York: The Metropolitan Museum of Art. 1973.

Donnan 1965 — Donnan, Christopher B. "Moche Ceramic Technology." *Nawpa Pacha* 3 (1965): pp. 115–134.

Donnan 1972 — ______. "Moche-Huari Murals from Northern Peru." *Archaeology* 25 (2, 1972): pp. 85–95.

Donnan 1973 — ______. *Moche Occupation of the Santa Valley, Peru.* University of California Publications in Anthropology, vol. 8. Los Angeles and London. 1973.

Donnan 1976 — ______. *Moche Art and Iconography.* UCLA Latin America Studies, vol. 33. Los Angeles. 1976.

Donnan 1978 — ______. *Moche Art of Peru: Pre-Columbian Symbolic Communication.* Revised edition. Los Angeles: Museum of Cultural History. 1978.

Donnan/Mackey 1978 — ______, and Carol J. Mackey. *Ancient Burial Patterns of the Moche Valley, Peru.* Austin and London: University of Texas Press. 1978.

Donnan/McClelland 1979 — ______, and Donna McClelland. *The Burial Theme in Moche Iconography.* Dumbarton Oaks Studies in pre-Columbian Art and Archaeology, vol. 21 (1979). Washington, D.C.

Downing/Gibson 1974 — Downing, T.E., and M. Gibson, eds. *Irrigation's Impact on Society.* Anthropological Papers of the University of Arizona, no. 25. Tucson: University of Arizona Press. 1974.

Duviols 1977 — Duviols, Pierre. *La destrucción de las religiones andinas (durante la conquista y la colonia).* Universidad Nacional Autónoma de México. 1977.

Easby 1967 — Easby, Elizabeth Kennedy. *Ancient Art of Latin America from the Collection of Jay C. Leff.* New York: Brooklyn Museum. 1967.

Eisleb 1977 — Eisleb, Dieter. *Altperuanische Kulturen II: Nazca.* Berlin: Museum für Völkerkunde. n.F. 34 (1977).

Emmerich 1965 — Emmerich, André. *Sweat of the Sun and Tears of the Moon: Gold and Silver in Pre-Columbian Art.* Seattle: University of Washington Press. 1965.

Engel 1963 — Engel, Frederic. *A Preceramic Settlement on the Central Coast of Peru: Asis, Unit 1.* Transactions of the American Philosophical Society, Philadelphia. 1963.

Feldman 1980 — Feldman, Robert A. *Aspero, Peru: Architecture, Subsistence Economy, and Other Artifacts of a Preceramic Maritime Chiefdom.* Ph.D. diss., Harvard University, 1980.

Ford/Willey 1949 — Ford, James Alfred, and Gordon Randolph Willey. "A Surface Survey of the Virú Valley." *Anthropological Papers of the American Museum of Natural History* 43 (1, 1949). New York.

Fuhrmann 1922a — Fuhrmann, Ernst. "Peru II." *Kulturen der Erde* II. Hagen i.W. 1922.

Fuhrmann 1922b — ______. "Reich der Inka." *Kulturen der Erde* I. Hagen i.W. 1922.

Gayton/Kroeber 1927 — Gayton, Anna H., and Alfred L. Kroeber. "The Uhle Pottery Collections from Nazca." *University of California Publications in American Archaeology and Ethnology* 24 (1, 1927): pp. i–ii and 1–46.

Gillin 1947 — Gillin, John. *Moche: A Peruvian Coastal Community.* Smithsonian Institution Institute of Social Anthropology Publication no. 3, Washington, D.C. 1947.

Grieder 1978 — Grieder, Terence. *The Art and Archaeology of Pashash.* Austin. 1978.

Hamy 1882 — Hamy, Jules. "Les Collections Péruviennes du Docteur Macedo." *Revue d'Ethnographie* 1 (1, 1882): pp. 68–71.

Hamy 1898 — ______. "Les Vases Peints d'Ica (Pérou Moyen)." *Bulletin de la Société d'Anthropologie de Paris, IV Série,* 9 (1898): pp. 595–597.

Harner 1972 — Harner, Michael. *The Jivaro: People of the Sacred Waterfalls.* Garden City: Doubleday/Natural History Press. 1972.

Hartline 1980 — Hartline, Beverly K. "Coastal Upwelling: Physical Factors Feed Fish." *Science* 208 (1, 1980): pp. 38–40.

Hawkes 1974 — Hawkes, Jacquetta. *Atlas of Ancient Archaeology.* New York: McGraw-Hill. 1974.

Hissink 1950 — Hissink, Karen. "Motive der Mochica-Keramik." *Paideuma* V (1950): pp. 115–135.

Hocquenghem 1977a — Hocquenghem, Anne Marie. "Quelques projections sur l'iconographie des mochicas, une image de le monde d'après leurs images du monde." *Baessler-Archiv* 25 (1977): pp. 163–191.

Hocquenghem 1977b — ______. "Les représentations de chamans dans l'iconographie mochica." *Nawpa Pacha* 15 (1977): pp. 123–130.

Hocquenghem 1977c — ______. "Une interprétation des 'vases portraits' mochicas." *Nawpa Pacha* 15 (1977): pp. 131–139.

Hocquenghem 1977d — ———. "Un 'vase portrait' de femme mochica." *Nawpa Pacha* 15 (1977): pp. 117–121.

Hocquenghem 1978 — ———. "Les combats mochica: Essai d'interprétation d'un matérial archéologique à l'aide de l'iconologie, de l'ethno-histoire et de l'ethnologie." *Baessler-Archiv* XXVI (1978): pp. 127–157.

Hocquenghem 1979a — ———. "Iconographie mochica et les rites andins: Les scènes en relations avec l'océan." *Cahiers des Amériques Latines* 20 (1979): pp. 113–129.

Hocquenghem 1979b — ———. "L'iconographie mochica et les rites de purification." *Baessler-Archiv* XXVII (1979): pp. 211–252.

Hocquenghem 1979c — ———. "Le jeu et l'iconographie mochica." *Baessler-Archiv* XXVII (1979): pp. 325–346.

Hocquenghem 1980a — ———. "Forme, décor et fonction: Les vases à sonnaille des collections mochicas du Museum für Völkerkunde de Berlin." *Baessler-Archiv* XXVIII (1980): pp. 181–202.

Hocquenghem 1980b — ———. "L'iconographie mochica et les représentations de supplices." *Journal de la Société des Américanistes LXVII* (1980): pp. 249–260.

Hocquenghem 1980c — ———. "Les offrandes d'enfants: Essai d'interprétation d'une scène de l'iconographie mochica." *Indiana* 6 Gedenkschrift Walter Lehmann, Teil 1 (1980): pp. 275–292.

Hommel 1969 — Hommel, William L. *Myths of Ancient Peru.* Baltimore Museum of Art. 1969.

Horkheimer 1965 — Horkheimer, Hans. *Vicús: Exposición auspiciada por la Universidad Técnica de Piura.* Instituto de Arte Contemporaneo de Lima. 1965.

Horkheimer 1973 — ———. *Alimentación y obtención de alimentos en el Perú prehispánico.* Universidad Nacional Mayor de San Marcos, Lima. 1973.

Isbell 1978 — Isbell, William. "The Prehistoric Ground Drawings of Peru." *Scientific American* 239 (4, 1978): pp. 140–153.

Jiménez 1937 — Jiménez Borja, Arturo. *Moche.* Lima. 1937.

Jiménez 1950–51 — ———. "Instrumentos musicales peruanos." *Revista del Museo Nacional de Antropología y Arqueología,* XIX and XX (1950–1951): n.p. Lima.

Jiménez 1955 — ———. "La Danza en el antiguo Perú Época pre-Inca)." *Revista del Museo Nacional de Antropología y Arqueología, XXIV* (1955): pp. 111–136. Lima.

Jones 1964 — Jones, Julie. *Art of Empire: The Inca of Peru.* New York: Museum of Primitive Art. 1964.

Jones 1969 — ———. *Pre-Columbian Art in New York: Selections from Private Collections.* New York: Museum of Primitive Art. 1969.

Jones 1979 — ———. "Mochica Works in Metal: A Review." In *Pre-Columbian Metallurgy of South America: A Conference at Dumbarton Oaks, 1975,* pp. 53–104, ed. E.P. Benson. 1979.

Joyce 1912 — Joyce, Thomas A. *South American Archaeology.* New York. 1912.

Joyce 1913 — ———. "On an Early Type of Pottery from the Nazca Valley." *Burlington Magazine* XXII (CXVII, 1913): pp. 249–255.

Kano 1979 — Kano, Chiaki. *The Origins of Chavín Culture.* Dumbarton Oaks Studies in Pre-Columbian Art and Archaeology, vol. 22. Washington, D.C. 1979.

Kauffmann-Doig 1973 — Kauffmann-Doig, Frederico. *Manual de Arqueología Peruana.* Fifth edition. Lima. 1973.

Keatinge 1980 — Keatinge, Richard W. "Archaeology and Development: The Tembladera Sites of the Peruvian North Coast." *Journal of Field Archaeology* 7 (1980): pp. 467–475.

Klein 1967 — Klein, Otto. "La ceramica mochica." *Scienta,* XXXII (1967): p. 130.

Klymyshyn 1982 — Klymyshyn, Alexandra M. Ulana. "Elite Compounds in Chan Chan." In *Chan Chan, Andean Desert City,* ed. Michael E. Moseley and Kent C. Day. Albuquerque. University of New Mexico Press 1982.

Kolata 1978 — Kolata, Alan L. *Chan Chan: The Form of the City in Time.* Ph. D. diss., Harvard University, 1978.

Kolata 1982 — ———. "Chronology and Settlement Growth at Chan Chan." In *Chan Chan, Andean Desert City,* ed. Michael E. Moseley and Kent C. Day. Albuquerque: University of New Mexico Press. 1982.

Kosok 1965 — Kosok, Paul. *Life, Land and Water in Ancient Peru.* Long Island University Press. 1965.

Kroeber 1925a — Kroeber, A.L. "The Uhle Pottery Collections from Moche." *University of California Publications in American Archaeology and Ethnology* 21 (5, 1925): pp. 191–234.

Kroeber 1925b — ———. "The Uhle Pottery Collections from Supe." *University of California Publications in American Archaeology and Ethnology* 21 (6, 1925): pp. 235–264.

Kroeber 1926 — ———. "The Uhle Pottery Collections from Chancay." *University of California Publications in American Archaeology and Ethnology* 21 (7, 1926): pp. 265–304.

Kroeber 1926–30 — ———. "Archaeological Explorations in Peru. Pts. I and II." *Field Museum of Natural History, Anthropology Memoirs* II (1-2, 1926–1930). Chicago.

Kroeber 1944 — ———. *Peruvian Archaeology in 1942.* Viking Fund Publications in Anthropology, no. 4. New York: The Viking Fund, Inc. 1944.

Kroeber 1953 — ———. "Paracas Cavernas and Chavín." *University of California Publications in American Archaeology and Ethnology* XL (8, 1953): pp. 318–348. Berkeley.

Kroeber 1956 — ———. "Toward Definition of the Nazca Style." *University of California Publications in American Archaeology and Ethnology* 43 (4, 1956): pp. 327–432.

Kubler 1948 — Kubler, George. "Towards Absolute Time: Guano Archaeology." *Memoirs of the Society for American Archaeology* 4 (1948): pp. 29–50.

Kubler 1967 — ———. *The Iconography of the Art of Teotiahuacan.* Studies in Pre-Columbian Art and Archaeology, no. 4. Washington: Dumbarton Oaks Research Library and Museum. 1967.

Kutscher 1948 — Kutscher, Gerdt. "Religion und Mythologie der frühen Chimu (Nord-Peru)." *Actes du XXVIIIe Congrès International des Américanistes, Paris, 1947,* pp. 621–631. Société des Américanistes, Paris. 1948.

Kutscher 1950a — ———. *Chimú: Eine altindianische Hochkultur.* Berlin. 1950.

Kutscher 1950b — ———. "Iconographic Studies as an Aid in the Reconstruction of Early Chimú Civilization." *Transactions of the New York Academy of Sciences,* Series II, XII (6, 1950): pp. 194–203.

Kutscher 1951 — ———. "Ritual Races among the Early Chimú." In *The Civilizations of Ancient America: Selected Papers of the XXIXth International Congress of Americanists,* ed. Sol Tax, pp. 244–251. Chicago: University of Chicago Press. 1951.

Kutscher 1954 — ———. *Nordperuanische Keramik: Figürlich verzierte Gefässe der Früh-chimu.* Monumenta Americana, vol. 1. Berlin. 1954.

Kutscher 1955 — ———. *Arte antiquo de la costa norte del Perú.* Berlin. 1955.

Kutscher 1958 — ———. "Ceremonial 'Badminton' in the Ancient Culture of Moche (North Peru)." *Proceedings of the XXXIId International Congress of Americanists, Copenhagen, 1956,* pp. 422–432. 1958.

Lanning 1963 — Lanning, Edward P. "An Early Ceramic Style from Ancón, Central Coast of Peru." *Nawpa Pacha* 1 (1963): pp. 47–59.

Lanning 1967 — ———. *Peru before the Incas.* Englewood Cliffs, N.J. 1967.

Lapiner 1976 — Lapiner, Alan. *Pre-Columbian Art of South America.* New York. 1976.

Lapiner n.d. — ———. *Art of Ancient Peru.* New York: Arts of the Four Quarters, Ltd. N.d.

Larco Hoyle 1938 — Larco Hoyle, Rafael. *Los Mochicas.* 2 vols. Lima. 1938–39.

Larco Hoyle 1941 — ———. *Los Cupisniques.* Trabajo presentado al Congreso internacional de americanistas de Lima, sesión XXVII. Lima. 1941.

Larco Hoyle 1945	______. *Los Mochicas (Pre-Chimú, de Uhle y Early Chimú, de Kroeber).* Síntesis Monográfica. Buenos Aires: Sociedad Geografica Americana. 1945.
Larco Hoyle 1946	______. "A Culture Sequence for the North Coast of Peru." In *Handbook of South American Indians,* ed. J.H. Steward, Bureau of American Ethnology Bulletin 143 (2, 1946): pp. 149–176. Smithsonian Institution, Washington, D.C.
Larco Hoyle 1948	______. *Cronología Arqueológica del Norte del Perú.* Hacienda Chiclin, Trujillo. 1948.
Larco Hoyle 1963	______. *Las Epocas Peruanas.* Lima. 1963.
Larco Hoyle 1965a	______. *La Cerámica de Vicús.* Lima. 1965.
Larco Hoyle 1965b	______. *Checan.* Geneva. 1965.
Larco Hoyle 1966	______. *Peru.* Archaeologia Mundi. Trans. James Hogarth. Cleveland. 1966.
Larco Hoyle 1967	______. *La Cerámica de Vicús y sus nexos con las demás culturas.* Lima. 1967.
Larco Hoyle n.d.(a)	______. *La Cerámica de Vicús 2.* Lima. N.d.
Larco Hoyle n.d.(b)	______. *La Cultura Santa.* Lima. N.d.
Larco Hoyle n.d.(c)	______. *La Divinidad Felinica de Lambayeque.* N.d.
Lathrap 1971	Lathrap, Donald W. "The Tropical Rain Forest and the Cultural Context of Chavín." In *Dumbarton Oaks Conference on Chavín, 1968,* ed. E.P. Benson, pp. 73-100. Washington, D.C. 1971.
Lathrap 1975	______. *Ancient Ecuador: Culture, Clay and Creativity 3000–300 B.C.* Chicago: Field Museum of Natural History. 1975.
Lathrap 1977	______. "Gifts of the Cayman: Some Thoughts on the Subsistence Basis of Chavín." *Pre-Columbian Art History: Selected Readings,* ed. A. Cordy-Collins and Jean Stern, pp. 333-351. Palo Alto: Peek Publications. 1977.
Lathrap n.d.	______. "Jaws: An Iconographic Structure Underlying Ceremonial Architecture of Nuclear America." In *Early Ceremonial Architecture in the Andes,* ed. Christopher B. Donnan. Washington, D.C.: Dumbarton Oaks. In press.
Lavallée 1970	Lavallée, Danièle. *Les représentations animales dans la Céramique Mochica.* Institut d'Ethnologie, Musée de l'Homme, Paris. 1970.
Lechtman et al. 1982	Lechtman, Heather, Antonieta Erlij and Edward J. Barry, Jr. "New Perspectives on Moche Metallurgy: Techniques of Gilding Copper at Loma Negra, Northern Peru." *American Antiquity* 147 (1, 1982): pp. 3-30.
Lehmann 1938	Lehmann, Heinz. *Ceramicas del Antiguo Perú de la Colección Wassermann-San Blás.* Buenos Aires. 1938.
Lehmann/Doering 1924	Lehmann, Walter and Heinrich Doering. *The Art of Old Peru.* London. 1924.
Leicht 1960	Leicht, Hermann. *Pre-Inca Art and Culture.* Trans. Mervyn Saville. New York. 1960.
Lettau 1978	Lettau, H.H. and K. Lettau. *Exploring the World's Driest Climate.* Institute for Environmental Studies, Report 101. Madison: University of Wisconsin. 1978.
Lothrup 1964	Lothrup, Samuel Kirkland. *Treasures of Ancient America: The Arts of the Pre-Columbian Civilizations from Mexico to Peru.* Geneva: Skira. 1964.
Lothrup/Mahler 1957	______, and Joy Mahler. *A Chancay-style Grave at Zapallan, Peru: An Analysis of its Textiles, Pottery and Other Furnishings.* Papers of the Peabody Museum of Archaeology and Ethnology, vol. 50, no. 1. Cambridge, Mass. 1957.
Lothrup/Mahler 1961	______. *Essays in Pre-Columbian Art and Archaeology.* Cambridge, Mass.: Harvard University Press. 1961.
Lumbreras 1970	Lumbreras, Luís Guillermo. *Los Templos de Chavín; guía para el visitante.* Publicación del Proyecto Chavín. Lima. 1970.
Lumbreras 1971	______. "Towards a Re-Evaluation of Chavín." *Dumbarton Oaks Conference on Chavín, 1968,* ed. E.P. Benson, pp. 1-28. Washington, D.C. 1971.
Lumbreras 1974	______. *The Peoples and Cultures of Ancient Peru.* Trans. Betty J. Meggers. Washington, D.C.
Lumbreras 1977	______. "Excavaciones en el Templo Antiguo de Chavín (sector R); informe de la sexta campaña." *Nawpa Pacha* 15 (1977): pp. 1-38.
Lumbreras 1979	______. *El arte y la vida Vicús: Colección del Banco Popular del Perú.* Lima. 1979.
Lumbreras/ Olazábal 1969	______, and Hernán Amat Olazábal. "Informe Preliminar Sobre Las Galerías Interiores de Chavín." *Revista del Museo Nacional de Antropología y Arqueología* XXXIV (1969): pp. 143-197. Lima.
Macedo 1881	Macedo, José Mariano. *Catalogue d'Objets Archéologiques de Pérou de l'Ancienne Empire des Incas.* Paris: Imprimerie Hispano-Américaine.
MacNeish 1971	MacNeish, Richard S. "Early Man in the Andes." *Scientific American* 224 (13, 1974): pp. 36-46.
Maitland 1979	Maitland, Maureen E. "Iconographic Relations Between Chavín-Related North Coast Ceramics and the Art of Chavín." Paper presented at the 19th annual meeting of the Institute of Andean Studies, Berkeley, January 5-6, 1979.
Maitland 1980	______. "The Chavín Influence on Early Horizon Peruvian North Coast Ceramics and Dating Implications." Master of Arts thesis, University of British Columbia, Vancouver, 1980.
Maitland et al. 1976	______, Sharon Mowatt, Arthur Phillips and Scott Watson. "A Proposed Revision of Rowe's Chavín Chronology." A paper presented at the 16th annual meeting of the Institute of Andean Studies, Berkeley, January 9-10, 1976.
Martin-Vegue 1949	Martin-Vegue, George B. "Nazca Pottery at Florida State University." *American Journal of Archaeology* 53 (4, 1949): pp. 345-354.
Mason 1957	Mason, J. Alden. *The Ancient Civilizations of Peru.* Baltimore. 1957.
Matos Mendieta 1965	Matos Mendieta, Ramiro. "Algunas consideraciones sobre el estilo de Vicus." *Revista del Museo Nacional de Antropología y Arqueología,* XXXIV (1964): pp. 89-134. Lima.
Means 1931	Means, Philip Ainsworth. *Ancient Civilizations of the Andes.* New York. 1931.
Menzel 1958	Menzel, Dorothy. "Problemas en el Estudio del Horizonte Medio en la Arqueología Peruana." *Revista del Museo Regional de Ica* IX (10, 1958): pp. 24-57.
Menzel 1964	______. "Style and Time in the Middle Horizon." *Nawpa Pacha* 2 (1964): pp. 1-106.
Menzel 1968a	______. *La Cultura Huari.* Las Grandes Civilizaciones del Antigolo Perú, tomo VI. Lima: La Compañía de Seguros y Reaseguros Peruano-Suiza, S.A. 1968.
Menzel 1968b	______. "New Data on the Huari Empire in Middle Horizon Epoch 2A." *Nawpa Pacha* 6 (1968): pp. 47-114.
Menzel 1976	______. *Pottery Style and Society in Ancient Peru: Art as a Mirror of History in the Ica Valley, 1350-1570.* Berkeley, 1976.
Menzel 1977	______. *The Archaeology of Ancient Peru and the Work of Max Uhle.* Berkeley: Lowie Museum of Anthropology, University of California. 1977.
Menzel et al. 1964	______, John H. Rowe and Lawrence E. Dawson. "The Paracas Pottery of Ica: A Study in Style and Time." *University of California Publications in American Archaeology and Ethnology* 50. Berkeley and Los Angeles. 1964.
Middendorf 1893	Middendorf, E.W. *Peru: Beobachtungen und Studien über das Land und seine Bewohner.* 3 vols. Berlin. 1893-1895.
Mint Museum 1970	The Mint Museum. *Pre-Columbian Art of the Americas.* Charlotte, N.C.: The Mint Museum of Art. 1970.
Montell 1929	Montell, Gösta. *Dress Ornaments in Ancient Peru: Archaeological and Historical Studies.* Göteborg. 1929.
Mortimer 1901	Mortimer, W. Golden. *Peru: History of Coca, the Divine Plant of the Incas.* New York. 1901.

Moseley 1975 — Moseley, Michael E. *The Maritime Foundations of Andean Civilization.* Menlo Park, Ca.: Cummings Publishing Co. 1975.

Moseley 1982 — ______. "Introduction: Human Exploitation and Organization on the North American Coast." In *Chan Chan: Andean Desert City,* eds. Michael E. Moseley and Kent C. Day. Albuquerque: University of New Mexico Press. 1982.

Moseley n.d. — ______. "The Exploration and Explanation of Early Monumental Architecture in the Andes." In *Early Ceremonial Architecture in the Andes,* ed. Christopher B. Donnan. Washington, D.C.: Dumbarton Oaks. In press.

Moseley/Mackey 1974 — ______, and Carol J. Mackey. *Twenty-Four Architectural Plans of Chan Chan, Peru.* Harvard University: Peabody Museum Press. 1974.

Moseley/Watanabe 1974 — ______, and Luis Watanabe. "The Adobe Sculpture of Huaca de los Reyes." *Archaeology* 27 (3, 1974): pp. 154-161.

Moseley/Day 1982 — ______, and Kent C. Day, eds. *Chan Chan: Andean Desert City.* Albuquerque: University of New Mexico Press. 1982.

Muelle 1936 — Muelle, Jorge C. "Chalchalcha." *Revista del Museo Nacional de Antropología y Arqueología* V (1, 1936): pp. 65-88. Lima.

Murra 1975 — Murra, John. *Formaciones económicas y políticas del mundo andino.* Lima: Instituto de Estudios Peruanos. 1975.

Nachtigall 1966 — Nachtigall, Horst. *Indianische Fisher, Feldbauer und Viehzüchter.* Marburger Studien zur Völkerkunde, vol. II. Berlin. 1966.

Netherly 1977 — Netherly, Patricia J. *Local Level Lords on the North Coast of Peru.* Ph.D. diss., Cornell University, 1977.

Nicholson/Cordy-Collins 1979 — Nicholson, H.B., and Alana Cordy-Collins. *Pre-Columbian Art from the Land Collection.* San Francisco: California Academy of Sciences. 1979.

Ortloff et al. 1982 — Ortloff, C.R., Michael E. Moseley and Robert A. Feldman. "Hydraulic Engineering Aspects of the Chimú Chicama-Moche Intervalley Canal." *American Antiquity* 47 (3, 1982): pp. 572-595.

Panofsky 1955 — Panofsky, E. "Iconography and Iconology: An Introduction to the Study of Renaissance Art." In *Meaning in the Visual Arts,* 26-54. Garden City: Doubleday Anchor Books. 1955.

Parsons 1974 — Parsons, Lee A. *Pre-Columbian America: The Art and Archaeology of South, Central and Middle America.* Milwaukee: Milwaukee Public Museum. 1974.

Parsons 1980 — ______. *Pre-Columbian Art: The Morton D. May and the St. Louis Art Museum Collections.* New York. 1980.

Ponce Sangines 1961 — Ponce Sangines, Carlos. *Informe de Labores.* Centro de Investigaciones Arqueológicas en Tiwanaku, Publicacion no. 1. 1961.

Posnansky 1945 — Posnansky, Arthur. *Tihuanacu: The Cradle of American Man.* New York: J. Augustin. 1945.

Pozorsky 1975 — Pozorsky, Thomas. "El Complejo Caballo Muerto: Los Frisos de Barro de la Huaca de los Reyes." *Revista del Museo Nacional de Antropología y Arquelogía* XLI (1975): pp. 211-252. Lima.

Pozorsky 1979 — ______. "The Las Avispas Burial Platform at Chan Chan, Peru." *Annals of the Carnegie Museum* 48 (8, 1979): pp. 119-137.

Proulx 1968a — Proulx, Donald A. *An Archaeological Survey of the Nepeña Valley.* University of Massachusetts Department of Anthropology Research Reports no. 2. Amherst. 1968.

Proulx 1968b — ______. *Local Differences and Time Differences in Nasca Pottery.* University of California Publications in Anthropology, vol. 5. Berkeley. 1968.

Proulx 1970 — ______. *Nasca Gravelots in the Uhle Collection from the Ica Valley, Peru.* University of Massachusetts Department of Anthropology Research Reports no. 5. Amherst. 1970.

Proulx 1971 — ______. "Headhunting in Ancient Peru." *Archaeology* 24 (1, 1971): pp. 16-21.

Proulx 1973 — ______. *Archaeological Investigations in the Nepeña Valley.* University of Massachusetts Department of Anthropology Research Reports no. 13. Amherst. 1973.

Purin n.d. — Purin, Gergio. *Vases anthropomorphes mochicas des Musées Royaux d'Art et d'Histoire, I.* Corpus Americanensium Antiquitatum/Union Académique Internationale. Brussels. N.d.

Putnam 1914 — Putnam, Edward K. "The Davenport Collection of Nazca and other Peruvian Pottery." *Proceedings of the Davenport Academy of Sciences* 12 (1914). Davenport, Iowa.

Raimondi 1874 — Raimondi, Antonio. *El Perú.* 6 vols. Lima. 1874-1913.

Ramos/Blasco 1977 — Ramos Gomez, Luis, and Concepción Blasco Bosqued. "Las Representaciones de 'Aves Fantásticas' en Materiales Nazcas del Museo de América de Madrid." *Revista de Indias* XXXVII (147-148, 1977): pp. 265-276. Madrid.

Ravines/Isbell 1975 — Ravines, Roger, and William H. Isbell. "Garagay: Sitio Ceremonial Temprano en el Valle de Lima." *Revista del Museo Nacional de Antropología y Arqueología* XLI (1975): pp. 253-275. Lima.

Ravines/Alvarez 1975 — Ravines, Roger, and Juan Alvarez Sauri. "Fechas Radiocarbonicas Para el Perú." *Arqueologicas* 11 (1967). Museo Nacional de Antropología y Arqueología, Lima.

Reiche 1968 — Reiche, Maria. *Mystery on the Desert.* Stuttgart: Offizendruck AG. 1968.

Roark 1965 — Roark, Richard P. "From Monumental to Proliferous in Nasca Pottery." *Ñawpa Pacha* 3 (1965): pp. 1-92.

Roe 1974 — Roe, Peter. *A Further Exploration of the Rowe Chavín Seriation and its Implications for North Central Coast Chronology.* Dumbarton Oaks Studies in Pre-Columbian Art and Archaeology 13. Washington, D.C. 1974.

Rostworowski 1961 — Rostworowski de Diez Canseco, Maria. *Curacas y Sucesiones: Costa norte.* Lima. 1961.

Rostworowski 1977 — ______. *Etnía y Sociedad: Costa Peruana Prehispánica.* Lima: Instituto de Estudios Peruanos. 1977.

Rostworowski 1981 — ______. *Recursos naturales renovables y pesca: Siglos XVI y XVII.* Lima: Instituto de Estudios Peruanos. 1981.

Rowe 1946 — Rowe, John Howland. "Inca Culture at the Time of the Spanish Conquest." In *Handbook of South American Indians,* ed. J.H. Steward, Bureau of American Ethnology Bulletin 143 (2, 1946): pp. 183-330. Washington: Smithsonian Institution.

Rowe 1948 — ______. "The Kingdom of Chimor." *Acta Americana* 6 (12, 1948): pp. 26-59.

Rowe 1954 — ______. "Max Uhle, 1856-1944: A Memoir of the Father of Peruvian Archaeology." *University of California Publications in American Archaeology and Ethnology* 46 (1, 1954).

Rowe 1958 — ______. "La serición cronológica de la cerámica de Paracas elaborado por Lawrence E. Dawson." *Revista del Museo Regional de Ica,* año IX (10, 1958).

Rowe 1960 — ______. "Nuevos Datos Relativos a la Cronología del Estilo Nasca." *Antiguo Perú: Espacio y Tiempo* (1960): pp. 29-45. Lima: Juan Mejía Baca.

Rowe 1962a — ______. *Chavín Art: An Inquiry into its Form and Meaning.* New York: The Museum of Primitive Art. 1962.

Rowe 1962b — ______. "Stages and Periods in Archaeological Interpretation." *Southwest Journal of Anthropology* 18 (1,1962): pp. 40-54.

Rowe 1967 — ______. "Form and Meaning in Chavín Art." *Peruvian Archaeology: Selected Readings,* eds. John H. Rowe and Dorothy Menzel, pp. 72-103. Palo Alto: Peek Publications. 1967.

Rowe 1971 — ______. "The Influence of Chavín Art on Later Styles." In *Dumbarton Oaks Conference on Chavín, 1968,* ed. E.P. Benson, pp. 101-124. Dumbarton Oaks, Washington, D.C. 1971.

Sawyer 1960 — Sawyer, Alan R. "Paracas Necropolis Headdress and Face Ornaments." *Workshop Notes,* paper no. 21. Washington: The Textile Museum. 1960.

Sawyer 1961 ______. "Paracas and Nazca Iconography." In *Essays in Pre-Columbian Art and Archaeology*, by S.K. Lothrop and others, pp. 269-298. Cambridge, Mass.: University Press. 1961.

Sawyer 1966 ______. *Ancient Peruvian Ceramics: The Nathan Cummings Collection.* New York: The Metropolitan Museum. 1966.

Sawyer 1968 ______. *Mastercraftsmen of Ancient Peru.* New York: Guggenheim Museum. 1968.

Sawyer 1972 ______. "The Feline in Paracas Art." In *The Cult of the Feline: A Conference on Pre-Columbian Iconography,* ed. E.P. Benson, pp. 91-115. Dumbarton Oaks, Washington, D.C. 1972.

Sawyer 1975a ______. *Ancient Andean Arts in the Collections of the Krannert Art Museum.* Urbana-Champaign: Krannert Art Museum. 1975.

Sawyer 1975b ______. *Ancient Peruvian Ceramics from the Kehl and Lena Markley Collection.* Pennsylvania State University: Museum of Art. 1975.

Sawyer 1982 ______. "The Falsification of Ancient Peruvian Slip-decorated Ceramics." *Falsifications and Misreconstructions of Pre-Columbian Art,* ed. Elizabeth Boone, pp. 19-36. Dumbarton Oaks, Washington, D.C. 1982.

Sawyer 1979 ______. "The Living Dead." Paper presented at the XLIII International Congress of Americanists, Vancouver, Canada, August 1979.

Schaedel 1951 Schaedel, Richard P. "Mochica Murals at Panamarca." *Archaeology* 4 (3, 1951): pp. 145-154.

Schmidt 1929 Schmidt, Max. *Kunst und Kultur von Peru.* Berlin, 1929.

Seler 1893 Seler, Eduard. "Peruanische Alterthümer, inbosondere Altperuanische Gefässe der Chibcha und der Tonia- und Cauca- Stamme, etc." Berlin: Dr. E. Mertens & Cie. 1893.

Seler 1923 ______. "Die Buntbemalten Gefässe von Nazca." *Gesammelte Abhandlungen zur Amerikanischen Sprach- und Altertunskunde* 4 (1923): pp. 160-438. Berlin: Verlag Behrend u. Co. Reprinted by Akademische Druk-u. Verlagsanstalt, Graz, Austria.

Sharon 1978 Sharon, Douglas. *Wizard of the Four Winds.* New York. 1978.

Sharon/Donnan 1974 ______, and Christopher B. Donnan. "Shamanism in Moche Iconography." In *Ethnoarchaeology,* eds. C. Donnan and C.W. Clewlow. Institute of Archaeology Monograph IV. 1974.

Squier 1877 Squier, E. George. *Peru: Incidents of Travel and Exploration in the Land of the Incas.* New York. 1877.

Steward 1955 Steward, Julian H., ed. "Introduction: The Irrigation Civilizations: A Symposium on Method and Result in Cross-Cultural Regularities." In *Irrigation Civilizations: A Comparative Study.* Washington, D.C.: Pan-American Union. 1955.

Strong 1957 Strong, William Duncan. *Paracas, Nazca and Tiahuanacoid Cultural Relationships in South Coastal Peru.* Memoirs of the Society for American Archaeology, no. 13; *American Antiquity* 23 (4, 1957): pt. 2.

Strong/Evans 1952 ______, and Clifford Evans, Jr. *Cultural Stratigraphy in the Virú Valley, Northern Peru.* Columbia Studies in Archaeology and Ethnology, vol. IV. New York: Columbia University. 1952.

Tello 1923 Tello, Julio Cézar. "Wira Kocha." *Inca* 1 (1, 1923): pp. 93-320 and (3, 1923): pp. 583-606.

Tello 1929 ______. *Antiguo Peru: primera epoca.* Editado por la Comisión organizadora del segundo Congreso sudaméricano de turismo. Lima. 1929.

Tello 1938 ______. *Arte Antiguo Peruano. Primera Parte: Technologica y Morfologia,* vol. 2, *Inca.* Lima: Museo de Arqueología de la Universidad Mayor de San Marcos. 1938.

Tello 1943 ______. "Discovery of the Chavín Culture in Peru." *American Antiquity* 1 (1, 1943): pp. 135-160.

Tello 1956 ______. *Arqueología del Valle de Casma.* Ediciónes de la Universidad Nacional Mayor de San Marcos, Lima. 1956.

Tello 1960 ______. *Chavín: Cultura Matriz de la Civilización Andina, Pt. I.* Publicación Antropológica del Archivo Julio C. Tello de la Universidad Nacional Mayor de San Marcos, vol. 2. Lima. 1960.

Topic 1977 Topic, John R. *The Lower Class at Chan Chan: A Quantitative Approach,* Ph.D. diss., Harvard University, 1977.

Topic 1982a ______. "Lower Class Social and Economic Organization at Chan Chan." In *Chan Chan: Andean Desert City,* eds. Michael E. Moseley and Kent C. Day. Albuquerque: University of New Mexico Press. 1982.

Topic 1982b Topic, Theresa Lange. "The Early Intermediate Period and its Legacy." In *Chan Chan: Andean Desert City,* eds. M.E. Moseley and K.C. Day, pp. 255-284. Albuquerque: University of New Mexico. 1982.

Towle 1961 Towle, Margaret. *The Ethnobotany of Pre-Columbian Peru.* Viking Fund Publications in Anthropology vol. 30. New York. 1961.

Ubbelohde-Doering 1954 Ubbelohde-Doering, Heinrich. *The Art of Ancient Peru.* New York. 1954.

Ubbelohde-Doering 1959 ______. "Bericht über archäologische Feldarbeiten in Péru, II." *Ethnos* 24 (1-2, 1959): pp. 1-32.

Ubbelohde-Doering 1960 ______. "Bericht über archäologische Feldarbeiten in Péru, III." *Ethnos* 25 (3-4, 1960): pp. 153-182.

Ubbelohde-Doering 1967 ______. *On the Royal Highways of the Inca.* New York. 1967.

Uhle 1913a Uhle, Max. "Die Ruinen von Moche." *Journal de la Société des Américanistes* X (1913): pp. 95-117.

Uhle 1913b ______. "Zur Chronologie der Alten Kulturen von Ica." *Journal de la Société des Américanistes de Paris,* Nouvelle Série, X (II, 1913): pp. 341-367.

Valcárcel 1932 Valcárcel, Luis E. "El Gato de Agua, Sus Representaciones en Pukara y Naska." *Revista del Museo Nacional de Antropología y Arqueología* I (2,1932): pp. 3-27. Lima.

Valcárcel 1935 ______. *Cuadernos de arte antiguo del Peru* 1-6 (1935-1938). Lima.

Vásquez n.d. Vásquez de Espinosa, Antonio. *Compendium and Description of the West Indies.* Trans. Charles Upson Clark. Smithsonian Miscellaneous Collections, vol. 102 (3646). N.d.

von Hagen 1965 von Hagen, Victor W. *The Desert Kingdom of Peru.* Greenwich, Conn. 1965.

von Heine-Geldern 1967 von Heine-Geldern, Robert. "American Metallurgy and the Old World." In *Early Chinese Art and its Possible Influence in the Pacific Basin.* Vol. 3, *Oceania and the Americas.* A symposium arranged by the Department of Art History and Archaeology, Columbia University, New York City, August 21-25, 1967.

von Schuler-Schömig 1979 von Schuler-Schömig, Immina von. "Die 'Fremdkrieger' in Barstellungen der Moche-Keramik." *Baessler-Archiv* XXVIII (1979): pp. 135-213.

von Schuler-Schömig 1981 ______. "Die sogenannten Fremdkrieger und ihre weiteren ikographischen Bezüge in der Moche-Keramik." *Baessler-Archiv* XXIX (1981): pp. 207-239.

Waisbard 1965 Waisbard, Roger, and Simone Waisbard. *Masks, Mummies and Magicians.* New York: Praeger. 1965.

Walker 1969 Walker, Lester C. *Art of Ancient Peru: The Paul A. Clifford Collection.* Athens, Ga.: Georgia Museum of Art. 1969.

Walker 1971 ______. *Pre-Columbian Art from the Collections of Paul A. Clifford and William Thibadeau.* Atlanta: High Museum. 1971.

Wallace 1962 Wallace, Dwight T. "Cerrillos, an Early Paracas Site in Ica, Peru." *American Antiquity* 27 (3, 1962): pp. 303- 314.

Wallace 1979 ——. "The Process of Weaving Development on the Peruvian Coast." In *The Junius B. Bird Pre-Columbian Textile Conference, May 19-20, 1973*, eds. Ann Pollard Rose, E.P. Benson and Anne-Louise Schaffer, pp. 27-50, Washington, D.C.: The Textile Museum and Dumbarton Oaks. 1979.

Wegner 1975 Wegner, Steven. "An Analysis of Vessel Shapes and Shape Changes in Phases 6 Through 9 of the Nasca Sequence." Paper written for Anthropology 220c, Professor John Rowe, University of California, Berkeley. Fall, 1975.

Wegner 1976 ——. "A Stylistic seriation of Nasca 6 Painted Pottery Designs." Paper written for Anthropology 220c, Professor John Rowe, University of California, Berkeley. Fall, 1976.

Weiss 1961 Weiss, Pedro. "La Asociación de la Uta y Verruga Peruana en los Mitos de la Papa, Figurados en la Cerámica Moshica y Shimu." *Revista del Museo Nacional de Antropología y Arqueología* XXX (1961): pp. 65-77. Lima.

Wiener 1880 Wiener, Charles. *Pérou et Bolivie.* Paris: Librairie Hachette et Cie. 1880.

Willey 1945 Willey, Gordon R. "Horizon Styles and Pottery Traditions in Peruvian Archaeology." *American Antiquity* 11 (1, 1945): pp. 49-56.

Willey 1951 ——. "The Chavín Problem: A Review and Critique." *Southwestern Journal of Anthropology* 7 (2, 1951): pp. 103-144.

Willey 1953 ——. *Prehistoric Settlement Patterns in the Virú Valley, Peru.* Bureau of American Ethnology Bulletin vol. 155 (1953). Washington: Smithsonian Institution.

Willey 1954 ——, and John Maxwell Corbett. *Early Ancón and Early Supe Culture: Chavín Horizon Sites of the Central Peruvian Coast.* Columbia Studies in Archaeology and Ethnology, vol. III (1954). New York.

Willey 1971 ——. *An Introduction to American Archaeology.* South America, vol. 2 (1971). Englewood Cliffs, N.J.

Wittfogel 1957 Wittfogel, Karl. *Oriental Despotism: A Comparative Study in Total Power.* New Haven: Yale University Press. 1957.

Wolfe 1981 Wolfe, Elizabeth Farkass. "The Spotted Cat and the Horrible Bird; Stylistic Change in Nasca 1-5 Ceramic Decoration." *Nawpa Pacha* 19 (1981): pp. 1-62.

Yacovleff 1931 Yacovleff, Eugenio. "El Vencejo (Cypselus) en el Arte Decorativo de Nasca." *Wira-Kocha* 1 (1931). Lima.

Yacovleff 1932a ——. "Las Falcónidas en el Arte y en las Creencias de los Antiguos Peruanos." *Revista del Museo Nacional de Antropología y Arqueología* I (2, 1932): pp. 35-111. Lima.

Yacovleff 1932b ——. "La Deidad Primitiva de los Nasca." *Revista del Museo Nacional de Antropología y Arqueología* I (2, 1932): pp. 103-106. Lima.

Yacovleff 1933 ——. "La Jíquima, Raíz Comestible Extinguida en el Perú." *Revista del Museo Nacional de Antropología y Arqueología* II (1, 1933): pp. 51-66. Lima.

Yacovleff/Herrera 1935 and 1939 ——, and Fortunato L. Herrera. "El Mundo Vegetal de los Antiguos Peruanos." *Revista del Museo Nacional de Antropología y Arqueología* III (2, 1935): pp. 241-322 and IV (1, 1939): pp. 29-102. Lima.

Zeil 1979 Zeil, W. *The Andes, A Geological Review.* Beitrage Zur Regionalen Geologie der Erde, Band 13. 1979.

Zuidema 1972 Zuidema, Reiner Tom. "Meaning in Nazca Art: Iconographic Relationships Between Inca, Huari and Nazca Cultures in Southern Peru." *Göteborgs Ethnografiska Museum, Arystryck* (1971): pp. 35-54. Göteborg.

PRODUCTION NOTE:
This catalogue was designed and its production supervised by Victor Trasoff. Production coordinator was Edward Tuntigian.
It was printed in limited editions in four-color process by Rapoport Printing Corp., N.Y. and bound by A. Horowitz & Sons, Fairfield, N.J.
Photo composition in *Baskerville* by Empire Typographers, N.Y.